FRANCE

1814–1940

By

J. P. T. Bury

A Perpetua Book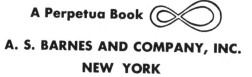

A. S. BARNES AND COMPANY, INC.

NEW YORK

Perpetua Edition 1962

by arrangement with
The University of Pennsylvania Press

Printed in the United States of America

FOREWORD

THIS book has no pretensions to originality. It is merely an endeavour to furnish the general reader, and anyone else who may be interested, with a straightforward and continuous survey of the vicissitudes of French history between 1814 and 1940. My excuse for such a work, apart from the courteous invitation of the publishers, must be that, although the period is wholly or partly covered in more general histories of France, there are, I believe, few books easily available in English which are entirely devoted to these momentous years. Furthermore, this century and a quarter of French history has a certain unity: it begins and ends with catastrophe and invasion and it is largely dominated by the working out of two great Revolutions, the political one of 1789 and the vast and still uncompleted process of economic change which goes by the name of the Industrial Revolution. Unhappily for France both of these revolutions brought schism in their train and so the tale is mainly one of a society divided against itself. Yet that society was also one which never ceased to be brilliantly creative in many spheres of human activity beside the purely political and economic. It is my regret that within the space allotted I have not found it possible to do more than hint at the splendour of some of these achievements. For such 'old-fashioned' neglect and for my numerous other sins of omission I take full responsibility.

My debt to many historians of France, some of them English and still more of them French, will be obvious to those who know their works and is to some extent laid bare in the bibliographies and footnotes which I have added in the hope that they may be useful. To them I express my admiration, and to Mr. P. E. Charvet, Mr. J. P. C. Roach, and the various members of my family who have been so helpful alike with encouragement and criticism my deepest gratitude.

J. P. T. B.

November, 1948

CONTENTS

MAPS

Drawings by Richard Cribb

GENERAL BIBLIOGRAPHY

(This is a list of books which refer either to the whole period or to periods covered by several chapters. I have also added short lists of books at the end of each chapter; these may sometimes include titles already in this General Bibliography.)

BAINVILLE, JACQUES: *La Troisième République*, 1870–1935. Paris, 1935.

BOURGIN, G.: *La Troisième République*, 1870–1914. Paris, 1939.

BOURGEOIS, E.: *Manuel historique de politique étrangère.* Vols. II—IV. 8th ed., Paris, 1927.

BROGAN, D. W.: *The Development of Modern France* (1870–1939). London, 1940.

BUTLER, K. T.: *A History of French Literature.* London, 1923.

CAHEN, L. and MATHIEZ, A.: *Les lois françaises de 1815 à 1914*, 4th ed., Paris, 1933.

CLAPHAM, J. H.: *The Economic Development of France and Germany, 1815–1914.* Cambridge, 1921.

CURTIUS, E. R.: *The Civilization of France.* London, 1932.

DANSETTE, A.: *Histoire religieuse de la France contemporaine*, Paris, 1948.

DICKINSON, G. LOWES: *Revolution and Reaction in Modern France.* London, 1892.

DUGUIT, L. and MONNIER, H.: *Les constitutions et les principales lois politiques de la France depuis 1789*, 5th ed. Paris, 1932.

ELTON, G.: *The Revolutionary Idea in France, 1789–1871.* London, 1923.

GAULLE, CHARLES DE: *La France et son armée.* Paris, 1938.

GOGUEL, FRANÇOIS: *La politique des partis sous la Troisième République*, 1871–1939. Paris, 1946.

HALÉVY, D.: *Trois épreuves, 1814, 1871, 1940.* Paris, 1942.

HALÉVY, D.; *Histoire d'une histoire esquissée pour le troisième Cinquantenaire de la Révolution Française.* Paris, 1939.

LEVASSEUR, E.: *Histoire du commerce de la France*, Vol. II. *De 1789 à nos jours.* Paris, 1912.

LEVASSEUR, E.: *Histoire des classes ouvrières et de l'industrie en France de 1789 à 1870.* Paris, 1903–4.

MADAULE, JACQUES: *Histoire de France*, Vol. II, *De 1715 à nos jours.* 5th ed. Paris, 1945.

MAILLAUD, PIERRE: *France.* Oxford, 1942.

MARION, M.: *Histoire financière de la France depuis 1715.* Paris, 1927.

MORAZÉ, CHARLES: *La France bourgeoise, XVIIIᵉ-XXᵉ siècles.* Paris, 1946.

PHILLIPS, C. S.: *The Church in France, 1789–1848.* London, 1929.

PHILLIPS, C. S.: *The Church in France, 1848–1907.* London, 1936.

RECLUS, M.: *La Troisième République de 1870 à 1918.* Paris, 1945.

RITCHIE, R. L. G. (ed.): *France, A Companion to French Studies.* London, 1937.

ROBERTS, S. H.: *History of French Colonial Policy (1870–1925).* London, 1929.

SCHUMAN, F. L.: *War and Diplomacy in the French Republic.* New York and London, 1931.

SEIGNOBOS, CHARLES.: *Histoire sincère de la nation française,* 15th ed. Paris, 1933 (also available in English translation).

SEIGNOBOS, CHARLES: *L'évolution de la 3ᵐᵉ République (1875–1914),* (Vol. VII of E. LAVISSE, *Histoire de France contemporaine.* Paris. 1921).

SOLTAU, ROGER: *French Political Thought in the Nineteenth Century.* London, 1931.

THOMSON, DAVID: *The Democratic Ideal in France and England.* Cambridge, 1940.

WEILL, GEORGES: *Le Journal, origines, évolution et rôle de la presse périodique.* Paris, 1934.

WEILL, GEORGES: *Histoire de l'idée laïque en France au XIXᵉ siècle.* Paris, 1929.

WEILL, GEORGES: *Histoire du mouvement social en France (1852–1924).* Paris, 1924.

WEILL, GEORGES: *Histoire du parti républicain en France de 1814 à 1870.* Paris, 1900.

WOODWARD, E. L.: *French Revolutions.* Oxford, 1934.

ZÉVAÈS, A.: *Histoire de la troisième République (1870–1945).* Paris, 1946.

THE FIRST RESTORATION AND THE HUNDRED DAYS

ON April 6th, 1814, Napoleon I, Emperor of the French, abdicated at Fontainebleau. Europe rejoiced: men believed that the 'Universal Tyrant' was finally overthrown, and even France thought gladly of relief from the burden of an increasingly onerous administration and hoped for peace at last. For the best part of twenty years France of the Revolution and the Empire had been almost incessantly at war and now by 1814, after the débâcle of the Grande Armée in Russia and the costly campaigns of 1813, she was weary, a 'mutilated and exhausted nation', poorer for the loss of some two million men, eager for peace, for the restoration of some degree of liberty and for the end of conscription, but uncertain where to look for such blessings.

The imminence of peace after nearly a quarter of a century of European upheaval brought its own tremendous problems. For the Allied leaders the main task was to re-establish a harmonious European order, and not the least of the necessary conditions of such an order was the settlement of the Government and frontiers of France in such a way as to ensure that she should not again disturb or endanger peace. Already on March 30th Paris had capitulated to the Allied armies and on the following day the Tsar of Russia and the King of Prussia had entered the city. Already a provisional government had assumed authority under the leadership of the most versatile of French statesmen, the wily Talleyrand, who combined a nimble sense of his own advantage with a penetrating awareness of his country's interests and an unrivalled ability as a diplomat. The Allies had already discussed the future government of France; a Republic with its revolutionary associations was out of the question, Great Britain had opposed the establishment of any Bonaparte dynasty and there had been no unanimous agreement about the suggested expedient of calling Bernadotte, most astute of Napoleon's marshals or the Duke of Orléans, rich and radical scion of the old royal family, to the throne. Accordingly, by the Convention of Châtillon of February, they had agreed that the 'French nation' should itself determine its future government. This was a striking recognition of

the new principle of popular sovereignty, but in the first days of April
the French nation was for all practical interests and purposes Talleyrand;
and Talleyrand it was who persuaded a doubtful Tsar and a French
Senate composed of Napoleon's nominees that there could be no more
satisfactory guarantee of order and good government for France than
the restoration of the hereditary Bourbon monarchy in the person of
Louis XVI's next surviving brother, Louis Stanislas Xavier, Count of
Provence. On April 6th, the day of Napoleon's abdication, Louis
was proclaimed King of France with the style of Louis XVIII, which
he had assumed in 1795 on the death of his young nephew, the unhappy
Dauphin best known to history as the 'Prisoner of the Temple', whom he
regarded as the rightful Louis XVII although he had never reigned.

Some sixty years later, when the future government of France was
once again in doubt, Thiers, the greatest French statesman of the day,
made a famous remark that the Republic was the régime which divided
Frenchmen least. In 1814 it could be hoped that the return of the
Bourbons would be not only the solution which all the Allies could
accept, even if they did so without enthusiasm, but also the solution
which would win the widest acceptance in France itself. During these
first months after Napoleon's fall French affairs were settled with a
decision and rapidity which the twentieth century might well envy.
On May 1st, 1814, peace was signed between France and the Allies
with the first Treaty of Paris; on the 3rd, Louis XVIII entered his
capital and on the 4th June he endowed his people with a Constitutional
Charter. Peace, the restoration of the dynasty, and its apparent reconciliation with the ideas of 1789, these events so momentous for France
had all taken place within the space of three months. The peace settlement was far from ungenerous. France retained her old frontiers of
1789 together with the former enclaves of Avignon, Montbéliard, part
of Savoy and some eastern frontier towns of great strategic importance.
With the exception of San Domingo, which was to become independent,
and of St. Lucia, Tobago, and Mauritius, which went to Great Britain,
she retained her colonial possessions. There was no war indemnity,
no continued Allied occupation of French territory. As Talleyrand
later said: 'The Treaties of 1814 were as happy as circumstances would
allow, for the enemy left the country at the end of six months. The
old France was enlarged, her borders rectified to her advantage.'[1] The
return of the King had been welcomed by many, and none, not even
the Republicans, had attempted to oppose it. The Charter was a guar-

[1] cit. PALLAIN, G.: *Ambassade de Talleyrand à Londres*, 1830-4, p. III, *n*.
     See Map II.

antee that his Restoration would not mean a purely reactionary return to the Ancien Régime as it had existed before 1789, an assurance that the most cherished gains of the last twenty-five years would not be swept away by a stroke of the pen. Equality before the Law; *la carrière ouverte aux talents*; a general system of taxation according to means; freedom from arbitrary persecution and arrest; freedom of worship; freedom to publish and print opinions 'in conformity with the laws which may repress abuses of this liberty'; inviolability of property, including the so-called 'national' property, which had been confiscated by the Revolutionary Government from the Church and *émigré* aristocrats and then sold by the State to new and often peasant proprietors— all these new benefits were preserved by the Charter which has been described as 'the most liberal instrument of government that existed anywhere on the continent.'[1] Nor was this all. It guaranteed the public debt, abolished one of the most onerous of Napoleon's measures, conscription, and attempted to provide a solution for the problem of political liberty which Napoleon had contemptuously ignored. The Charter of 1814 in fact represented the triumph of one of the Liberal theories of 1789 and of the partisans of a constitutional settlement on the English model: the restored Bourbon returned as a constitutional monarch with a parliament of two houses like that of Great Britain. This parliament itself, moreover, emphasized the continuity of new and old, for the members of the old Legislative Body of Napoleon's day became the new Chamber of Deputies, which was, like the English House of Commons, to be subject to election on the basis of property qualification, while the new upper house or Chamber of Peers, made hereditary in 1815, was largely recruited from the old Imperial Senate.

A rapid and lenient peace, followed by the reassertion of France's influence among the Great Powers of Europe through the diplomacy of Talleyrand at the European Congress of Vienna, the restoration of the ancient dynasty, and its reconciliation with the ideas of 1789 formally proclaimed in a Constitutional Charter—here were solid achievements which might well seem to augur well for the future of France. On paper, the provisions of the Charter might seem admirably devised to conciliate all classes of Frenchmen and to enable the Bourbons to strengthen and enlarge the unity which Napoleon had done something to recreate. On paper, there might seem to be no obstacle to the King's wish that all Frenchmen should live as brothers: but unfortunately for France this harmonious pattern of paper schemes was far removed

[1] ARTZ, FREDERICK B.: *France under the Bourbon Restoration*, p. 41. For the text see Appendix III.

from the sharp cleavages of reality. In less than ten months from the proclamation of the Charter, the restored Bourbon régime which came as the harbinger of peace and unity had toppled like a house of cards. On March 1st, 1815, Napoleon escaped from the island of Elba, to which he had been relegated, and landed with a handful of supporters on the French Riviera near Antibes. Within three weeks the former Emperor of the French was in Paris, the King of France a refugee in Ghent. It was not the people of France, but the armies of the European Allies who ensured that Napoleon's second reign should last but a hundred days. It was not the people of France, but the 'baggage wagons' of these armies that brought Louis XVIII back once more from exile and enabled him to resume his throne.

This dramatic interlude in Louis' reign, this episode of the 'Hundred Days', was a calamity both for the Bourbons and for France. It deepened the cleavages that already existed among Frenchmen. It brought war in its train and retribution from the Allies, whose new terms of peace were much more severe.

In fact, the task with which the Restoration Government had been faced in 1814 was singularly difficult. 'If you knew them,' the Tsar had said of the Bourbons before their return, 'you would be convinced that the burden of a crown is not for men such as they.'[1] The collapse of 1815 might seem to many to justify that statement and yet, as we shall see, it would be hard to maintain it as a final verdict. Louis XVIII and some of his immediate advisers suffered from the initial disadvantage of having lived for the best part of twenty-five years in exile. They had had no part or lot in the glorious achievements of the Revolution and the Empire. They had lived obscurely in foreign lands, unknown to or ignored by the great majority of their fellow countrymen, brooding on their wrongs, hating much of the remarkable work accomplished by the French people, because it had been wrought under the guidance of usurping powers. And so it was that, when they returned to their own country, these men who had so long been out of touch with France were virtual strangers to the people they came to rule. They were the heirs of the 'forty Kings who in a thousand years had created France', and yet, said Chateaubriand: 'When I described the royal family to my countrymen, it was as though I had enumerated the children of the Emperor of China.'[2] This strangeness need not have been and was not an insuperable handicap—the English put up fairly easily with Dutch William and Hanoverian George I, who were not merely unfamiliar,

[1] cit. WOODWARD, E. L.: *Three Studies in European Conservatism*, p. 121.
[2] *Mémoires d'outre-tombe*, III, p. 340.

but foreigners, speaking a foreign tongue—nevertheless it was a disadvantage. Louis XVIII, a dignified, witty, courteous, cynical, and
somewhat indolent widower of fifty-nine, ponderously stout, prematurely
aged, and so gouty that he was often obliged to move about in a wheeled
chair, was not a person to inspire immediate and enthusiastic devotion
in subjects who set eyes on him for the first time and were not already
converts to or devotees of the cause of legitimate monarchy. He had
neither the personal magnetism nor the military glory of the predecessor
whose reign he affected to ignore. He had not waged war, but it was
his Government which inherited the legacies of a quarter of a century
of upheaval followed by a shattering military defeat: and, though peace
had been welcomed for its own sake, there had been many to criticize
the terms of the treaty, lenient though it was. The genuine Royalists
were far from being a majority among Frenchmen. The Bourbons
were reimposed by Talleyrand and the Allies *faute de mieux* and
were accepted by most Frenchmen with indifference or resignation
rather than enthusiasm. Such indifference was only too likely to turn
into censure from one of the most politically critical and acrimonious
of peoples unless there was some positive reason for their conversion to
loyal admiration of the new sovereign and his Government. No such
reason presented itself. On the contrary, the problems of demobilization were bound to create an army of discontented—the disbanded
soldiery, the returned prisoners, the civil service that had administered a
French Empire extending over half the Continent, could not all expect
to find immediate and lucrative employment. 'For each office there
were two claimants, for each grade two holders, for each field two
proprietors'.[1] Moreover, in spite of the guarantees of the Charter,
there were many who soon began to fear that the change of régime
would affect them for the worse. With the King there returned a
number of *émigrés*, who in a well-known phrase could be truly said
to have forgotten nothing and to have learnt nothing; they had shared
the King's misfortunes, proved their loyalty to the dynasty, and heedless
of the changes of twenty-five years hoped to be rewarded by the restoration of their former lands, rights and privileges. The presence of such
men embarrassed a monarch who was tolerant at heart and did not wish
to seem ungrateful, but it did little to reassure the numerous classes of
persons whose stake in the country largely depended upon the maintenance of the Revolution settlement. The fact that the King had
preferred to grant the Charter as a favour bestowed by his prerogative
power instead of accepting it from the representatives of the nation,

[1] MARION, M.: *Histoire financière de la France depuis 1715*, IV, p. 376.

and that the document itself contained certain ambiguities or omissions, also gave rise to criticism or suspicion. Moreover, the natural tension, the exaggerated hopes and fears attendant upon a complete change of régime in dramatic circumstances were aggravated by certain ill-advised acts of Louis XVIII and his counsellors. There were ceremonial acts which jarred: acts of policy which caused alarm. The King's declaration that after God he owed his throne to the English Prince Regent was scarcely gratifying to the proud French people—nor were Parisians pleased when one of his first acts was to review the Allied troops of occupation or when his niece entered the regicide city clad in deepest mourning. His first Government lacked both coherence and authority and the King himself failed to give it a unity of direction: his chief confidant, the Comte de Blacas, was ill-fitted to advise the King at such a time, and the tactless talk and conduct of many returned *émigrés* caused alarm. The substitution of the white flag of the Bourbons for the tricolour of the armies which had conquered Europe, and the restoration of many of the symbols and much of the etiquette of the Ancien Régime acted as irritants. The restoration of certain national property to *émigrés* in October 1814, the reduction of the tariff barriers with the ending of the Continental Blockade, the reimposition of the censorship and the maintenance, however financially essential, of the unpopular *droits réunis* or indirect tax on alcoholic drinks and tobacco all gave grounds for discontent.

In fact, the circumstances under which Louis XVIII succeeded to his heritage were such as to require all the political wisdom and tact of an Henri IV. Henri IV, for whose memory there was indeed something of a Royalist cult in the first years of the Restoration, had largely succeeded in reconciling the factions which had been so bitterly opposed during the fifteenth-century Wars of Religion; but the stiff, ageing and indolent Louis XVIII, however sensible and sincere his intentions, was not the man to exercise the charm and energetic leadership necessary to bridge the gulf between friends and foes of the Revolution. Nevertheless, in spite of the prevalence of much discontent, there was no conspiracy to overthrow the Government and there is no reason to suppose that Louis would have had to flee to Ghent but for his failure to retain the loyalty of the army. Here, too, he had a singularly difficult situation to meet. The army he inherited was one discouraged by defeat, humiliated by the peace treaty, irritated at the disbandment of some 200,000 men and the retirement of 13,000 officers on half pay, concessions essential both to humour the Allies and meet the exigencies of the national economy. To these men the displacement of the tricolour was a provocation, as was the creation of a large military household and the appointment of several officers from among Royalists who had seen no service with Napoleon's army. Small wonder, then, that, once Napoleon by sheer personality had won over the first troops sent to oppose him after his landing, what had seemed a mad adventure became a triumphal progress, and the army returned to the loyalty to which it had been accustomed, loyalty to the man who had led it across Europe, whose courage and commands were still irresistible.

Napoleon's return thus showed how insecure were the foundations of this restored monarchy. In his brief second reign he did his best to undermine what credit it had had, to play upon its suspected reactionary intentions and to pose as a champion of Liberal enlightenment against Bourbon obscurantism. He induced the Liberal Benjamin Constant, till lately one of his bitterest opponents, to frame a new Constitution, he ordered democratic institutions to be set up and had them confirmed by plebiscite. Thereby he paved the way for the Napoleonic legend and for that alliance of Bonapartists and Liberals which was to be so important during the next forty years. Thereby, too, he deliberately added fuel to the flames of 'that old quarrel which the Empire had smothered and the Charter was designed to extinguish, the quarrel of the old and the new France, of the "emigration" and the "revolution".'[1]

Yet all these acts betrayed a sense of insecurity which hung heavily upon the country during these fateful days. The Emperor had won the army, but the people as a whole were too weary to rally with enthusiasm. Inevitably Napoleon's reappearance was a defiance of Europe which meant war and brought invasion upon France for the second time within eighteen months. The Allies, who had been at loggerheads at Vienna over the terms of the general European settlement, hastily composed their differences and prepared to deal with the offender. Napoleon, well aware of their intentions, took the initiative, marched into Belgium and met his fate at Waterloo on June 18th. The Hundred Days, had, however, reopened the whole French question. During his second exile, Louis XVIII continued to hold court and council and to act as King of France, but there were many Allied statesmen and French politicians who played with the idea of providing some other ruler for France. Louis, however, had a firm supporter in the Duke of Wellington, and was induced by him to co-operate with Talleyrand and with Napoleon's notorious Police Minister, Fouché, who held the keys to power in Paris. With the help of these three and by acting promptly, he forestalled any serious attempt by the Allies to undo the

[1] GUIZOT: cit. WOODWARD, E. L.: *Three Studies in European Conservatism*, p. 120.

arrangements of 1814. On the 28th June he re-entered France and on July 8th he was back in a capital which was once again occupied by Allied troops. His welcome was cool, but he had anticipated any attempt to supplant him and possession of the throne was nine-tenths of a reign.

The Allies accepted the *fait accompli*, but this time they imposed much sterner measures to secure the Continent against any further French disturbance of the peace. In 1814 they had taken the line that they were warring against Napoleon rather than against the French people. Now they considered that the French people had unashamedly been Napoleon's accomplices in his new aggression and that they must be punished accordingly. From the end of June until September two-thirds of France were occupied by more than a million Allied troops, and when a new peace treaty, the second Treaty of Paris of November 20th, 1815, was concluded it was much more severe than the first.[1] In spite of the pleadings of Louis' able Minister, the Duc de Richelieu, and of the personal remonstrances of the King himself, France was obliged to surrender to Prussia, now for the first time installed as a sentinel in the Rhineland, the border fortresses of Sarrelouis and Landau and to give up Philippeville and Marienbourg. She had to destroy the fortifications of Huningue near the Swiss border and to restore the Department of Mont Blanc to the Kingdom of Sardinia; and in addition to these losses of territory she was obliged to pay an indemnity of 700 million francs within five years, to submit to the occupation of her eastern departments for a period of from three to five years by 150,000 Allied troops, and to return the works of art removed by Napoleon from other countries.[2] Moreover, the Ambassadors of Great Britain, Russia, Austria and Prussia were to meet regularly in Paris as a kind of Control Commission, watching the conduct of the French Government and admonishing it when necessary, and one of them, the Russian representative, Pozzo di Borgo, came in fact to exercise a remarkable influence on French politics for many years to come.[3] Thus, as a result of Napoleon's escapades, the Government of Louis XVIII was placed under a species of tutelage, and for a second time within a few months of their return to power the Bourbons were obliged to conclude an inglorious peace. The circumstances of the Restoration of 1815 were thus by no means propitious for the stability of the régime, and the events of a hundred

[1] Forty-six departments were entirely and fifteen partly occupied. PONTEIL, F.: *La Chute de Napoléon I et la crise française de* 1814-15, pp. 286-7.

[2] See Map II.

[3] TEMPERLEY, H. W. V.: *The Foreign Policy of Canning,* 1822-7, pp. 61-2.

days had rendered a difficult task doubly difficult. Before, however, we proceed to consider how the Bourbon monarchy fared in the years after Waterloo it will be well to take a brief glance at the country and people under its sway.

BEUGNOT: *Mémoires du Comte.* Paris, 1866.

CHATEAUBRIAND: *Mémoires d'outre-tombe*, Vol. III. Paris, 1860.

COOPER, DUFF: *Talleyrand.* London, 1932.

FIRMIN-DIDOT, G.: *Royauté ou Empire, La France en 1814 d'après les rapports inédits du Comte Anglès.* Paris, s.d.

GUEDALLA, P.: *The Hundred Days.* London, 1934.

HOUSSAYE, HENRY: 1814, 27th ed. Paris, 1899.

LACOUR-GAYET, G.: *Talleyrand.* Paris, 1930.

NICOLSON, HAROLD: *The Congress of Vienna, A Study in Allied Unity*, 1812–22. London, 1946.

PONTEIL, FÉLIX: *La chute de Napoléon Ier et la crise française de 1814–15.* Paris, 1943.

THIRY, J.: *La première abdication de Napoléon Ier.* Paris, 1945–8.

VITROLLES: *Mémoires et relations politiques du Baron de.* Paris, 1884.

WEBSTER, C. K.: *The Congress of Vienna, 1814–15.* London, 1934.

II

FRANCE IN 1815

IN 1789 Mirabeau had described France as 'an agglomeration of dis-united peoples',[1] observing different customs, subjected to differing laws, using different weights and measures, separated from one another by customs barriers, obedient to local rather than national loyalties. Within a few years the Revolution had swept away many cobwebs and the strong hand of Napoleon had seized upon the central institutions of the country and had reinforced, remoulded, and where necessary supplemented them, with the result that France had emerged as the pattern of a nation state, endowed with a highly centralized administration, subject to uniform laws, using common weights and measures, divided equally into departments centrally administered, her people enrolled in a national army and her *élite* drilled in a national system of education. Three-quarters of a century after Napoleon's fall an English historian could write that 'the Civil Code, the Penal Code, the Conseil d'État, the Judicial System, the Fiscal System—in fact every institution which a law-abiding Frenchman respects from the Legion of Honour to the Bank of France and the Comédie Française was either formed or reorganized by Napoleon.'[2] Thus when the Bourbons came into power in 1814 they found already in being an efficient civil service; they had ready to hand a working machine of government which immensely facilitated their task of retrenchment and reconstruction. Parts of it might require to be adjusted but in spite of much talk of the need for de-centralization neither they nor their successors were ever anxious to weaken so efficient an instrument of control.

Yet the France of 1815, in spite of its centralized administration was still rich in the diversity of its racial types, its dialects and its customs. Provinces might cease to be administrative units, but they still retained, and retain to this day, their own traditions and strongly marked character-istics. The Alsatian was notably different from the Breton who was

---

[1] cit. CHAMPION, E.: *La France d'après les Cahiers de 1789*, p. 44.

[2] BODLEY, J. E. C.: *France*, p. 89.

as different again from the man of the Midi. Moreover, France, now reduced once more to bounds not widely different from those of 1789, comprised a land still singularly blessed in the rich variety of its soil and climate. 'We have iron, forests and harvests,' wrote Chateaubriand with pride, 'our sun ripens the vines in every region; the coasts of the Mediterranean give us oil and silk and the shores of the Ocean nurture our flocks. Marseilles . . . attracts the commerce of the old world, while our ports on the other sea receive the wealth of the new.' Some districts had indeed been ravaged by the campaigns of 1814 and 1815, the development of industry had been retarded during the war by lack of coal and labour, and France lagged well behind England as an industrial power. None the less, she had suffered less from fighting and economic disruption than most of the countries she had overrun. The balance of trade remained steadily in her favour from 1815-21. Rich in agricultural production, proud of her ancient civilization, she seemed a veritable Land of Cockayne to the soldiers of the Prussian army of occupation and they talked of living 'like God in France'. With some 29,000,000 inhabitants she was the most populous state in Europe apart from Russia. She was still regarded as the centre of European culture and her language was still the language of diplomacy and of polite society, the most common currency for the exchange of thought between the educated people of many lands. Her capital city of well over 600,000 inhabitants was surpassed in size only by London. With its splendid public buildings, many of them erected by Napoleon—some such as the Bourse, the Arc de Triomphe and the Church of the Madeleine still unfinished when he fell—its public gardens, theatres, restaurants and cafés, it ranked as the finest and most animated city in Europe. Socially and artistically it was the most brilliant. Chateaubriand was the glory of French letters, Talma the master of the stage; the paintings of David and hi school still won widespread admiration.

In this France the main classes of society were still as they had been under the Ancien Régime, nobles, clergy, bourgeoisie of varying degree, and finally the great mass of peasants, workers, artisans, domestics and others who were collectively known as 'the people'; but their conditions had greatly altered. The nobility had lost their ancient privileges and retained only their pretensions. Their numbers had been reduced by the toll of revolution and war and those who had emigrated had lost their estates. The greatest families, whose fortunes had been most closely identified with the old order, had naturally suffered most from the trials of the last twenty-five years. Beside them there still survived a numerous lesser nobility or *noblesse de province*, who lived on their estates, came seldom to Paris and retained considerable influence, social and political, especially in the west, which was long to remain a stronghold of royalism. In spite, however, of their general impoverishment, the nobility as a whole clung to the notion that the exercise of any professions save those of arms and diplomacy was beneath their dignity and thus they themselves barred the way to other means of bettering their fortunes. The older *émigrés* were often enough politically and socially out of touch, easy game for a popular Bonapartist poet, Béranger, to criticize in his famous song, the 'Marquis de Carabas'; and yet even here there were notable exceptions. For instance at Broglie it was the son of the late Seigneur 'who introduced new ideas and democratic tendencies which astonished and sometimes even scandalized his former vassals'.[1] Nevertheless, their misfortunes during the past quarter of a century had had a sobering effect on the nobility as a whole. No longer tempted to flirt with Voltairean and radical ideas, the majority turned their backs on free-thinking and freemasonry and resumed that practice of the Roman Catholic religion which has ever since been a mark of the French aristocracy. Thus, along with their political belief in the Bourbon monarchy, went a renewed belief in the importance of the Church and of religion as a necessary check upon the evil doctrines of revolutionary free-thinkers and as a necessary safeguard of stability in state and society. In general, then, this nobility of 1815 was imbued with a greater seriousness than its forebears of 1789. As Chateaubriand noted: 'In high society morals are purer and domestic virtues more common. . . . We are less frivolous, more simple and natural. . . . Our young people, brought up in camps or in solitude have something forceful and original in them which they did not possess before. Vast interests have preoccupied us; the whole world has passed before us. It is one thing to fight for one's life and to see thrones set up and overthrown and another to be concerned with nothing more than a court intrigue, a stroll in the Bois de Boulogne and a literary novelty.'[2] Men, he claimed, were fuller men than they had been thirty or forty years before.

The clergy had suffered still more than the nobility. Not only had the Revolution deprived them of their wealth; it had also decimated their ranks and disrupted their organization, and in 1815 there were far too few to enable each parish to have its own priest. The numbers of the Bishops had been reduced by more than half and they no longer

[1] *Mémoires du Duc de Broglie*, I, p. 11.

[2] cit. HALÉVY, D.: *Trois épreuves*, pp. 19-20.

enjoyed the princely status which had been theirs under the old dispensation. Roman Catholicism was no longer the sole religion recognized by the State, for although the vast majority of the French people were, at least nominally, Roman Catholics, Jews and Protestants[1] were now officially recognized. The Concordat of 1801 by which Napoleon and the Pope had determined the relations of Church and State in France, and the Organic Articles subsequently issued by Napoleon,[2] subjected the Church to a degree of State control as strict as any that had been imposed by the Ancien Régime, and in their endeavours to resist this control the clergy tended to look more and more beyond the Alps to the Pope as the defender of their cause. So already there was beginning that ultramontane movement among French Catholics which was to be so important in the history of the French Church during the nineteenth century and which was to appeal to Bishops and ordinary clergy alike. Within his diocese, however, the Bishop now, as the result of the Concordat, had a more absolute control over his clergy. These were for the most part recruited from the peasantry and little better educated than their flocks, so poor too, that their poverty was more than once to be a subject of sympathetic reference in the Chamber even by speakers who were ordinarily anti-clerical in their outlook. In order to supplement the meagre stipend of 1,000 or 1,500 francs a year allowed them by the State they depended on Church offerings, gifts from parishioners and grants in aid from their commune or parish. None the less this peasant priesthood, like the priesthood in Ireland to-day, still retained a great hold over the faithful in many country districts, especially in the west and in the more remote and mountainous regions.

It was the bourgeoisie who had been the chief gainers from the Revolution. They had led the Third Estate to victory and were now on the way to complete political ascendancy. Their social aspirations were no longer blocked by the privileges cf the aristocracy and the higher clergy. It was they who had been the largest purchasers of the lands confiscated by the Revolution and who were most suspicious of any Bourbon design to undo the land settlement. Many of those who had thus stepped into the shoes of the nobility and clergy were now content to live on the revenues of these estates, thus forming a new class of landed gentry. Such men, successful in some profession

[1] It has been estimated that there were at this time in France about 680,000 Protestants and 60,000 Jews. ARTZ, FREDERICK B.: *France under the Bourbon Restoration*, p. 103.

[2] For the text of the Concordat and the Organic Articles see Appendix I and II in BODLEY, J. E. C.: *The Church in France*.

or in government service, were more numerous than the industrialists who derived their wealth from factories, and who were mainly to be found in the great cities and among the iron masters of Lorraine and the textile manufacturers of the north and east. In general the liberal professions, especially medicine and the law, were those in which they aspired to place their sons, while they sought to provide their daughters with dowries sufficient to enable them to marry into their own class. To religion they were often indifferent and sometimes actively hostile, but scepticism or anti-clericalism did not necessarily mean that the influence of religious thought and practice was excluded from their homes, since, for lack of any suitable alternative, their daughters were usually educated in convent schools. More than ever prosperous and politically powerful (in fact under the franchise of the Restoration monarchy the wealthiest of them constituted a new privileged class) the bourgeoisie nevertheless in general lived simply and travelled little. Their outlook was limited and at a time when such amenities as seaside resorts, watering places and English sports and games, except for horse-racing and whist, were still virtually unknown, their main distractions were those of the dining-table. Thus all over France they helped to maintain the reputation, won for their country in the seventeenth century, as the land where the art of good cooking and the growing of fine wines is unsurpassed. The France of the Restoration was the France of Carême, the celebrated master of Talleyrand's kitchens, and the former magistrate, Brillat-Savarin, whose *Physiologie du Goût*, published in 1825, has ever since been the classic of epicurean taste.

The rest of the people, *les gens du peuple*, comprised the artisans, industrial workers, small shopkeepers, petty employees and, last but not least, the peasantry, who accounted for more than seventy-five per cent of the population and were the main source of recruitment for the army and navy, for domestic servants and, as we have seen, for the lower clergy. All those who tilled the soil were loosely termed 'peasants', but they differed considerably in their relationship to the land. While many owned the land they cultivated, it often happened that their own plot was too poor or too barren or too embarrassed by mortgages to meet their needs, and so there was still a considerable though dwindling class of tenant farmers and *métayers*—these last cultivating the land with means provided by its proprietor and sharing the produce with him. Many were thus dependent on large land-owners, and the laws of inheritance which imposed further subdivision of the land served only to increase their dependence. Moreover, in some parts of the country, especially in Burgundy and Normandy, there was still a high proportion of landless labourers. The Revolution had altered the legal status of the peasantry and relieved them of onerous burdens in the way of feudal dues, but it had not affected their methods of cultivation or led to any striking improvement in their material lot. Even after 1850 a great French mediævalist, Delisle, could write that 'a thirteenth century peasant would visit many of our farms to-day without much astonishment.'[1] In diet, clothes and housing the French peasant of 1815 was no doubt generally worse off than the British agricultural labourer. The British labourer's diet 'was often meagre enough, but nowhere did he live for six months every year' exclusively on potatoes and chestnuts 'like some poor peasants of the . . . Tarn. Nor did he go either barefoot or in sabots', and 'Only in the Western Highlands could any houses be found so bad as the houses in Nogent-sur-Seine'.[2] It was only gradually, in certain districts, that the French peasant was accustoming himself to grow the new crops of sugar beet, turnips and potatoes which were to make a valuable addition to a diet in which meat was still for the most part a luxury. Only on the large farms in the north and east was he beginning to make some use of artificial manures, to learn how to enrich the soil by changing crops and how to improve his stock by cross-breeding. Around the compact villages of the more level lands he still ploughed vast open fields and used the traditional three-course rotation; elsewhere he still tilled the soil according to the age-long dictates of tradition, geology and climate, using the hoe, long-shafted spade and short scythe. For the most part, he and his fellows lacked the knowledge and the capital to make improvements. Communications in districts away from the few main roads were still very poor and the peasant was therefore entirely dependent upon the local market. Thus in a bad year there was still, as in the days of the Ancien Régime, serious risk of local famine: in 1816–17 the Government was obliged to import corn from overseas and to spend large sums in order to relieve distress caused by the shortage of bread and consequent high prices.

Distress and state aid for the needy were also conditions only too well known in the towns of France. In Paris over 100,000 people, or one-sixth of the population of the city, were in receipt of poor relief, either at home or in hospitals and institutions. Artisans and small shopkeepers were mainly concerned to supply the needs of their local clientèle and were often little better off or better educated than the peasantry, working long hours in cramped conditions. The lot of the

---

[1] ARTZ, FREDERICK B.: *France under the Bourbon Restoration*, p. 174.

[2] CLAPHAM, J. H.: *Economic History of Modern Britain*, I, p. 317.

industrial worker in a big factory was still harder. France was still
essentially a country of small industries: compared with Great Britain
the workers in large-scale industry were a small class and industry a
backward growth—apart from Paris there were only two towns, Lyons
and Marseilles, with over 100,000 inhabitants and only five with between
50 and 100,000, namely Bordeaux, Rouen, Nantes, Lille and Toulouse.
Nevertheless industrial development, such as it was, raised the same sort
of problems as in Great Britain. The introduction of machinery led
to riots like the Luddite disturbances in England, and the growth of urban
manufactures accelerated the decline of rural industries, particularly of
textiles. Towns became overcrowded, workshops were unhygienic,
women and children were employed for long hours to the detriment
of their health. The English Combination Laws had their counterpart in the Revolutionary and Napoleonic legislation maintained by the
Bourbons, which forbade the workers to strike or combine in their own
interests and imposed a strict police control over them by means of a
system of passports and *livrets* or work-books.[1] The only kind of
workers' unions which were tolerated were mutual aid or benefit
societies. Thus the industrial workers had no effective means of im-
proving their lot, and, while the administrative supervision of industry
was often marked by a kindly paternalism, the general attitude of the
Government was one of *laissez-faire*. The individual worker was left
to make his own arrangements with his employer. While the old
traditions of *compagnonnage* still survived in certain industries, all
attempts to reintroduce the guilds of the Ancien Régime which had been
abolished by the Revolution, were unavailing. The interests of the
bourgeoisie were much better served by the combination of industrial
freedom and police control instituted by Revolutionary and Napoleonic
legislation and they had nothing to gain from a return to the restrictive
practices of the guilds. The freedom they sought was, however, by
no means the freedom of general free trade. One of the main concerns
of the industrialists was to be shielded from foreign competition and in
this they were at one with the landed proprietors, who feared the import
of cheaper foreign corn. Thus the needs of the French people were
to a large extent supplied by the French themselves and France continued
to be a highly protectionist country throughout the first half of the nineteenth century.
   In this France of 1815, as in all other countries of the time, the benefits
of secondary education were naturally accessible only to an *élite*, and

[1] The worker was to present this book to his employer upon being engaged.
In it the employer kept a record of the worker's conduct.

even for them it was often a summary matter.[1] Greek and Latin and
Mathematics were the staple subjects taught in the secondary schools,
whether they were colleges (or Lycées as they had been known under
the Empire) or *petits séminaires*[2] which, designed primarily for the
education of priests, took many pupils who eventually adopted a lay
career. University education was, as in this country, virtually confined to those who were destined either to be gentlemen of leisure or to
enter one of the 'liberal' professions. Elementary education was rudi-
mentary and in 1821 there were still as many as 25,000 communes which
lacked any sort of school. In the absence of any compulsory system of
schooling the unscrupulous industrialist was tempted to exploit child
labour. Thus the majority of the people were illiterate and the sight of
a messenger or errand-boy reading might still be a phenomenon to a
returned *émigré—'Voyez! voyez, ce coquin qui lit!'*[3]

The general picture of the Bourbon inheritance is of a rich and
populous country endowed with an efficient administration and proud
of its glorious military and cultural traditions. The vast majority of the
subjects of Louis XVIII are a thrifty, hard-working, illiterate peasantry.
'We are a tranquil people,' said Laboulaye many years later, 'with agitated legislators,' and this saying is profoundly true of France throughout the nineteenth century. The great mass of the French people was
indifferent to the constitutional struggles and the contests of political
doctrinaires. The questions they asked were: How can I secure a living
wage? Will this mean increased taxation or affect the price of corn?
Does this mean conscription or a longer term of service in the army for
my son? When the grant of universal suffrage gives the whole adult
male population a vote, we shall see that time and time again that vote
is cast in favour of order and tranquillity.

[1] 'In 1813 the Empire had thirty-six *lycées*, with 14,492 pupils . . .; in the
private schools—if private they can be called, when their teachers had to be
members of the University, their studies and discipline to admit University inspection, and their students to pay the University tax—there were 30,000 pupils.'
ARNOLD, MATTHEW: *A French Eton, and Schools and Universities in France*, pp. 248-9.

[2] A law of October 1814 permitted one of these *séminaires* to be set up in
each department.

[3] SIBOUTIE, DR. POUMIÈS DE LA: *Souvenirs d'un médecin deParis*, p. 153.

CLAPHAM, J. H.: *The Economic Development of France and Germany, 1815-1914.*
     Cambridge, 1921.
SÉE, H.: *La vie économique de la France sous la monarchie censitaire, 1815-48.* Paris,
     1927.
SEIGNOBOS, CHARLES: *Histoire sincère de la nation française.*

III

THE SECOND RESTORATION

BEFORE his return to Paris in July 1815, Louis XVIII had been induced to get rid of Blacas and on the day after his return he formed a Ministry headed by Talleyrand, who had represented France so brilliantly at the Congress of Vienna, and in which the regicide Fouché, Duke of Otranto, emerged once again as Minister of Police. Chateaubriand recorded his horror at the 'infernal spectacle' of 'Vice leaning on Crime', when he caught sight of Talleyrand and Fouché 'silently' making their way to the King's study.[1] Fouché had indeed worked his passage and Talleyrand had indisputably rendered the greatest service to the State; but for the loyal Royalists a Ministry with such men in Bourbon France after the Hundred Days was a shocking combination and one which was certain not to survive once all the adroitness of the Minister of Police had failed to secure a moderate Chamber out of the elections of August.

The elections of August 1815 immediately illustrated the damage wrought by the Hundred Days. The Charter had laid down that the deputies should be elected by electoral colleges; that their numbers should be unchanged and that they should sit for five years, a fifth being renewed annually. After his return from Ghent Louis had, however, been induced to issue an ordinance lowering the age of eligibility from forty to twenty-five and increasing the number of deputies to 402. As a result the first Chamber of the second Restoration was unexpectedly large and youthful. The electorate, in effect a plutocracy of some 88,000 to 110,000 people—for only Frenchmen of thirty or more who paid at least 300 francs a year in direct taxation had the right to vote—animated by fear, indignation or the desire to be revenged, reacted violently against the dislocation and eventual humiliation caused by Napoleon's last wild fling. Many of the electoral colleges in which the electors assembled were presided over by ardent Royalists and the result was to bring into being what Louis XVIII dubbed '*La Chambre*

[1] In *Mémoires d'outre-tombe*, IV, p. 25, cit. WOODWARD, E. L.: *Three Studies in European Conservatism*, p. 122.

introuvable',[1] an assembly which contained a large majority of young, untried, and fanatical Royalists—Ultra Royalists, as they were to be known. Now for the first time for many years the forces of the Revolution and Counter-Revolution openly confronted one another in France. With such a Chamber it was impossible for the King to keep his Ministers. The regicides were proscribed and Fouché had to accept dismissal not only from office but from France. It was his last appearance on the French political stage, and he was speedily followed into retirement by Talleyrand who had lost his diplomatic usefulness by incurring the enmity of the Tsar. Talleyrand, however, was compensated with the office of Grand Chamberlain and his salon in the Rue St. Florentin soon became a rallying point for opposition and the birthplace of half the witticisms directed against the Court and the Ministry of the day. Fifteen years later this extraordinary man was once again to play an important part in serving yet another régime.

The fall of Fouché and the resignation of Talleyrand meant the disappearance of the noted men of former régimes who had made the Restoration but were not of it. To pass from the men of the Empire to the men of the Bourbons, was, said Chateaubriand, to pass from a stage of giants to one peopled by pigmies.[2] This was, however, a harsh judgement. The new Ministry chosen by Louis XVIII contained several men of considerable ability who rendered notable services. The Duc de Richelieu, who headed it, did not merely look 'the very personification of nobility',[3] but was remarkable among *émigré* Royalists for having taken service in Russia, where he had become Governor of Odessa and proved himself a great administrator.[4] Now that peace had again to be negotiated his personal friendship with the Tsar Alexander was likely to be an important asset; the Comte Decazes, of bourgeois origin but a particular favourite of the King, who wrote to him daily and called him *mon fils*, was a young man of great parts; and Baron Louis who insisted that a State which wanted to enjoy credit must pay for everything, even for its follies, did remarkable work in re-establishing French finances. Moreover, all these men were moderate in outlook. It was a factor of great importance not only that the King was not obliged to take his Ministers from the majority in the Chamber, but that even

[1] i.e. he had never supposed that a Chamber so Royalist could have been found.

[2] *Mémoires d'outre-tombe*, IV, pp. 115–16.

[3] MORGAN, LADY: *France*, p. 162.

[4] Talleyrand's wry comment on his successor's qualifications was: 'He is certainly the Frenchman who is best acquainted with the Crimea.'

when that majority was Ultra-Royalist, he preferred not to do so. Louis XVIII, for all his shortcomings, was sincerely loyal to the Charter, sincerely anxious to put an end to the dissensions of Frenchmen, firmly determined to steer a middle course and not to be forced to go on his travels again.

The Chambre Introuvable was not slow to demand punishment for those who had connived at Napoleon's return and courted his favour, and when Great Britain and Prussia made representations the Government, who wished to be lenient, were under pressure at home and abroad. The passions roused by the Hundred Days inevitably led to a provisional suspension of some of the liberties granted by the Charter. From the general amnesty eighteen prominent men were excepted, including the famous Marshal Ney and the young Count de Labédoyère, men whose desertion to the Emperor had largely contributed to the success of his venture in March. Since their action had brought upon their country much additional suffering and loss of life it might well be thought that they, if any, were worthy to die; but a milder sentence or a royal reprieve would have been more politic, for their execution[1] at once furnished martyrs to the enemies of the régime. As it was, their deaths helped to slake a thirst for revenge which was also exhibited in the questionable proceedings of some of the special courts set up in each department to try rebels and seditious people, and in the condonation of a series of outrages perpetrated in the south by Catholic Royalists against wealthy Protestants, Republicans, and Bonapartists. This wave of 'White Terror' claimed some 200–300 victims in all,[2] not a great number, yet its occurrence and the exultation in it by the more fanatical Royalists showed how dangerously the Hundred Days had exacerbated passions as between Frenchmen and Frenchmen.

The problem which now confronted the rulers of France was one that was virtually new. It was the task of founding a stable constitutional monarchy upon the basis of revolutionary and imperial achievement. The experiment of constitutional monarchy had indeed been essayed in 1789, but conditions had soon become chaotic and the experiment had been short-lived, a tragic failure. This time the legislators of France had preferred to follow the model of Great Britain. France in the months after Napoleon's fall was swept by a wave of Anglomania, of which not the least important effect was the adoption of a constitution on the British model. But, though equipped with a constitutional sovereign

---

[1] One, the Comte de la Valette, escaped through the courage of his wife who changed clothes with him in prison.

[2] BARANTE, BARON DE: *Souvenirs du*, 1782–1866, II, p. 212.

and a bicameral legislature in which many of the outward forms of English procedure were faithfully copied, the French operated the system very differently. As has been said, there was no obligation on the King to choose his Ministers from the party which had the majority in the Chamber. Nor indeed has France ever developed well-organized disciplined parties, much less a two-party system. There were, however, at the outset three main groups of strenuous partisans, Ultras, Independents, and Doctrinaires or Constitutionalists, and it was they who fought in the legislative battles which were ever and anon dominated by the question how far the great Revolution was to be accepted or rejected, ever and anon embittered by invocations of The Terror or the Hundred Days. In Society and in the press the words Jacobin and reactionary were bandied about with the same irresponsible licence with which men were to call each other Fascists or Communists in the twentieth century.[1]

The 'Ultras', who had emerged triumphant from the elections of August 1815, were essentially the party of the *émigrés* and most of their leaders had long lived abroad. They accepted the Charter as an evil, but they hoped temporary, necessity and although they did not scruple to make use of its machinery to serve their own interests, they retained a rooted belief in the divine right of Kings, unfettered by constitutions. They had no intention of trying to resurrect the Ancien Régime with all its anomalies, but they did hope to effect the return of property confiscated by the Revolution, to gain preferments for themselves, to reassert their social superiority, to restore the political influence of the clergy, and to obtain a revision of the Concordat. Their two foremost thinkers, the Vicomte de Bonald and the Savoyard, Comte Joseph de Maistre, 'prophets of the past' as Barbey d'Aurévilly called them, vividly illustrated the Romantic reaction, which had now set in against the rationalist philosophy of the French Revolution, and constantly preached that France's only way to salvation lay through the monarchy and close union with Rome. This 'alliance of Throne and Altar' was indeed a fundamental point of Ultra policy and a theme which was to recur more than once in nineteenth-century French history. Recruited mainly from the clergy, the nobility, and country bourgeois, and representing landed interests to a large degree, the party included men of distinction such as Chateaubriand, the chief literary glory of the day,

[1] The word Jacobin, which originally denoted the name of a club, became that of the extreme Republican party which set up the dictatorial régime of 1793-4, commonly known as The Terror. In consequence, it was commonly applied by Conservatives in both the New World and the Old to Republican or democratic movements which they disliked.

a man whose pen wielded considerable power but whose views were often unorthodox since his character was essentially egotistical and given to opposition, and Villèle, later for some years to be the chief Minister of Louis XVIII and Charles X; but among the mass of its representatives there were many returned *émigrés* of the type satirized by Béranger in the 'Marquis de Carabas' and other poems, and many whose fanatical hatred of the Revolution and all its works warped their political judgement and blinded them to the real temper of the nation. The ardent Royalists who aimed at a veritable counter-revolution were, as Louis XVIII himself said, more Royalist than the King, and all the more embarrassing to him because their acknowledged leader was no less a person than the King's own brother, the Comte d'Artois, the heir to the throne, and because other members of the royal family such as the Duchesse d'Angoulême and the Duc de Berry[1] gave them open support. As a result of their extravagances the King after his second restoration was soon to be at loggerheads with those who, had they been more moderate, should have been his warmest friends.

Very different, and at first very few in the Chamber, were the Independents. For them the Charter was an indispensable guarantee of essential liberties, and if they disliked it, it was because it had. been granted by the King of his royal prerogative instead of emanating from the nation. The will of the nation—that was their guiding principle, for had not the Declaration of the Rights of Man declared that 'the principle of all sovereignty resides essentially in the Nation'? While they were not necessarily hostile to monarchy they had little love for the restored Bourbon régime, which they affected to despise because it had returned in the wake of the enemy, which they disliked because it had done away with the tricolour, and which they suspected because of the influence of the Ultras. They were largely recruited among the urban bourgeoisie who were jealous of the pretentions of the returned nobility, among purchasers of national property who feared that they would be dislodged, and among former soldiers who regretted the glories of the Empire. They included Bonapartists, Liberals[2] who would have preferred to see an Orléans on the throne, a handful of Republicans, and

---

[1] See Appendix I for a genealogy of the Bourbons.

[2] The term 'Liberal' in Continental politics has a wider application than in this country, where it has come to be associated with a highly organized political party. In general, it refers to those who believe in the Liberal or Girondin theory of parliamentary government developed at the time of the Great Revolution: a theory according to which national sovereignty should be constitutionally exercised through freely elected assemblies.

a number of freemasons and anti-clerical admirers of Voltaire. They were the Rationalists as opposed to the Romantics, the Left-wing party of the day. In Lafayette they had their 'flag', in Benjamin Constant and Manuel two brilliant parliamentary orators, in Paul-Louis Courier their pamphleteer, and in Béranger their song-writer. In the press their views were expounded by the *Minerve* and subsequently by the *Mercure* and the *Constitutionnel*.

The third party, the Constitutionalists, who came to embrace or combine with a small group known as the Doctrinaires, was the party of the centre, which tried to preserve a balance and which was most sincerely concerned to secure stability for the régime on the basis of the Charter. Opposed alike to revolution and to reaction, it included several men whose past allegiance was varied but who had an equal desire to make the new order work, men of great intellectual ability and oratorical powers such as Camille Jordan, Royer-Collard and Guizot, the future Minister of Louis Philippe. It was the party with which the King himself was most in sympathy and on which he chiefly relied for the carrying on of his Government during the first five years after his return from Ghent. It was the party on which Richelieu and Decazes depended mainly for support, but, although it had the backing of an influential section of the bourgeoisie, it had no deep roots in the country as a whole.

The fact that the Ultra Chamber of 1815 was confronted by a moderate ministry led to a curious inversion of roles—the Ultras espousing the doctrine of parliamentary sovereignty and the Constitutionalists maintaining that, provided the King did not govern unconstitutionally, he might choose his Ministers as he wished. The apparent liberalism of the Ultras went still further when they advocated the extension of the franchise and a measure of decentralization. These proposals, however, were dictated solely by immediate party interest; their authors calculated that a wider franchise would increase the influence of the lesser nobility and their adherents, and that decentralization would likewise augment the political power of local aristocracies at the expense of the prefects, many of whom were still recruited from among officials of the Empire. Moreover, other demands made by the Ultras, demands for the abolition of the University and the national debt and for the restitution of the national property to the owners from whom it had been confiscated at the time of the Revolution, showed that their true intentions were very far from liberal. While the Ministry did what it could to temper the zeal of the majority in the Chamber it was the Upper House which at first played the main part in frustrating Ultra policy. Strangely enough, the House of Peers was by no means packed with representatives of the old aristocracy, and all these proposals and the new electoral law voted by the Chambre Introuvable were rejected by a Chamber largely composed of men who had held high administrative posts under the Empire. Thus at the outset of the new régime the Second Chamber appeared to justify the bicameral system and fulfilled its role as a block or brake upon ill-considered or excessively partisan legislation.   In this way the course of aristocratic reaction, which had incidentally provoked two minor insurrections, was stayed, but the enemies of the Ultras were not content with this victory, and finally, in 1816, the King was induced to intervene.   In April he brought the session of the Chamber to a close, and in September he yielded to the pressure put upon him both by his Ministers and by the Allied Conference of Ambassadors, and dissolved a house of representatives which had embarrassed him by its conservative ardour.   It was difficult for him to be as severe as the Constitutionalists could have wished against men who had shown such devotion to his person and his dynasty, but at last he acted and the Ultras learnt to their bitter regret that they had presumed too much upon their strength.

The new Chamber which met in November 1816 contained a large majority of Constitutionalists who gave the Richelieu Ministry a support it had never yet enjoyed.   The Liberals were still only a small group and the Ultras whose strength in the Chamber was much reduced entered the Opposition in dudgeon.   The number of deputies had been once more limited by royal ordinance to 258, as in 1814.

Having obtained a majority to their liking, the King and the Government sought to pursue a policy of appeasement and reconciliation and to make one people of the two who, as Louis XVIII was to admit in 1818, still unhappily lived side by side under the same sovereign.   Now that the relations between Government and Chamber were more harmonious serious legislation became possible.   There were certain important tasks of reconstruction which the Ministries of Richelieu and Decazes carried out with singular success.   The finances were overhauled and French credit was re-established owing to the skill of two exceptionally able Ministers, Baron Louis and Count Corvetto.   A new system of accounting was adopted and in 1818 for the first time it became obligatory on each Minister to present an annual report for his department.   As a result of all this, French finances only three years after Waterloo were sounder than those of any other European state except Great Britain.[1]   Furthermore, this re-establishment of credit and the prompt payment of the heavy war indemnity enabled France to be rid

[1] MARION, M.: Histoire financière de la France depuis 1715, IV, p. 433.

of the Allied army of occupation in the shortest possible time. In 1817 Wellington had already consented to reduce it by 30,000 men. By November 1818 the evacuation was complete and Richelieu, content to have accomplished the liberation of the territory, resigned his office. In the meantime an important law was passed which established the basis on which the army was to be recruited for the next fifty years. Since the abolition of conscription by the Charter in 1814 and the disbandment of Napoleon's men after Waterloo, the army had been recruited entirely by voluntary enlistment. This method had produced but a very small force and the Law Gouvion St. Cyr of 1818 supplemented it by the annual conscription of a levy not exceeding 40,000 men. The conscripts were chosen by lot, but those who wished could escape service by the time-honoured device of paying a substitute to take their place, and priests and teachers were in any case exempt. The peace-time effective of the army was fixed at 240,000 men and the period of service at six years for the infantry and eight for other arms. As a result, the French army was to become essentially a professional army, recruited mainly from the peasantry, since most of the upper classes who drew 'a bad number' paid for substitutes (curiously enough, the nobility, in spite of their traditional interests in the army do not seem to have attempted to reserve any specific privileges for themselves). The numbers and the periods of service might be altered—in 1820 the complement was increased to 400,000 and the annual levy from 40,000 to 60,000 —but the Law Gouvion St. Cyr laid down the basic principle of a small professional army, sedulously cultivating the *esprit militaire*, and regarded by successive Governments as a bulwark against internal disorder as well as against external aggression. The main omission of this and subsequent legislation for many years to come was the provision for an effective trained reserve. Whatever the merits of such a reserve, Governments shied at the prospect of arming the nation in time of peace.

The new Chamber also tackled the question of the electoral régime, which the Chambre Introuvable had failed to solve, and legislated for the control of the Press. The Ultras again pressed for a wider franchise, but they were defeated. What, asked Royer-Collard, would be the effect of 'calling upon the multitude' but to 'stir all the depths and to make it drunk with false hopes and promises of proscriptions and spoils?'[1] The laws of February 5th, 1817, and March 25th, 1818, confirmed the provisions of the Charter which stipulated that the vote should be confined to men over thirty who paid 300 francs in direct

[1] cit. WEIL, G. D.: *Les élections législatives depuis 1789*, p. 81.

taxes and that only men of forty or more who paid 1,000 francs should
be eligible as deputies. They also continued the arrangement whereby
the Chamber was renewed by fifths each year and laid down that, for
the first time since 1793, there should be direct election by *scrutin de
liste* held in the chief town of the department, the electors meeting as
a single electoral college for the purpose. This was a blow to the
Ultras who would have preferred *scrutin d'arrondissement*—a system
whereby the elector would have cast a single vote at the chief town of
his local arrondissement,[1] instead of voting for as many deputies as were
allotted to the department. *Scrutin d'arrondissement* was always believed
to tell more strongly in favour of rural interests and, as we shall see,
the conflict between these two rival systems of election continued
throughout the greater part of the next hundred years.

The question of the control of the Press was a subject which aroused
scarcely less passion than that of the electoral régime and it continued
to be regarded as a major problem for many years to come. The Charter
had laid down that Frenchmen had the right to publish and print their
opinions 'in conformity with the laws which should restrain abuses of
this liberty', but the Hundred Days and the conflict with the Ultras had
delayed the passage of definite Press laws. In France, however, as in
most countries at this time, the political Press was regarded as a potentially
dangerous and subversive force which must be kept under strict supervision. Thus Napoleon had maintained it as an arsenal reserved for
those who had the confidence of the Government, and the philosopher
Maine de Biran could write of 'these papers which can bring life or
death'.[2] In fact, although the number of daily papers under the Restoration was extremely small—in 1827 the twelve biggest daily papers had
only 56,000 subscribers between them—and although they were expensive
and obtainable only by subscribers, within their limited circle of readers
they exercised great influence. Moreover, this circle naturally corres-
ponded very closely to the privileged electorate, whose views might
largely be moulded by the able journalists of a Press which in France has
always tended to place doctrine before news. Hence Governments were
bound to be sensitive to the influence of the Press upon the electorate,[3]
while the more they betrayed their sensitiveness, the more the power
and prestige of the Press were enhanced. The laws of 1819, framed by
de Serre and modelled, like so much else at this time, upon English

---

[1] The *arrondissement* is a subdivision of the department. It contains a
number of cantons which are in turn subdivided into communes.

[2] *Journal intime*, II, p. 171.

[3] They were not above helping friendly papers by grants from secret funds.

usage, were in fact the most liberal of the Press laws of the Restoration monarchy, but they reflected the prevalent notion that the production and perusal of a newspaper should alike be reserved for men of substance, men who could be presumed to be educated, who were likely to enjoy a vote and who ought also to have a sense of political responsibility. Newspaper proprietors were obliged to pay a deposit which was fixed at such a high figure—10,000 francs for daily papers in the Parisian area —as to ensure that only men of wealth could afford to start a paper. In addition, the imposition of a stamp duty meant that the papers would continue to be expensive to buy. The liberalism of the laws lay in the important provisions abolishing censorship and permitting Press trials to be decided by jury instead of by the police tribunals.

Meanwhile the balance of forces in the Chamber had been shifting. The annual renewal of the Chamber by fifths meant a partial election each year, and each year saw an accretion in the strength of Bonapartist Liberals, which reflected the growth, even before the Emperor's death, of a Napoleonic legend and of the influence of men such as Béranger. Béranger's songs, satirizing the Royalists and providing the first popular glorification of the armies of the Empire and the Revolution, had indeed a vogue which extended far beyond the electorate, and it was said of him: 'He is more than the poet of the people, he is the people turned poet.' From twenty-five deputies in 1817, the Bonapartists and Liberals rose to forty-five in 1818 and to ninety in 1819, and they included men of note, such as Lafayette, Benjamin Constant and Manuel, or of notoriety, such as the Abbé Grégoire, a former regicide. This rising tide of Liberalism alarmed Richelieu to such an extent that he advocated revision of the electoral law and a rapprochement with the Ultras. As so often happens with Governments or parties of the Centre the moderates tended to be torn in two directions by the opponents on either side of them. So now the result was a split in the Ministry and its resignation in December 1818. The King preferred to continue to steer a middle path and a new Cabinet was formed in which his 'dear son' Decazes still played a leading part, ably assisted by the Comte de Serre; but it met with considerable opposition in the Chamber of Peers, which was only overcome when Louis XVIII increased the number of Peers from 208 to 270, restoring to the Chamber a number of Bonapartists who had been ejected after the Hundred Days. Decazes was subjected to ardent criticism from both Left and Right and the growth of the Liberal representation served only to emphasize the continued existence of the 'two peoples' whom the King would fain merge into one; men who remembered the vicissitudes of the last thirty years now became uneasy and began to doubt the stability of the existing régime, however much they desired it.[1] The King was put under increasing pressure from the Royal Family and the Ultras to change his Ministers, and the assassination on February 13th, 1820, by a lunatic, of the Duc de Berry, the Comte d'Artois' second son, together with the outbreak of a series of Liberal risings and revolutions in various parts of Europe in the same year, forced him to give way. For the Ultras and Right-wing Constitutionalists, the assassination was the final proof of Liberal conspiracy to overthrow the régime and the Ministers were denounced for their weakness, if not indeed their direct complicity in the crime. Consequently, as a result of the storm of Royalist indignation on the Duc de Berry's death, Louis XVIII, to his bitter grief, was obliged to get rid of Decazes and his colleagues. Richelieu returned to power, but at the head of a Cabinet in which Ultra influence was strong and which openly proclaimed its intention of making war upon the Liberals.

The Right, which was now to enjoy power for seven years, immediately set about undoing or modifying the work of the previous governments. Control of the Press was at once tightened; the censorship was re-established, new papers were forbidden to appear without Government authorization, and all printed or engraved drawings had similarly to be approved before they could be published, displayed, distributed or sold. These measures taken in 1820 were followed by a law of 1822 which made papers liable to prosecution for their general tendency and once again removed Press cases from trial by jury and handed them back to the royal courts. The electoral law was also promptly modified to suit the party in power. Instead of widening the franchise, the Government substituted *scrutin d'arrondissement* for *scrutin de liste* and introduced a system of double voting. The electors were now to meet in colleges of arrondissements instead of in a single departmental college—this measure gave greater scope for local and official pressure[2]—and, whereas they all elected the 258 deputies, those who were in the class which paid 1,000 francs direct tax were empowered to meet again as a departmental college to elect a further 172 representatives. The total number of deputies was thus increased to 430 by a system which gave a double vote to the 16,000 wealthiest citizens. The result of the first elections held under this arrangement in 1821 was entirely satisfactory to those who devised it. The Ultras emerged with a

---

[1] e.g. BIRAN, MAINE DE: *Journal intime*, II, pp. 111 and 138.

[2] For interesting details of the forms official pressure took see FREDERICK B. ARTZ: *France under the Bourbon Restoration*, pp. 71ff.

large majority in the new Chamber, the compromise Richelieu ministry gave way to one headed by Villèle, and the triumph of the Right was complete when the posthumous birth of a son to the Duc de Berry assured the continuance of the male succession in the elder branch of the Bourbon family which hitherto had been childless.[1] But the *enfant du miracle*, as the infant Duc de Bordeaux (later known as the Comte de Chambord), was called by ardent and pious Royalists, was destined never to reign. The folly of his grandfather was to deprive him of the throne and his own obstinacy to prevent him from regaining it.

The effect of the severe measures taken by the party in power was naturally to drive some of the elements of opposition underground and to encourage those very conspiracies which the Ultras had feared. Thus a secret society, known as the Charbonnerie and modelled on the Neapolitan Carbonari, was formed with the definite object of over-throwing the Bourbon dynasty. Its activities were probably not un-known to intellectuals like Victor Cousin and Jouffroy[2] and were con-nived at by Liberal deputies like Manuel and Lafayette, but its attempts to foment revolution by the insurrectionary outbreaks which occurred in four or five towns during 1822 were quelled without difficulty. The time for a successful rising was not yet, and under the new Government France was in fact free to take the leading part in crushing an insurrection-ary régime in Spain. None the less, secret societies with more or less revolutionary aims continued for many years to be a feature of French political life and objects of governmental fears and repressions.

Meanwhile, as a result largely of Richelieu's able diplomacy, France had escaped from the tutelage which had been imposed on her after Waterloo and was now once again in a position to play an independent part in European politics. In March 1814 the four principal Allies had, by the Treaty of Chaumont, formed a sort of league to guard against further peril from France. Renewed again in Paris in November 1815, it had then provided for periodic meetings for the discussion of matters of common interest and the maintenance of peace. As a result, the con-ference of Aix-la-Chapelle took place in 1818 for the final settlement of the war damages to be paid by France, and France, having with the aid of the English banking house of Baring acquitted her obligations, was invited to join the Big Four and to sign with them a protocol declaring the intention of the five powers to maintain the peace of Europe on the basis

[1] Neither Louis XVIII nor the Duc d'Angoulême, the Comte d'Artois' elder son, had any children.

[2] SAINTE-BEUVE: *Portraits littéraires* I, p. 313.

of the existing treaties and to confer again as need be. Accordingly, although the four Allies, still suspicious, secretly renewed the Chaumont Treaty, France was publicly readmitted to the Concert of European Great Powers. With her finances re-established and a new army in the making, she could afford to take an independent line, and once the Ultras gained the ascendancy, French foreign policy, although it never lay in a single directing hand, began to reassume its traditional aspect of hostility to Great Britain both in the New World and the Old. In the New World it showed an ambition to establish spheres of French influence in South America which was disquieting to the British Foreign Secretary, Canning, and which he was able to frustrate. In the Old it intervened so successfully that, when Canning in 1826 described how he had called the New World into being to redress the balance of the Old, he represented his action as a direct riposte to French action in Spain.

In 1820 a military revolt had obliged the Bourbon King of Spain, Ferdinand VII, to re-establish the Spanish constitution of 1812 and to submit to the election of a Cortes or parliament. Such a régime was wholly distasteful to the monarch and, in consequence of disturbances which arose when he was discovered to have been plotting against his Liberal ministers, he was kept more or less a prisoner in his own capital. A party armed itself in his support, but was as unable to win control as the Liberals were to exert their authority effectively over the whole country. In these circumstances, the French Government saw an opportunity of reviving French prestige by means of an easy military and diplomatic triumph, and also of acquiring merit in the eyes of the continental Great Powers, who were increasingly disturbed by the manifestations of unrest in various parts of Europe. At the same time they were not unaffected by what has been and still is a recurring preoccupation of French Governments whatever their political colour, namely the desirability of securing in Spain a régime whose political outlook would accord with their own. So at the Congress of Verona in 1822, Chateaubriand, now Foreign Minister in the Cabinet headed by Villèle, secured the blessing of the Great Powers other than Great Britain for an expedition to Spain to re-establish the authority of Ferdinand VII. In 1823 a French army, commanded by the Comte d'Artois' elder son, the Duc d'Angoulême, crossed the Pyrenees. The expedition was at first, like so many French military ventures in the nineteenth century, hampered by the inefficient organization of its supplies, but compared with the forces opposed to it it was a model army. Spain had relapsed into a veritable state of anarchy and the Liberal Government, unable to put up any really effective opposition, took the King with them and withdrew to the south-western and remotest corner of the Kingdom, where after the capitulation of the Trocadero fortress at Cadiz, they eventually gave in.

The ease of this military promenade through a country which had caused Napoleon so much trouble undoubtedly made some impression in Europe and had the desired effect of enhancing French prestige abroad, while the Government did their best to magnify their success at home. But apart from this the gains were slight; the operations of Ouvrard, the biggest French financier of the day, who had demanded exorbitant terms for his services in compensating for the defects of the army intendance, were much criticized; the Liberals in France were naturally bitterly opposed to this 'crusade' on behalf of a reactionary Bourbon King— indeed some of them even went off to fight under the Spanish tricolour against their own forces, thus setting a precedent for their spiritual descendants 113 years later—and the reactionary King himself showed little gratitude to his liberators.   Furthermore, the failure of the French Government to exact any guarantees that the King would be moderate in his conduct, or to prevent him from inaugurating a régime of repression, lost them much of the sympathy they might otherwise have gained at home and abroad.

Meanwhile Villèle and his colleagues took further steps to ensure the perpetuation of the power of the Right in the Chamber.   In 1823 they obtained a dissolution of the existing house, held fresh elections in which civil servants were openly admonished to vote for the Government candidates, did away with the system of partial renewals and decreed that henceforth the life of the Chamber should last seven years instead of five.   The result was the assembly early in 1824 of a Chamber so reminiscent of the Chambre Introuvable, by reason of its large majority of fanatical Ultras, that it was dubbed '*la Chambre retrouvée*'.   This time there would be no Louis XVIII to restrain them from acts of intemperance which ill accorded with the mood of the nation as a whole, for it was evident that for some while past the King's physical powers had been failing and with them his power of independent decision. Since he had been forced to abandon the *via media* of conciliation in 1820 he had fallen increasingly under the influence of the Comtesse du Cayla, who sympathized with the Ultras, and he had bowed more and more frequently to the stronger will of his brother, the Comte d'Artois.   At length, after much suffering, he died in September 1824. Artois ascended the throne as Charles X and Artois was the chief of the Ultras.

32 FRANCE 1814–1940

ARTZ, FREDERICK B.: *France under the Bourbon Restoration.* Harvard, 1931.

CHARLÉTY, J.: *La Restauration* (Vol. IV of LAVISSE, E.: *Histoire de France contemporaine.* Paris, 1921).

CHATEAUBRIAND: *Mémoires d'outre-tombe,* Vol. IV. Paris, 1860.

COOPER, DUFF: *Talleyrand.* London, 1932.

FOUQUES DUPARC, J.: *Le troisième Richelieu,* 2nd ed. Lyon, 1940.

LA GORCE, P. DE: *La Restauration,* 2 vol. Paris, 1926-33.

LUCAS-DUBRETON, J.: *La Restauration et la monarchie de juillet.* Paris, 1926.

MAINE DE BIRAN: *Journal intime,* 2nd ed. Paris, 2 vols., 1927 and 1931.

NOAILLES, MARQUIS DE: *Le Comte Molé, 1781-1855, Sa Vie—ses Mémoires.* Paris 1922. Vols. II-V.

PASQUIER: *Mémoires du Chancelier,* 4th ed. Paris, 1894. Vol. III-V.

IV

THE REIGN OF CHARLES X

CHARLES X, a widower like Louis XVIII, tall and active in spite of his sixty-seven years and a great huntsman, like so many Bourbons before him, possessed a charm, elegance and graciousness unknown to his brother. But his political views were far from reassuring in one who was called upon to be a constitutional monarch and to consolidate a dynasty. More passionate, but at the same time more light-hearted than Louis XVIII, he lacked his brother's balance and sound judgement. When he acted like a sensible King, said Guizot, he did so from a sense of propriety, 'from timid and short-sighted complaisance, because he was momentarily carried away, or from the desire to please, and not from conviction or natural choice'.[1] As Comte d'Artois he had been the acknowledged leader of one of the main parties in the State, and that the very party which had the most reactionary views and was most inclined to scoff at the Charter which as King he was now bound to uphold. Moreover, dissolute in his earlier years, the new sovereign was now a devotee much under clerical influence. As an Ultra and a pious son of the Church he therefore fully believed that the Revolution was the work of the Devil and disbelieved as fully in constitutional limitations upon the divine right of Kings. The Duke of Wellington in 1818 might well wish that 'Monsieur would read the histories of our Restoration and subsequent Revolution, or that he would recollect what passed under his own view and probably at his own instigation in the Revolution'[2]—Charles, if he did indulge in such reading or reflections, came only to the conclusion that he would rather chop wood than be a King like the King of England. With such a past and such an outlook it would have been difficult indeed for him to raise himself to be a King above party, even had he so wished.

Nevertheless the circumstances under which the new King ascended the throne were not unfavourable. France was at peace and economically prosperous. The value of foreign trade notably increased during

[1] *Memoirs of my own time*, I, p. 265.
[2] cit. ALDINGTON, RICHARD: *Wellington*, p. 244.

the first year of his rule. The elections had produced the results which had been intended; the new reign began with harmony between the sovereign, the Government and the majority in the Chamber, and the head of the Government, Villèle, was widely recognized as a man of great ability. Furthermore, the King was induced to begin his reign by abolishing the censorship and according a limited amnesty to political prisoners, gestures which made a favourable impression. Thus it might have been expected that under such conditions the Ultras of the Chambre Retrouvée, supported by King and Government, would have had little difficulty in imposing the programme which they had failed to carry in 1815; that they would hand over the control of education and the keeping of civil registers to the clergy; that they would indemnify the *émigrés* for their confiscated property; that they would re-establish a territorial aristocracy and amend the provisions of the Civil Code relating to the equal division of inheritance; and that such measures would be accepted quietly, since the ranks of the parliamentary Opposition were so much reduced although the principle of parliamentary government was still maintained.

In fact, however, although the Opposition were weak in the Chamber, they were strong outside it. Villèle had made a serious blunder when early in 1824, because of Chateaubriand's lukewarm support of a conversion loan, he had persuaded Louis XVIII to dismiss his Minister of Foreign Affairs in summary fashion. Chateaubriand, who 'aspired to all things and complained of all' and who, as Guizot remarked, was much hurt if he were not regarded as the rival of Napoleon as well as of Milton,[1] might be an awkward colleague, but he was still more dangerous as an opponent; and the humiliating brusqueness with which he had been dismissed at once led him to place his tongue and his redoubtable pen at the service of the Opposition, who thereby gained a powerful ally. In the press the Opposition papers, such as the *Constitutionnel*, in which the young Thiers had made his début, and the *Journal des Débats*, which Chateaubriand carried with him into opposition, commanded no less than 40,000 subscribers, whereas the organs which supported the Government could boast no more than a mere 15,000. In such circumstances the Ultra programme was less easy to fulfil; it was bitterly opposed outside Parliament, while within three years the ardent Royalists in Parliament were themselves so divided upon certain of its proposals that Villèle was forced to dissolve a Chamber with which he had hoped to govern for seven years.

This is not to say that the programme was not in part carried out.

[1] GUIZOT, F.: *Memoirs to illustrate the history of my time*, I, p. 86.

Control of education was in effect given to the Church when a Bishop, Mgr. Frayssinous, was in 1822 made Grand Master of the University and in 1824 appointed Minister of Education and Ecclesiastical Affairs; and the vexed question of the compensation to be paid to the *émigrés* who had been dispossessed of their estates was not unfairly settled when they were voted an indemnity. This indemnity was often referred to by its opponents as the *émigrés*' 'milliard' but in tangible form it would not appear to have amounted to more than 650,000 francs at the most. It had, however, been all the more strenuously opposed by many of the bourgeoisie because the money was to be provided by the conversion of 5 per cent annuities into 3 per cents. As yet the principle of a conversion loan, subsequently so familiar in government financial operations, was new and strange in France, and the holders of annuities were sore and indignant at losing interest in such a cause. Other issues, however, aroused still more contention, and above all it was the clerical question which excited passions and caused the ranks of Tuscany to break.

Louis XVIII had been too infirm to undergo the strain of a five hours' coronation service; Napoleon had crowned himself; but one of Charles X's first acts was to be crowned at Rheims with most of the elaborate religious ceremonial of the Ancien Régime. In a country long unused to such scenes, the ceremony seemed symbolic of an intention to restore something of the substance as well as of the forms of pre-revolutionary society. In particular, there were many, like the terrible Béranger (who scoffed at the ceremony in his *Coronation of Charles the Simple*) who feared that it heralded the revival of clerical influence in matters of state. Those who shared the fear of clericalism included not only deists and free-thinkers, Bonapartists and Liberals, but also Catholics who had come to accept the idea of the neutral lay state as a necessary concomitant of civil equality and Royalists who were full of the old Gallican fire against the pretensions of Rome to direct the clergy. Under Louis XVIII proposals for the restoration of unsold national property to the Church had been rejected for fear of the opposition of the Chambers, and for similar reasons the Government had dropped a suggested new Concordat which it had negotiated and of which the main effect would have been a reversion to the Concordat of 1516. Among the general public, however, it was above all the unauthorized reappearance of the Jesuits and the missionary activities of the so-called Congregation which reawakened the spirit of anti-clericalism. As a result of the acute shortage of clergy and of the neglect of religious observances into which many parts of the country had fallen owing to the vicissitudes of the previous twenty-five years, the Church authorities had approved a campaign of home missions of which the main instrument was a body of specially trained priests known as 'the Congregation of Priests of the Mission of France'. These missionaries did much excellent work, but their zeal in planting missionary crosses in expiation of the crimes of the Revolution and in burning the works of Voltaire was often provocative and had at once aroused the suspicions and hostility of anti-clericals and of those who feared a reversal of the Revolution settlement. So they had drawn upon themselves the satire of Béranger and the attacks of many pamphleteers. Now under the new King a multiplication of religious manifestations (in some of which the King and members of the Royal Family took part), ecclesiastical control of education, the measures taken against critics like Cousin, Béranger, P.-L. Courier and Guizot, who were imprisoned or obliged to suspend their lectures, the persecutions of publishers who reprinted the works of the eighteenth-century rationalists such as Helvetius and D'Holbach, the suppression of the École Normale or teacher's training school on account of its *mauvais esprit*, and an extraordinary law, passed despite Villèle's opposition, which made sacrilege a crime punishable by death, all increased the fears that 'hidden forces' directed by Rome were gaining control of the State. Fantastic rumours circulated about the aims of the Jesuits[1] and the Congregation, and the King himself was reported to have become a Jesuit. This issue of clericalism came to a head in 1826 when a Royalist but ardently Gallican peer, the Comte de Montlosier, published a book denouncing the existence of 'a religious and political system tending to the overthrow of religion, society, and the throne' and declared that it was due to four 'scourges'—a number of religious and political congregations which had spread throughout France, various establishments of 'the odious and forbidden society of Jesuits', the more or less open profession of Ultramontanism, and priestly encroachments upon civil authority.[2] Already the Villèle ministry had been under heavy fire from the Left and from the Royalists who followed Chateaubriand and, as we have seen, the figures of the relative circulation of Opposition and Governmental papers—40,000 compared with 15,000 only—showed how far it was from carrying even educated opinion with it. Now Montlosier's action divided the Royalists still further: several Bishops even went so far as to make a declaration against the Jesuits and the Royal Court debated a new Denunciation of the Jesuits addressed

---

[1] The number of Jesuits in France was probably not more than 300. A. DANSETTE, *Histoire religieuse de la France contemporaine*, p. 278.

[2] *Mémoire à consulter sur un système religieux et politique tendant à renverser la religion, la société et le trône, par M. le Comte de Montlosier*, Paris, 1826.

to it by Montlosier and showed its sympathy with his case, although it
had no power to prosecute. The anti-clericalism of the Opposition
papers increased and there was a veritable spate of pamphlets and brochures—no less than 5,000 in 1826 alone—denouncing the influence of
the religious orders in general and of the Jesuits in particular. In salons
and in clubs, and even in the Académie Française as well as in the press,
Villèle and his colleagues were bitterly attacked for countenancing the
growth of clerical influence; and their denials carried little conviction
when it was they who had had the unwisdom to sponsor the law on
sacrilege. Faced by such a virulent campaign, they decided that it
could only be checked by more drastic control of the press. Accordingly, a bill was introduced which imposed the obligation to prior
deposit (dépôt préalable) and a stamp duty on all printed matter. This
bill, described by an Ultra deputy as a 'law of reason and love', but
condemned by Chateaubriand as a 'law of the Vandals', would virtually
have stifled the printing business, and though it was carried in the
Chamber it was, to Villèle's extreme vexation, as good as rejected by
the Peers. Once again, as in 1815, the members of the Upper House
showed that they were prepared to stand out against excessively reactionary measures. Ironically enough, while Villèle's policy at home was
disliked on account of its reactionary vigour his foreign policy was no
less criticized on account of its caution. In particular, the cause of Greek
independence had won widespread sympathy in France as well as in
Great Britain, and Villèle's failure to give the Greeks more active support did much to increase the unpopularity of his Government. An
ill-advised attempt of the King to try and rally opinion by a grand review of the National Guard only made tension worse, for the Guards
shouted for the downfall of the Ministry and the Jesuits, and Villèle
insisted on their dissolution. Finally, towards the end of 1827, the
Minister decided that he could retain control only by packing the
House of Peers and by securing a still more disciplined Chamber. In
November the King issued three ordinances, the first dissolving the
Chamber and ordering new elections, the second creating seventy-six
new peers—a precedent for an English sovereign four years later—and
the third once again reimposing the censorship.

Villèle's confident expectation that official pressure would give the
Ultras a fresh majority was grievously disappointed. The forces of the
Opposition gained a majority of sixty, and after a brief attempt to carry
on notwithstanding this check Villèle resigned in January 1828. He was
the most unpopular Minister the Restoration monarchy had so far known,
yet even his enemies admitted that he was a great administrator and in

particular perhaps the ablest French Finance Minister since Colbert. He had crowned the work of Baron Louis and Corvetto by further stabilizing French finances and putting public accounting on a regular basis. Whatever the shortcomings of the Bourbon Governments in other directions it could no longer be said that they were incapable of financial reform, and after 1821 the credit for this was due to Villèle. It had been his weakness that he was largely dependent upon a majority which was still more out of touch than he with the main currents of French opinion and that he allowed himself to carry out a policy with which he was not wholly in sympathy, in order to retain the power of which he was over-fond.

The fall of Villèle was a bitter blow to Charles X, but for a while he made the best of his discomfiture and succeeded in forming under the Vicomte de Martignac, a new Ministry, recruited mainly from men of the Right Centre who were prepared to follow a conciliatory policy. The censorship of the Press was once again abolished, Guizot was allowed to resume his lectures; unauthorized congregations were forbidden to direct schools and a limit was placed upon the number of pupils who could be taken by seminaries. Such measures effectively served to relieve tension, but they were far from palatable to the monarch, and the Ministry of the centre was, as usual, liable to be attacked from the Right and Left. So, at length, in April 1829, weary of a policy so alien to his own way of thought, Charles X, who, from a successful tour in Western France, the traditional stronghold of royalism, had gained the illusion that he was universally popular, gladly sought the pretext of the rejection of a Government bill by a combination of Right and Left to be rid of his too moderate Ministers. Like Louis XVIII in 1815 he preferred a Cabinet which contained men after his own heart and selected as his new chief Minister an intimate personal friend, a former *émigré* and Ultra of the deepest dye, Prince Jules de Polignac.

The new Ministry was formed when the Chamber was no longer sitting, but the announcement of its composition came like a thunderbolt to France and to Europe. Apart from Polignac it included Bourmont, a general who was notorious for having deserted Napoleon before Waterloo, and La Bourdonnaye, who had been the most bloodthirsty of the Ultras in demanding vengeance after the Hundred Days. The choice of men so unpopular was either a piece of blind tactlessness or deliberate provocation. Under Louis XVIII the first Richelieu Ministry, if it had not the backing of the majority of the Chamber, was well regarded by public opinion as a whole both at home and abroad. But the Polignac Cabinet was bound to antagonize both. Abroad, the

Austrian Chancellor, Prince Metternich, at once recognized its formation as tantamount to a counter revolution. At home, Opposition papers like the *Journal des Débats*, hailed it with scorn: 'Coblentz! Waterloo! 1815! Those are this Ministry's three principles: Squeeze it, twist it, nothing but humiliation, misfortune and danger oozes out!'[1] Many feared that it was in fact the prelude to a *coup d'état*, and, during a winter of extraordinary severity, all the forces opposed to clericalism and reaction, all the forces loyal to government according to the Charter, and all the forces which aimed at the overthrow of the régime girded themselves for a fight. Political societies, such as the one which rejoiced in the name of 'Help thyself and heaven will help thee', and which was supported by Constitutionalists as eminent as Guizot and the Duc de Broglie, began to contemplate passive resistance and refusal to pay taxes. The Opposition Press was powerfully reinforced by the creation, in January 1830, of a new paper called *Le National*, which had the blessing of the aged Talleyrand and, under the direction of Armand Carrel and two distinguished young historians, Thiers and Mignet, extolled the Glorious English Revolution of 1688 and hinted that an unsatisfactory monarch might well be replaced by a member of his own family with broader views. The allusion to the Duke of Orléans was understood by all.

The clash between Cabinet and Chamber came as soon as the new session opened in March 1830. The speech from the throne carried a scarcely veiled threat that opposition would be overcome by force. The Chamber replied with an address of no confidence. 'The permanent harmony of the political views of your Government with the wishes of your people is the indispensable condition for the conduct of public affairs. Sire, our loyalty, our devotion oblige us to tell you that this harmony does not exist.'[2] Thus the constitutional problem latent throughout the Restoration came to a head. Could the King choose and keep his Ministers as he pleased or must they be chosen from the majority in the Chamber and resign when defeated or censured? The Prince de Polignac took his inspiration from the heavenly visions which were vouchsafed to him in the night and which bade him stand firm. Charles stood by Polignac, dissolved the Chamber and kept his Ministers.

The Government and country now prepared for new elections, but no amount of official pressure could secure a majority for the supporters of so unpopular a Cabinet. In the elections of July 1830 the Opposition returned 270 strong instead of 221. Still the King was undaunted.

[1] cit. LUCAS-DUBRETON, J.: *La Restauration et la monarchie de juillet*, p. 134.
[2] CAHEN, L. and MATHIEZ, A.: *Les lois françaises de 1815 à 1914*, p. 57.

In spite of this vivid proof of public opinion, in spite of advice from the
Tsar and Metternich, he was determined to have his way.   On July 25th
he invoked Article XIV of the Charter which empowered the King, if
need be, to make 'the necessary regulations and ordinances for the
execution of the laws and for the safety of the State'.   As it depended
upon the King and his advisers to decide when Article XIV should be
called into play, he could still argue that he was acting according to the
letter of the constitution.   But in all the circumstances the four ordinances published on the 26th July,[1] virtually suppressing the liberty of
the Press, dissolving the Chamber, modifying the electoral law in such
a way that the electorate was reduced to some 25,000 people almost
exclusively composed of landed proprietors, and fixing a date for new
elections, were tantamount to a *coup d'état* and everyone recognized
them as such.   The immediate reactions in Paris did not threaten
revolution.   Deputies still contemplated only passive resistance and
refusal to pay taxes; and, although at the office of the *National* Thiers
and his fellow journalists drew up a collective protest declaring that the
Government had lost the legal character by which it commanded obedi-
ence and invited the country to decide 'how far she ought to carry
resistance against tyranny', the first demonstrations of printers on strike
and of stray bands of workmen and students did not appear serious.
It was the astonishing lack of preparedness on the part of the King
and Government which allowed a demand for the dismissal of the Ministry to swell rapidly into a revolution beyond their control.   Nothing
indeed is more extraordinary than the blind insouciance of Charles X
and Polignac.   It was they who were effecting a *coup d'état*, it was they
who controlled the armed forces, and yet they took no steps to ensure
that their forces should be adequate to ensure their success.   They
believed that if the coup were prepared with secrecy the public would
be too surprised to react, and so, having signed the ordinances, the King
went off to hunt at Rambouillet, leaving the Deputy Minister of War to
learn of them for the first time from the official *Moniteur* and to deal with
the situation as best he could.   No troops had been concentrated in case
of emergency, no measures taken to occupy all strategic points in and
about the capital or to arrest potential leaders of opposition.   The Paris
garrison was actually much below strength, since some men had been
drafted to take part in an expedition against Algiers and others were
away on manœuvres.   As if this were not folly enough, the King threw
fuel on the flames by appointing Marmont, the Duke of Ragusa, to com-

[1] For the text in English see BUTTERFIELD, H.: *Select Documents of European
History*, 1715–1920, pp. 111ff.

mand these diminished forces. Marmont, like Bourmont, was another of the generals who had destroyed Napoleon, and 'raguser' for the Parisians was a word which meant 'to betray'. Thus the forces of opposition were given time to organize and the tactless intransigence of Charles encouraged the opposition to take a revolutionary turn. Barricades went up all over the city; the National Guards, disbanded but not disarmed in 1827, brought out their weapons; workers with Republican sympathies, students of the École Polytechnique and many bourgeois, all joined in the fray. Swept by a wave of romantic revolutionary enthusiasm, the majority of the Parisians clamoured for the fall of the dynasty and Marmont's small force struggling in the labyrinth of narrow streets soon suffered heavy casualties. On the 29th July, 1830, the decisive day, two of his regiments went over to the insurgents. Meanwhile, Charles, now back at St. Cloud, within sound of the firing, put his trust in the Virgin who appeared to Polignac at night, and continued to remain obstinately optimistic, refusing either to call up reinforcements or to make the concessions urgently entreated of him by some of the moderate leaders in Paris, the Constitutionalists, who feared a Republic every whit as much as they detested absolutism. Not until the 30th did he at last consent to give a written promise to dismiss Polignac and revoke the ordinances. But by then it was too late. When the royal messengers reached the capital the moderate leaders had decided to replace him by Louis Philippe, Duke of Orléans. Charles X could only have regained control by the exercise of an overwhelming force which he did not possess. There was nothing left but to abdicate, escape the mob which set out to search for him at St. Cloud and Rambouillet, and make his way into exile for the third and last time.

Thus ingloriously and unnecessarily the restored Bourbon monarchy came to an end through the folly of the monarch only fifteen years after Waterloo. A fresh shock was given to French political stability and new cleavages were added to those which already divided Frenchmen from Frenchmen. And yet, despite its miserable ending, the Restoration was no inglorious period of French history. Under the firm guidance of her Ministers France had achieved a remarkably rapid national recovery from the strain and disorganization of prolonged war and the effects of invasion. Her population had increased by three millions; until the depression of 1825 she had enjoyed a period of great commercial prosperity:[1] her credit had stood high, there had been a considerable increase in public wealth and from 1819 the budget showed

[1] The trade balance remained steadily in France's favour from 1815-21, cp. G. BOURGIN Le régime de l'industrie de 1814 à 1830.

a surplus year after year. Banking operations of all kinds had enormously increased in scope and the support of Villèle had helped to found the fortunes of the French branch of the house of Rothschild. A first savings bank had been established in Paris in 1818 and joint stock companies had begun to make a somewhat hesitant appearance. Communications, too, had been improved: main roads neglected during the last years of the Empire had been repaired and maɔadamization had been introduced; the canal system had been lengthened by an additional 921 kilometres; a first steamboat crossed the English Channel and a regular service had made its appearance on the Loire;[1] and, most revolutionary of all the changes in modes of transport, the advent of the railway had been heralded with the construction of three short lines for the carriage of coal by horse-drawn wagons. In these same years industry and agriculture had made some progress behind the solid shield of protection with which France had, like most continental states of the time, guarded herself, and which manufacturers and land-owners alike had forced successive governments to maintain or reinforce. Paris had witnessed three industrial exhibitions. She had seen the introduction of street pavements and horse-drawn omnibuses; and a plant run by an Englishman named Manby had helped to supply the gas lighting which had become general in the city by 1829. Thus in the material sphere the Governments and people of France during the Restoration period had much solid, if unspectacular, achievement to their credit.

In the realms of politics and culture there had been many distinguished men to uphold the country's reputation. Great orators or able men such as Berryer, Benjamin Constant, Royer-Collard, de Serre and Chateaubriand had been among the protagonists in the Chambers and had contributed to the high standard of debate which had extorted admiration far beyond the French frontiers. Chateaubriand and Madame de Stael had been the eminent precursors of a Romantic movement, which in France received fresh impetus from a new study of Shakespeare and from the influence of Byron and Scott; and their followers, Hugo, Lamartine, Vigny and Musset, the young Royalist champions of the revolt against classicism, had contributed to a striking literary revival which followed upon the fall of the Empire with its attempts at over-regimentation. The Restoration had seen the momentous years of the great struggle between the Classics and the Romantics which had culminated in the battle over Victor Hugo's play, *Hernani*. Here Charles X, foolish in so many things, had been wise enough—wiser no doubt than a Napoleon in that he refused to interfere: 'In matters of

[1] GRAND-CARTERET, J.: *Le XIXe Siecle*, II, p. 634.

comedy, gentlemen, I am no more than one of the audience in the stalls.'
These had been the days when Ingres returned to France from Italy to
continue his painting and when Delacroix arose to carry the standard
of Romanticism into the realm of art; when fashionable companies
had been delighted by the plays of Scribe and the music of Auber, by
the dancing of Marie Taglioni or La Malibran and the acting of Made-
moiselle Mars; when Italian music was the vogue, the interest in opera
revived and the Concerts of the Conservatoire were founded; when the
greatest names of literature, art and politics assembled in the brilliant
salons of ladies such as Madame Récamier, the Duchesse de Duras,
Madame Ancelot and the Princesse de Belgiojoso: when science and
natural history were still adorned by men such as Cuvier and Geoffrey
St. Hilaire, philosophy by Maine de Biran and de Maistre and when
through the lectures of men such as Guizot, Villemain and Cousin the
Sorbonne gained a fresh reputation as the centre for the diffusion of new
ideas. These, too, had been days which saw the foundation of such
notable institutions as the Ecole des Chartes (1821), the École des Arts et
Manufactures (1824) and the École des Beaux Arts (1830).

Finally, however unfortunate the domestic policy which eventually
brought Charles X to his fall, it must be remembered that the Restoration
Governments had done much to restore French prestige abroad. 'In
their foreign policy,' as an eminent French historian has written, 'the
Bourbons, as though by hereditary vocation, displayed an understanding
of French interests.'[1] In the affairs of Spain as we have already seen,
and later, after the fall of Villèle, in those of Greece and the Eastern
Mediterranean, France had played a conspicuous part. Her navy had
shared in the victory of Navarino over the Turks in 1827, and her troops
had cleared the Morea of Turkish and Egyptian forces in 1828. Moreover, Charles X and Polignac, for all their shortcomings at home, had a
wide vision of foreign affairs. An ambitious plan they had devised for
the overthrow of the Vienna settlement and the rearrangement of the
map of Europe by France and Russia had indeed come to nought,[2] but
with the conquest of Algiers in July 1830 Charles had defied the hostility
of Great Britain, had laid the foundation stone of a vast new African
Empire and finally put an end to a nest of pirates which had been a
menace to Mediterranean trade for more than three centuries. The
transport to Africa of a force of 38,000 men and 4,500 horses by 103
warships and 469 merchant vessels was no mean symbol of France's
renewed strength, and the expedition had had the additional merit of

[1] GORCE, P. DE LA: Napoléon III et sa politique, p. 48.
[2] cf. BOURGEOIS, E.: Manuel historique de politique étrangère, II, p. 771ff.

paying for itself, since a treasure greater than its whole cost was found in the hoard of the Algerian Dey.   Such a success, however, had counted for nothing with Frenchmen who had been wholly preoccupied by the constitutional crisis.   The glory of an African conquest had diverted men, but not public attention, from France.   Indeed it is unlikely that the French public could have been roused to enthusiasm even had there been no clash of King and Chamber.   The exploitation of Africa still lay far in the future and the men of 1830 'could only conceive of war and glory as something in Europe, across the Rhine and across the Alps'.[1]   But, although they knew it not, Charles X's last foreign venture had been one of momentous importance for the future of France.   He had been quick to seize a great opportunity.   Had he not done so the conquest of Algiers might have been postponed for many years or not been possible at all, for it is highly doubtful whether his cautious successor would have embarked upon such an enterprise.

[1] HALÉVY, D.: *Trois épreuves*, p. 36.

ARTZ, FREDERICK B.: *France under the Bourbon Restoration*.   Harvard, 1931.

CHARLÉTY, S.: *La Restauration* (Vol. IV of LAVISSE, E.: *Histoire de France contemporaine*).   Paris, 1921.

CHATEAUBRIAND: *Mémoires d'outre-tombe*.   Vol. V.   Paris, 1860.

GORCE, P. DE LA: *Charles X*.   Paris, 1928.

LUCAS-DUBRETON, J.: *La Restauration et la monarchie de Juillet*.   Paris, 1926.

NOAILLES, MARQUIS DE: *Le Comte Molé, 1781-1855, Sa Vie—ses Mémoires*.   Paris, 1922.   Vol. V.

PASQUIER: *Mémoires du Chancelier*.   Vol. VI, 4th ed.   Paris, 1894.

V

THE JULY MONARCHY

'CHARLES X can never return to Paris; he has shed the blood of his people. The Republic would expose us to dangerous divisions; it would involve us in hostilities with Europe.

The Duke of Orléans is a Prince devoted to the cause of the Revolution.

The Duke of Orléans has never fought against us.

The Duke of Orléans was at Jemappes.

The Duke of Orléans is a Citizen King.

The Duke of Orléans has carried the tricolour under the enemy's fire; the Duke of Orléans alone can carry it again. We will have no other flag.

The Duke of Orléans does not commit himself. He awaits the expression of our wishes. Let us proclaim those wishes and he will accept the Charter as we have always desired it. It is from the French people that he will hold his crown.'[1]

Thus succinctly did Thiers and his fellow journalists put the case for a French 1688 and such was the proclamation that the belated envoys of Charles X found placarded in Paris on July 30th, 1830. That same day, after some hesitation, Louis Philippe, Duke of Orléans, who was above all animated by the desire not to be obliged to go into exile once more, entered Paris and accepted the post of Lieutenant-General of the Kingdom offered to him by a group of deputies. But the Chamber dissolved by Charles X's ordinances was not the only power in the insurgent capital, and the problem of government could only be solved with the consent or acquiescence of a municipal commission of Republican tendencies which had installed itself in the Hôtel de Ville and of the veteran Lafayette, whom the victorious National Guard had acclaimed as their commander and who as such was the hero of the hour. Accordingly, on the 31st, the Duke, who had never lacked personal courage,

[1] CAHEN, L., and MATHIEZ, A.: Les lois françaises de 1815 à 1914, p. 63. See also BUTTERFIELD, H.: Select Documents of European History, 1715–1920, p. 114.

proceeded through the crowded streets to the Hôtel de Ville. Lafayette, 'a Republican at heart who never had the strength or daring to proclaim the Republic', preferred a constitutional monarchy to a Jacobin dictatorship, and was prepared to welcome him. The crowds went mad with enthusiasm when Louis Philippe appeared on the balcony holding the tricolour flag and publicly embraced the venerable Commander of the National Guard. This was the famous kiss that made the July monarchy. Republican opposition was stifled by a gesture which momentarily made the Duke of Orléans appear the best of Republicans.

Two days later Charles X, bowing tardily to realities, in turn appointed Louis Philippe Lieutenant-General of the Kingdom and abdicated in favour of his grandson, the boy Duc de Bordeaux, henceforth to be known to his adherents as Henri V. Charles left the protection of his grandson's rights to Louis Philippe; but when he and the boy were both on their way to exile it could be argued that the throne was vacant. Louis Philippe accepted this view, and accordingly on August 7th the Chambers declared the throne to be vacant and two days later he was proclaimed King. Perhaps it was true that no compromise of Regency would have been acceptable to the men of the Left, but the Royalists who remained loyal to Charles never forgave what to them was a base act of treachery.

The Revolution thus accomplished by Paris was accepted by the country as a whole with singularly little demur. It was a blow to the Church, which for some time was greatly discredited. It was also a blow to the Royalist nobility and split their ranks, thus introducing yet another cleavage among Frenchmen, for the majority, henceforth known as Legitimists or Carlists, remained faithful to Charles and his grandson and retired to their tents, nursing a bitter hatred against those of their fellows who had rallied to the new régime. It was also a disappointment to the handful of ardent Republicans who had hoped for the abolition of Kings and were, as we shall see, by no means satisfied with this fresh experiment in constitutional monarchy. Above all, however, the July Revolution was a triumph for the bourgeoisie and for the doctrine of popular sovereignty. With the overthrow of Charles X and the Ultras the bourgeoisie finally achieved the political and social supremacy for which they had fought in the Great Revolution. The days when men feared that the *émigrés* would succeed in overthrowing the revolutionary land settlement had gone for ever. The bourgeoisie had now made a King, and their sovereignty as representatives and leaders of the nation was demonstrated in the terms of his creation. The new monarch was not to be Philip VII, King of France, but Louis Philippe, King of the French 'by the Grace of God and the will of the nation'. The Chamber of Deputies took upon itself to revise the 1814 Charter and did away with the preamble on the grounds that it was 'wounding to the national dignity'.[1] Thus instead of Louis Philippe granting a revised Charter, like Louis XVIII, of his royal prerogative, he had one imposed on him by the deputies who represented the will of the nation. And these deputies displayed a somewhat niggardly delight in curtailing the privileges of royalty in other ways. Charles X had enjoyed a civil list of forty million francs: but the deputies, in Guizot's words, 'scrutinized and passed' the bill for Louis Philippe's allowance as though they were 'disputing and determining the price of a machine'[2] and reduced it to a mere twelve million francs. In the same way they made a fresh attack upon the hereditary principle by securing the transformation of the Chamber of Peers into an upper house of life members nominated by the King. Characteristically the passage of this reform by which the peers virtually committed suicide was obtained by the creation of a further batch of new noblemen.

The new King, scion of a branch of the royal house which was traditionally on bad terms with the reigning sovereign, was a son of that Duke known as Philippe Égalité, who had intrigued against Louis XVI, adopted revolutionary ideas, and none the less perished on the scaffold.[3] He was fifty-seven years of age when he came to the throne. His boyhood and early manhood had thus been passed in the years of the Revolution; he had known poverty and exile and had had exceptional opportunities of observing the workings of democracy abroad. Now one of the wealthiest men in France, careful in the management of his fortune, though often generous to individuals in distress, excellent father of a large family, simple and unaffected in his habits and tastes, although a man of wide interests, he appeared admirably fitted to preside over a régime directed by the bourgeoisie, so many of whose virtues he seemed to epitomize. Shrewdly opportunist, he understood how to play to the gallery. Committed to being a Citizen-King, he performed the part with assiduity, received delegation upon delegation of fellow citizens, discarded the pomp and etiquette of the Bourbon Court, mixed freely with the Parisians in his daily walks, and appeared like an ordinary bourgeois in top-hat and with an umbrella instead of in uniform. In

---

[1] For the Declaration of the Chamber of Deputies and the modified clauses in the Charter see Appendix IV.

[2] *Memoirs of my own time*, II, p. 213.

[3] See the genealogical tree in Appendix I.

the first months of revolutionary enthusiasm the Parisians were entranced by such a novel and model sovereign; later they were to find him drab, to pine for more splendour, cruelly to caricature his homely virtues and criticize even his manifold and manifest abilities.[1]

The main immediate changes in régime of the revised Charter were naturally enough in the direction of greater liberty. The creation of extraordinary tribunals and judicial commissions was forbidden and the censorship was abolished 'for ever'. The age qualifications for electors and those eligible as deputies was lowered to twenty-five and thirty respectively; and laws were passed reducing the property qualification for electors from 300 to 200 francs. The National Guard was reorganized; the term of military service was reduced from eight to seven years; and the tricolour flew once again as the national flag of France. The alliance of Throne and Altar was at an end and Roman Catholicism was now recognized as no more than the religion 'of the majority of Frenchmen'. Certain religious orders were expelled and the funds allotted to the Ministry of Public Worship were reduced. Press cases were once again referred to trial by jury; the *Conseils généraux* or county councils were re-organized, and though they were to have little power, the new bodies were henceforward to be a permanent feature of local administration. Last, but not least, provision was made for the establishment of state-aided primary schools in every commune. This was the beginning of a momentous educational reform, but only a beginning, for there was no compulsion, and illiteracy continued to be widespread for many years to come.

These measures which constituted the main legislative changes of the first three years of the new reign were by no means unimportant, yet there still remained the great question—to what end had the revolution been made? The 'Three Glorious Days' of July 1830 had released an extraordinary ferment of ideas and passions which continued to work long after the formal establishment of the new régime. All the latent discontents and grievances came to a head, and all who wanted change, or believed they would profit from it now it had come, vociferously demanded new men, new methods and new ideas. Mobs of place hunters besieged each Ministry and the new Government made sweeping changes of prefects and sub-prefects, generals and high army officers, magistrates, Counsellors of State and Rectors of Academy; changes which accentuated the new bourgeois character of the new administration. At the same time the belief that a new era of Liberty had dawned

[1] For a striking character of Louis Philippe see TOCQUEVILLE, A. DE.: *The Recollections of,* ed. MAYER, J. P., pp. 4ff.

led to an extraordinary efflorescence of political clubs and societies, accompanied by constant street demonstrations and by a spate of literary propaganda on behalf of all kinds of political and social reform. Bonapartists and Republicans, and social reformers such as the followers of Fourier and Saint Simon all believed that their hour was at hand. Even within the Church, the extraordinary fire and eloquence of Lamennais seemed in his paper *L'Avenir* to herald a revolutionary movement of Liberalism and democratic trend. Moreover the incursion into the political arena of a Romanticism which had deserted Royalist for new Liberal, Philhellenist enthusiasms—the *Globe*, for instance, so influential in the first four years since its foundation in 1824 in doing battle against the Classicists, had begun to join issue in political matters in 1828[1]—momentarily carried a cloak and dagger extravagance of action into political demonstrations.[2] At the same time economic difficulties which the revolution and a hard winter accentuated led to a number of manifestations of another kind, processions of workers demanding 'bread'. Thus the months immediately following the Revolution were extremely disturbed. There was a large number of Frenchmen who, for one reason or another, believed or hoped that the Revolution was but the beginning of a series of further changes and who did not cease to agitate for fresh reforms; but there was also an important body of opinion which was alarmed by such demonstrations and held that in effecting a change of dynasty and a new guarantee of essential liberties through the revised Charter the Revolution had accomplished its object. These contradictory views both had their representatives in Louis Philippe's first government. On the one hand there was the so-called Party of Movement, with Lafayette, Laffitte, Dupont de l'Eure and others, who carried with them many Romantic idealists and held that the events of July were but a prelude to further reform and to an active foreign policy. On the other, there was the Party of Resistance whose most prominent members, Casimir Périer and former Doctrinaires such as Guizot and the Duc de Broglie, maintained that the Revolution was complete with the victory of constitutional legality and that it was essential to conciliate the great powers of Europe. But the revolutionary momentum could not be stopped at once, however much the King might wish it, and in

---

[1] SAINTE-BEUVE: *Portraits littéraires*, I, p. 317.

[2] The romantic cult of the eighteen-thirties, like the Existentialist cult of the nineteen-forties led to strange exaggerations of dress and behaviour. 'Even schoolboys were now dressed as pages with little daggers. . . . Young men endeavoured to float companies for reviving the tourney or formed societies like the so-called Francs-Archers.'

November, not long after Parisian mobs had demonstrated under his windows and marched to Vincennes to demand the heads of Polignac and his colleagues who were imprisoned there, Louis Philippe thought it prudent to give the Party of Movement some rein and to form a new Ministry under the leadership of Laffitte. This was a sop to public opinion but did not prevent further disorders. There were furious demonstrations when the Chamber of Peers condemned Charles X's late Ministers to life imprisonment instead of to death, and again, in February 1831, hostility to the late régime showed itself afresh when a mob, angered at a Legitimist commemoration and swept by one of the most violent waves of anti-clericalism witnessed in the nineteenth century, sacked the Palace of the Archbishop of Paris and the Church of St. Germain l'Auxerrois. The Laffitte Government, unable or un-willing to maintain good order, and unable either to prevent a financial crisis and a sharp rise in unemployment or to indulge a popular clamour for a crusade in aid of national risings in Belgium, Poland and Italy was soon discredited. Accordingly, in March 1831, Louis Philippe turned to the Party of Resistance and with a Ministry headed by another banker, Casimir Périer, secured a much stronger Government. Casimir-Périer was indeed a man of most forceful character, a veritable Prime Minister, ruling King and colleagues alike and by no means patient of royal inter-ference. This struggle for power between the Parties of Resistance and Movement was to continue throughout the reign, but, although the King himself spoke of pursuing the policy of the happy mean (*juste milieu*) his temperament and native caution naturally inclined him to the Party of Resistance and it was this which enjoyed office for the greater part of his rule.

Louis Philippe, as we have seen, represented a compromise. In other words it was once again a case of the solution which would divide Frenchmen least. But after the failure of the Restoration to recreate unity, and after the events of July 1830, the task of founding a régime acceptable to all was still more difficult. Once again the Government had to face insurrectionary fire from two flanks. The absence of any sort of rising in support of Charles X in 1830 had shown how little real hold the Ultra-Royalists had had in the country, but none the less they were now ready to plot against the Government, even on occasion joining forces with the Republicans, who were much more experienced con-spirators. During the first ten years of the new régime there was a whole series of plots and disturbances of varying gravity, and between 1835 and 1846 no fewer than six attempts were made on the life of the King. In spite of the fact that men such as Berryer still championed the Legitimist cause,[1] and of an attempt in 1832 by the young and once popular Duchesse de Berry to raise the Vendée for her son, 'Henri V', Legitimist hostility was much less serious than that of the Republicans. The Vendée rising proved to be a fiasco only less ridiculous than the later efforts of Louis Napoleon to raise the Bonapartist standard at Strasbourg and Boulogne in 1836 and 1840, and the strength of the Legitimists was to some extent further weakened by the growth of a Liberal Catholicism which ran counter to the Ultramontane tendencies of the Bourbon exiles. The real peril lay to the Left and it was the abiding and eventually fatal weakness of Louis Philippe's Government that it failed to conjure the peril by broadening its electoral basis or by timely social legislation.

It was now indeed for the first time in French history since the Great Revolution that the condition of the workers in industry came to the fore as an important social and political problem. The fundamental reason for this lay in the striking development of certain big industries, which had begun during the last years of the Restoration and which had resulted in a crowding and migration of population into certain areas, unchecked by considerations of health, sanitation or a minimum living wage. This did not mean that France had ceased to be a country in which small industries were the rule—by 1846 the numbers employed in large-scale industry were not much over a million[2] but it did mean that 'the industrial revolution' (a phrase first used in France by Blanqui in 1837) was developing apace and that the scale and scope of industrialization had rapidly increased, especially in the cotton and textile industries of Alsace, Normandy and the Nord, in the silk industry in the Lyons area, and the metallurgical industries of the Loire basin and Lorraine. Thus, for example, the numbers employed in the Haut Rhin textile industry increased by 135 per cent during the seven years 1827–34, and the population of Roubaix jumped from 8,000 to 34,000 in the ten years 1831–41 and that of St. Etienne from 16,000 to 54,000. Crowded and insanitary living conditions gave a free field to terrible epidemics such as the cholera, which raged both in Great Britain and France in 1831–2, but caused a heavier mortality among the French;[3] and these conditions, together with the uncontrolled exploitation of female and child labour and long hours of work, led to widespread tuberculosis, immorality and

---

[1] Chateaubriand refused to acknowledge Louis Philippe and resigned his peerage, but he remained Achilles-like in his tent and did not actively work for a Legitimist restoration.

[2] WOODWARD, E. L.: *Three Studies in European Conservatism*, p. 213. These figures are quoted by L. BLANC in *Organisation du Travail*, p. 66.

[3] CLAPHAM, J. H.: *Economic History of Modern Britain*, I, p. 317.

drunkenness. The damage to health is vividly brought out by the fact that 'in 1840 out of every 10,000 young men called up for military service from ten French departments which were predominantly manufacturing in character, 9,000 were rejected as physically unfit.'[1] Apart from their wretched living conditions, the main misfortune of these workers was the uncertainty of employment. Research has shown that on the whole their average consumption per head increased under the July monarchy, that there was a general rise in agricultural and industrial productivity and that many workmen were able to entrust earnings to the growing number of savings banks; but all too often salaries (which varied enormously in different industries and different localities) failed to keep pace with rises in the cost of living, and all too seldom did they allow a margin to guard against the big emergencies of unemployment or illness. Contemporary observers calculated that a working class family would be in distress if their earnings were less than 750 francs per annum and there were times of economic crisis or of epidemic when all too many families failed to reach this figure.

Living in such precarious conditions, many workers, especially in Paris, had been led to believe that the July Revolution would mean an improvement of their lot. Had not *Le National*, for instance, declared on July 30th: 'It is the people which has done everything ... it has been powerful and sublime; it is it which has won the victory and all the benefits of the victory should be for it?'[2] But the workers of different trades in Paris who demonstrated, demanding shorter hours and minimum wages, got no encouragement from the new authorities. The Revolution had dislocated business and the political uncertainty which naturally followed the establishment of the new régime only brought with it an intensification of unemployment which continued into 1831. Disappointment and desperation led to a series of demonstrations in Paris and Lyons of workers demanding bread or work and finally in November 1831 to a veritable insurrection in Lyons during which the city was for a time in the hands of the 'canuts' or silk-weavers. These months were indeed critical. They determined whether the authorities would be sympathetic to large numbers of Frenchmen in distress, and upon the answer largely depended the extent to which the Republican opponents of the régime could swell their ranks by recruits from the workers.

The Lyons insurrection of 1831 which has been called 'the first appearance of armed Socialism'[3]—since many of the men involved in it

---

[1] WOODWARD, E. L.: *French Revolutions*, p. 137.

[2] cit. DOLLÉANS, E.: *Histoire du mouvement ouvrier*, I, p. 43.

[3] cit. RUDE, F.: *Le mouvement ouvrier à Lyon de 1827 à 1832*, p. 739.

are known to have been influenced by Socialist ideas—was a tragic blow to the cause of conciliation. In the silk trade, which at this time accounted for twenty-nine per cent of France's exports, wages had lagged sadly behind the cost of living. The workers therefore demanded that joint committees of workers and employers should meet to fix a minimum wage scale. The proposal was approved by the Chambers of Commerce, and the Prefect himself lent his good offices, with the result that a tariff was duly fixed. The principles of collective bargaining and peaceful settlement of disputes appeared to have won a signal success. But 104 out of some 1,400 manufacturers refused to observe the agreement and threatened to close their works. Then it was that the whole body of weavers rose in exasperation and for a short time controlled the city, the challenging words '*Vivre libres en travaillant ou mourir en combattant*' inscribed upon their banners. The Government was scared and replied by an overwhelming display of force, dispersed the rebels, denounced the tariff, and declared collective bargaining illegal. Thus in their alarm the authorities rallied to protect the interests of the manufacturers and reaffirmed the sacred doctrine of *laissez-faire*—each individual must be free to contract as he liked. In the Chamber, the workers were told by Casimir Périer that patience and resignation were their only remedies.

This insurrection was not primarily political in its objective; but its repression and the repression of many lesser disturbances in Paris and elsewhere all led the workers to seek more effective organization for their own interests, to distrust the Government and to realize that to improve their conditions they would have to rely on their own efforts. So they became amenable to Republican propaganda which made great efforts during these first years 1831–4—no less than six million copies of Republican pamphlets were distributed in three months—and many were tempted to join secret Republican groups such as the Société des Droits de l'Homme, the 'Familles' or the 'Saisons'. Thus to some extent events moved in a vicious circle. The Republicans, frustrated in the achievement of their goal in July 1830, less numerous than the Legitimists, but better versed in revolutionary technique, kept the authorities on edge by a series of disturbances and so led them to deal severely with all manifestations, even those which had no strictly political objective. In consequence many who were not primarily concerned with political issues turned to Republicanism in the hope that it would help them in their struggle for existence.

Casimir Périer, the strong man of the first years of the reign, died in May 1832 during the first cholera epidemic in France, a fearsome visitor which carried off some 20,000 victims. The Vendée rising was still flickering and in Paris in June the funeral of a popular Opposition deputy, General Lamarque, afforded a pretext for further Republican demonstrations so serious that for three weeks the city was put in a state of siege. It was clear to the King that the unsettled state of the country demanded a continuation of the policy of Resistance. Accordingly in October a new Ministry was formed with Marshal Soult as titular head, but Broglie as the real director. The death of the Duc de Reichstadt, Napoleon's son, and the arrest of the Duchesse de Berry, who was soon discredited by a liaison with an Italian count, by weakening the Bonapartists and Legitimists seemed to strengthen the Orleanist dynasty and to introduce a period of relative calm. But it was not to be for long. After a brief respite there was a fresh eruption of Republican propaganda and incitements to violence, and the *Tribune*, the Republican paper directed by Armand Marrast, which in four years was the subject of 114 prosecutions, now published a programme for the establishment of a 'social Republic'.[1] For more than three years the Press had enjoyed unbridled liberty, the King and Government had been unmercifully caricatured by Daumier and Monnier, Republican papers had deliberately fomented disturbances, the life of the capital and often the existence of the régime had been threatened by insurrectionary movements. At length, their patience exhausted, the Government decided that liberties must be curtailed in the interests of order and stability. In April 1834 legislation was passed restricting the right of association. In Lyons, where there had just been a strike, the news of the law produced fresh disturbances organized by friendly societies of Republican sympathies and six days of bitter fighting followed. In Eastern Paris there was an almost simultaneous rising, at the call of the Société des Droits de l'Homme. Its repression, largely directed by Thiers, was savage, involving as it did the so-called massacre of the Rue Transnonain, a foretaste of the repression after the June Days of 1848 and the Commune of 1871, when Thiers was again in control. It was, however, effective and the Republican movement was driven underground for several years to come. In the following year a fresh attempt to kill the King, which caused the loss of many lives, provoked a further revulsion against the romantic cult of political assassination, and the Government profited by the occasion to introduce laws bringing the Press under stricter control and modifying judicial procedure in order to secure more speedy results. Henceforth insults to the King or attacks on the principle or form of government by

[1] It was during the 'thirties that the terms 'Socialism' and 'Socialist' first came to be widely applied to advocates of social reform.

Charter were to be treated as threats to the security of the State. The Press, which had shown its power in the July Revolution, had subsequently abused its new-won liberties and indulged in the unbridled violence so characteristic of French journalism. It had overshot the mark and was now to pay the penalty.

The main period of disorders was now at an end, and during the next four years interest in internal matters centred rather on the battles in Parliament and the instability of Ministries. Louis Philippe had appreciated the need for the firm hand of Casimir-Périer and his successors, but he had chafed under their domination. He had no notion of being a King who would reign but not govern, and after the fall of the Broglie Ministry in February 1836 he sought ministerial combinations in which he hoped himself to keep control. The young and ambitious Thiers seemed likely to be a more supple instrument and was tempted into leading the next Cabinet—a momentous decision, for it meant a break between Thiers and Guizot. Henceforward one of the dominant features of the reign was to be the rivalry between these two historians who were to be its most notable Ministers. This first Thiers Cabinet, however, did not last long. Thiers came to grief over foreign policy and in August he resigned.

Foreign affairs had been of vital importance from the outset and nowhere had the King shown greater firmness and good sense. The July Revolution had had immediate repercussions throughout the Continent. In imagination men's thoughts had inevitably flown back to 1789 and Europe had been torn by a complex of fears and hopes. Conservative Governments were indignant and alarmed at the outbreak of revolution in France, and when it inspired Belgians, Poles and Italians to rise in revolt and German Liberals to make demonstrations, the Russian Tsar beheld the menace of universal revolution and was eager to parry it with all the armed might of the quondam Holy Alliance. At the same time in France itself there were many hot-headed and enthusiastic supporters of the Party of Movement who burned to help the Poles and other foreign insurgents and who envisaged a march across the Rhine as a natural corollary of revolution. The new Government had therefore to walk warily. Mistrusted by the Eastern Powers, insecure at home, it could not afford to launch upon any ill-considered revolutionary crusade, even had it so wished. Equally its origin forbade it to play a reactionary role. Louis Philippe himself was the last man to wish to embark upon foolhardy adventures abroad. He wanted peace to consolidate his government and he wanted to obtain from other European Governments recognition that the July Monarchy could be a stable and stabilizing force in Europe. Although the presence of large numbers of Polish exiles in Paris and the romantic and dramatic quality of the Polish risings aroused more sympathies on behalf of the Poles than of the Belgians or Italians, Poland was too remote for there ever to be any serious question of French intervention. On the other hand, the Belgian and Italian revolutions presented the new régime with test cases from which it emerged with flying colours and enhanced prestige.

The rising in Belgium, originally a demonstration for Home Rule under the House of Orange, had soon turned into a move for complete separation from Holland. Such a disruption of the Kingdom of the Netherlands meant a flagrant breach of the 1815 settlement. The Dutch King appealed for military aid and the Eastern powers thought seriously of giving it. But in the west, close at hand, there was another power, Great Britain, which was much less disposed to join in or encourage armed intervention on behalf of the *status quo*. By co-operating with her, France saw an opportunity to play an honourable part in procuring a peaceful settlement and by none was this course more skilfully urged and executed than by the veteran Talleyrand, who now emerged to serve his fifth régime as French Ambassador in London, a post he had first held nearly forty years before, in 1792. 'Whether other States are or are not disposed in favour of peace, France and England must declare that they wish it, and this wish of the two most powerful and civilized countries in Europe must be heard with the respect to which their power entitles them.'[1] Thus Talleyrand argued, and, playing with the principle of non-intervention as skilfully as in 1814 he had played with that of legitimacy, he won Britain's support. His reckoning was correct. Instead of troops to the Netherlands the eastern sovereigns sent envoys to a conference in London to settle the Belgian question; and the settlement was virtually a recognition of the *fait accompli*. The new kingdom of Belgium came into being—French troops and an English fleet forced the Dutch king to submit—and its neutrality was guaranteed by the four Great Powers in 1839. Thus in its first great diplomatic trial the July Monarchy had at once emerged from isolation, effected a rapprochement with Great Britain, with whom France's relations at the end of the Restoration had been distinctly cool, and played an important part in imposing a peaceful settlement, which at the same time confirmed the breach in the 1815 treaties. As a result, on her north-west frontier France now had a new, weak, and friendly state, with a constitution still more liberal than her own, in place of the larger one which the

[1] PALLAIN, G.: *L'ambassade de Talleyrand à Londres* 1830-34, p. ix.

settlement of Vienna had designed as a barrier against any recurrent French aggression. In securing this result Louis Philippe had had to resist great temptations; many Belgians and French had hoped for a union of Belgium and France and one of Louis Philippe's sons, the Duc de Nemours, had actually been elected King by the Belgian National Congress. Acceptance of either proposal would have meant not merely alienation from but probably hostilities with Great Britain: and such a prospect the new King could not contemplate. It was much to his credit that he kept his head, contented himself with marrying one of his daughters to the Coburg Prince Leopold who eventually became King of the Belgians, and withstood the lure of realizing the age-old French dream of incorporating the Belgian lands in France.

In the Belgian problem France intervened in the name of non-intervention and yet avoided a clash with Great Britain. So, too, in Italy the French Government proclaimed a policy of non-intervention which Italian patriots hoped would mean that France would prevent Austria from intervening. But Louis Philippe had no desire to come to blows with Austria and so, to the disgust of the Italian patriots, Casimir-Périer had explained that non-intervention actually meant what it said and that France could not give armed help to every foreign revolution. In 1832, however, when a second rising occurred in the Papal States, the Vatican once again called in Austrian troops and the French Government replied by occupying Ancona. By now the July Monarchy was more firmly established and by this action it demonstrated its fidelity to another classical principle of French foreign policy: that France had an abiding interest in Italian affairs and could not allow any other power to dominate the peninsula exclusively. The Austrian soldiers were not withdrawn until 1838, and so for six years French troops were maintained at Ancona facing them. As has been remarked, 'they had only to raise a tricolour on top of the hill-fort at Ancona and it might easily send a flame of revolution running northwards to the Alps and southwards to the Gulf of Taranto'.[1] But Louis Philippe did not aspire to give revolutionary signals. He had successfully made his demonstration on behalf of French prestige and the balance of power and at the same time avoided a clash with Austria. That was enough—he had no Napoleonic plan of fathering Italian unity—probably he had too shrewd a notion of France's real interests. In the west, meanwhile, further somewhat uneasy co-operation with England had resulted in a fresh triumph for constitutional monarchy. The Quadruple Alliance of 1834 between Great Britain, France, the Queen of Portugal and the Regent of Spain was speedily followed by

[1] BERKELEY, G. F. H.: *Italy in the Making* 1815 to 1846, p. 123.

the collapse of the absolutist forces of the two Iberian pretenders, Don Miguel of Portugal and Don Carlos of Spain.   Thus by 1835 the most serious disturbances which followed on the French Revolution of 1830 had been either quelled or settled.   The main battle between the Liberal and the Conservative forces in Europe was over for the time being.   Both had consolidated their positions and were prepared to observe a truce.   Co-operation with Great Britain had been one of the main planks of French policy; but it had not been easy in practice.   Lord Palmerston had been an exacting and suspicious associate and there were many in France who deplored that their Government should work hand in hand with the power whom they still regarded as the 'hereditary foe'.   Accordingly Louis Philippe, once his régime was established, was disposed to play a more independent role and eventually to seek rapprochement with the conservative powers, especially Austria. The English *entente* began to cool, and was soon virtually shattered by a crisis in the Near East.

In general, France and Great Britain had been agreed in wishing to bolster up the sick man of Europe against his most persistent adversary, the Tsar.   But in the 'thirties Turkey was menaced with destruction from the south as well as from the north, and the attitude of the two Western powers to this new danger to Turkish interests was by no means identical.   The most powerful of Turkish vassals, Mehemet Ali, the Pasha of Egypt, the Porte's main supporter in the war of Greek Independence, had been promised Syria as a reward for his help, and when the Sultan had tried to evade his promise he had seized the province and threatened Constantinople itself.   Peace was patched up between the Sultan and his vassal by the good offices of the Powers, but the Sultan could not brook his humiliation and in 1839 tried to take his revenge, only to be once again decisively defeated by the Egyptian forces.   The European Powers once again prepared to intervene, but only one of them, France, was sympathetic to Mehemet Ali.   France had maintained a close interest in Egypt ever since the time of Napoleon, and the Egyptian army had been largely trained and the Egyptian administrative services organized by Frenchmen.   Mehemet Ali had responded by a policy which tended to be pro-French and markedly anti-British.   Thus Great Britain had little love for him while Russia dreaded the prospect of a strong Egyptian ruler at Constantinople who might really reinvigorate the Turkish Empire.   Aware of this situation Thiers, now for the second time head of a French Government, tried to by-pass the intervention of the powers by bringing about a direct settlement between the Sultan and the Pasha which would safeguard the Egyptian's position.

Instead of succeeding, however, this manœuvre led only to France's isolation and humiliation. Palmerston denounced the French action as a bid for exclusive control in the Near East and induced the other powers to conclude the Treaty of London imposing a settlement distinctly unfavourable to Mehemet Ali. The news of this Treaty was received with intense indignation in France. There was much talk of tearing up the 1815 Treaties and fighting 'the new Quadruple Alliance'[1] on the Rhine. Even the King allowed military preparations to be set on foot: the army was increased to 500,000 and twelve million francs were voted for the fortification of Paris. In fact, however, Louis Philippe was as loth as ever to embark upon risky adventures. He would not go to war to preserve Syria for Mehemet Ali, and, after a further attempt on his life had given him new popularity, he took the opportunity to be rid of the bellicose Thiers and to form a new ministry headed by Soult, but really directed by Guizot. Peace was thus assured and in 1841 France joined with the other four Great Powers in signing the Straits Convention. She thus returned to the Concert of Europe, but her client, Mehemet Ali, had been irreparably weakened and was now confined to Egypt alone. Moreover her own brief explosion of martial spirit had been answered by an unexpected thunder of warlike patriotism from the Germanic Confederation. The English bombardment of Beirut and the German songs, 'Die Wacht am Rhein' and 'Deutschland über alles' were warnings of the dangers of war and the risks of isolation. In France, however, 'the young, the passionate, the lovers of liberty and action', had ignored the dangers and thought only of the glory.[2] Disillusioned by an outcome which they thought humiliating, they believed the Orléans monarchy was pursuing a policy of peace at any price and they began to despise it accordingly. 'France,' said Lamartine in a famous phrase, 'is bored'—and she failed to recognize the importance of the work which her Government was accomplishing in slowly and painfully building up the foundations of a new Empire in North Africa which would be of vital importance to her a century later, or to derive much satisfaction from the acquisition of a few remote territories such as Nossi Bé, Tahiti or the Ivory Coast. None the less the most significant decision of the July monarchy, in foreign policy, apart from the decisions to avoid war, was indeed the decision to retain Charles X's conquest of Algiers. 'It is our opera box,' Louis Philippe is reported to have said, 'but a terribly expensive one,'[3]

---

[1] i.e. An alliance against France like the Quadruple Alliance of 1814.

[2] BOURGEOIS, E.: *Manuel de la politique étrangère*, III, p. 176.

[3] SENIOR, N. W.: *Conversations with Thiers, Guizot, etc.*, II, p. 139.

and Corcelle told an English visitor to France in 1857 that he did not
believe that France would have retained it had not Great Britain hoped
that she would give it up.[1] At first the policy pursued was one of a
limited occupation of the coastal area, but constant raids by the tribes of
the interior eventually led the Government to the decision that the whole
of Algeria must be brought under French control. This work of pacification opened up a field for eventual colonization and a base for the later
development of a vast new continental territory, but its immediate
significance was mainly military. Not only did it add picturesqueness
to the French army by giving rise to the creation of special corps such as
the Zouaves and the Foreign Legion, but it was for a long time to be the
main theatre in which French troops could gain direct experience of
military operations. Moreover, since the conditions of this warfare
were highly specialized, there came into being, under the command of
men like Bugeaud, what was virtually a separate African army with its
own technique and equipment, necessarily very different from those
required by the army of the metropolis. Training in Africa, however,
was no necessary asset to the men and officers who would be required
to fight in Europe, and the existence of an African training ground
certainly did not compensate the old adherents of the party of Movement and the young men who were bored for the absence of a European
battlefield.

But their boredom was unlikely to be relieved by the Minister who
now directed French policy in conjunction with the King. 'Let us not
talk about our country having to conquer territory, to wage great wars,
to undertake bold deeds of vengeance. If France is prosperous, if she
remains free, rich, peaceful and wise, we need not complain.'[2] These
words, spoken by Guizot on November 17th, 1840, well summarize the
policy of the man who was to be Louis Philippe's chief adviser during the
last seven and a half years of his reign.[3] Guizot was a man of impressive learning, a Protestant of austere character, a man whom both
Lord Acton and John Morley thought the greatest all-round statesman
of the nineteenth century.[4] Yet he maintained his majority in the
Chamber by a system of judicious bribery reminiscent of Sir Robert
Walpole. Under him, said Tocqueville, the Government of France

[1] SENIOR, N. W.: *Conversations with Thiers, Guizot, etc.*, II, p. 139.

[2] LAVISSE, E. and RAMBAUD, A.: *Histoire générale du iv. siècle à nos jours*, X, p. 399.

[3] He did not actually become President of the Council of Ministers until
September 1847.

[4] WOODWARD, E. L.: *French Revolutions*, p. 135.

'came to resemble a limited company in industry which undertakes all its operations with a view to the profit to be extracted from them by the shareholders'.[1] The theory that power was the prerogative of the upper classes was indeed the essence and the weakness of Guizot's view of politics. For him the notion of political equality was a dangerous illusion and universal suffrage an instrument of destruction or deceit. Such a theory required above all the maintenance of peace, order and prosperity and aimed at the conservation and consolidation of the gains made by the middle class in 1830 rather than at any extension of liberties. Thus it was not surprising that towards the end of his official career Guizot came to work in harmony with the leading figure among European Conservatives, Prince Metternich, or that he obstinately resisted proposals for an extension of the franchise to people whom he believed to be without political capacity since he was certain it would lead to internal disturbance. Unfortunately for him, this inflexibility was in the end to lead directly to the very trouble he sought to avoid. Unfortunately, too, for the stability of the régime, Guizot's views were largely shared by the King. Louis Philippe enjoyed politics too much not to wish to exercise personal influence. Casimir-Périer, Broglie and Thiers had all been difficult to manage: in Guizot he found a perfect collaborator. Indeed, under the new dispensation, it was for the most part the King himself who, like George III of England, pulled the strings and manipulated the 'pays légal', as the electorate was called.[2] Unhappily this meant that once again the French sovereign was prone to be a party man and unable to lift himself above party politics. Moreover, Louis Philippe was vain enough to let it be known that he, too, was a king who governed. In consequence, when the corruptness of the system of government was exposed, the sovereign who boasted of his share in the direction of policy, inevitably shared also in the discredit.

To begin with, however, under the new combination all seemed to prosper. The Anglo-French Entente was renewed when Lord Palmerston was replaced at the Foreign Office by Lord Aberdeen with whom Guizot formed close and friendly relations. Although the old struggle between Church and University for control of secondary education (by which the electorate was formed) was once again renewed the country as a whole was tranquil, since the turbulent Republican elements

[1] cit. CHARLÉTY, S.: La Monarchie de juillet, p. 315.

[2] The fact that civil servants were not debarred from sitting in Parliament provided obvious opportunities for Government pressure: at one time no less than 184 out of 459 deputies were 'placemen'. cp. G. BOURGIN in F. FEJTO, 1848 dans le Monde, le Printemps des Peuples, I, p. 183.

had now been driven underground or into exile. Commerce and industry boomed and the great era of railway construction was at hand. France was certainly in appearance rich and peaceful. But was she also wise and free?

In a pamphlet published in 1821 attacking the Ultra Government of the time, a young critic had written as follows: 'France is prosperous and does not stir; that is enough for them (the Ministers). There is no need to fear anything; no need to do anything; and if contrary to expectation, contrary to right, some misfortune were to happen, the misfortune would be in the wrong. . . . Nothing is more deceitful than the material happiness of peoples . . .'[1] and he had complained that 'the Counter-Revolution' feared 'movement' above everything. How well might these words have been applied some twenty years' later to Guizot's Government and how extraordinary that their author was none other than Guizot himself! His wisdom was indeed short-sighted. In the Chamber he won oratorical victories and in elections, by adroit manipulation, he secured safe majorities. But beneath the superficial veneer of ministerial stability and industrial and commercial prosperity there still lay the great depth of misery among the workers. Their freedom was a mockery. Here there was a social question of growing seriousness which sooner or later was bound to lead to grave complications unless the Government took steps to solve it. As early as 1819 Sismondi in his *Principes d'économie politique* had attacked the policy of *laissez-faire* and urged that the state should intervene to regulate the use of property for the well-being of the whole community. Already the writings of Saint-Simon, who died in 1825, had sowed a seed-plot of ideas which provided a basis for the Positivist philosophy of Auguste Comte and inspired on the one hand many Socialist thinkers and on the other many masters of new forms of capitalist enterprise. For Saint-Simon's whole emphasis was transferred from politics to economics. He looked upon society as one great workshop or industrial community whose efficient organization was the main task of modern times. And so there had arisen a whole series of thinkers and writers who were preoccupied by the problems of industrialism and economic inequalities and whose criticisms of the existing order served to focus discontent. When the Government did nothing, the investigations of individual researchers and philanthropists and the writings of theorists and reformers such as Louis Blanc with his *Organisation du Travail* (1839), Flora Tristan with her *Union ouvrière,* Lamennais with his *Paroles d'Un Croyant* (1834), and Proudhon with his *Qu'est ce que la Propriéte?* (1841) and

[1] *Des moyens du gouvernement et d'opposition,* p. 90.

his ruggedly individualistic Socialism, all helped to rouse a social conscience which was inevitably more and more critical of the July Monarchy and tended to look elsewhere, to Republicanism, for salvation. At the same time, it must be remembered that the primary education law of 1833 and the development of a cheaper press was tending to increase the numbers of the literate. When enterprising speculators like Emile de Girardin and Dutacq introduced advertisements and spiced their newspapers with serial stories, a device which helped to bring wealth and fame to men like Eugéne Sue, Alexandre Dumas and Balzac, they were able to sell their new journals such as the *Presse* (1836) and the *Siècle* (which was soon dubbed 'the grocers' paper') at half price. By 1864 some twenty-six dailies were published in Paris with about 180,000 subscribers, more than three times the number there had been twenty years earlier, and these now included quite new kinds of paper such as the workers' *L'Atelier*, founded in 1840, which advocated many of the social reforms which would appear in the Republican programme of 1848. Simultaneously there had taken place a corresponding development of the provincial press, and the number of papers of one kind and another published in the provinces had doubled during the decade 1835–45. Thus the circle of the reading public, that is to say of potential critics of the Government, had greatly widened since Louis Philippe's accession. Furthermore, there were other factors which belied the apparent stability of the régime during the 'forties. In 1842 the dynasty had suffered a serious loss through the death of the heir to the throne, the Duc d'Orléans, the eldest and decidedly the most popular of the King's numerous sons. At the same time there was a disquieting tendency for Frenchmen to make a cult of other régimes than the one under which they lived: a little book by Prince Louis Napoleon published in 1839 under the title *Des ideés napoléoniennes* contributed not a little to the legend of a Liberal Emperor, while the cult of Napoleon grew with the return of his ashes from St. Helena in 1840 and their interment at the Invalides in a ceremony of portentous splendour; moreover, the publication of Michelet's *Le Peuple* in 1846 and of his *Histoire de la Révolution* and Lamartine's *Histoire des Girondins* in 1847 revived interest in the Great Revolution.[1] When we remember also that Paris in the 'forties was a refuge for every kind of *émigré* forced to leave his own country on account of his political or social views, we

---

[1] The appearance of Lamartine's book could be described by a contemporary, Lanfrey, as 'the greatest political event of the time'. Louis Blanc also published a *History of the Great Revolution* in 1847. cp. D. HALÉVY: *Histoire d'une histoire esquissée pour le troisième cinquantenaire de la Révolution Française*, p. 15.

shall see that it was open to all sorts of foreign influences and a harbour for advanced or revolutionary thought. Thus beneath the apparent tranquillity there was much social and political discontent and an intense intellectual ferment which boded no good for the Government.

The real turning-point in the second half of Louis Philippe's reign came with the year 1846. Then good fortune seemed to desert the Government, which was confronted by a grave economic crisis and embarked on a very questionable foreign policy. The result was that it incurred more and more criticism and soon became as unpopular as the ministry of Villèle in the days of Charles X.

The root cause of the economic crisis lay in the widespread bad weather of 1846 and 1847 which led to the failure of a great part of the corn harvests and the blighting of the potato crops of most of the countries of Northern and Western Europe. By May in 1847, a year long afterwards remembered in France as 'the year of dear bread', the price of wheat had risen to more than double the price in 1844. As a result, consumers had less money to spare for less essential purchases and there was an acute depression in the textile and other industries with a consequent increase in unemployment and sometimes reductions in wages. 'The metallurgy, coal mining and building industries were hard hit. Railway construction was stopped. Prices and profits collapsed to an . . . unprecedented degree.'[1] All this came on top of a financial crisis which had for some time been brewing in consequence of overspeculation in railway shares and a shortage of capital for investment. In the second half of 1846 the gold reserves of the Bank of France sank to a dangerously low level and the French Bank was obliged not only to follow the example of the Bank of England and raise its discount rate which went up to five per cent for the first time since 1817, another year of dear corn, but also to obtain a credit of £1,000,000 from the Bank of England through Baring's. There had been many economic crises in France before. The July Monarchy had come into being during a period of depression and there had been another difficult period during 1837–9, but none since 1815 had been so severe as this. In spite of the Government's prompt measures ·to import corn and alleviate distress, discontent remained widespread, all the more so since the depression persisted on into 1848. By then Guizot no longer had any reason to contemplate the state of France with complacent satisfaction.

[1] LABROUSSE, E.: *Summary of a paper on the Economic Crisis and the Political Crisis in France, 1847–51, given to an Anglo-French Historical Conference in Paris,* Sept. 1945, p. 1.

In the meantime his foreign policy had in 1846 led to a rupture of the Entente with Great Britain over the so-called Spanish Marriage Question. The shades of the war of the Spanish Succession and of various eighteenth-century dynastic quarrels seemed to have been resurrected by this strange nineteenth-century quarrel between two constitutional monarchies for influence in Spain. The issue was indeed, as Lord Aberdeen remarked, no adequate cause for national quarrel, but Aberdeen was no longer in office in England, and with his successor, Palmerston, the man who had helped to break the Entente in 1840, Guizot's relations were far from friendly. The Queen of Spain and her sister were both in the marriage market and Great Britain hoped either to secure a Coburg relation of Queen Victoria's as one of the husbands, or at least to ensure that the House of Orléans should not carry off both the prizes. Thus it had been a British stipulation that the marriage of the Infanta to a French prince should take place only after the Queen had married and had a child; and when in 1846 notwithstanding this supposed understanding with France, a double wedding took place between the Queen and the Duke of Cadiz and the Infanta and one of Louis Philippe's sons, the Duc de Montpensier, Palmerston was furious and believed that he had been tricked, while Guizot's supporters hailed the event as a splendid triumph of French diplomacy. Certainly it was an empty triumph; for the establishment of a precarious domestic influence in the troubled Spanish kingdom was hardly worth the determined hostility of the British Foreign Secretary and the rupture of the Entente which had been the mainstay of French foreign policy during the greater part of Louis Philippe's reign. Temporarily the rupture left France in isolation and although the conservative tendencies of Louis Philippe and Guizot led them to gravitate all the more easily towards co-operation with the Conservative Governments in Eastern Europe,[1] this evolution was far from palatable to an increasingly critical public opinion at home. The capture of Abd-el-Kader, the most redoubtable of the native leaders of resistance to French rule, in Algeria in 1847, was of no avail to offset the rebuffs to French prestige elsewhere. In Italy, where nationalist and liberal movements were growing, it was to England rather than France that the patriots looked for support in the cause of constitutional reform, and when Switzerland was rent by civil war it was England and not France which won the chief credit for the success of the Federal (and Liberal) cause. Thus there were no military or diplomatic successes in Europe to compensate for misfortune at home and France, from being

[1] For instance, both Guizot and Metternich went as far as they dared in supporting the Catholic Cantons' league in Switzerland.

merely bored, became all the more carping and critical of the foreign as
well as the domestic policy of her governors.
Nor was this all. In spite of the economic crisis and the criticisms
of home and foreign policy, the Government made no attempt to meet
its opponents half-way. 'What has been done during these last seven
years?' asked an Opposition Deputy in 1847, 'Nothing! Nothing!
Nothing!'[1] and in fact, apart from the first Factory Act of 1841, a measure which restricted the use of child labour in undertakings which
employed more than twenty persons, but which was largely ineffectual
for lack of a proper system of inspection, and from measures taken to
relieve distress and encourage benefit societies, there had been no social
legislation of any significance. Moreover, in spite of the growing criticism and of the revival of a movement for parliamentary reform which
had first begun before 1840 with a petition for the grant of the vote to
National Guards, the Government refused to consider any extension
of the franchise.
This was their last and most fateful error; for they claimed to be the
Government of the middle classes and of the *juste milieu*, yet continued
to exclude from the *pays légal* an important section of that middle
class, confining it to the wealthy among whom the new class of rich
manufacturers formed a veritable new aristocracy, 'one of the harshest,'
said Tocqueville, 'that has yet appeared on earth'.[2] The tax qualification had been arbitrarily fixed in 1814 and as arbitrarily modified in
1830. There was no logical reason why it should not again be lowered,
especially since at its existing level it confined the franchise to some
200,000 people and debarred from it a number of National Guards and
educated middle-class people whose support would have broadened the
basis of the régime. As a brilliant writer of the Second Empire later
pointed out, with his income he would in 1847 almost certainly have
been neither eligible for parliament nor qualified to be an elector and
'the fact that I was a doctor of letters, a former Faculty teacher, a member of the Institute and even a landed proprietor would have been of
no avail'.[3] Thus the government of the country was still confined to
an extremely small circle, and the occurrence of political scandals, such
as that which led to the conviction of a former Minister, Teste, of
corruption and social scandals such as that of the murder of the Duchesse

---

[1] cit. SEIGNOBOS, C.: *Histoire politique de l'Europe contemporaine*, p. 135.
[2] cit. WEILL, G.: *L'éveil des nationalités et le mouvement libéral* (1815–48), p.
324. A new phenomenon is the growing jealousy and fear of the new mono-
polistic plutocracy shown by the smaller traders and *petite bourgeoisie*.
[3] PRÉVOST-PARADOL: *La France nouvelle*, pp. 324-5, n.

de Choiseul-Praslin by her husband, at a time when there was already
so much discontent, made it very easy for the reformers and the critics
to denounce the whole circle as rotten. The government of the 200,000
electors became almost as much a subject of abuse by the Left as the
'government of the 200 families' eighty or ninety years later.[1]

The English Anti-Corn Law League with its lectures and tea-parties
had recently shown what might be done by vigorous propaganda, and
so now in France in 1847 several members of the Opposition sponsored
a widespread campaign of banquets throughout the country in favour
of parliamentary reforms. These meetings, which met with considerable success to the accompaniment of cries of 'Down with corruption!' and
'Long live reform' were to culminate in a banquet to be held in Paris on
February 22nd, 1848. After some hesitation the Government decided to
ban the meeting. The decision was to be their undoing, for it did not
avail to prevent large crowds from gathering near the rendezvous and
from demonstrating against the Guizot ministry. At the same time, the
appearance of barricades and red flags in certain working-class districts of
the capital showed that there was a dangerous revolutionary spirit in the
air. Even the entreaties of the Queen and the Princes, who were alarmed
lest the hostility to Guizot should extend to the King, had failed ten days
earlier to induce Louis Philippe to part with his Minister, but now he re-
lented. Guizot was dismissed and the royal summons first to Molé and
then to Thiers, the chief Opposition leader, to form a new Cabinet,
seemed to show that the King was ready to change his system, that the
cause of reform had triumphed and that the crisis was over. Unfortunately this bloodless 'revolution' was already being transformed into one of
violence which was to sweep away the throne as well as the Government. On the evening of the 23rd, as the result of an incident in front
of the Ministry of Foreign Affairs, troops were impelled to fire upon a
crowd of demonstrators. At once the mood of the Parisians changed
for the worse. Republican agitators had already made much profit
out of the abnormal public excitement; streets in the eastern part of the
city were quickly blocked by insurrectionary barricades and armed
mobs began to descend to the centre. Louis Philippe, who was now
seventy-five years old, had been recently much depressed by the death
of his sister and confidante, Madame Adélaide. He was further dis-

[1] The '200 families' were the families of the 200 largest shareholders in the
Bank of France, who alone of the whole number of 40,000 shareholders had the
right to vote at the annual meeting. For this reason they were attacked as the
representatives of the financial oligarchy which was accused of exercising a new
pouvoir occulte in French politics.

heartened by the lukewarm reception he had received from the National Guards whom he had ridden out to review on the 24th. When they, who had been his special protégés, no longer greeted him with warmth he felt that all was over. Paris could only be regained by military conquest and on that he was not prepared to embark. So, in spite of the opposition of some members of his family, he decided to abdicate in favour of his grandson, the Comte de Paris, the ten-year-old son of the late Duke of Orléans. On that same February 24th the old King and his family followed in the footsteps of Charles X and trod the melancholy road of exile into England.

In many ways there were striking resemblances between the Revolutions of 1830 which brought Louis Philippe to the throne and of 1848 which led to his fall. In both, when a large part of Paris comes into rebel hands, the King decides to abdicate in favour of a child. But in 1830 it was the King who had courted revolution without preparing to meet it should it break out, whereas in 1848 the King had already yielded to the outcry against Guizot and the further disturbances took him and the authorities generally so much by surprise that they had been unable to react with the necessary vigour to restore order. In consequence, it was the initiative of the extremists which carried the day and swept not only Louis Philippe but also his dynasty from the throne. The majority of deputies in the Chamber were ready enough to accept the Comte de Paris and the Regency of his mother, but, when the Chamber was invaded by a crowd and the Republic was proclaimed at the Hôtel de Ville, it was clear that constitutional forms had no validity against the will of an excited people. This time the Republicans were determined that their Republic should not be side-tracked by any monarchical compromise. They swept aside the claims of the boy Comte de Paris and by revolutionary acclamation the Second French Republic came to birth.

Thus for the second time since 1815 a monarchy in France had fallen because of its failure to bridge in time a widening gulf between itself and public opinion. A second attempt to found a lasting system of government on the English model had come to grief and once again a revolution made in Paris was meekly accepted by the provinces. Nowhere was there any attempt to raise the standard in defence of the Orleanist cause. The Orléans family did not represent either a principle or a national glory; they had merely been a useful expedient, 'an administrative monarchy', as Armand Carrel had predicted,[1] and when they ceased to be useful to an important section of the middle classes

[1] SAINTE-BEUVE: *Portraits littéraires*, II, p. 144.

who had been their mainstay their power collapsed—there was no other section of French society on whom they could depend. But their fall also meant the end of the experiment by which the middle and upper classes had sought to reserve to themselves the exclusive enjoyment of political influence by means of a limited franchise. The bourgeoisie might quickly recover and long enjoy great political as well as economic influence, but if they did so it would no longer be founded upon exclusive electoral rights. The days of *la monarchie censitaire* were over for ever.

It is easy to criticize the failings of the July Monarchy, but this criticism must not blind us to the facts that during these eighteen years from 1830 to 1848 it presided over or witnessed great material changes which did much to transform the conditions of life of large numbers of the French people and add to their amenities; and that during this period individual Frenchmen continued to achieve eminence in the most varied spheres of activity.

It would be impossible for us to leave the reign of Louis Philippe without mention of the law of 1836 for the improvement of country roads or of the inauguration of the first railway worthy of the name, the Paris-St. Germain line in 1837, or of the sailing of the first transatlantic steamer in 1840.[1] These were developments, due either to the Government or to private enterprise, which were speedily to bring distant countries into communication with France and distant parts of France into contact with one another in ways and to a degree undreamed of fifty years earlier. By the end of the reign France could boast 1931 kilometres of railway track—the first stage in a process which was to revolutionize the conditions of commerce and of war—and the construction of her steam navy had contributed not a little towards the veritable invasion scare which swept through England after the rupture of the Entente in 1846. By 1848 the improvement of local roads had led to an acceleration of local transport, to a widening of the areas to which farmers could send their produce and so to the beginning of a gradual revolution in agricultural technique which included a greater specialization and a greater reliance on artificial aids. An incidental consequence of these changes in communications was the introduction of a regular postal service and the appearance of what was soon to be the familiar figure of the *facteur* or postman. These were changes which affected life in every commune. There were others, too, but we cannot do more than mention one example, namely the fall in cotton prices in 1842, which Michelet, with some characteristic exaggeration of language, described as meaning a revolution in France: 'a revolution in property,

[1] GRAND-CARTERET, J.: *Le XIXᵉ Siècle*, II, p. 636.

a sudden embellishment of the poor man's household; whole classes now had underclothes, and linen for their tables and windows, who never had had such things since the world began. All the women formerly wore black or blue dresses which they kept for ten years without washing them for fear they would fall to pieces—to-day their husbands, poor workmen, for the price of a day's labour can clothe them in dresses of flowers. All these women who now display a rainbow of a thousand colours in our streets used to go about in mourning.'[1]

So too, we cannot dismiss the July Monarchy without recalling a few of the most splendid cultural achievements of its day. This was the time which saw the publication of some of the greatest works in French literature, further plays or poems by the great Romantics, Lamartine, Vigny, Hugo and Musset, novels such as Stendhal's *Le Rouge et le Noir* (1831), many of the first important works of Balzac, Hugo's *Notre Dame de Paris* and Dumas' *Count of Monte Cristo* (1844), Merimée's *Colomba*, and tales by Gautier and George Sand. It was a period which could boast of an historian such as Tocqueville and of others so popular in their own day as Thiers, Lamartine, and Michelet, as well as of a prince of literary critics in Sainte-Beuve; in which the début of the young tragedienne Rachel in 1838 and the failure of Hugo's play *Les Burgraves* in 1843, marked the decline of the Romantic movement and the revival of an interest in classical drama; when the exhibition of paintings by the Barbizon School in 1831 brought a new galaxy of talent, including the exquisite Corot, to the fore; when the same year helped to make the reputation of a noted sculptor in David d'Angers; when the skill of Monnier, Philipon, Gavarni and Daumier now for the first time raised caricature to the level of art, and when the ingenuity of Daguerre with his invention of photography in 1839 was to doom the silhouette and to bring the possession of a family portrait gallery within the means of the most modest purse, thereby providing a democratic complement to the aristocratic art of portrait painting. Nor was this all: the eloquence of the Chambers was outdone in the pulpit, and Lacordaire and Ravignan, the first to deliver the famous Lenten sermons at Notre Dame, are to be numbered amongst the greatest of all French preachers; in architecture Viollet-le-Duc began his career as the exponent of the Gothic revival; the Abbé Huc, intrepid missionary explorer, penetrated to the capital of the mysterious kingdom of Tibet; the Orientalist Burnouf won a foremost place among those who advanced the study of eastern languages; and the astronomer Leverrier discovered Neptune. These are but a

[1] MICHELET, J.: *Le Peuple.* cit. DUVEAU, G.: *La vie ouvrière en France sous le second Empire*, pp. 162–3.

few of the many names which might be mentioned to illustrate the continued diversity of French talent. During these same years Paris, the chief centre of so much intellectual activity, grew apace; several new quarters were constructed; the Pont du Carrousel was opened; the Luxor obelisk was erected in the centre of the Place de la Concorde; and last but not least, the Panthéon was reconverted from its use as a Church to serve as a mausoleum for great men with the words 'A ses grands hommes la patrie reconnaissante' inscribed over its portal. There were many in the roll we have just cited, many of the men of Louis Philippe's day, who were to deserve this gratitude and find a resting-place within its vaults.

ALLISON, JOHN. M. S.: *Thiers and the French Monarchy*. London, 1926.

BLANC, LOUIS: *Histoire de dix ans.*

BLANC, LOUIS: *Organisation du travail*, ed. J. A. R. Marriott. Oxford, 1913.

BONAPARTE, PRINCE NAPOLEON-LOUIS: *Des idées napoléoniennes*. Paris, 1860.

CHARLÉTY, S.: *La Monarchie de juillet* (Vol. V of LAVISSE, E.: *Histoire de France contemporaine*. Paris, 1921).

COOPER, DUFF: *Talleyrand*. London, 1932.

DOLLÉANS, EDOUARD: *Histoire du mouvement ouvrier*. Vol. I, 1830–71. Paris, 1936.

GUIZOT, F. P. G.: *Memoirs of My Own Time*. Vol. II–IV, tr. by J. W. Cole. London, 1859–61.

LUCAS-DUBRETON, J.: *La Restauration et la monarchie de Juillet*. Paris, 1926.

MALO, HENRI: *Thiers*. Paris, 1932.

NOAILLES, MARQUIS DE: *Le Comte Molé, Sa Vie—ses Mémoires*. Vols. V and VI. Paris, 1922.

WOODWARD, E. L.: *Three Studies in European Conservatism*. London, 1929.

VI

THE SECOND REPUBLIC

THE proclamation of a Republic in Paris evoked an extraordinary variety and intensity of emotion both in France and throughout Europe, emotion which ranged from the deepest alarm and anxiety to the most extravagant hopefulness and enthusiasm. The young Prince de Broglie, then a diplomat in Rome, was one of those who heard the news with alarm: 'Country, family, honour,' he wrote later, 'ambition, interests, personal security—all seemed to be threatened at once and to fall engulfed in the same abyss. Men could think only of 1793. The Republic meant bloodshed, confiscation, terror and war.'[1] All those who had possessions were indeed anxious. Within a week, more than 1,300 English people had hurried home. Business, already slack, came almost to a standstill; unemployment increased and there were outbreaks of machine smashing. Stocks fell; rich people sold their effects, while at the same time there was a run upon banks, many of which were obliged to suspend payment; even the gold reserve in the Bank of France sank to such a low level that on March 1st, 1848, dealings in paper money had to be stopped. This was one side of the picture, the gloomy side. On the other we see an extraordinary Romantic ebullience and optimism which manifested themselves in many ways: in the sudden efflorescence of clubs—no less than 450 appeared within a month in Paris and its suburbs, clubs with names that echoed those of the Great Revolution, clubs of Jacobins and Montagnards, and clubs for the emancipation of European peoples or of the feminine sex; in an abundance of banquets, banquets of 'the Federation of European Peoples', of the 'Friends of Poland', of 'Democratic Women', of 'Les travailleurs de la pensée' and a hundred more, banquets which always ended with some resounding toast—'To the Mountain of 1793'—'To Mistrust, sister of Vigilance'—'To Jesus Christ'—'To democratic Germany'—'To Jean-Jacques Rousseau'— 'To the oppressed peoples'—and to many others; in the spate of newspapers and pamphlets which poured forth as soon as the new rulers abolished the stamp duty and removed the restrictions imposed by the law of 1835 on the liberty of the Press, papers and pamphlets which

[1] *Mémoires du Duc de Broglie*, I, p. 185.

abounded not with news but with social and political programmes and doctrinaire declarations; in the planting of Trees of Liberty and their blessing by the clergy—for the Church, too, had been swept by liberal enthusiasms since the election in 1846 of a Liberal Pope; and in the grandiloquent language of the new Government itself, as instanced by the opening words of the preamble to its proclamation of February 26th announcing its intention to abolish the death penalty: 'The Provisional Government, convinced that generosity is the supreme part of policy and that each revolution effected by the French people owes it to the world to consecrate yet one more philosophic truth, considering that there is no principle more sublime than that of the inviolability of human life; considering that, in the memorable days in which we are living, not a cry of vengeance has arisen from the mouth of the people. . . .'[1] In short, among the people, the *gens du peuple* of Paris, the Revolution was hailed as the dawn of a new era. It was not long before their hopes were to be bitterly disappointed.

In many ways the consummation of the Revolution recalled that of 1830. Once again journalists played a great part, once again rival sets of insurgents bid against one another for power; once again the Hôtel de Ville was a place of decisive importance for determining the nature of the new Government; once again the period of unrest and popular demonstrations continued long after the Revolution itself was over; and once again there were two conflicting views of the object of the Revolution, each of which had its supporters within the Government itself. Accordingly, this Provisional Government which emerged represented a compromise. All its members save one, Albert, a workman, included in recognition of the part played by the people in the Revolution, were of bourgeois origin, more or less well-known Republicans, for the most part lawyers, orators and journalists by profession. On the one hand there were the men of the newspaper, *Le National,* people like Arago, Crémieux, Marie, Garnier-Pagès and Lamartine, for Lamartine had more or less abandoned poetry for politics and now became Minister for Foreign Affairs; on the other it included the men who supported the rival paper, *La Réforme,* such as Louis Blanc, Albert, Flocon and Ledru-Rollin. For the former the Revolution was a political event: it means the completion of the political work of the Great Revolution by the substitution of a free and democratic Republic based upon universal male suffrage for a monarchy based upon a restricted franchise: but for the men of the *Réforme* it implied a social and economic as well as a political transformation, and in Louis Blanc,

[1] *Les murailles révolutionnaires de 1848*, p. 58.

the author of *L'Organisation du Travail,* they had a social observer who was acutely aware of the evils of the new industrial age and who was most eager to abolish them. The great drama of 1848 lies in the conflict between those who want to seize the opportunity to solve the social problem by radical reforms of the conditions of labour and those who are determined to resist social changes which they fear will lead to chaos and anarchy. And herein also lies the great contrast between 1830 and 1848: in 1830 the middle classes were undisputed victors, in 1848 they are for a while on the defensive.[1]

The men of the *Réforme* were a minority in the Provisional Government, but they had sufficient influence and sufficient popular backing to make themselves felt at the outset. On the 25th February only the eloquence of Lamartine saved the tricolour from being displaced by the Socialist red flag; this was symbolic of the conflict between the old and the new revolutionaries—but, if the Government compromised by allowing a red rosette to be affixed to the standard of the tricolour, they had to make more conspicuous concessions to the demand for social reform when they reduced daily working hours to ten in Paris and eleven in the provinces and when they issued a proclamation recognizing the right to work. Moreover, although they refused the request for the establishment of a separate Ministry of Labour, they set up a permanent commission which was to sit at the Luxembourg Palace and examine labour problems under the presidency of Louis Blanc. Finally, in order to deal with the acute problem of Parisian unemployment, they created National Workshops. All this marked a radical departure from the *laissez-faire* attitude of the July Monarchy. The Government for the first time in French history were ready to guarantee work and to set about the task of organizing labour; but their organization of labour in the National Workshops was to be a parody of the 'Organisation du Travail' envisaged by Louis Blanc. None the less, these first social successes were sufficient to confirm the hopes of the enthusiastic workers. Was not one of their own kind, Albert, in the Government? Was not Louis Blanc in charge of labour questions? Was not George Sand who had echoed his charitable formula 'To each according to his needs',[2] busy helping the new ministers draft their decrees? And if

---

[1] MADAULE, J.: *Histoire de France,* II, p. 184, but a Marxist author like M. Daniel Guérin (*La Lutte des classes sous la première République*) would argue that they were already on the defensive in 1793-5.

[2] In *Le Péché de M. Antoine* one of the characters says '*Si après votre formule à chacun selon ses capacités vous n'ajoutez pas aussitôt à chacun selon ses besoins, c'est l'injustice qui règne.*' cit. PONTEIL, F.: '1848', p. 15.

the Government had not yet abolished the work-book or done away with the Combination Laws,[1] had it not guaranteed the right to work? All these considerations appeared signs of still better things to come and were hailed by many as a mere prelude to the complete transformation of society. But the fact that some of these social measures were extorted more or less under pressure by armed demonstrators had been enough to alarm both the moderates in the Government and most of their sympathizers outside it. The political course of the Revolution was soon to give the moderates and conservatives, the forces of order, the defenders of the existing society, an opportunity to rally and eventually to go over to the offensive.

After abolishing 'monarchy of every kind without possibility of return'[2] and removing stamp duties and many other restrictions on the liberty of the citizen, the Provisional Government had hastened to arrange for the establishment of the Republic on a regular basis. Accordingly, on March 5th, they decreed that elections to a National Constituent Assembly should be held on April 9th and that every Frenchman over twenty-one years of age should be entitled to a vote. Thus, by a stroke of the pen, universal male suffrage was introduced into France and the electorate was increased from some 200,000 to some 9,000,000. Moreover, in spite of the elementary education bill of 1833 and the growth of the popular press to which we referred in the last chapter, the majority of this vast new electorate was still illiterate. In his *Les Paysans*, written in 1845, Balzac has a striking passage on the meaning of legislation for the provinces: 'For twenty million beings in France the law is merely a piece of white paper stuck on the door of the Church or the Town Hall (Mairie). . . . Many mayors of cantons turn their copies of the *Bulletin des Lois* into bags for holding raisins and seeds. As for the mere mayors of communes you would be shocked by the number who cannot read or write and by the way in which the civil registers are kept.'[3] If such were the mayors, it is clear that the ordinary peasant or worker was unlikely to be more lettered. In these circumstances, although the Republic was giving them the vote, it was not at all

[1] See ch. ii, p. 16.

[2] For the Provisional Government's proclamation of February 26th. cf. BUTTERFIELD, H.: *Select Documents of European History*, 1715-1920, pp. 125-6.

[3] cit. *Bulletin No. 10 of the Société d'histoire de la Troisième République*, p. 87. According to F. PONTEIL, '1848', p. 108, the number of primary schools had increased from 30,586 to 63,028 between 1829 and 1847 and the number of pupils from 1,937,000 in 1832 to 3,000,000 in 1847. 'But as late as 1857, 33.5 per cent of the conscripts could neither read nor write.'

certain that their vote would be for the Republic. Blanqui indeed had at once seen that if elections were held quickly they would be likely to produce conservative results, and Ledru-Rollin as Minister of the Interior, did his best to educate the new electors and secure an Assembly 'animated by a revolutionary spirit' by sending out special 'Commissioners of the Republic' to all the departments. But the Government would only consent to postpone the elections for a fortnight and meanwhile events in Paris and various parts of the country served but to increase the moderates' distrust of the Republic and its capacity to maintain order. Thus the postponement of the elections was itself extracted from the Government by outside pressure. On the 16th March the bourgeois National Guards of the western districts of Paris had demonstrated against a measure dissolving some of their companies: on the following day Clubs and crowds from the east had penetrated into the Hôtel de Ville and compelled the Government to postpone the general elections. On the 21st a Radical Republican 'Club of Clubs' was founded which opened branches in the provinces and associated itself with Ledru-Rollin in his attempt to republicanize the electorate. On the 9th April another club, in which Armand Barbès was a prominent figure, called upon the Government to take over the Bank of France and to nationalize the insurance companies, railways, mines and salt works and canals; and on the 16th there was a workers' demonstration in favour of a further postponement of the elections, which alarmed the Government so much that they summoned the National Guard to their aid. Meanwhile in many country districts also the Revolution had been a signal for disturbances, for attacks on Jews and forest guards, and on justices of the peace, who were responsible for the collection of the unpopular *droits réunis* tax. The tales of these disturbances, of Paris disorder and of Socialist threats to property soon spread to the remotest parts of the country and naturally were not diminished in retelling. Furthermore, the Provisional Government had found themselves in financial difficulties which had led them as early as March 16th to add an additional forty-five centimes to direct taxation. This was a measure which inevitably made them unpopular with a thrifty peasantry already alarmed by rumours of disorder. In fact, the difference between 1789 and 1848 was very marked, in spite of the conscious echoes of the Great Revolution which resounded in the clubs. In 1789 the great mass of the nation, the country dwellers as well as the bourgeoisie, had been eager for the abolition of feudal privileges and political inequality: but in 1848 the number of Frenchmen who genuinely desired a social revolution and the abolition of economic inequality was comparatively small. The peasantry, so many of them now proprietors, were only scared by the stories of the Parisian Socialists and their rumoured talk of redistributing or doing away with individual property by some new agrarian law. And so when election day came and eighty-four per cent of the electorate went to the polls, most of them for the first time and village folk often headed by their parish priests as they marched to the booths, the votes cast were above all votes for order. In other words, the result of the elections was a crushing defeat for the extreme Radicals and Socialists, who won only 100 out of 876 seats.

The new Assembly, which thus comprised a large majority of moderate Republicans, former Orleanists, and Legitimists, was bound to come sooner or later into conflict with the extremists who were still able to exercise great influence in Paris. A few days after it met in May the Provisional Government resigned their power and the executive authority was entrusted to a so-called Executive Commission which included several members of the late Government, but not Louis Blanc or Albert. Already the Assembly was beginning to show its Conservative tendencies, and on the 12th May there took place the first of a series of demonstrations against it which culminated in one on the 15th when the Palais Bourbon was invaded by a mob, a club orator pronounced the Assembly's dissolution, and most of the crowd, headed by Barbès and Albert, then proceeded to the Hôtel de Ville to concoct a new Government. But the National Guard rallied and the newly raised Mobile Guards cleared the Assembly. The Hôtel de Ville was re-occupied and many of the leaders of this attempt at a second Revolution including Barbès, Blanqui and Albert, were arrested and prosecuted. The apostles of a Social Republic had, as George Sand perceived, committed a moral as well as a political blunder: 'They had without serious cause . . . given the signal for a rising against the law of the Republic; they had thrown people into a permanent state of anxiety and in some sort justified future *coups de force*![1]

Meanwhile labour problems again came to the fore. In the Assembly on May 10th Louis Blanc once again proposed the creation of a Ministry of Labour and Progress, but the Assembly contented itself with setting up a committee which was to conduct inquiry into labour conditions in agriculture and industry, canton by canton, throughout the country. It was optimistic enough to hope that the inquiry would be completed in a few weeks, but such a vast operation in unquiet times was bound to be protracted, and in fact it was to continue into 1850. A special problem was, however, presented by the National Workshops in Paris.

[1] cit. PONTEIL, F.: '1848', p. 116.

In his *Organisation du Travail* Louis Blanc had conceived of National Workshops as a means of combating unemployment and utilizing skilled labour in an orderly fashion under State direction. But the Workshops of Paris in 1848, as they were organized under the direction of Marie and Thomas, were a travesty of Louis Blanc's conception and were like nothing so much as the *ateliers de charité* of the Ancien Régime. They had been set up too hastily, under revolutionary pressure and without adequate administrative services to control them, with the result that some 50,000 workmen had soon been enrolled when there was real work for only 10,000. The remainder had to be occupied and were therefore employed on tasks such as levelling the Champ de Mars for two francs a day, work of such little value that, as someone said, they might just as well have spent their time in bottling the waters of the Seine. The presence of such a large body of men doing such unprofitable work was soon recognized by the Government as demoralizing for the men themselves, a drain on public funds, a danger to public order (many of the workers having taken part in the disturbances of May 15th) and in consequence an impediment to the recovery of business; and so it was decided that, after a census had been taken, the Workshops should be dissolved, that bachelors between eighteen and twenty-five should have the choice of dismissal or enrolment in the army; and that the rest should either accept what work could be offered by private employers or be sent to work on public enterprises in the provinces. After some delay the Assembly passed a decree on these lines and towards the end of June the Executive Commission of the Government decided to proceed immediately with the dissolution of the Workshops.

The result was infinitely tragic. When once they heard of the decision the workers were furious at what they regarded as the Government's and Assembly's treachery in going back on the guarantee of the right to work. The persistence of the economic crisis, in spite of the rule of a Republican régime, had steadily hardened social antagonisms, making the employers sterner in their resolve to end what they regarded as social anarchy and the young workers all the more bitter at the choice now presented to them between conscription and unemployment. And so the men of the National Workshops, and the unemployed who had been refused admission to them, determined to resist the order for dissolution, and all the working-class quarters of Paris rose in sympathy with them. For a second time within a few months Paris saw the barricades go up. No persuasion could induce the men to disperse peaceably and on June 24th, 1848, the Assembly gave General Cavaignac the title of Chief of the Executive Power with full authority to use force.

Reinforcements of troops, for the first time in French history, were hurried to the city by train, and three days of bitter fighting ensued. It was a remarkable insurrection—not led by any of the Socialist chiefs or deputies, but, in Tocqueville's words, one in which 100,000 insurgents fought 'without a war-cry, without chiefs, or a standard, and yet with a cohesion and a military skill which surprised the oldest officers'. It was 'not the work of a group of conspirators, but the rising of one part of the population against the other. Women took part in it as much as men . . . they hoped for victory to ease the lot of their husbands, and help to bring up their children'. 'It was not a political struggle . . . but class war, a kind of slave-war.'[1] As such it had all the ruthlessness of class or slave warfare, and was bitterly fought, and ruthlessly suppressed. Many were killed, 15,000 people were arrested and 4,000 deported, mostly to Algeria.[2] All Socialists were now under suspicion and Louis Blanc hurriedly took refuge in England. Clubs were placed under supervision. New press laws were introduced, reimposing a cautionary payment on those who wished to publish newspapers and making attacks upon certain institutions indictable offences. In September the working day in Paris was once again increased to twelve hours and in many instances in the years to follow it became still longer. When the Assembly applauded Cavaignac for his achievement in suppressing the insurrection Lamartine exclaimed: 'The Republic is dead.' When Lamennais was obliged by the new press laws to cease publishing his paper *Le Peuple Constituant* he did so with the bitter words 'Silence to the poor man', and commented that the spectacle presented by France after the June Days was not that of Republican France but of the 'saturnalia of reaction around its bloodstained tomb'.[3] The forces of order had triumphed and the Utopian dreams of a Social Republic and all the optimism of February and March had vanished in the horrors of civil war. But the memories of the bitter fight put up by the 'Army of Despair' long remained to keep alive the distrust of the bourgeoisie in many a Parisian worker's household.

Henceforward there is much to be said for the view of Lamartine and Lamennais that, although the Republic still continued for more

[1] cit. NAMIER, L. B., 1848: *The Revolution of the Intellectuals*, p. 10.

[2] The statistics given for killed and arrested vary. The official number of killed is 1,460, but as G. BOURGIN points out (in F. FEJTO, 1848 *dans le Monde*, I, p. 214,) no one ever counted the number of those who died in hospital or who were buried immediately. One of the most notable casualties was Mgr. Affre, the Archbishop of Paris, who was shot while attempting mediation.

[3] cit. PONTEIL, F.: '1848', p. 154.

than four years, it was really only a Republic in name. After the June Days it was experienced Orleanists or Legitimists like Thiers, Falloux, Montalembert, Odilon Barrot, and Berryer, who carried most weight in the Assembly; and, when the Assembly had completed its work of endowing the country with a Republican constitution, the nation was to elect as President a man who would work patiently to give this strange accidental republic the *coup de grace.*

In November, after six months of labour and much debating, the new Constitution was ready.[1] It reflected both the retreat from the social aspirations of February and the reaction against English parliamentarism, as it had been imitated by the Charters of 1814 and 1830. The Republic now no longer guaranteed the right to work, but only undertook more cautiously to guarantee 'the existence of citizens in distress, either by procuring them work within the limits of its resources or by giving relief to those who were not able to work'. In its political arrangements the Constitution laid down that separation of powers was the first condition of a free Government and provided that the legislature should consist of a single chamber or Legislative Assembly. Thus the constitution-makers harked back to the traditions of the Great Revolution, but they failed to ensure that the separated parts of their new structure would work in harmony together. What, for instance, would happen if the new Legislative Assembly, to be elected by universal suffrage, should come into conflict with the new President of the Republic, who was also to be elected by universal suffrage and to enjoy very wide executive power? In vain had the moderate Republican, Jules Grévy, argued that it would be more prudent not to have a President at all. His objections had been swept aside by the eloquence of another Republican, Lamartine, who himself aspired to the Presidency and who also said that it would be an error to have the President elected by the Assembly instead of by direct universal suffrage; for an Assembly would be suspect, whereas 'a nation is as incorruptible as the Ocean'.[2] Again, if there were difficulties in operating the new machinery, would it not be well to make it easy for the Constitution to be revised? But the Constituent Assembly had too much respect for its own work and held that a constitution was not a thing to be lightly tampered with. Accordingly the provisions laid down for revision were elaborate and required a vote of no less than three-quarters of the new Legislative Assembly before any changes could be made.

In December the sovereign people, Lamartine's 'incorruptible

[1] For the text see Appendix V.
[2] cit. FALLOUX, COMTE DE: *Mémoires d'un Royaliste,* I, p. 352.

nation', went once again to the polls: this time to elect the first President of the Second French Republic. Three of the Republicans, who had played a prominent part in the events of the last ten months were among the candidates, Cavaignac, Lamartine and Ledru-Rollin. But these names spelt little to a nation which was by no means Republican at heart compared with another which had a meaning for the humblest peasant, a name known to all, a name covered with glory and which had gained such fresh popularity in recent years as the result of a romantic cult that it was capable of sweeping the country, almost regardless of the character and personality of its present bearer: the name of Napoleon. Already in by-elections to the Constituent Assembly in June and September a number of departments had chosen Prince Louis Napoleon, nephew of the great Emperor and, since the death of his elder brother in March 1831 and of the Duc de Reichstadt in 1832, head of the House of Bonaparte, to be their deputy. Now in December, aided by the clever and assiduous propaganda of his agents, the Prince was carried to the Presidency by an overwhelming majority.

To those who knew the Prince, without knowing the strength of the Bonapartist legend and how weary France was of a Republic which had done nothing but accumulate disorders, perpetuate instability and increase taxation, such a result might well have appeared wholly astonishing. His attempts to raise the Bonapartist standard in 1836 and 1840 had been ludicrous fiascos. He had spent most of his life out of France and spoke French with a German accent. He was unprepossessing in appearance—with his black clothes, heavy thick moustache and pale immobile features, almost a caricature of a Romantic conspirator. His manners were awkward, shy, and irresolute, and his first speeches in the Assembly led experienced politicians to dismiss him as a nonentity. Indeed, ironically enough, the protest he made against a motion that all members of former ruling houses should be ineligible for the Presidency was so halting and embarrassed that the mover of the motion was led to withdraw it, saying that it was clearly superfluous 'after what we have just seen and heard'. But he still had two great assets, his name and his extraordinary faith in his star, which had so far enabled him to triumph over every obstacle. For the peasants and old soldiers[1] he stood for order and glory; for many of the workers 'Poléon', the Prince who in 1844

---

[1] 'I canvassed for Louis Napoleon one of my own peasants,' Montalembert told Nassau Senior. 'Comment veut-on,' he answered, 'que je ne vote pas pour ce monsieur: moi, qui ai eu le nez gelé à Moscou!' 'Et quand,' added his wife, 'nous avons eu deux fois la maison pillée!' SENIOR, N. W.: Conversations with M. Thiers, vol. I, p. 365.

had written an essay called *L'Extinction du Paupérisme* and who might like his uncle continue the work of the Great Revolution, was preferable to Cavaignac, the Butcher of June; for most of the Royalists he appeared likely to be a useful stopgap until such time as the Legitimists and Orleanists should succeed in composing their differences and restoring the monarchy; and even some Republican politicians, like the Jewish Crémieux, gave him their vote on the grounds that he represented the clearest protest against the Treaties of 1815.[1] And so the vote for Louis Napoleon in December 1848, had been in the words of Emile de Girardin 'not an election, but an acclamation'.[2]

Now that the President had been chosen it remained for the other parts of the new constitutional structure to be set up. The elections to the Legislative Assembly in May 1849 still further emphasized the discredit of the Republicans. Nearly two-thirds of the deputies in the new Parliament were Orleanists or Legitimists; the moderate Republicans were reduced to a mere eighty and outdistanced by the extremists now known as 'the Mountain', who retained a considerable hold upon Paris and had won some ground in parts of the south and south-east of France which have ever since tended to remain bastions of the Left. The Spanish Ambassador might well comment on the strange spectacle of an Assembly filled with monarchists who could not establish a monarchy and who groaned under the weight of a Republic which had no Republicans to defend it. Yet it was not so much true that the Republic had no defenders as that its deputies were a cowed and impotent minority. The meeting of the new Assembly like that of the Constituent Assembly a year earlier, provoked another Parisian insurrection, but this time it was not as in June 1848 the people who wanted leaders so much as the leaders, Ledru-Rollin and his friends, who wanted troops. The rising was a fruitless gesture which strengthened the forces of order still further, led Ledru-Rollin[3] and others implicated to follow Louis Blanc and flee to England, and was followed by a tightening of the press laws and a ban on public meetings of a political character.

Meanwhile the President, although many of the politicians as yet did not realize it, set about patiently preparing for the final step which would lead him to the fulfilment of what he believed to be his destiny, the restoration of the Empire. He had a number of faithful personal

---

[1] NAMIER, L. B., 1848: *The Revolution of the Intellectuals*, p. 34.

[2] cit. BELLESSORT, A.: *La Société française sous Napoléon*, III, p. 27.

[3] It was at this time that Ledru-Rollin, a reluctant revolutionary, uttered his famous phrase, "*Je suis leur chef, il faut que je les suive*," cp. HALÉVY, D.: *La République des Comités*, p. 16.

followers, but there was as yet no organized Bonapartist party. He could not expect to appeal to Orleanists and Legitimists as such, but by his acts he might well win over the sympathies of the influential body of French Catholics. And so the years 1849 and 1850 are marked by extremely important developments in foreign and educational policy which did much to consolidate Louis Napoleon's position in France.

As we have seen, the Revolution of February 1848, was followed by much grandiloquent talk of emulating the deeds of the ancestors of the Great Revolution, and it was believed by many at home and abroad that the proclamation of a Republic would inevitably lead to war and a crusade to tear up the 1815 Treaties and carry the blessings of liberty to less fortunate peoples. It is indeed arguable that such a crusade would have solved the problem of unemployment and averted the civil strife of the June Days; but the rulers of 1848 were influenced as much by the new Romantic pacifism with its cult of the peaceful brotherhood of peoples as by militant Jacobinism, and with more than enough trouble on their hands at home they had no wish to add to their burdens the perils of war. Thus, although the February Revolution had been an European event of the first magnitude because it had given the impetus to revolution in Berlin, Vienna, Budapest and many other lesser cities, Lamartine had resolutely resisted the pressure of extremists like Barbès and Blanqui, who demanded that France should help to recreate an independent Poland, and he and his successors had been no less firm in refusing to go to war on behalf of the Italians against Austria. But the extreme Republicans never lost sight of their international connections. One of the avowed objects of the manifestation of May 15th, 1848, against the Constituent Assembly had been to secure a Government which would reconstitute a free Poland; and now again the rising of June 1849 was partly a demonstration on behalf of the Republic which had been set up four months earlier in Rome, after the murder of his Prime Minister, Rossi, had led the Pope to flee to Gaeta. In March 1849, the expiring Constituent Assembly had voted credits for the dispatch of a French expeditionary force to maintain Roman liberties against the danger of suppression by Austria—once again the desire to maintain France's traditional influence in Italy was a powerful force in the diplomacy of 1848-9. But this was not the goal designed for the expedition by the Prince-President, for the French Catholics, for whose support he was angling, wanted not the preservation of Mazzini's Republic but the restoration of the Pope. And so it was that the expeditionary force intended by French Republicans to defend the Roman Republic was

used to destroy it. After sham negotiations, its commander, General
Oudinot, at the end of June, proceeded to besiege the city of Rome
and on July 3rd it fell. France, the chief of European Republics, then
put an end to one of the few others born of the revolutionary wave of
1848 which still survived. The Pope was restored but, like Ferdinand
VII of Spain in 1823, stubbornly refused to reintroduce any liberal
reforms, in spite of Louis Napoleon's expressed wish. However,
Catholic support was more important to the Prince-President than
Liberal institutions. The result was that French troops henceforth
appeared as the natural defenders of the temporal power of a Papacy
which had reverted to reaction and was soon to denounce most of the
works of modern civilization.

In foreign affairs Louis Napoleon had thus played his part. The
countenance he gave to the Loi Falloux of 1850 was the equivalent
gesture to the French Catholics in domestic matters. In spite of anti-
clericalism, which had continued into the 'thirties and revived again
with renewed attacks on the Jesuits in the 'forties, the Church had
continued to try and improve its position in the State. Above all, it
had fought against the University monopoly of higher and secondary
education and in its struggle it had been most eloquently served by some
of the new school of Liberal Catholics of whom the Comte de Montalembert was the chief. Now at last its efforts were to be rewarded. The
Loi Falloux was to secure the position of the Catholics in education for
more than thirty years and seemed so great a victory that the illustrious
Dominican preacher Lacordaire could hail it as a nineteenth-century
Edict of Nantes.[1] The State monopoly was broken down and henceforward two categories of school were accorded official recognition:
the public schools founded and maintained by Communes, Departments or the State itself; and the free schools founded and maintained by
private individuals or associations. In effect this meant that any authorized or tolerated religious association could now open a school—as for
private individuals few were wealthy or interested enough to do so—
and that the religious orders came to play an increasingly important part
in French education. To the detached English observer this might well
seem a fair enough solution, but to contemporary Frenchmen of the
Left it naturally appeared to be another sign of the strength of the
Conservative reaction, a measure of a piece with the electoral law of
the same year, 1850, which, by requiring evidence of three years' resi-

[1] There was, however, a body of intransigent Catholics, led by the great
polemical journalist Veuillot, who were not satisfied and denounced it as a
miserable compromise.

dence in order to qualify would-be voters for inclusion in the electoral roll, had effectively disfranchized some 3,000,000 people, a large number of whom, mobile industrial workers, would undoubtedly tend to vote for the Mountain.

The discredit of the Republicans and the inability of the Monarchists to agree upon a King naturally facilitated the Prince-President's task of achieving his personal ambitions. The two acts to which we have just referred were largely successful in bringing many French Catholics to regard him with sympathy as the defender of their interests. By a series of tours of the provinces he made himself more widely known, learnt to play his new part more easily and won a considerable personal triumph by his gracious demeanour and the unexpected felicity of the speeches in which he dwelt upon the blessings of order and prosperity and recalled how they had been provided of old by a greater than he whose name he bore. At the same time he had not been slow in showing the Legislative Assembly that he did not intend to be its mere tool. As time passed and Louis Napoleon's confidence in his ability to pursue an independent policy increased, the growing friction between the Executive and the Legislative became more and more apparent. In February 1851, the Assembly rejected a proposal to increase the President's civil list, and in July they defeated a proposal to revise the constitution so as to permit of Louis Napoleon's immediate re-election and turned down his suggestion that they should rescind the electoral laws of 1850. Meanwhile the term of both was running out. The President had been elected at the end of 1848 for four years, the Legislative Assembly in May 1849 for three years. Eighteen fifty-two would therefore be a critical year. Louis Napoleon who had played his cards against the Legislative Assembly with so much adroitness that there were many who thought he had been ill-used by it, decided not to wait for the expiration of his term. By the end of November his plans were made, he had made sure of the army, he had prepared his justification and during the night of December 1st–2nd he acted. The chief party leaders were arrested and the Chamber was occupied by troops. On the 2nd Frenchmen awoke to find the capital placarded by proclamations announcing the dissolution of an Assembly which the President accused of 'forging arms for civil war'. 'My duty,' said Louis Napoleon, 'is to maintain the Republic . . . by invoking the solemn judgement of the only sovereign I recognize in France . . . the people';[1] and he posed as the people's champion by at once re-introducing the full universal suffrage which the Assembly had refused

[1] Proclamation to the people. cit. CAHEN, L. and MATHIEZ, A.: *Les Lois françaises de 1815 à 1914*, p. 121.

to restore in the summer, and by announcing that a new Republican constitution would be submitted to the verdict of a plebiscite.

Wiser in his generation than Charles X, Louis Napoleon had pre- pared his coup with skill and thoroughness. Yet, even so, it was not wholly unopposed: the Jacobins of Provence and the South Centre once again took up arms, and a handful of Republican deputies, in- cluding Victor Hugo, attempted to raise the eastern quarters of Paris. But there the workers were by now for the most part passive, sceptical or indifferent, and the death of one of the deputies, Baudin, on a flimsy barricade, hardly caused a stir. This did not mean that there was not still a strong Republican feeling, which indeed showed itself in the plebiscite and in the elections to the new Legislative Assembly in February 1852 when two staunch Republicans, Carnot and Cavaignac, were both returned; but the workers had no taste for a second June Days war.

Such attempts as were made at resistance were ruthlessly repressed. Nearly 27,000 people were arrested or prosecuted in default; some 15,000 were condemned to various sentences; and some 9,000 were deported to Algeria.

Although the Republic, which Louis Napoleon acknowledged it was his duty to maintain, survived in name for another year, everyone knew that the restoration of the Empire was only a question of time. The 2nd December 1851 was virtually the *coup de grâce* for the Second Republic, so long already only a shadow of its original self, and it led to the institution of an authoritarian régime very different from the parliamentary governments enjoyed by France since 1815. The re- luctance of Louis Philippe and Guizot to grant parliamentary reform and the violence of the Parisians had thus led to a further violent inter- ruption in the peaceable and regular development of constitutional government in France. The political changes in French society resulting from the French Revolution had been emphasized anew and in addition the bitter social cleavages resulting from the industrial Revolution now stood revealed. The first Napoleon had been nearer than any French ruler since 1789 to recreating a unity among Frenchmen. It remained to be seen whether 'The man of December' would have equal success.

ARNAUD, R.: *La deuxième République et le second Empire.* Paris, 1929.
BROGLIE: *Mémoires du Duc de.* Vol. I, 1825-70. Paris, 1938.
DANSETTE, A.: *Deuxième République et Second Empire.* Paris, 1942.
FALLOUX, COMTE DE: *Mémoires d'un Royaliste.* Paris, 1925.
FEJTO, F.: ed. 1848 *dans le Monde. Le Printemps des Peuples.* Paris, 1948.
FLAUBERT, G.: *L'éducation sentimentale.*

PONTEIL, FÉLIX: "1848" (Collection Armand Colin, No. 204).   Paris, 1937.
QUENTIN-BAUCHART, P.: *La crise sociale de 1848*.   Paris, 1920.
SEIGNOBOS, C.: *La Révolution de 1848—le Second Empire* (1848–59).   (Vol. VI of
    LAVISSE, E.: *Histoire de France contemporaine*.   Paris, 1921.)
SIMPSON, F. A.: *The Rise of Louis Napoleon*.   London, 1909, new ed. 1925.
TOCQUEVILLE, ALEXIS DE: *The Recollections of*, ed. MAYER, J. P.   London, 1948.

The series of slim volumes known as the *Collection du Centenaire de la Révolution de 1848* (Presses Universitaires de France.   Paris, 1948), may also be consulted with profit.

VII

THE SECOND EMPIRE

THE experiment of the Second Republic had, as we have seen, ended in profound disillusionment. The extravagant hopes of the birth of a new society at home and of the liberation of peoples abroad had come to nought. Within a few months there had been civil war in the capital and the economic crisis had been intensified. This crisis had persisted in many branches of the national economy throughout the greater part of the Republican régime: credit was impaired, the metallurgical, mining, and building industries continued to be depressed, while agriculturists were now dismayed by harvests so abundant that corn prices were lower than at any time since 1787. Thus for a large section of the community the Republic had come to be synonymous with an instability which was injurious to the economic as well as the political well-being of the nation. The Prince-President for his part did not scruple to encourage this disenchantment or to diffuse the belief that only by giving him a free hand and by the restoration of the Empire could France recover confidence in the future. So, on Louis Napoleon came to centre many hopes, and the *coup d'état* together with his assumption a year later, on December 2nd, 1852, of the Imperial title, with the name of Napoleon III, were generally welcomed. He had won the support of the army and gratified it by a special proclamation on the morrow of the *coup d'état*: now under a Napoleon it could hope for greater scope and prestige. His accession was accepted by most of the remaining Saint Simonian economists and by members of the financial aristocracy who had previously supported the July Monarchy—men such as Fould, Magne and Billault, 'Orleanists of the second generation', as they have been called, were to hold office throughout the greater part of the Second Empire. It was welcomed by the industrialists, business men and shop-keepers, who hoped for economic recovery under a strong government and mistakenly believed that the Emperor was a whole-hearted pro-tectionist. It was hailed by the peasants, who looked for higher prices, and even by many workers who hoped that the Emperor might yet prove to be the champion of their interests against the employers. It pleased the majority of the Catholics who were now increasingly Ultra-montane and looked forward to a new alliance of Throne and Altar although the new ruler was no believer. <u>Napoleon had posed as a saviour of society, and for the most part society accepted him as such.</u> The Empire stood above all for order and social security, and because, after the turmoil of the last years, the majority of Frenchmen now counted these as the chiefest blessings, it was with comparative equanimity that they saw the disappearance of the relatively free institutions which they had enjoyed since 1815. <u>The plebiscite of December 1851 had approved the *coup d'etat* by an overwhelming majority of 7,481,000 to 647,000, and the plebiscite upon the restoration of the Empire was almost as striking</u> a victory for the Emperor. As an English historian has well remarked, 'For better or for worse the people had made the act their own . . . If the *coup d'etat* was a crime France was less its victim than its accomplice.' Only for a small minority, the half million or so who voted 'No' and the sullen abstainers, did he remain 'the man of December 2nd', yet, as the same historian has pointed out, while Louis Napoleon 'appealed to the French people not as a tyrant, but as a tyrannicide . . . the fact remains that the Constitution was suppressed by the one man in the world who had sworn to uphold it'.[1] This was the fundamental weakness of his position which Napoleon's enemies never forgot. Men like Victor Hugo, the author of *Les Châtiments* with its bitter attack on the Second Empire, and his fellow Republicans, never ceased to inveigh against the 'criminal' and the 'crime' of December 2nd, 1851. At the same time it is to be remembered that the 'tyrant' was not really the Republic. If Louis Napoleon saved France from anything, he saved it from the perils of an unsatisfactory Constitution and from the possibility of a monarchical restoration. As Bainville has remarked, 'To read the *Châtiments* of Victor Hugo or the *Histoire d'un crime* one would think the Prince-President had strangled the Republic. In reality he smothered a monarchy in the cradle'.[2] Yet, in spite of the death of Louis Philippe in 1850, the Royalists were still unable to put an end to their divisions. But for the emergence of yet another competitor in the person of Napoleon, the Republic might have survived on the basis of Thiers' famous negative formula, which we have already had occasion to quote, namely that it was the regime which divided Frenchmen least.

The institutions of Empire were already partly in being before the Empire itself was restored. The Constitution of 1852 was an avowed

[1] SIMPSON, F. A.: *Louis Napoleon and the Recovery of France 1848-56*, pp. 163, 168-9.

[2] BAINVILLE, J.: *Histoire de France*, p. 486.

replica of the first Napoleon's Constitution of 1800, with the important difference that the lower house or Legislative Body was now to be elected by universal suffrage,[1] for that, together with the abolition of slavery in the French colonies, was the one great innovation of the Second Republic which no subsequent régime dared to reject. But the Legislative Body had only 260 members compared with the 700 of the Legislative Assembly of 1849; it was to sit for only three months in the year; it was not allowed even to choose its own President or to have its debates published; and the general elections of deputies, to be held every six years, were, in accordance with a tradition now well established, liable to be subject to strong official pressure. Moreover, to make doubly sure of satisfactory results, the Imperial Government drew the boundaries of constituencies in quite arbitrary fashion. The upper chamber, the Senate, was to be a still smaller body of men who held their seats for life, either ex-officio or through nomination by the President. Its main function was to serve as a vehicle for constitutional change—any such changes being promulgated by *Senatus consultum* which might afterwards be submitted to a plebiscite for confirmation. This was indeed a typically Napoleonic device. 'The present constitution,' declared Louis Napoleon in a proclamation to the French people, 'proclaims that the Chief whom you have chosen is responsible to you; that he always has the right to appeal to your sovereign judgement, in order that, on solemn occasions, you may be able to continue or withdraw your confidence. . . . Since he is responsible his action must be free and untrammelled.' In other words he might at any time override the legislature by resort to a plebiscite; while his freedom of action meant among other things that Ministers were responsible to him and not to the Legislative Body, of which they need not be members, and that he alone initiated legislation, bills being, by what Prévost-Paradol called 'a strange inversion of public powers',[2] prepared by the Conseil d'Etat and presented complete to the Legislative Body, which could modify them only on the Conseil d'Etat's advice. There is, as Lowes Dickinson has remarked,[3] 'no sufficient reason to suppose that he was deliberately announcing a fraud; as he believed in his own mission, so he believed in its acceptance by the nation': but the plebiscite was hardly 'an adequate means of establishing his responsibility to the people'.

The Emperor also appointed to all offices, was Commander in Chief of the forces and had the right of declaring war and making treaties. This

[1] For the text of this Constitution, see Appendix VI.
[2] *La France nouvelle*, p. 96.
[3] *Revolution and Reaction in Modern France*, p. 229.

authoritarian regime, which gave the Prince-President, soon to be Emperor, such wide powers, was buttressed by other measures of importance. In particular, a 'decree-law' of 1852 subjected the Press to more stringent control. Any newspaper was now obliged to obtain Government authorization before it could appear, and all those which dealt with political or social economy had to give a financial guarantee. Direct Government censorship was, however, replaced by an ingenious system of warnings. If a paper offended, its director received a warning, and after this had happened twice the paper was liable to be suspended. Such warnings might be given by the prefects, whose powers were generally increased. They meant that the censorship desired was exercised by the directors themselves, and the system then decreed by the French authorities was subsequently imitated elsewhere by Bismarck and the Tsar Alexander II. In addition, Napoleon, who had not scrupled to break his own oath to the Republic, demanded that all Senators, deputies, magistrates and state officials should take an oath of allegiance to him. This meant that conscientious opponents of the régime, like the Republican Cavaignac, who could not bring themselves to take the oath, were unable to take their seats in the Legislative Body, which was thus more than ever an instrument of the Imperial will. Under such conditions active political life was effectively stifled, as indeed the Emperor intended that it should be. By the end of 1853 the number of avowedly political daily newspapers had dropped to fourteen: on the other hand, as in the days of Charles X, there was an increase in the numbers and circulation of literary and philosophical papers in which the critics sought to make political points indirectly. State education, too, assumed a still more rigid and disciplined character, reminiscent of the First Empire, and the rule of Napoleon III's first Minister of Education, Fortoul, it has been said, 'was the time in which every class in France did exercises at the same hour; the time when teachers were ordered to shave off their moustaches in order to remove the last vestiges of anarchy from their costume as well as from their morals'. The France of Napoleon was strictly regimented in political matters and the police organization whose extensive powers had more than once been criticized under previous régimes, was strengthened in order to keep watch on malcontents and subversive elements.

But if political activity was repressed, there was great activity in other spheres, and at this moment in French history this was a compensating fact which counted for much. The year 1851 had already marked a real improvement in the economic state of the country. The long depression was over and the fortunate coincidence of the beginning of a new period of prosperity with the advent of the new régime redounded greatly to the advantage of the Emperor. In spite of cholera and poor harvests again in 1853-5, a slight depression in 1854, and the worldwide crisis of 1857, which hit France less severely than many other countries, relative prosperity continued until 1860, when a change in economic policy, coinciding with a set-back in foreign policy, unsettled France's internal stability. Until then, however, the reign of Napoleon III could be said to have gone a long way to fulfil the hopes of many of those who had voted 'Yes' in 1851 and 1852; and the successes of the new régime were more striking than those of its predecessors in that they were shared or appreciated by more people. Plebiscites and elections by universal suffrage helped to maintain the illusion of popular sovereignty. The economic prosperity contrasted favourably with the lean years of the end of the July Monarchy and of the Second Republic. The Emperor's marriage in 1853 to the beautiful, red-haired Spanish Countess, Eugénie de Montijo, and the consequent development of a gay and brilliant Court contrasted with the stiffness of Bourbon etiquette and the bourgeois dullness of Louis Philippe's household. A series of fêtes and military reviews and the great Paris Exhibition of 1855, the French answer to the London Exhibition of 1851, all displayed to a contented public the splendour and well-being of the new order. Moreover, prosperity at home was matched by success abroad. The Anglo-French Entente was re-established, Russia was defeated in war, and in 1856 the statesmen of Europe gathered together in Paris at the first general Congress to be held since 1822. Once again their object was to make a peace settlement, but this time France was one of the victors. There is no doubt that in 1856 under Napoleon III the prestige of France stood higher than at any time since the First Empire. Once again she appeared to be without question the foremost power on the Continent. And yet in the end it was the weakness and contradictions of Napoleon's foreign policy which was to bring his whole edifice crashing to the ground.

'The Empire means peace': such were the oft-quoted words uttered by the Prince-President in a speech at Bordeaux in October 1852. They were enough at the outset of the new régime to reassure opinion both at home and abroad and may have been sincerely meant at the moment at which they were spoken. But the name he bore, his system of government and his personal interest in new movements abroad, all impelled the Emperor to an active foreign policy which was soon to lead him into war. The very name of Napoleon was in itself a challenge to the Treaties of 1815; the Napoleonic system of government required success abroad as well as prosperity at home to compensate for the deprivation of liberty, while Napoleon III's quixotic sympathy with the aspirations of other nationalities encouraged him to go crusading on their behalf. So here, too, the Second Empire is in striking contrast to previous régimes; it is dominated not by internal political struggles or by the development of industry and commerce, important though they are, but by foreign affairs.

The character of Napoleon provides the main clue to a foreign policy in which he himself took the main decisions. But it was a character compounded of contradictions which often made the Emperor's purposes appear obscure and enigmatic to his contemporaries. If the third Napoleon was un-Napoleonic in appearance he was no less dissimilar from his great uncle in other ways. Although personally brave and imperturbable in moments of danger, he had none of the military genius of Napoleon I. Often obstinate and tenacious in adhering to designs once formed, he yet lacked the vigour and ruthlessness to carry them out to the full. In exile and prison he had meditated long upon the lessons of his uncle's reign with the result that while in some ways the Second Empire was a sort of somnambulist's revival of the First, in others, especially in foreign policy, its ruler deliberately pursued a different path, hoping thereby to avoid the mistakes of the great Napoleon. Thus while England was Napoleon I's great enemy Napoleon III sought to base his policy upon English friendship.[1] This un-Napoleonic aspect of the new Emperor's demeanour was enhanced by his attachment to certain dreams of his youth and by his almost Republican belief in the virtues of nationality, the greatness of Prussia and the possibilities of disarmament. Withal, the Emperor was grave, courteous and gentle: 'If surnames were still given to Princes,' said Emile de Girardin, 'Napoleon would be called Napoleon the well-meaning.' No journalist would ever have attributed such qualities to the Little Corporal or given such a name to Napoleon I. And it was precisely this gentleness and idealistic humanitarianism, which by blurring the traits of the Napoleonic model, made the Emperor so strange a figure among the crowned heads of his day. The Saint-Simonian 'Socialist' who wrote 'L'Extinction du paupérisme' still cared for the welfare of the workers, the conspirator who had belonged to the Carbonari still wished to do something for Italy and believed that the idea of nationality was a good one, which it was his mission to bring nearer fulfilment. Unfortunately for France

---

[1] This influence of Napoleon III's study of history upon his policy was the subject of an interesting article by F. A. SIMPSON in *The Times' Napoleon Supplement* of May 5, 1921.

these dreams were woven into the realities of Napoleon's foreign policy. Heine had once described Louis Philippe as a 'secret, boxed-up character',[1] but the words were far more truly applicable to Napoleon III. There was in French foreign policy of the 'fifties and 'sixties almost always '*un secret de l'Empereur*', just as a hundred years earlier there had been '*un secret du Roi*', and French Foreign Ministers were too often 'not counsellors, but mere executors of designs of which they only see fragments'.[2]

To begin with, however, as we have seen, Napoleon's foreign policy met with a great measure of success. The British Government had at first viewed his accession with alarm and there had been another invasion scare; but when it seemed that Napoleon was as pacific as his Republican predecessors, they had been prepared to be friendly. As after 1830 and after 1848, so after 1851, the best means of restraining France seemed to be to co-operate with her, and soon, when the affairs of the Near East came to a crisis, the two powers were to be allied on the battlefields. Thus a renewal of the dangerous Anglo-French rivalry which had embarrassed Louis Philippe's last years was averted and the new partnership greatly enhanced Napoleon's prestige.

In the first new phase of the Eastern Question France played a leading part. When a dispute arose between Latin and Orthodox monks over the guardianship of the Holy Places of Jerusalem, Napoleon was quick to seize the chance of restoring France's traditional interests in the Levant, which had been reviving with the renewed activity of French missionaries in the 'forties, hoping thereby to make the support of the French Catholics still more secure. But Russia soon intervened on behalf of the Orthodox and widened the issues by demanding that the Turks should grant her a virtual protectorate over all Orthodox Christians within their Empire. To Britain, long suspicious of Russian designs, and to France, whose parvenu Emperor had been treated scornfully by the Tsar as an upstart, such claims were intolerable. France had long taken the British view of the Eastern Question and held that the balance of power and her own Mediterranean interests required that Constantinople and the Straits should be kept out of Russian hands; and so, when in 1853-4 Russian troops entered the Principalities of Moldavia and Wallachia and attempts to negotiate a settlement broke down, the two powers went to war to prevent the Turkish Empire from being crushed by Russia.

Marking as it did such an early departure from the announcement that

---

[1] *French Affairs*, II, p. 35.
[2] GORCE, P. DE LA: *Napoléon III et sa politique*, p. 70.

the Empire meant peace, the Crimean War was far from being universally popular in France. Yet Catholics, as we have seen, had had reason to welcome Napoleon's championship of the interests of Latin Christianity, while Liberal opinion rejoiced at the attempt to curb the pretensions of the most reactionary power in Europe. Moreover, the war brought considerable prosperity to certain sections of the community which were concerned with the equipment of the troops. The new screw-propelled warships first laid down under Louis Philippe had proved their worth as also did the first iron-clad boats, whose construction, with the Emperor's support, was to revolutionize naval architecture.[1] The alliance with England, the traditional enemy, made an extraordinary impression and led Queen Victoria to pay an official visit to Paris. Moreover, although it brought no territorial gains and although the defects of the French military administration were once again exposed, the war ended victoriously. Such a result and the splendid assemblage of peace-makers in Paris, coinciding as it did with the birth of an heir to the Emperor, the Prince Imperial, seemed to emphasize the solidity and brilliance so quickly acquired by the new régime and was therefore very gratifying to French pride.

The Crimean War could be said to have been a war which accorded with French interests. Far otherwise was it with the Italian campaign of 1859 which was to carry the Empire to its turning-point. Here Napoleon's Italophil sentiment, due partly to his ancestry, partly to his early associations with the Carbonari and to his participation in the 1831 rising in the Romagna, and partly to his liberal dreams, led him into a course of action which ran wholly counter to France's traditional policies. In his own entourage he had many people who were Italian in origin or sympathies, the beautiful Countess Castiglione, Prince Napoleon his cousin, Arese, Conneau, his doctor, and others, and who urged him to do something for Italy, the northern part of which was still largely under Austrian rule. In January 1858 a sanguinary attempt on the Emperor's life by an Italian named Orsini enhanced the Emperor's popularity in France and provoked a wave of anti-Italian feeling. But, curiously enough, it was precisely this which impelled the Emperor to develop his Italian policy. Orsini's attempt had been made because of Napoleon's inaction; now the Emperor allowed Orsini's appeal to him from prison to espouse the Italian cause to be read in court and to be published. Thus he began to prepare public opinion for eventual

[1] *vide* TEMPERLEY, H. W. V.: *The Crimea*, p. 295, for the part played by the screw in inducing the Turks to decide the Holy Places issue in favour of the French, and BAXTER, J. P.: *The Introduction of the Iron-Clad Warship*, p. 4.

French intervention. In July at the Vosges watering place of Plombières he had a secret interview with the Sardinian Foreign Minister, Cavour, and promised him French aid in a war which was to be undertaken against Austria with the object of freeing Italy 'to the Adriatic' and of setting up a Central Italian Kingdom, which, together with Sardinia-Piedmont, enlarged to form a Kingdom of Upper Italy, Naples and the Papal States, was to form an Italian Confederation under the presidency of the Pope. In return for her services, it was suggested that France should receive Nice and Savoy from Piedmont, thereby attaining her 'natural' south-eastern frontier.

It had long been a cardinal point of French policy to keep Italy and Germany weak and divided, and even the Republicans of 1848-9 had been loth to see the creation of a strong North Italian kingdom. It might, however, still be hoped that an Italian Confederation which owed its existence to French support would be a valuable friend and client of the Empire. All might have been well had Napoleon been able to secure and maintain the rearrangement of the map of Italy as he had planned it at Plombières, for it was neatly devised to satisfy his own conscience and to appease all sections of French opinion. The expulsion of the Austrians might be expected to please the Liberals as much as the place reserved to the Pope in the projected Federation would appeal to the Catholics; while those who thought first of material gains would be placated by the acquisition of Nice and Savoy. Furthermore, and this was a fundamental point for the Emperor, the social aspirations of the Bonapartes were to be gratified by the marriage of Prince Napoleon with a Princess of Savoy. The marriage duly took place, but subsequent events outran the Emperor's control. Pius IX was no longer the popular liberal Pope of 1846, but, as a result of his experience of the revolutions of 1848-9, a die-hard reactionary, maintained in his temporal dominions by the aid of French bayonets; and as soon as the war began a series of plebiscites in Central Italy resulted in an overwhelming popular vote for union with Piedmont which swept away Napoleon's Papal Confederation before it had begun to take shape. Moreover, the ravages of malaria among troops most inadequately provided with medical services, Catholic pressure at home and the menacing attitude taken up for the second time in twenty years by Prussia on the Rhine, all impelled Napoleon to seek peace without attempting to storm the redoubtable Austrian fortresses of the so-called Quadrilateral, which stood between the French army and the Adriatic. Thus he failed to keep his promise to free Italy as far as her eastern coasts and caused the Italians bitter disappointment. Furthermore, by the preliminaries of the Peace of Villafranca,[1] he impaled himself upon the horns of a dilemma. He wished to obtain Nice and Savoy; at the same time he had promised Austria that Central Italy should be formed into a separate kingdom: but if this happened when the people of Central Italy were clamouring for union with Piedmont, Piedmont could hardly be expected to relinquish Nice and Savoy. In this dilemma he managed through English good offices to induce Austria to disinterest herself in Central Italy so that it might after all be incorporated with a Piedmont already enlarged by the annexation of Lombardy. But there still remained the fact that many of the people in the Papal States had risen in revolt and voted likewise for union with Piedmont. Could Napoleon, hitherto so stalwart a champion of the Pope, allow such a diminution of Papal territory? To secure his ultimate territorial aim he was ready to sacrifice the Pope and to hazard a complete change of policy at home. Accordingly he replaced his pro-clerical Foreign Minister, Walewski, by the more liberal Thouvenel and allowed much publicity to be given to an inspired pamphlet entitled *The Pope and the Congress*, in which he suggested that the requirements of Papal independence could as well be met by the retention of Rome 'and a garden' as by the maintenance of a large temporal dominion. The Pope, who stigmatized the pamphlet as 'a notable monument of hypocrisy and an ignoble tissue of contradictions', which he hoped that Napoleon would condemn,[2] received an unpleasant shock when it was followed up by a letter in which the Emperor urged him to renounce his claims to his rebellious provinces in return for a European guarantee for the remainder. But he was obliged to yield to *force majeure*—the current of Italian nationalism was too strong for Pope and Emperor alike—and soon saw his temporal power reduced to Rome alone. Even then the maintenance of his temporal authority still depended on the French soldiery.

The Italian question had thus landed Napoleon in unforeseen difficulties. The war had indeed been short and successful as far as it went. The Emperor and his troops were hailed as victors on their return to Paris in August 1859, the last occasion on which the city would welcome a victorious French army for fifty-seven years,[3] and the acquisition of Nice and Savoy[4], confirmed by the vote of an overwhelming majority of the population, had marked a fresh breach in the 1815 Treaties and was

[1] For the English text see BUTTERFIELD, H.: *Select Documents of European History*, 1715-1920, pp. 137-8.

[2] cit. ARNAUD, R.: *La deuxième République et le second Empire*, p. 164.

[3] That is, apart from troops who returned from successful colonial expeditions.

[4] See Map II.

France's first territorial gain in Europe since the fall of Napoleon I. None the less, unable to control the developments of events in Italy, the Emperor was obliged to look helplessly on at the incorporation of the whole of the peninsula, save Rome and Venetia, with Piedmont, and at the creation of a new Kingdom of United Italy. He had already abandoned his firm championship of the Pope, yet dared not withdraw French troops from Rome, which every Italian regarded as the natural capital of the new kingdom, with the result that France once again appeared to bar the way to the achievement of Italy's natural aspirations and that the Roman question continued to be an embarrassment to French policy for the remainder of Napoleon's reign. Furthermore, his acquisition of Nice and Savoy, in spite of solemn denials that he had any designs upon them, had much offended Great Britain, which was shocked by his duplicity and distrustful of his ambitions. The affair thus played much the part which the Spanish Marriages had played in Louis Philippe's reign towards breaking the Anglo-French Entente. Last, but not least, his Italian policy had greatly offended those people in France who had hitherto been his warmest supporters, the French Catholics. He had in consequence made overtures to the Liberals; but, as events were to show, it was highly questionable whether Liberalism and Bonapartism were genuinely reconcilable.[1]

The year 1860 thus marked a turning-point in Napoleon's fortunes and in his policy towards the Catholics. Henceforth the relations of Church and State were less friendly. The Church no longer enjoyed such freedom of action, and the State system of education made notable progress under the direction of a man personally selected by the Emperor, Victor Duruy, who proved to be one of the greatest of all French Ministers of Public Instruction. The year was no less a turning-point in economic policy. The conclusion of a commercial treaty with Great Britain in that year, followed in 1861 by trade agreements with Belgium, Italy and Switzerland, and in 1862 by one with Prussia, gave an important impulse to greater freedom of international trade. But the Anglo-French Treaty, in many ways reminiscent of an earlier Treaty of 1786, marked a striking departure from the rigid protectionist policy pursued by successive French Governments ever since the early years of the Restoration. As such it met with bitter hostility from some of the big land-owners and from many industrialists, especially the textile manu-

---

[1] It is to be noted that the achievement of Roumanian unity in 1859 was a triumph for Napoleon III who had been the chief foreign sponsor of the Roumanian cause. But this success of his nationality policy was entirely overshadowed by the Italian problem.

facturers of Normandy and the North and the iron masters of the East. The change was a victory for the Saint-Simonians and evidence of Napoleon's desire to bolster up the Anglo-French Entente, and although its most obvious effects were political it had some important economic and social consequences. More intensive competition from England hastened the concentration of certain industries in fewer firms and in many cases led to a renewal of plant or modernization of equipment. When factories had to be rebuilt there was generally a resulting improvement in the working conditions of the employees. On the other hand, many weaker firms went to the wall and others were obliged to reduce wages so that there was a considerable amount of temporary distress. This had unusually significant consequences, for it was partly responsible for the attempt of French workers to get into touch with the working classes of Britain which resulted in the formation of the First Workers' International. Nevertheless, in spite of the temporary distress and the political resentments caused by the new policy, the statistics of French exports in general, and to Britain in particular, continued to show an upward trend. On French industry as a whole there can be little doubt that the 1860 Treaty acted as a healthy stimulant.

This wind of free trade was not the only breath of fresh air which the Emperor now let into France. Aware of and irritated by the opposition of the clergy and their sympathizers to his Italian policy, Napoleon had already in 1859 sought to conciliate the other main body of opinion, the Left, by an amnesty and greater liberty for the Press. In 1860 he went further and issued a decree permitting the Senate and Chamber to discuss and vote an annual address in reply to the speech from the throne, and allowing reports of debates to be published in full. In the following year the Legislative Body was granted a wider measure of control over national expenditure. Thus public opinion once again had a certain restricted opportunity to form judgements about political issues and to exercise pressure. But instead of winning converts to Bonapartism these so-called Liberal reforms, by giving greater freedom to the enemies of the régime, only tended to confirm them in their intransigence. Already indeed, in 1857, five Republican deputies had been elected to the Legislative Body and had taken their seats, treating the oath of allegiance as a mere formality. The extreme Left may have welcomed the Italian war and the 1860 Treaty of Commerce, but they remained Republicans. Equally, many of the men who re-emerged on the Right were monarchists avowedly or at heart. The old parties which had confronted one another under the Second Republic, the conservative and clerical party of order on the one side and on the other the

Republican and democratic Left, had both re-formed, and this was in itself a grave set-back for Napoleon who had wished to destroy both. After nearly a decade Napoleon had failed, as his predecessors had failed, either to win over or to annihilate the adherents of previous régimes. The Emperor now had to face a double opposition which was drawn from the most live elements of the nation; and the opposition of the Republican Left was particularly dangerous, since it, and not the official Bonapartist candidates, more and more won the sympathy and suffrages of the industrial workers. Moreover, his new policies caused serious rifts in his own entourage. His Liberal concessions, favoured by Walewski and Magne, were ridiculed by Prince Napoleon, who adopted an irresponsibly democratic attitude, and strongly opposed by men like Baroche, Fould and Rouher. His Italian policy, on the other hand, was no less unpopular with the Empress, who took an increasing interest in politics, and with Walewski, both of whom were ardent supporters of the Pope. Thus the strength of the régime at home was conspicuously weakened in the 'sixties—it was being sapped by parliamentary opposition, by Press criticism, and by divided counsels, which meant that Government policy was increasingly hesitant and lacking in direction. This weakness became still more conspicuous towards the end of the decade when the Emperor, who was ageing fast, was frequently crippled by an extremely painful disease which impaired his power of decision. Already, however, the strength of the new forces of opposition was strikingly shown in the elections of 1863. Then a broad coalition of the opponents either of the régime itself or of the Emperor's personal policy, was formed under the name of Union Libérale. It contained men as varied as the Legitimist Berryer and the moderate Republican Jules Simon, and, although it won only thirty-five seats, it polled some two million votes.[1] Moreover, most significant fact of all, the big towns, Paris, Lyons and Marseilles voted almost solidly Republican.

The Opposition deputies in the new Legislative Body, who now included such notable advocates of former régimes as Berryer, Thiers and the Republican Jules Favre, naturally demanded further Liberal reforms and urged a return to full parliamentary government with the right of interpellation and ministerial responsibility. But although his half-brother, the Duc de Morny, who presided over the Legislative Body, urged him to be generous, Napoleon was not ready for further

[1] The candidates of the Union Libérale had their consciences about taking the oath of allegiance set to rest by Jules Simon, who explained that it really meant an undertaking not to conspire against the Empire. Yet rather than take the oath a few years earlier he himself had resigned his chair at the Sorbonne.

political concessions.   Instead he sought to gain the favour of the workers by concessions in social legislation.   Thus in 1864 they were permitted to form combinations and the right to strike was legally recognized. Yet, important as such measures were, they failed to achieve Napoleon's object.   Increasing pressure at home and serious set-backs abroad eventually obliged him to give way to the demands of the Opposition and in January 1867 he announced his intention of conceding further Liberal reforms.   In the meantime the European balance of power, so recently and strikingly modified by the creation of the Kingdom of Italy, had undergone further significant changes.

The Italian question had shown the contradictions inherent in Napoleon's attempt to defend French interests and at the same time to give a practical demonstration of his sympathies with the idea of nationality. Nevertheless, in the name of the balance of power, Napoleon had acquired Nice and Savoy as the reward for his services to the cause of Italian unity.   In like manner he hoped that a fresh extension of French territory might be his recompense for assisting the unification of Germany and even that it might be obtained merely through astute diplomacy without any need to draw the sword.   It is remarkable how readily Frenchmen talked of annexing Belgium or the Rhineland as the most natural thing in the world should there be another war.[1]   If Napoleon could succeed in securing one or the other for them without war he might expect to win their undying gratitude and could well afford to abandon further projects of Liberal reform.   After 1860 two main objectives emerge from the fog of Napoleon's secret diplomacy: his wish to complete the unification of Italy by securing Venetia for her from Austria; and his ambition to obtain either the Rhineland or part, if not the whole, of Belgium for France by way of reward for helping or giving a free hand to either Prussia or Austria in Germany.   It is impossible not to be struck by the cynical indifference with which he turned first to Austria and then to Prussia and then back again to Austria, seemingly quite indifferent as to which power gained the hegemony of Germany provided that France obtained additional territory as compensation.   But unfortunately for him and for France, as in Italian affairs he had met his diplomatic match in Cavour, so in German affairs he was to meet his master in Bismarck.

The Polish question of 1863, the Schleswig-Holstein question of 1864–6 and the Austrian war of 1866 all marked stages on Bismarck's progress towards the unification of Germany, and in each of them France

---

[1] *vide* e.g. SENIOR, N. W.: *Conversations with Thiers, Guizot, etc.*, I, p. 27; II, p. 94.

was unable to play an effective part either because of the breakdown of the Entente with England or because of the Emperor's errors of judgement and lack of military preparedness. It was indeed difficult for England or for France with all her Polish exiles, to do anything but protest when the Tsar not only crushed a Polish rising in 1863 but also revoked the Polish Constitution of 1863: but their protests antagonized Russia, whereas Bismarck not only did not protest but assisted the Russians in dealing with the rebels. Thus he won Russia's friendship and thereby ensured that if France were once again engaged in war with a German power she would not, as in the days of the Ancien Régime, have a traditional ally to help her in the East. In the Schleswig-Holstein affair the hostility of Lord John Russell and Palmerston to Napoleon made effective Anglo-French co-operation impossible, so that once again Bismarck had things his own way. In 1865 he prepared for the conflict with Austria which he hoped would make Prussia master of Germany. Russia could be counted on to remain friendly, but the attitude of France was less certain. In October Bismarck had an interview with Napoleon at Biarritz. The Emperor not only promised French neutrality but gave his blessing to the idea of an alliance between Prussia and Italy—yet a few months later he had no scruple in signing a convention with Austria whereby he promised to make every effort to induce Italy to abstain from intervention. In fact, he calculated that the struggle would be protracted, that France could step in and mediate or tip the scales on one side or the other, and that in the meantime it was to her interests to stand as well as possible with both parties.

Unfortunately his judgement of the balance of forces between Austria and Prussia was completely astray. He was indeed not alone in being amazed at the swiftness and completeness of Prussia's victory in the war of 1866. Within a few weeks the Austrian army had been routed at Sadowa and the Austrian Emperor, Francis Joseph, had appealed to Napoleon for his good offices in securing an armistice. When Austria ceded Venetia to Napoleon and Napoleon magnanimously handed it over to Italy the French Emperor might once again appear to be the arbiter of Europe, and in a circular issued not long afterwards he claimed credit for the overthrow of the 1815 settlement, the break-up of the Holy Alliance of the Eastern Powers, the progress made towards the realization of German national aspirations, and also for confining Prussian expansion to the north of the Main. In reality, however, these successes were purely illusory. Not one of them brought any real advantage to France. As a result of the war of 1866 Prussia had emerged as the leader of a closely knit confederation comprising more than half Germany; and none could doubt that her next objective would be the incorporation of the states south of the Main which still enjoyed a nominal independence. Moreover, this new and ominous change in the balance of power had occurred without any territorial compensation for France. Napoleon had lost his opportunity. Had he been ready, as his Foreign Minister, Drouyn de Lhuys, and others had urged, to place an observation corps on the Rhine frontier as soon as war broke out and to back his mediation by force of arms he might well have secured the Rhineland territory which had been the object of so many fruitless negotiations during the past five years. As it was, he had hesitated until it was too late. Once the victory was won Bismarck could afford to snap his fingers at what he called Napoleon's 'hotel-keeper's bill', asking for the frontiers of 1814 and the fortress of Luxemburg, and at a French draft convention which contained a secret clause providing for the French annexation of Belgium. More than that, he used this evidence of Napoleon's covetousness against him. He kept the draft convention for publication at a later date when it should suit him publicly to expose French ambitions, and he promptly utilized an alternative French suggestion that France might acquire the Bavarian Palatinate to put pressure upon Bavaria to sign a treaty of friendship with Prussia. Thus Napoleon's diplomacy played into the hands of the man who was to be his mortal enemy and he was out-manœuvred at every turn. In a memorandum of 1829 Polignac had written that it was of great importance to France to prevent the reunion of Germany into one or two big states. 'If ever this circumstance was to occur, this country, which is to-day divided between Princes who have need of our protection, would confront us with rival forces which would be jealous and soon hostile, and our relative power would be seriously affected.' The jealousy and hostility of nationalist forces in Germany had already been shown in 1840 and 1860; but Napoleon and indeed many other Frenchmen had failed to appreciate its significance. His departure from the fundamental French policy which the Ultras, heirs of the Ancien Régime, had understood so well was fatal for France. Napoleon had failed to give protection to the small South-German states, who had all at one time or another looked towards France; he had misjudged Bismarck and Prussia; and he had been unsuccessful in securing an adjustment of frontiers in order to compensate France for the change in the balance of power. As has been well said, 1866 marked the end of that old order of things in Central Europe which had been so agreeable and so safe from the French point of view.

Nor had the Emperor been able to compensate for this check in Europe by his many ventures overseas, although some of them were of great importance for the future growth of France's new colonial Empire. The conquest of Algeria had been virtually completed by 1857, but this was an event which caused little enthusiasm, particularly among those sections of the community who viewed the new colony as a tiresome commercial rival, since its products were not so much complementary as similar to those of the metropolis. Moreover, the Emperor's well-meant but misguided attempt to apply the theory of nationality to Africa and treat Algeria not as a colony but as an 'Arab Kingdom', discouraged French colonization and retarded the material development of the country, which was to be further hampered by a terrible famine in 1867-8. Elsewhere, indeed, there was great activity. French troops fought in places as distant as China and Mexico. The death of French missionaries was avenged by an expedition to Pekin in 1859-60; an expedition to Syria in 1861 once again reaffirmed France's interest in the Levant; in Africa France's footing in the Senegal area was extended by Faidherbe and new settlements were made on the coasts of Guinea and Dahomey; in the east of the continent and off it the old rivalry with England continued and France replied to the English settlement of Perim by the establishment of a port at Obock and contested with her for influence in the rich island of Madagascar.[1] Farther east again New Caledonia had been occupied in 1853 and the persecution of French missionaries by the Emperor of Annam had led to another military expedition. In 1859 Saigon had been captured and within a few years France had gained full sovereignty over three of the provinces of Cochin China and established a protectorate in Cambodia. Furthermore, in Egypt, which French capital was rapidly helping to transform into a great cotton-growing country, the Frenchman, Lesseps, by cutting the Suez Canal, was engaged in a work which was to transform the strategic and commercial communications of the world. Thus in the new era of exploration and exploitation which was the prelude to the great 'Scramble' for Africa and other lands outside Europe in the last quarter of the nineteenth century, France of the Second Empire played an active and enterprising part. But the French public, as ever, was little concerned or interested in these distant happenings. Algeria was still widely looked upon as a source of military weakness and doubtful economic advantage which France would have been glad to abandon had she been able to do so without loss of prestige, and the potentialities of more remote territories were even less understood by the general public. Moreover, the success of French arms in the distant valleys of

[1] See Map IV. French explorers did notable work in W. Africa in these years.

the Senegal or the Mekong was soon completely overshadowed by the tragic failure of Napoleon's policy in Mexico.

Begun as a debt-collecting expedition of three powers, Great Britain, France and Spain in 1861-2, the Mexican venture developed into an attempt by France alone to establish a new Latin Catholic Empire in the New World. This enlargement of the original scope of the expedition was largely due to the influence of Napoleon's Spanish wife, the Empress Eugénie. This was to be 'her war', a reassertion of Catholic power and an enterprise which would provide easy compensation for the humiliation of the Pope and the set-back to French policy in Italy in 1860. In so far as it was a sort of Catholic crusade it did indeed at first help to appease Catholic opinion in France, while at the same time it held promise of satisfaction to French financial interests. But unfortunately the Emperor and his advisers were sadly ignorant or misled about the real conditions, both geographical and political, of the country they set out to conquer. The Mexican expedition was to be no easy promenade like the Spanish war of 1823. The French intruders met with savage resistance. For five years they fought for the establishment and maintenance of the Hapsburg Archduke Maximilian on the newly created throne as Napoleon's puppet Emperor; but, although more than 38,000 men were involved and 6,000 were killed or died of sickness, their efforts were in the end of no avail. The Mexican Republicans remained indomitable and once the American Civil War was drawing to an end, the United States Government, angered by Napoleon's flouting of the Monroe Doctrine, began to adopt a threatening attitude. Unable to face the prospect of war with the U.S.A. and worried by events in Europe, Napoleon had no choice but to withdraw his troops. Left to its own feeble resources the artificial Mexican Empire speedily collapsed and the news of the death of the hapless Maximilian at the hands of his Republican opponents reached Napoleon to mar the Paris Exhibition of 1867 when he was acting as host to many visiting sovereigns and grandees. Once again he had been seduced by a chimera. The 'most profound conception of the reign', the establishment of a Mexican Empire might indeed have served French financial interests and strengthened the Latin Catholic forces in America, making them better able to resist the encroachments of Yankee 'Manifest Destiny': but the tangible advantages for France were not obvious and once again Napoleon had shown that his schemes were apt to fail through lack of adequate preparation. The war of 1866 had already dimmed France's prestige; the Mexican disaster and further failures of the diplomacy of *pourboires* or compensations in Europe in 1867 tarnished it still more.

In September of that year Napoleon might well confess that France had met with reverses and that the horizon was darkened by *des points noirs*.

Under the cloud of such disappointments, Napoleon was impelled in his hesitant fashion to seek to appease public opinion at home by further Liberal reforms. Since the 1863 elections there had grown up a new so-called Third Party, generally moderate in its tendencies but eager to limit the extent of the Emperor's personal power and to convert the Empire into a parliamentary régime. Already in 1866 its demand for further Liberal reforms had won sixty-three votes. Now, early in 1867, the Emperor made a gesture to it by granting the Legislative Body the right of interpellation and by relaxing the laws controlling the Press and public meetings. Characteristically, however, he kept the old Ministers, the men who were opposed to concessions, so that his ultimate aims remained in doubt. None the less the Legislative Body continued to show a growing independence: so much so indeed that on two matters of vital importance it was able to frustrate the Emperor's policy and to impose its aim. In the first instance, showing, as is too often the case with Parliaments, an ill-timed sense of economy,[1] it rejected a proposal by the Government, alarmed at Prussia's victory, to strengthen the French army by the creation of an effective trained reserve. In the second it wrung from Rouher the rash promise that France would never abandon Rome. 'This,' says a French historian, 'was the solemn undertaking which, in spite of clerical pressure, Napoleon had so far always refused to give; his Government yielded at last to the Legislative Body. Contemporaries were alive to the significance of this: "There you have Parliamentary government in full swing," wrote Sainte-Beuve to the Princess Mathilde.'[2] This was however an exaggeration: the elections of 1869, a fresh Third Party demand for parliamentary government, this time backed by 116 deputies, and a further set of half measures, were necessary before the Emperor finally brought himself to the experiment of ministerial responsibility and government through the Third Party. After an appeal in November 1869 to the Legislative Body to help him to found liberty in France, in January 1870 he asked Emile Ollivier, formerly one of the five Republican deputies of 1857, to head a Ministry which would for the first time be responsible to Parliament.

[1] SIMPSON, F. A., in *The Times' Napoleon Supplement*, May 5th, 1921, also speaks of 'surreptitious economies designed to conceal the true costs of that forlorn adventure in world-policy'; i.e. the Mexican expedition.

[2] HAUSER, H., MAURAIN, J. and BENAERTS, P.: *Du libéralisme à l'impérialisme* (1860-70), pp. 27, 28.

Ollivier, an able lawyer, was an example of an erstwhile opponent of the Empire who had rallied to its support, and it was therefore fitting that he should lead the experiment of reconciling the country at large to a revived parliamentarism under the Bonapartes and of giving a new lease of life to the Empire on a new basis. But that basis was still equivocal, and, when the Emperor ingeniously contrived once again to make use of the plebiscite, two of the Orleanist members of the Ministry resigned in protest against resort to such extra-parliamentary machinery. The plebiscite of 1870 was, however, an event of considerable importance. The people were asked whether or not they approved the Liberal reforms introduced since 1860 and in particular the *Senatus Consultum* of April 20th, 1870, whereby the Constitution of 1852 was revised and constituent power transferred from the Senate to the people. In spite of the vigorous opposition of the Republicans who had been increasingly active since 1863, who had once again carried most of the great urban seats in the 1869 elections, and who had all along denounced the new parliamentarism as a sham, the result was a resounding endorsement of the Emperor's policy It was not so much a specific vote of confidence in the Ollivier Ministry as in the Empire, and as such it greatly heartened the authoritarian Bonapartists who had viewed the Emperor's latest concessions with the utmost dismay. Over seven million people, nearly as many as had approved the *coup d'état* of 1851 and the proclamation of the Empire in 1852, again voted 'Yes'. Against them there were one and a half million 'Noes': the various opposition forces, who in the 1869 elections had polled three million votes, appeared to have received a grave set-back.

It may be idle, but is none the less interesting, to speculate whether the Empire might now have continued for many years more had not Bismarck intervened and the Emperor made a last fatal blunder in foreign policy. In spite of the impressive support it received in the plebiscite, signs of weakness in the Empire had been growing. For the last five years at least it had been apparent that Napoleon was failing, that his powers of decision had been affected by disease, that he was tired and saddened, torn between the contrary advice of those who opposed and those who favoured concessions to Liberalism, and no longer imbued with that confident belief in his star which had been such a remarkable feature of his rise to power. And as the Emperor had begun to lose grip, so too, as it seemed, had the Government and administration in general. The growing weakness of the master had communicated itself to the servants. Several of the ablest of the Old Guard of Bonapartists who had assisted Napoleon to power were either dead, like Morny, or in retirement, like Persigny, and the men to whom he had since given preferment were of lesser stature. Moreover, the Liberal reforms set the administration more difficult problems. The 1859 amnesty had given an impetus to Republican journalism and, although the Government-sponsored papers had a wider public and were more effectively edited than their forebears of Restoration days, it was a moderate Republican paper, Le Siècle, which by 1866 had a far larger circulation (44,000) than any other. The relaxation of the Press legislation in 1868 had put an end to the warning system and the necessity for prior government authorization before a paper could be launched and had led to an efflorescence of new journals reminiscent of 1848. No less than 140 new ones appeared in Paris within a year. Most of them were ephemeral, but there were others, less transitory, like Le Rappel of Victor Hugo and Le Réveil of Delescluze which indulged in violent attacks on the Empire; and the Government could find no friendly journalist to vie with the renegade Republican aristocrat Rochefort for biting wit. The first number of his La Lanterne, with its famous opening sentence, 'The Empire contains thirty-six million subjects, not counting the subjects of discontent' sold no less than 120,000 copies instead of the 15,000 expected.[1] The authorities indeed did their best to curb or suppress the most virulent or impudent critics of the régime. Prosecutions and Press trials multiplied, but they did not always have the desired results, for they sometimes created martyrs or, as in the Baudin trial of 1868, provided the publicity for some new recruit to the Opposition, in this case the young Gambetta, to win his spurs by a fresh denunciation of the imperial régime. Thus, in the climate of opinion of the late 'sixties, the ablest of the younger men, whether in the universities, in journalism, in politics, or at the bar, were more tempted to oppose than to support a régime which had so obviously lost prestige that the mere fact of deriding it might itself provide a passport to renown. To maintain or regain authority the Empire needed to renew its personnel and to attract the rising generations. At the end of 1869 it was in a situation not unlike that of the July Monarchy under Louis Philippe, but unlike Louis Philippe, Napoleon had been ready to concede reform without waiting for insurrection to force him to it. At the same time, as in 1847, the critics, growing vehement, had been all the more eager to smell out scandals and cry corruption. The famous Prefect of the Seine, Baron Haussmann, who had transformed the centre of Paris and done so much to make it the city we know to-day, was forced to resign owing to 'alleged financial impropriety'; and in 1870 when an obscure but

[1] ZÉVAÈS A. Henri Rochefort, le pamphlétaire, p. 43.

irascible cousin of the Emperor, Prince Pierre Bonaparte, shot and killed a young Republican journalist named Victor Noir, the sensation caused was as great as that of the murder of the Duchesse de Praslin in 1847. Further disquieting facts were that the great cities remained strongly Republican, that revolutionary bodies and secret societies, many of them now more or less connected with the Workers' International, were beginning to operate again and that they were active in fomenting street demonstrations and disturbances from which Paris of the Empire had so far been singularly free; and that in the same year, 1870, troops had, for the first time since Napoleon came to the throne, been called in to repress a serious outbreak of strikes.

All these signs seemed to suggest that the Empire was slowly decomposing. Yet it is possible that some French Republican historians have been easily led to exaggerate the strength of the Opposition and the unpopularity of the Empire. The voters in the plebiscite of 1870 were above all votes for peace and order—too many people remembered the disorders of the Second Republic to wish for their recurrence—but the Republican deputies' recognition of this fact meant that they at least would not begin a revolution though they would be ready enough to profit by one. Moreover, the plebiscite, as we have suggested, was still a vote for the Empire and, in the opinion of the latest historian of the working classes during this period, nearly twenty years of power had done little to impair the hold of Napoleon upon the loyalty of the masses: 'Napoleon III, still strong in his seven million votes, retained a singular prestige.'[1] Furthermore, the economic situation showed a marked improvement in 1870, the Prince Imperial was growing up and likely to be popular, and, last but not least, the concessions to Liberalism seemed to open the door to precisely that renewal of personnel which was so necessary. The Ollivier Government had gone so far as to appoint notable Orleanists like Guizot and Odilon Barrot to various commissions: Ollivier himself, as we have seen, had once been a Republican; and there was more than one observer who believed that, given time, even a young 'irreconcilable' like Gambetta might one day emerge as a Minister of the Crown.[2] Ill though he was, Napoleon had by no means lost his personal charm and power of fascinating individual opponents.

But the experiment of parliamentary empire was all too brief. On July 3rd, 1870, the appearance of a fresh *point noir* came to darken

[1] DUVEAU, G.: *La vie ouvrière en France sous le second Empire*, p. 56.

[2] cp. SAINT-VALRY, G. DE: *Souvenirs et réflexions politiques*, I, p. 134, who says that the rural masses up to 1870 were '*dans un état de confiance réel*' towards the Empire.

the political horizon. News reached Paris that a Hohenzollern prince had consented to stand as a candidate for the vacant throne of Spain. As we have already seen from the history of the Restoration and July Monarchies, France had long been accustomed to regard Spain as a natural field for French influence. The sudden intrusion of a prince related to the ruling house of Prussia appeared to be part of a Machiavellian manœuvre to encircle France and, in a well-known phrase, 'to recreate the Empire of Charles V' at her expense. French public opinion was therefore immediately aroused. Since 1866 there had indeed been a growing belief that a collision between France and Prussia would sooner or later be inevitable. 'There must,' Prévost-Paradol had written in 1869, 'be a struggle for supremacy. Until this collision has taken place everyone will instinctively feel that nothing has been decided. For Germany to become unified in spite of France, or while France remains passive, would be an irrevocable abdication of French greatness.'[1] This fatalistic feeling was perhaps itself a factor which helped to precipitate events in 1870. Meanwhile the French Government at once attempted to secure the withdrawal of the candidature. Many Ministers and diplomats were on holiday, but after a few days, Benedetti, the French Ambassador to Berlin, succeeded in inducing the King of Prussia, the Head of the House of Hohenzollern, to arrange that his relative's candidature should be withdrawn. This renunciation was regarded by the two most experienced statesmen of the July Monarchy, Guizot and Thiers, as the greatest diplomatic victory they had ever seen. Had the French Government rested content with it the prestige of the Empire would have enjoyed a remarkable recovery. But Ollivier and Gramont, his Foreign Minister, disastrously overplayed their hand. Instead of being satisfied with the word of one of the foremost European sovereigns, they sought to improve upon their success by requiring a formal guarantee that the candidature would never be renewed. Moreover, they did nothing to calm public opinion at home. Thus the incident which should have been swiftly and successfully closed was prolonged and its prolongation gave Bismarck the opportunity to intervene, to influence opinion on both sides of the Rhine and to goad the French into war. The famous Ems telegram was an immediate cause of hostilities, but not the only one. Still more important was the lack of calm and balance on the part of the French Ministers who had made a false move and then feared to draw back in face of their own public opinion which they had allowed to become increasingly bellicose.

    Thus it came to pass that in spite of Thiers' grave warning that the

[1] *La France nouvelle*, pp. 386, 389.

moment was very ill-chosen, on July 19th, 1870, France, having failed to secure the guarantee she had demanded, declared war upon Prussia, taking up the sword against a formidable opponent without any ally to support her. Here, too, Napoleon's diplomacy had failed. Since 1868 tentative negotiations had been in progress for a triple alliance between Austria, France and Italy; but Austria, more interested in securing an ally against Russia than in giving help against Prussia, had hung back, and Napoleon, in view of the attitude of the Legislative Body, had hesitated to play what has been called France's last strong diplomatic card—'the fact that Rome was still hers to give or to refuse'[1]—in order to make sure of Italy. Thus, when July 1870 came, the projected alliance had still not been concluded. Diplomatically unsupported, France was still further handicapped by her lack of military preparedness. In conversation with an Austrian Archduke earlier in the year Napoleon had said that he could put 400,000 men on the frontiers within fifteen days, but, in fact, by August 5th he was unable to mobilize more than 250,000. Unfortunately for France, the Emperor's own complaint in 1859 of the inefficiency of French military organization which, he said, meant 'that we are never ready for war', still held good in spite of all his efforts to improve it in the meantime. Napoleon, indeed, in military as in other matters, was often more far-sighted than the experts,[2] but he had been unable to overcome the resistance of the comfortably routine-loving War Office and High Command to his proposals for reform. Even the shock of 1866 had failed to stimulate a thorough-going overhaul of the military system. In 1865 the military school at Metz had been solemnly taught that the Prussian army was no better than a training school for a Landwehr: 'It is a magnificent organization on paper, but a doubtful instrument for defence and would be very imperfect during the first period of an offensive war.'[3] In 1870 the power of that army was still underestimated, and, although in the meantime the Emperor had secured the introduction of the chassepot or quick-firing rifle (rejected as quite useless by a committee of experts eleven years earlier), his endeavours to introduce conscription and create a proper reserve had been frustrated. In 1867 he changed his War Minister, but through

[1] SIMPSON, F. A.: *Louis Napoleon and the Recovery of France* 1848–1856, pp. 88–9.

[2] He has been well described by a French historian as 'l'homme de son temps qui a le mieux prévenu l'avenir et le plus mal dirigé le présent.' A. DANSETTE, *Histoire religieuse de la France contemporaine*, p. 334.

[3] cit. MONTEILHET, J.: *Les institutions militaires de la France*, 1814–1932 (Paris, 1932), p. 39.

Marshal Niel, too, he was able only to obtain half-measures. The Niel Plan for forming a mobile National Guard which would receive a summary training in peace-time and be drafted into the regular army upon mobilization was ludicrously amended by the Legislative Body. On the one hand Conservative deputies jibbed at the extra expenditure; on the other, the Republicans maintained their distrust of standing armies and argued that France should renounce offensive wars and be content, if attacked, to rely upon the nation in arms for her defence. Thus the four months' training period for the Mobile Guard proposed by Niel was reduced to fifteen days and an absurd provision was introduced providing that no muster should entail more than one day's absence from work. In 1870, therefore, when war broke out, the Guard was in fact little better than a paper force and its equipment and training were to take many weeks. The diplomatic blunders of the Emperor and his Ministers were indeed responsible for France's commitment to war; but the need for preparedness had been obvious to all who had eyes to see for at least four years. Yet all save the Emperor, Niel, and a handful of prophets, had been only too eager to bury their heads in the sand. So too, in a somewhat different way, it was to be again seventy years later. On each occasion the Nemesis was swift and terrible.

'Formerly,' wrote Prévost-Paradol, 'when the military power of the Continental States was discussed the only question was whether France could resist a European coalition: to-day the question is whether France will defeat Prussia.'[1] But the majority of his compatriots had no doubts. Accustomed to victory in every European campaign in which France had taken part since 1815, forgetful of Waterloo, but mindful of Jena, still ill-informed about Prussian efficiency, they looked for a triumphal march to Berlin. All the more bitter and stunning, then, was the news of defeat upon defeat. By the end of the first week in August Alsace and most of Lorraine lay open to German invasion. The French armies had fought and continued to fight with gallantry, but they were out-numbered, out-generalled and out-manœuvred by a force which was superior in discipline, equipment[2] and mobility. At home in Paris the gravity of the situation led the Empress, who was acting as Regent in the absence of the Emperor with the armies, to recall Parliament for a special session and the Ollivier Ministry was at once

[1] La France nouvelle, p. 377.

[2] The French were much inferior in artillery but their infantry was on the whole better equipped. cp. BROGAN, D. W.: The Development of Modern France, p. 20.

defeated and resigned. In an unhappy moment in July Ollivier had said that he entered the war 'with a light heart'—that phrase was never forgiven him, his political career was at an end, and he spent most of the rest of his long life writing the history of the short-lived parliamentary Empire in seventeen volumes. Before the special session began some of his colleagues had urged that the Republican deputies should be arrested and sent to Belle Ile. But the Empress rejected the proposal on the ground that it would be more likely to provoke than to prevent the risk of civil war. This failure to take strong action and the formation of a new Ministry by the Comte de Palikao, an elderly general who had none of the popularity or dynamic qualities of leadership necessary in such a crisis, showed that the authorities, too, were stunned by France's reverses and that they had lost confidence in their ability to maintain control. In the Legislative Body it was now the Opposition deputies who took the initiative, and radical proposals which a few weeks before would have aroused storms of protest were now listened to with silen fear or apathy by the chastened Bonapartists. As early as August 16th the British Ambassador reported that the new Foreign Minister, Prince de La Tour d'Auvergne, was the only person he knew who still spoke like a loyal subject.[1] In fact the belief rapidly grew that the end of the Empire was at hand. At such a moment there are always men to desert the sinking ship, and the number of the defenders of the Bonapartist cause rapidly dwindled.

By the 20th August it was known that the army commanded by Marshal Bazaine was blockaded at Metz. The fate of the Empire depended upon the movements of the Emperor and upon the only remaining force of any size, the army of Châlons under Marshal MacMahon. The Liberal General Trochu, to whose appointment as Governor of Paris the Empress had reluctantly consented, and others were insistent that the Emperor should return to the capital, but the Empress, who feared for his life, would have none of it, and in order that he might be kept away MacMahon's army was sent off on a foolhardy attempt to make a junction with Bazaine. Thus the Emperor was, in the words of a contemporary observer, 'like King Lear driven out of his palace'[2] and the last main French army set out to court disaster.

Retribution was not slow in coming. On August 31st and September 1st a great battle raged near the Belgian frontier only to end in the French defeat so vividly described by Zola some years later in his novel *La Débâcle*. On the 2nd the whole of MacMahon's army of 84,000 men, 2,700 officers

---

[1] BURY, J. P. T.: *Gambetta and the National Defence*, p. 43.

[2] *Letters from Paris*, 1870-75, edited by R. HENREY, p. 56.

and thirty-nine generals capitulated. With them Marshal MacMahon and the Emperor himself were captives. 'There had been no disaster in French history more complete or more humiliating.'[1]

The political consequences were speedily to follow. The unhappy and unpopular Empress had no chance of maintaining a régime which had brought France to such disaster and which now had scarcely any defenders. On September 4th after a bloodless revolution, the Republic was once again proclaimed in Paris. The Empress fled to England, now the habitual refuge of France's fallen sovereigns, where she was joined by the Emperor in the following year. Two years afterwards, in 1873, Napoleon III died, once again an exile and now a broken man. He too had failed to unite all Frenchmen and to end the struggle of Revolution and Counter Revolution; but none the less he had come nearer than any of his predecessors since 1815 to winning the sincere allegiance of the great mass of Frenchmen.

It was easy for the Republicans to dismiss the Second Empire as a tissue of meretricious grandeur and political and social corruption which invited an inevitable collapse. But we who can take a more detached view must remember that economically and culturally, as well as on account of its achievements overseas and its political successes or failures in Europe, the eighteen years of its existence from 1852 to 1870 were of singular importance in French history. It was during these years that the economic structure of the country as it was to continue until the Great War of 1914-18 was largely moulded. It was during these years that the capital began to assume its modern form and that the social structure was further crystallized, while developments in thought foreshadowed the ideological battles of the Third Republic.

If first we glance at the Paris of 1870 and compare it with that of 1840 we shall see that economic developments and the great building programme of Baron Haussmann, one of the most notable town planners of his age, had changed much of it out of all recognition. The modern tourist would have little difficulty in finding his way in the Paris of 1870, but were he transported to that of 1840 with its tortuous labyrinth of narrow streets he would indeed be lost. Haussmann's new Boulevards, broad and straight, bewailed by the Goncourts as suggestive of 'some future American Babylon',[2] opened up the centre of the city and gave it the spaciousness of a modern cosmopolitan capital. Some 20,000 old houses were pulled down and more than 40,000 new ones built.

---

[1] BURY, J. P. T.: *Gambetta and the National Defence*, p. 45.

[2] cit. DUVEAU, G.: *La vie ouvrière en France sous le second Empire*, p. 209. The Emperor himself took the greatest interest in Haussmann's plans.

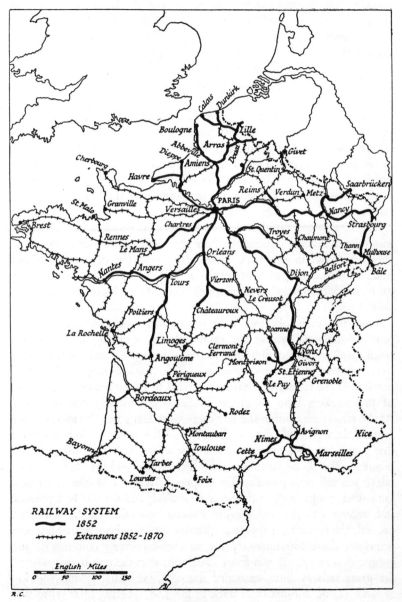

RAILWAY SYSTEM

—————— 1852

++++++++ Extensions 1852-1870

English Miles
0   50   100   150

R.C.

MAP I

New squares and new churches multiplied; the new Opera and the new
Louvre were begun: the Parc Monceau and the Buttes de Chaumont
were converted into public parks; the Bois de Boulogne and the Bois
de Vincennes were made into agreeable places for promenades; and
cafés, hitherto select and closed, opened up on to the streets and earned a
new popularity. Omnibuses and local railways increased greatly in
number, and, now that long-distance railways and steamship services
were developing, Paris more than ever became a centre of attraction
to foreigners, 'the café-concert of Europe', the city of gaiety and vice
from which France was to derive such a reputation for depravity among
the peoples of austerer northern nations. At the same time the area
of the city was greatly extended. By a decree of 1860 it took in all the
outskirts and villages between the octrois (customs barriers) and the
fortifications, thus increasing its administrative area from twelve to
twenty arrondissements. The social effects of reconstruction and
enlargement were considerable. In the old city, which in 1851 contained
just over a million inhabitants, bourgeois and worker had often lived
cheek by jowl in the same buildings. Now the destruction of old
houses and building of new ones at higher rents forced many workers
to the outskirts, several parts of which were already becoming industrialized.

Thus the Paris of 1870 with more than 1,800,000 residents was
nearly double the size of the capital at the beginning of Napoleon's
reign, and in it the divisions between bourgeois and working-class
quarters were much more marked. The 'banlieue rouge'—the 'Red'
precinct of the twentieth century, so-called from the political sympathies
of the workers who congregated there—was already foreshadowed.
At the same time, within the city there were many new buildings which
marked the arrival of a new economic era. It is from the Second Empire
that there date the earliest of those vast stores, the 'Bon Marché', the
'Louvre', the 'Belle Jardinière', the 'Printemps' and the 'Samaritaine',
which are still such paradises for shoppers. It was then that great new
joint-stock banks, such as the Société Générale and the Crédit Lyonnais,
and enterprises like the Crédit Foncier and the Crédit Mobilier,
opened their doors, supplying thereby on the best Saint-Simonian
principles the credit necessary for an ever-increasing commercial and
industrial activity. It was from Paris, too, that there radiated most of
the great railway lines, extended during these years by the addition
of some 14,000 kilometres of track to the 3,685 existing in 1851, so that
it became more than ever the economic, social and intellectual hub of
France. So it came to pass that the capital of Napoleon III with all its

material transformations, its imperial fêtes and splendid exhibitions, did indeed shine forth before the world as La Ville Lumière.

Similar developments, though on a different scale in different places took place in the provinces. The organization of country pleasures for the fashionable world was marked by the foundation of seaside resorts, such as Deauville, the creation of the Duc de Morny, while Imperial visits gave a new vogue to spas like Vichy.

On the other hand, while resorts multiplied, the populations of industrial cities also made striking increases: that of Roubaix was trebled; in Lyons, Lille, Toulouse and St. Etienne the number of inhabitants doubled; and in other towns such as Marseilles, Bordeaux and Rheims the rise was of the order of fifty per cent to seventy per cent. In fact the Californian gold discoveries of the 'forties were largely responsible for facilitating the acceleration of industrial development and of business enterprise in the two following decades. As a result France had enjoyed a period of remarkable prosperity especially in the 'fifties: industry had boomed; there was an orgy of speculation and a great increase in the number of small investors; and the total value of the French import and export trades had risen from 2,615 million francs in 1851 to 8,008 millions in 1869. At the same time the growth in numbers and in power of the big industrialist or capitalist was still more notable than in the reign of Louis Philippe. Vast interests were concentrated in the hands of a few families such as the Péreires, the Foulds and the Paulin Talabots, and already before the end of the Empire a contemporary observer could estimate that most of the money of the country was handled by some 183 firms. In certain industries, such as that of iron—the most remarkable new building material displayed in the Paris Exhibition of 1867 —this development was particularly marked, and the famous Comité des Forges, founded in 1864, was soon to become a power in the land, the weight of whose influence has still to be correctly estimated. Such great interests naturally soon formed connections which transcended national boundaries, and it is in this intensely active period of the Second Empire that the international aspects of French finance and industry begin to assume a real importance. Thus although the artisan and the small workshop had by no means disappeared—individualism and the persistence of small industries were long to be characteristics of French economy—the Second Empire had witnessed a profound transformation. France, which in 1848 was still essentially a land of artisans and peasants, could now in 1870 also be counted as 'a big industrial power',[1] not nearly so big as Great Britain already was or as Germany was soon to

[1] DUVEAU, G.: La vie ouvrière en France sous le second Empire, p. 105.

become, but none the less a highly important factor in the increasingly industrialized world. In this development the reign of Napoleon III had been the period of decisive advance, and the patronage of the Emperor and of highly placed people like the Duc de Morny had done much to encourage it.

It was amid such changes, then, that the intellectual and cultural life of the country continued to flourish; and, as the emphasis in social and economic matters was on material progress, so in these spheres a new realism marks much of the most notable work of this period—the realism of Courbet in the realm of painting, soon to be followed by the first pictures of the Impressionists led by Manet; of Flaubert in 'Madame Bovary', and Gautier with his 'Emaux et Camées'; of Augier, and of Dumas' *La Dame aux Camélias* in the theatre; and the scientific determinism of Taine and Renan in historical study. But if this was a dominant note it was far from being the only one; as ever France was rich in the variety of her talents. While Hugo, now in exile, was publishing lyric and epic poetry as prolifically as ever, Daudet was beginning to write, and Sainte-Beuve was doing much to make literary criticism an art to which a man might be proud to devote all his gifts and energies. It was now that Baudelaire produced his *Les Fleurs du Mal* and that Leconte de Lisle and the Parnassians and Gérard de Nerval and the Symbolists started new fashions in poetry. It was in 1860 that Gounod's *Faust* was first performed, and it was during these years that Offenbach launched the *opéra bouffe* which was to have such an extraordinary success in the fashionable world, and that Labiche delighted enthusiastic audiences with his gay comedies. In the world of art Corot was joined by other landscape painters of great talent such as Millet and Harpignies, and Puvis de Chavannes began his monumental frescoes; while Méryon and Doré showed their skill as etchers and illustrators. In the realm of philosophy, Renouvier expounded Neo-Kantianism, and after the death of its founder, Auguste Comte, in 1857, Positivism, a pseudo-scientific creed, steadily extended its influence under the direction of his disciples such as the lexicographer, Littré. Here too the effect of the material progress of the age was marked in popularizing man-made systems which affected to dispense with the aid of religious beliefs, and Positivism in particular was to play a great part in strengthening the secularist, anti-clerical tendencies of many a Republican. Throughout Napoleon's reign, indeed, the age-long struggle between clericals and anti-clericals continued, and the Roman Question of the 'sixties and the challenging pronouncement of the Pope caused it to become ever more passionate. But the superior intellectual talent was on the whole on the side of the unbelievers and the Church was fighting a losing battle. Last, but not least, we must note the achievements of French scientists, such as the physiologist Claude Bernard, Deville the discoverer of aluminium, Marcellin Berthelot and, greatest of all, Louis Pasteur, who now began his work on fermentation and bacteria. With men such as these France, in spite of the shortcomings of her rulers and the collapse of her armies, could still hold her head high: whatever her political failings there was no intellectual or artistic débâcle.

ARNAUD, R.: La Deuxième république et le second Empire. Paris, 1929.

BELLESSORT, ANDRÉ: La société française sous Napoléon III. Paris, 1932.

DUVEAU, GEORGES: La vie ouvrière en France sous le second Empire. Paris, 1946.

GUÉRARD, ALBERT: Napoleon III. Harvard, 1943.

HALÉVY, LUDOVIC: Carnets, 1862–70. 2 vols. Paris, 1935.

HAUSER, H., MAURAIN, J., and BENAERTS, P.: Du libéralisme à l'impérialisme (1860–78). Paris, 1939.

LA GORCE, P. DE: Histoire du second Empire. 7 vols. Paris, 1894–1905.

LORD, R. H.: The Origins of the War of 1870. Harvard, 1924.

OLLIVIER, E.: L'Empire libéral, études, récits, souvenirs. 17 vols. Paris, 1895–1915.

PRÉVOST-PARADOL: La France nouvelle. New ed. Paris, 1876.

SEIGNOBOS, C.: La Révolution de 1848—Le Second Empire (Vol. VI of LAVISSE, E.: Histoire de France contemporaine. Paris, 1921).

SEIGNOBOS, C.: Le Déclin de l'Empire et l'établissement de la Troisième République (Vol. VII of LAVISSE, E.: Histoire de France contemporaine. Paris, 1921).

SIMPSON, F. A.: Louis-Napoleon and the Recovery of France, 1848–56. London, 1923.

VIII

THE FRANCO-PRUSSIAN WAR AND THE COMMUNE

'FRANCE,' wrote Prévost-Paradol in 1868, 'is approaching the most formidable trial she has ever had to encounter.'[1] He was a true prophet; and the men who from September 1870 onwards had to face it were, like the Republican leaders of 1848, comparatively little-known lawyers, journalists and politicians whose experience of government was either non-existent or dated from the Second Republic. In February 1848 the Republicans had come into power as the result of a revolution which had taken everyone by surprise and had found themselves under the necessity of ruling France at a time of severe economic depression and of almost universal unrest in Europe. In September 1870, the situation with which the new Provisional Government was confronted was much more alarming; and yet it contained many striking parallels with 1848. Although the revolution of September 4th was bloodless, it was not 'legal'—that is to say, all the constituted authorities had been swept aside or ignored. As in 1848, while the deputies were dispersed in their committee-rooms debating the transference of powers—this time to some sort of Executive Commission which should carry on the government of the country until a Constituent Assembly could be elected—the Chamber was invaded by a motley crowd, probably with the connivance of some of the Republican deputies. The clamours of this mob soon made debate impossible and deprived the legislators of all authority. But, as in 1830 and 1848, the people looked again to the Opposition deputies to give a lead, and so two of them, Jules Favre and Gambetta, assented to the demands for the proclamation of a Republic, but declared that as in 1830 and in 1848 it should be proclaimed at the Hôtel de Ville—to such a point had Revolution in France now developed its ritual. Once again crowds converged on the Hôtel de Ville and once again there was a race between moderate and extreme Republicans to seize power. In order to forestall growing disorder, a convenient formula was hastily devised by the parliamentarians—the new Govern-

[1] *La France nouvelle*, p. 373.

ment should be formed by the deputies of Paris, including those who had originally been elected there, but who, under the system whereby a man could be a candidate in more than one constituency at the same time, had chosen to sit for some other constituency. Thus the thirty-two year old barrister Gambetta, who sat for Marseilles, and Jules Simon, one of the members for Bordeaux, both became members of the new administration which assumed the title of Government of National Defence. In addition, because of the military situation General Trochu, the Governor of Paris, was made President of the Government. On the other hand, Thiers, who was also a deputy for Paris, while ready to serve it on diplomatic missions abroad, prudently abstained from entering a Government so uniformly Republican in its composition. This abstention was indeed a loss; but it meant that on the whole the men in the new Government were people of much the same outlook. With the exception of the journalist Rochefort, who had to be fetched from the prison of Ste. Pélagie, where he was serving one of his numerous sentences for infringement of the Press laws, they were all relatively moderate in their Republican views. There was not the sharp cleavage between the advocates of social revolution and the others which had weakened the Government of 1848.

The name 'Government of National Defence' rightly stressed the urgent overriding task of the new authorities. In spite of the pacifist tendencies not so long since exhibited by some of the more doctrinaire among them, and in spite of the seemingly hopeless military situation, there was little thought of peace. Had Napoleon still been on the throne he might perhaps have appealed to England to mediate and peace might have been concluded as rapidly as it was between Austria and Prussia in 1866. But this would have been possible only if the Emperor had been able to persuade opinion to accept territorial concessions. It would have been difficult for a Bonaparte to do this. It was no less difficult for a Republican Government. In Paris, the great stronghold of Republicanism, apathy and dejection had been transformed into a frenzy of patriotic fervour, and many naïve enthusiasts appeared to think that the mere existence of a Republic was as good as a rout of the enemy in the field. Indeed the new Government's very first proclamation encouraged such a way of thinking when it declared 'The Republic was victorious against the invasion of 1792. The Republic is proclaimed. The Revolution has been made in the name of the right of public safety'. With characteristic love of historical parallels the minds of Frenchmen at once went back to 1792. Once again German armies were advancing towards Paris; once again the country was in danger and would be rescued by the united efforts of all her citizens. The regular soldiers might be captive or besieged, but still the nation would rise in arms and the *levée en masse* would sweep the sacrilegious invader from the land. Such thoughts even found their way into the first circular issued by the new Foreign Minister, Jules Favre, to French representatives abroad: 'We shall yield neither an inch of our territory nor a stone of our fortresses. . . . Paris can hold out three months and conquer. If it fell, France, ready at its call, would avenge it; she would continue the struggle and the aggressor would perish.' Between such a spirit and the German determination to annex Alsace and a large part of Lorraine on the grounds that they were historic German lands and that their chief cities, Metz and Strasbourg, were, in Bismarck's phrase, 'the keys of the German house', there could be no compromise. Thus the Revolution of September 4th meant not peace, but *guerre à outrance*, war to the knife.

Such a war presented tremendous and pressing problems. The German armies were rapidly advancing upon Paris. The city must be prepared to stand a siege, but was the Government to stay and be immured in the capital? The provinces must be galvanized into mobilizing all their resources of men and materials, but who was to galvanize them if the Government remained in Paris? The Government's solution of these two questions was a strangely unsatisfactory compromise. To the deputies of Paris, even more than to most Frenchmen, Paris naturally seemed all-important. It was the heart of the country: in it were concentrated some 75,000 of the remaining regular troops and the best of the Garde Mobile. The Government had some justification for thinking that if they quitted it they would be accused as deserters, that political control of the capital would be in danger of falling into the hands of the extreme Left, and that civil disorder and a weakening of morale might ensue. So they decided to stay in Paris, but to send the seventy-four-year-old Minister of Justice, the Jewish Crémieux, as a Government delegate to Tours. A few days later they dispatched two more of their oldest and least-known colleagues to join him. They left only just in time. Two days afterwards the Germans completed the investment of the capital, and on September 23rd its last certain means of communication with the outside world disappeared when the telegraphic cable in the bed of the Seine was cut. Henceforward, the Parisians and all but three members of the Government of National Defence were dependent upon carrier-pigeons and balloons for their contact with the rest of France and the world beyond. Such a siege of a city of nearly two million inhabitants, the cultural capital of Europe, such isolation of the Government of a Great Power, constituted one of the most extraordinary spectacles of the nineteenth century.   There were few indeed outside Paris, either among the Germans or in neutral countries, who believed that the siege could last for more than a week or so.   But the Parisians tightened their belts, and, although it is very questionable whether they made the most of their manpower and military resources under the military direction of a general, Trochu, who had no belief in the possibility of victory and profoundly distrusted the National Guards, they held out for four months, far into the depths of one of the severest winters of the century.   Thereby they won the respect and admiration of the world and did much to make foreign opinion, which at the outbreak of the war was largely unfriendly to France, more sympathetic.

Meanwhile the provinces were far from being galvanized by the elderly Delegation at Tours, and the question had arisen whether their authority should not be reinforced by some sort of elections.   The Government of National Defence, like the Government of February 1848, was a purely *de facto* administration, the offspring of a revolution. But in war it was diplomatically desirable for the country to have a regular Government and it could well be argued that such a Government with the nation behind it would have much more authority and prosecute the defence more successfully than an improvised régime like that of September 4th.   The Government of National Defence had debated this issue from the outset and, in spite of considerable divergence of opinion, had on September 9th decreed that elections for a Constituent Assembly should be held in October.   A few days later Jules Favre had interviewed Bismarck at Ferrières in an endeavour to obtain an armistice which would enable the elections to be held all over the country, in the invaded as well as in the free· departments.   But Bismarck's conditions for such an armistice had been unacceptable and in consequence the Government had decided to postpone the elections indefinitely and to devote their whole energies to the war.   They were therefore much astonished when only a week later they heard that their Delegates at Tours had reversed their decision on the grounds of 'a general demand of the departments' and of 'unavoidable necessity'.   In fact the three elderly Ministers were quite unable to dominate a situation which was going from bad to worse.   Toul and Strasbourg had fallen and the advance of Bavarian troops towards the Loire had necessitated the evacuation of Orléans.   The Delegation themselves inspired neither respect nor confidence—to many of the military and Conservative elements they represented a crowd of demagogues and the coincidence of demagogy and invasion seemed to have brought the country to the

Cherbourg

Havre

Laval

Le Ma:

Tour:

Nântes

Poitiers

La Rochelle

Angoulême

F R A N C E
1814 ~ 1940

English Miles

0   20   40   60   80   100

Bordeaux

R. Dordogn

.... Boundaries between Departments

▦ Territory retained by France in 1814 and ceded in 1815

▨ "   ceded to France by Sardinia in 1860

☰ "   "   by France to Germany in 1871.

∞∞∞∞∞ Line of military occupation by Allies according to Treaty
    of Paris, Nov. 20th 1815

.... " "   "   " by German troops Feb. 26th 1871

×××× " "   "   "   "   "   "   according to Armistice of
    June 1940

MAP II

'very bottom of the abyss, the last circle of Dante's Hell'.[1] The Generals and military authorities were constantly at loggerheads with the new Republican prefects appointed throughout the country by Gambetta. Disturbances were reported from various southern towns, and the formation of a so-called Ligue du Midi, however patriotic its purpose of regional defence, threatened still further to weaken the Delegation's hold upon the country. Thus very naturally the Delegates felt that elections were essential to reinforce their waning authority. But they reckoned without their beleaguered colleagues, who at once sent Gambetta to Tours by balloon to express their disapproval and impart to the direction of the war in the provinces that energy which had been so lacking. With him he bore a fresh decree, cancelling the elections, and instructions which gave him a casting vote in the councils of the Delegation and full power as Minister of the Interior to recruit, call up and equip all the forces of the nation which might be required for the country's defence. On his arrival at Tours on October 10th he found that one of his colleagues, Admiral Fourichon, had just for the second time resigned the post of Minister of War and that no one else was willing to assume it. Gambetta had no such hesitation. Within forty-eight hours of his coming he had become Minister of War as well as of the Interior and had virtually concentrated all powers in his own hands. It was now up to this young Cyclops of thirty-two to improvise the defence of the invaded country and emulate the feats of a Carnot or a Danton.

Gambetta's arrival very quickly had a tonic effect. At once the country felt that here was a man who, however little he knew about waging war, was full of energy and determination and that action would succeed to apathy and confusion. Within a short time he had appointed a tireless, supple, ambitious civil engineer, Charles de Freycinet, to be his deputy at the Ministry of War and together they had organized the small part of the War Office which had been evacuated to Tours with the Delegation. The civilians and the amateurs were now in control and the last chance of salvation lay in the hope that their readiness to dispense with military routine and red tape would so accelerate the defence measures already under weigh and so hasten new ones, as to enable fresh armies to take the field while Paris still held out. They did their utmost: many changes were made in commands; all formations which did not constitute part of the regular army were enrolled into a new auxiliary force; and the National Guards, who had been revived as a result of Opposition pressure in August, were mobilized for active

[1] *Mémoires du Duc de Broglie*, II. p. 21.

service. Indeed there was no lack of manpower; the crux of the problem of organization was to train and equip a sufficient number of men to enable the new provincial 'Army of the Loire' to go into action well before December 1st, the date which, as Gambetta and Freycinet believed, would mark the limit of effective resistance by the Parisians.

At first their efforts met with success beyond expectation. At the beginning of November the new Army of the Loire was able to relieve Orléans and to win a battle at Coulmiers, but it could not exploit its victory and all attempts to break through to relieve Paris were as ineffectual as the efforts of the Paris garrison to effect a sortie. Disaster soon followed upon disaster. Already at the end of October, the capitulation of Bazaine and his army of 154,000 men at Metz had released large additional German forces and darkened the military prospects still further. By the beginning of December the Army of the Loire was being rapidly forced back and cut in two; and the re-entry of the Germans into Orléans and their advance down the Loire compelled the Delegation to quit Tours for Bordeaux. The defeated Army of the Loire was reorganized—one half executing a brilliant retreat westwards under a new commander, Chanzy, the other being formed into a new Army of the East under General Bourbaki, which Freycinet dispatched to attempt the relief of Belfort and to threaten German communications. But it too was thrown back and only escaped the annihilation which threatened it at the end of January 1871, as the result of Jules Favre's omission to cover it in the terms of a general armistice, by crossing the Swiss frontier and being interned. Finally, on January 28th, Paris itself capitulated. During the last month of its ordeal it had experienced many of the trying experiences now so familiar in modern war, including bombardment, sheltering in basements, firewatching and food rationing.[1] By the end of that time supplies were nearing exhaustion and the failure of a last effort to effect a sortie had seriously impaired morale. The news of the capitulation reached Bordeaux on the 29th together with information that the Government in Paris had agreed to a twenty-one days' armistice and that a National Assembly to be elected on February 8th was to meet on February 12th. Gambetta was furious. He had often told his colleagues that the provinces could carry on the war even after the fall of Paris and he still believed that he could raise and equip new armies and wear the Germans down by refusal to surrender. Yet now, as he thought, the Government in Paris had betrayed him and meekly

---

[1] There was also a serious epidemic of smallpox both in Paris and in the provinces. cp. ASHWORTH, E.: 'Pestilence and War', in the *Spectator*, Nov. 2nd, 1945.

given in. At least if there were to be elections he would ensure that they would have a reasonable chance of giving a Republican result and so, since he had not received a copy of the Paris Government's election decree, he issued one of his own for which he obtained the reluctant consent of his elderly colleagues of the Delegation. This laid down that no one who had served Napoleon III as a Minister, Senator, Councillor of State or official candidate should be eligible. The armistice terms, however, had stipulated that the elections should be free, and free the Government in Paris were determined that they should be. For a moment, when Gambetta refused to listen to Jules Simon whom they dispatched to Bordeaux to explain their policy and to effect liaison with the Delegation, it looked as though a major conflict between the Government in Paris and the Government in the provinces would still further complicate the affairs of the unhappy country. But when more Ministers from Paris reached Bordeaux and upheld the armistice conditions, Gambetta rejected the promptings of enthusiasts who urged him to make a coup and assume a dictatorship; he bowed to superior numbers and resigned. That resignation removed both the danger of civil war and the last obstacle in the way of peace.

Thus the desperate, heroic, and largely improvised national defence, the French 'people's war', as it has been called by a military historian,[1] came to an end. The sufferings of the often ill-equipped, ill-prepared, hastily raised new forces had been intensified by the bitter weather. By the beginning of February 1871 the garrison of Paris and three other armies had capitulated or been interned, the remaining forces, Chanzy's Army of the Loire and Faidherbe's Army of the North were in retreat, and forty-three departments or half the country had been overrun by the enemy. Furthermore, although Great Britain had made a friendly offer of mediation, no ally had come to France's aid. Under such circumstances further resistance might well seem hopeless. It was true that the Germans had at first been angered, inconvenienced and perplexed by the rising of new forces whose extent and worth they were for some time unable to gauge and whose existence had created a veritable 'fog of war'; but this fog had not been thick enough to mislead them into a single serious defeat and all Gambetta's energy and indomitable resolve could not have availed to restore the morale of the people after such a series of unrelieved disasters. France was weary of war and the elections of February 8th were first and foremost a vote for peace. By her resistance under Gambetta's leadership and by the siege of Paris she had saved her honour and had reminded men of what had

[1] HALE, COLONEL LONSDALE: *The People's War in France*, 1870-71.

not been seen in Western Europe since the days of the Spanish war of Napoleon I, the immense possibilities of organized resistance by a whole people to a foreign invader. For the future, his organization of the provincial armies and his stand as the champion of war without thought of surrender would serve Gambetta and the Republicans in good stead and give rise to a legend: but for the moment, in spite of the fact that he was elected by no less than nine constituencies, they were to bring him and most of his colleagues of the Government of National Defence into temporary eclipse. The Republic, formerly associated with social disorder, had not succeeded in dispelling this impression in 1870 and now in addition it was coupled with military defeat. Gambetta and his prefects had not succeeded in their short period of power in converting the mass of the people to Republicanism, any more than had Ledru-Rollin and his Commissioners of 1848. So the electorate turned to the forces of order which had not been compromised by the war. In their result the elections of February 8th were reminiscent both of the elections to the Chamber of 1815 and of those to the Legislative Assembly in May 1849, and incidentally they were held under the same electoral law as the elections of 1849. Once again the Monarchists and Conservatives gained a large majority of the seats —some 400 compared with 200 won by the Republicans and a mere thirty by the Bonapartists. The eclipse of the Empire was confirmed, the Republicans were scarcely stronger than the Mountain in 1849. Once again the Monarchists appeared to have a great opportunity to put France's house in order and to set her back upon the path of constitutional monarchy from which she had by such an unhappy accident departed in 1849. Unfortunately for them they were still, twenty years' after, divided as to who should be king.

Apart from being a vote for peace and a triumph for the Monarchists, the elections were also an extraordinary personal success for a single man, Adolphe Thiers. Thiers, now a veteran elder statesman of seventy-three, was returned by no less than twenty-six departments. Alone among the foremost politicians he enjoyed a prestige which was unimpaired. Prominent ever since the days of Charles X, this little man who had been the protégé of Talleyrand and the opponent of Guizot and Palmerston had an unrivalled experience of public affairs. Since 1863 he had distinguished himself as a leader of the Opposition and as one of the most trenchant and clear-sighted critics of Napoleon III's foreign policy: his warnings of the German menace had fallen unheeded at the time, but now they were remembered all over the country. By refusing to enter the Government of National Defence he had avoided being compromised by its ill success, while by his diplomatic missions on its behalf he had shown his patriotic readiness to serve his country. Even had the Monarchists not been divided they might well, remembering Louis XVIII and the Treaties of Paris, have preferred that someone other than the King should bear the responsibility for making a peace which must be humiliating. As it was, all were agreed that Thiers was the obvious head of the new provisional Government which must function until a new constitution had been devised and could come into operation. Accordingly, on the 16th February, the National Assembly, which had met at Bordeaux and accepted the resignation of the Government of National Defence, nominated Thiers as 'Chief of the Executive Power of the French Republic'—this title being without prejudice to the eventual form of Government which might be decided upon by the deputies or their successors. Thiers at once accepted the post, undertook by what was to be known as the Pact of Bordeaux to observe neutrality as between the different parties, and formed a Government which, amongst a number of men of various shades of opinion, included three of the members of the late Government of National Defence; they were to share in the responsibility for the peace which followed the war they had waged and not to be left free to criticize it like the Left under the Restoration. On the 17th he was given a free hand to negotiate for peace, and the representatives of Alsace and Lorraine made a first moving protest against the cession of their provinces, which everyone knew that the Germans intended to demand, and which was in fact inevitable.

Before France was free to consider her future form of government she had more bitter trials to undergo. Already on January 18th she had experienced the humiliation of seeing the King of Prussia proclaimed German Emperor in the Hall of Mirrors at Versailles. Now Bismarck was ready to consolidate the new Empire forged in war by territorial aggrandisement at France's expense. Not only was she obliged by the preliminaries of peace,[1] eventually confirmed in the Treaty of Frankfurt, to pay a war indemnity of five milliard francs within three years and to submit to the occupation of several departments by German troops, who would be withdrawn gradually as the instalments of the indemnity were paid, but she also had to surrender two of her richest provinces. Alsace and Lorraine could not be saved, and with them she lost great iron-ore deposits, important textile works, rich forest and agricultural land and a population of some 1,600,000. Thiers' tenacity

[1] For text see BUTTERFIELD, H.: *Select Documents of European History*, 1715–1920, pp. 165–6.

as a negotiator had succeeded in securing a reduction of one milliard francs in the indemnity and in retaining in return for the concession of a triumphal entry of German troops into Paris on March 1st, the fortress of Belfort, but more than this he could not wrest from the conqueror. When the terms of peace were announced to the Assembly the deputies from Alsace and Lorraine once again made a moving protest and swore that their people would ever remain faithful to France.   By this annexation of two unwilling provinces and their erection into a German Reichsland, or territory common to the new Empire, Bismarck may have helped to cement the unification of the new Germany but he also bequeathed to Europe a problem which bid fair to endanger her peace and made almost impossible any reconciliation between France and Germany such as took place between Austria and Prussia after 1866. Henceforward until 1918 the statue of Strasbourg in the Place de la Concorde in Paris was to be veiled in crêpe.   Henceforward, although the mass of the people was quickly resigned to the new situation, the thoughts of many Frenchmen were long to be dominated by the idea of *revanche*.   Like the partition of Poland, the 'rape of Alsace-Lorraine' was a wound in the body politic of Europe, a wound which would not be healed for nearly fifty years.

The preliminaries of peace, voted by the National Assembly on March 1st, 1871, were only one of the trials which France had to face. A few days later the Assembly decided to adjourn and to resume its sittings at Versailles on the 20th.   Before it met again the country was involved in civil war.   On March 18th there broke out the revolutionary movement in Paris known as the Commune.

This tragic and complex affair was the outcome of a variety of causes and to understand some of them we must go back to the June Days, which in certain aspects this new Parisian rising so much resembled. The June Days insurrection of 1848 had, as we have seen, been ruthlessly suppressed, but it had left among certain classes of Parisian workers a deeper hatred than before of the bourgeoisie, which none of Napoleon III's gestures had been able to eradicate.   The economist, Michael Chevalier, was obliged to admit that there were two opposing mentalities, the bourgeois and the proletarian,[1] and it seemed more than ever difficult to reconcile them.   In the by-elections of 1864 sixty French workers had issued a manifesto declaring that social emancipation had still to come and that political rights implied social rights which could only be won by the workers' own efforts.   In the following years the opening in Paris in 1865 of the first French office of the International and the

[1] cit. DUVEAU, G.: *La vie ouvrière en France sous le second Empire*, p. vii.

gradual extension of branches to other parts of the country, the influence
of Proudhon and Blanqui, combined with continued long hours and
poor conditions in several industries, had all tended to keep open the
gulf between workers and bourgeoisie and to revive dreams of the
Socialist Republic of which the workers had been disappointed in 1848.
The International, still an essentially working-class organization,[1] had
soon fallen into the hands of extremist leaders in France, and when it
had aroused the suspicion of the Government and was prosecuted, it
had quickly become another thorn in the flesh of the weakening Empire.
So, as we have seen, Paris in the late 'sixties, as in the 'thirties and 'forties,
was once again honeycombed by extremist societies and clubs of political
and social revolutionaries, all of them anti-clerical, all of them hostile
to the Empire, but at the same time far too individualist and varied in
the sources of their inspiration to constitute anything like an organized
party or even a movement.   As the Empire had become more Liberal
and restrictive legislation had been relaxed, so the extremist attacks upon
the régime had been ever more virulent and the likelihood of some
attempt at insurrection had increased.   On September 4th, 1870, there
is little doubt that had the Republican deputies been less prompt, some
of the extremist group would have seized power.   As things were, they
all hoped, like their forebears of 1848, to be able to bend the new
Government to their will.   The Government of National Defence,
like that of Lamartine and his colleagues, were subjected to frequent
pressure from clubs, from demonstrations of armed National Guards
from working-class quarters, and from self-appointed district Watch
Committees, often composed of extreme Republicans, who set up
a Central Committee in the offices of the International and sought to
impose their own military and political ideas.   The National Guards
in particular had in the siege conditions of Paris and with the shortage
of regular soldiers become a veritable power whom the Government
had great difficulty in handling.   They, too, developed a general organization in Federations, and many extremists worked their way into positions
of command.   Once Paris was cut off, the Government were under
constant criticism from all these extremists and patriots; their failures to
proclaim a *levée en masse*, to attempt sorties sufficiently frequently
and to hold municipal elections were all held against them; and when
the news of the capitulation of Metz had reached the city on October
3rd, they had nearly been overthrown by a crowd of excited demonstrators who had surrounded and invaded the Hôtel de Ville demanding
elections to a Commune or municipal council and a *levée en masse*.

[1] *vide Société d'Histoire de la Troisième République, Bulletin No.* 8, p. 66.

In both these demands the preoccupation was with the prosecution of the war; for the Commune at this moment was envisaged less as an organ of municipal autonomy than as a means of imposing a Jacobin dictatorship which would save the country and wage war with more ruthless energy.   For a short time, until loyal forces came to the rescue, most of the members of the Government of National Defence had been held prisoner by the mob.   After this escape they had reinforced their authority by a plebiscite which gave them a handsome majority, and had sought to govern with a stronger hand by entrusting the administration of the city to the firm and capable Jules Ferry.   Nevertheless, clubs and extremist papers had continued their attacks and as the siege dragged on, food gave out, the cold became more severe, news of the outside world was rare, and the Germans began their bombardment, these grew more bitter.   In one way or another many of those in the beleaguered city came to be overwrought and to suffer from what was known as 'siege fever'.   And so, soon after the dismal failure of another attempt at a sortie, on January 22nd, there was another revolutionary demonstration.   Breton Mobile Guards were obliged to fire on National Guards who had sided with the demonstrators; and General Vinoy, who had just succeeded Trochu as Governor of Paris, closed several clubs and suspended a number of newspapers.   When the city capitulated a few days later feelings inside it were passionately divided; and in the subsequent elections there was a violent campaign against the 'men of the capitulation', the Government of National Defence, with the result that workers and extremists like Tolain, Benoît Malon, Gambon and Félix Pyat, were elected alongside Republicans of all shades from Gambetta to Henri Martin.   Out of forty-three deputies all but six were in favour of the continuation of the war.   Such a result was a striking indication of the emotional state of the populace.

But in the provinces, as we have seen, the elections were overwhelmingly a vote for peace.   Thus there was yet one more parallel with 1848.   Once again the contrast between the will of the capital and the will of the country stood out in sharp relief.   Paris was dismayed by the election of what it regarded as an Assembly of reactionary rural notables, and the Assembly had little understanding or sympathy for the feelings of the Parisians.   Capital and country had both fought the same war, but in totally different conditions and the fact that they had been isolated from one another for four months greatly increased their mutual incomprehension.   A series of acts of the new Government was soon to cause the city's latent tendency to insurrection to flare up again in exasperation.   The Parisians were humiliated by the Germans'

entry into the city on March 1st, although the exceedingly prompt
ratification of the peace preliminaries had obliged them to withdraw
two days later; they were slighted by the decision of the National
Assembly to sit at Versailles instead of in Paris; and they were greatly
embittered by the decision of a Government anxious to return to 'nor-
malcy' as quickly as possible that commercial bills which had matured
in August 1870 must be settled forthwith, and that the National Guards
should no longer be paid their one franc fifty cents a day. This second
decision seemed particularly hard: not only did many of the Guards
regard themselves as great heroes, but, until conditions of full employment could be restored, many of the poorest of them were mainly
dependent upon their Guards' pay for their means of subsistence. And
so when the Government then proceeded to demand that the Parisians
should hand over to the military authorities some 220 guns, which had
been subscribed for by the people and concealed from the Germans,
they met with a blank refusal. The test of force was about to begin,
for the Government had committed a cardinal blunder in depriving the
National Guard of their pay without having first deprived them of their
weapons. Jules Favre, to his eternal sorrow, had refused to consider
their disarmament when he negotiated the armistice with Bismarck and
no step had been taken to enforce it since.

But for local incidents in which two Generals were killed it is possible
that some peaceful settlement might have been reached. But once again,
as so often in French history, the unforeseen local clash, unexpectedly
involving the loss of human life, at once changed the course of events,
quickly embittering the opposing forces beyond hope of reconciliation.
To a large number of Parisians it now seemed that a reactionary Government was bent on humiliating the capital in spite of its gallant defence.
To the Government it appeared that insubordinate and dangerous
revolutionary elements were bent on defying them and discrediting their
authority while the invader looked on. They believed that after the
débâcle their first task must be to restore the authority of government
with uncompromising firmness throughout the length and breadth of
the land. And so when Thiers heard that the troops sent to recapture
the guns had begun to fraternize with the people, that National Guards
and demonstrators had disarmed soldiers in various barracks, and that
insurgents were masters of several parts of the city, he gave orders that
the Government should leave it. This was what he had urged Louis
Philippe to do on February 24th, 1848, to withdraw with the regular
troops, reorganize them and then take the city by force. Now, in a
similar situation, he lost no time in carrying out the policy which Louis

Philippe, with fatal results for his dynasty, had hesitated to adopt. The seat of government was transferred to Versailles and the evacuation left Paris once more in the hands of revolutionaries. There was thus to be civil war, war between the regular troops of the Versailles Government and the Federalists, as the National Guards of Paris were to be known on account of their federal organization; and after the repulse of the Federalists' attempt to march on Versailles Paris was to undergo its second siege within six months.

The extremists thus had their chance to create a Commune under the impetus of the Central Committee, a number of followers of Blanqui, and several more or less obscure Radical and Socialist politicans and journalists. The handful of moderate members soon resigned, but because the Commune still included doctrinaires of every kind, Blan-quists, Proudhonians, old Jacobins of the 1848 variety and various independent revolutionaries (but only one Marxist) it was more successful in hunting 'reactionaries' and priests than in evolving an agreed and coherent constructive programme. Indeed the Communards were soon at loggerheads with one another; and when the threat from Ver-sailles grew and it was known that Communards taken prisoner were shot out of hand, their violence became more extreme and they tended to imitate the Terror of the Great Revolution. Numbers of suspects, including the Archbishop of Paris, were thrown into prison as hostages, and buildings and monuments such as Thiers' house and the Vendôme Column were destroyed. The Communard forces had an abundance of arms, but they were exceedingly ill-disciplined, and it was soon evident that they would be no match for the reorganized Government forces under Marshal MacMahon, whose numbers the Germans had permitted to be increased from 40,000 to 80,000 by the incorporation of returned prisoners of war. By the middle of May their position was hopeless, and then, in a terrible frenzy of despair, when Government troops began to pass into the city they began an orgy of destruction. Fifty-six of the hostages, including the Archbishop of Paris, were shot, and several of the finest buildings in Paris, among them the Tuileries, the Palais de Justice and the Hôtel de Ville were set in flames. By the 28th May, after a brief existence of little more than two months, the Commune was at an end. Paris was subjugated and order was restored, but at a terrible price. As in the June Days, the fighting on both sides had been characterized by all the savagery and ruthlessness of civil war, and now, as after the June Days, the repression was equally ruthless. The forces of order had been all the more exasperated by this insurrection at a time when the foreign enemy was still within the gate and when the country was in crying need of peace and reconstruction after the war against Prussia. Small wonder, then, that in the last week of the fighting, the 'semaine sanglante' or 'bloody week' when the Government troops fought their way into the city street by street, they indulged in wholesale executions and undoubtedly made many innocent victims. The exact number of those who perished will never be known but it cannot have been less than 20,000.. In addition 36,000 were arrested, 13,450 sentenced to various terms of imprisonment and 7,000, among them the journalist Rochefort, deported to New Caledonia.

Hitherto, since the Great Revolution, it had been an oft-repeated axiom that in politics Paris led the way and gave the law to France.[1] The failure of the Commune marked the end of that supremacy.[2]   As a movement of defiance against a conservative Assembly and a protest against peace it had had its imitators in other towns, particularly in the south, where extremist influence was still very strong.   But the Communes of Toulouse, Narbonne, Lyons, St. Etienne and Marseilles had been suppressed with little difficulty and 'the Commune', without qualification, remains for history above all a specifically Parisian phenomenon.   Although it displayed the red flag, although members of the International took a prominent part in its direction, and although most of its troops were supplied by the Parisian workers, it was, like the insurrection of the June Days, a spontaneous uprising, not a long-planned, carefully-co-ordinated, conscious attempt at social revolution; an uprising dictated in the first instance, as we have seen, as much by patriotic indignation as by political ambition or doctrinaire theory.   Unhappily the results had been death and destruction on a scale still greater than in 1848.   As after the June Days, executions, arrests and deportations disorganized and virtually silenced the extremists thereby greatly delaying the growth of organized Socialism in France.   Among the victims we must also note the National Guard whose abolition was decreed by the National Assembly in August despite the opposition of Thiers.   Thus there finally disappeared a 'democratic' force which had played a notable part in French history during the best part of a century.   The Commune was an unhappy prelude to the Third Republic, a tragic climax to the misunderstandings of half a century between capital and provinces and between workers and bourgeoisie.   Yet without it, it is possible

[1] The elections of 1848 and the June Days were, of course, notable exceptions.

[2] It is, however, to be noted that the Communards no longer claimed supremacy for Paris like the Jacobins of old, but demanded liberty for all the Communes of France. In doing so they spoke a language much like the Anarchists of Bakunin, HALÉVY, E.: Histoire du Socialisme Européen, p. 158.

that the birth of the Third Republic might have been much more difficult than it was. The proscription and exile of so many extremists enabled the new Republic to attain constitutional legality and to develop in a peaceable and orderly fashion during its first formative years. Last but not least, this absence or quiescence of the turbulent extremist elements enabled it at length to cast off that association in men's minds with violence, instability and social peril, by which it had been inextricably bound and hampered for so long. Only then could it be certain of winning the allegiance of the majority of hard-working, peaceable, Frenchmen.

BOURGIN, G.: *La Guerre de 1870-1871 et la Commune.* Paris, 1939.

BURY, J. P. T.: *Gambetta and the National Defence.* London, 1936.

DREYFUS, ROBERT: *Monsieur Thiers contre l'Empire, la Guerre, la Commune, 1869-71.* Paris, 1928.

GOLTZ, COLMAR, BARON VON DER: *Léon Gambetta und seine Armeen.* Berlin, 1877.

HALE, LONSDALE: *The 'People's War' in France, 1870-1.* London, 1904.

MASON, EDWARD S.: *The Paris Commune.* New York, 1930.

IX

THE ESTABLISHMENT OF THE THIRD REPUBLIC

ONCE France could take stock of her position after the terrible year
of 1870–1 she found herself in a world which had greatly changed since
the triumph of Napoleon III at the Treaty of Paris in 1856, only fifteen
years earlier. Then she had been incontestably the foremost power in
Europe. Italy and Germany were still only geographical expressions,
Russia had been vanquished, Great Britain was an ally. Now France's
débâcle had completed that rapid transformation of the map of Europe
which had begun with the Italian war of 1859. It had obliged her to
recall her troops from Rome—without any *quid pro quo*—and this withdrawal had spelt the doom of the Temporal power of the Papacy. The
establishment of the Italian Government in the Eternal City had completed the unification of the new Italian kingdom. At the same time
Russia had seized the chance afforded by war between two of the great
powers of Europe to secure a modification of the Black Sea clauses of
the Treaty of Paris. Most momentous of all, Germany, through war
with France, had at last attained national unity and France had been
without an ally. Consequently, while France was prostrate, three of
the other principal European states had profited from her fall. The
balance of European power was completely altered. The new German
Empire had proved to be the most formidable military state; it already
outnumbered France by over four million people[1] and bid fair also to
become the greatest industrial country on the Continent. The hegemony
of Europe had passed from France to Germany, and Bismarck, not
Thiers, was now the chief arbiter of continental destinies.

Willy-nilly, therefore, France had to adjust herself to a position
which was painful and humiliating. Isolated, to some extent an object
of mistrust to other Powers because of the Revolution of September
4th and the Commune, she could no longer think of ambitious foreign
policies. As after 1815, so now her main preoccupations were internal

---

[1] Germany's population in 1871 was 41 millions, France's in 1876 nearly
37 millions. CLAPHAM, J. H.: *Economic Development of France and Germany*,
p. 278.

—reconstruction after the ravages of war, fulfilment of the terms of the peace treaty, and last but not least the establishment of a stable form of government. The elections of February, 1871, had shown clearly enough that the crying desire was for peace and this was long to remain true for the vast majority of the people—peace and quiet and steady work at home were the heartfelt needs, and they go far to explain the public dislike of new colonial adventures and the slight enthusiasm evoked by clerical campaigns for the restoration of the Temporal power. But was France capable of the positive effort of setting her house in order? Notable among the many who were exceedingly pessimistic were great men of letters such as Renan and Taine.[1] After all, what had the last half-century been but a dismal tale of the failure of one régime after another? And now the Terrible Year had brought defeat by Germany, civil war at home, and insurrection in Algeria.

In fact, however, France once again showed the economic resiliency which had been so striking after 1815. Many a thrifty citizen had managed to put a good deal aside during the prosperous years of the Second Empire, and Europe and France herself were surprised and impressed by the way in which the two principal loans raised to meet a war indemnity, which all had regarded as crushing, were covered not once, but twice and thirteen times. As a result it was possible to secure the evacuation of France by the occupying German troops much before the date originally contemplated. By July 30th, 1873, the whole country was cleared, except for Verdun, and in September the last German soldier left French soil. Thiers, whose steadying hand and skilled negotiations had largely contributed to this success, well deserved the title of Liberator of the Territory.

In general the early measures of reconstruction were marked by a conservative imprint. As Johnson in England is still Dr. Johnson and Gladstone still Mr. Gladstone, so Thiers in France is still M. Thiers, that is to say the type of the prudent bourgeois. For good or for ill, any chance the disappearance of the Empire might have afforded for a radical change in administrative organization was ignored. The traditionalist Thiers stood out against any wide measure of decentralization, although there had been a strong Opposition movement in favour of the so-called Nancy Regionalist Programme in the last year of the Empire. Indeed for a time the Right, like the Ultras in 1815, appeared to be more liberal than the Chief of the Executive Power who refused to allow free election of mayors to be accorded to any but towns of

[1] See RENAN's *La Réforme intellectuelle et morale de la France*, and TAINE's *Origines de la France contemporaine*.

under 20,000 inhabitants, not including chief towns of departments and arrondissements. So it was, too, that while the general councils (something like English county councils)[1] were now at last allowed to choose their own Presidents and to set up standing departmental Commissions, they were still—as they are to this day—very much under the control of the prefects and far from achieving the independence as a unit of local government which some of the advocates of decentralization desired that they should enjoy. It was no less significant that neither he nor his Republican successors made any attempt to control the powers of the Prefecture of Police. In fact the highly centralized administrative structure inherited by France from Napoleon survived another crisis of régime virtually intact.

In financial and commercial policy the traditionalism of Thiers was also marked. The proposal to introduce an income tax was rejected and under stress of competition from the New World he secured the first steps towards a return to the protectionist policy so characteristic of France before 1860. Thus innovations were few. 'The Republic will be conservative or it will not be at all,' said Thiers, and his attitude was no doubt reassuring to the bulk of the French middle classes and the ever-growing ranks of investors: but it is arguable that in the long run France would have benefited still more had a greater breath of freedom been introduced into local government and had the French people accepted an income tax in the 'seventies instead of waiting for the crisis of the 1914-18 war.

No less striking, both as a measure of reconstruction which was to have European significance and as a further example of the strength of traditional habits in colouring French institutions, was the law of August 1872 and subsequent legislation reforming the army. This law, the counterpart of the Law St. Cyr of 1818 reorganizing the army after the Napoleonic wars, bore the stamp of Prussian example. Victorious Germany enforced three years' general conscription. So in theory France must have conscription too, and for no less than five years. But in practice the application of the theory was singularly modified in the interests of economy. France could not, did not wish to carry the perennial burden of an enormous standing army, and so the old system of drawing lots was re-introduced. Only those who drew 'bad numbers' were obliged to serve the full period of five years, while their more fortunate brethren were let off with a year or six months. In addition, numerous categories of people, including priests and seminarists, were exempted altogether and volunteers who provided their own equipment

[1] See p. 48 ante.

were also required to serve only for a year. Thus, as regards terms of service at any rate, the new French army was in many ways strikingly like the old. Three years later, however, the financial position had so much improved that the National Assembly was able to pass a bill providing for the increase of the size of the army by 150,000 men, and in the following years much thought was given to the modernization of equipment. This increase, coupled with the patriotic agitation of exiles from Alsace and Lorraine and the open talk of *revanche* which still persisted in certain circles, led to the so-called war scare of 1875. There is no evidence that Bismarck actually intended to embark upon a preventive war, but it suited him to unleash the German Press and to adopt an attitude sufficiently menacing to cause considerable alarm and to lead Decazes, the French Foreign Minister at the time, to rouse England and Russia to awareness of a possible danger to peace. Both powers answered his appeal for good offices. The British Government made representations in Berlin and the Tsar intervened personally with the German Emperor. The incident was significant. It emphasized another aspect of French recovery; it suggested that other great powers would not always let Germany invade France with impunity; and in particular it pointed to Russia as a possible future ally.

In the meantime, once the Commune had been quelled and the peace treaty signed at Frankfurt on May 10th, 1871, the problems of government could be tackled anew. In view of the composition of the National Assembly the logical solution in 1871, as in 1849, would have been the restoration of a monarchy, and in June, in spite of the opposition of Thiers, the Assembly hastened to repeal the legislation exiling the princes of the royal houses of Bourbon and Orléans. But the Royalists, as in 1849, were still divided among themselves. Although mostly drawn from the aristocracy and wealthy bourgeoisie, half were Legitimists devoted to 'Henri V', the Comte de Chambord, and half were Orleanists who recognized Louis Philippe's grandson, the Comte de Paris, as their chief. Again, while one group was strongly Ultramontane, another was closely associated with the Liberal Catholic school which had just been worsted at the Vatican Council of 1870. Moreover, the cause of the Republic was by no means hopelessly lost. The Assembly had allowed the name of Republic to continue to be attached to the provisional régime and it had elected a moderate Republican, Jules Grévy, to preside over it, mainly because he had been highly critical of the continuation of the war and of the Government of National Defence. More important still, the Chief of the Executive Power, M. Thiers himself, former Orleanist Minister that he was, apart from personal ambition now honestly convinced that in the circumstances the Republic would prove to be the régime which divided Frenchmen least, was a convert to the Republican faith. Furthermore, the results of the by-elections of July 1871 were highly significant. As a consequence of the election in February of many deputies for more than one constituency, and of subsequent resignations and deaths, as many as 118 seats had to be filled and of these the Republicans won no less than 100. This was a most striking reversal of the trend in February and showed beyond doubt that the voting then had been for peace rather than for monarchy. If this current continued the handsome Royalist majority would soon be seriously reduced. Thus it behoved the Royalists to make their Restoration quickly if it were to be achieved at all.

But this was just what they were unable to do. Although the fact that the Comte de Chambord was childless should have made the fusion of the Legitimist and Orleanist groups an easy matter, the Comte himself was the main obstacle. After forty years in an exile spent largely in a narrow circle far remote from the realities of French politics, the Pretender paid a secret visit to France, and on July 5th issued a manifesto which caused consternation among his supporters. If he returned to reign he would, he said, be ready to accept a constitutional form of government based upon universal suffrage, but he must retain the white flag of his ancestors: 'Henri V cannot abandon the white flag of Henri IV.' 'With the symbol of the Revolution,' he had told one of his followers, 'it would be impossible for me to do any good, or set aright any evil.'[1] This public reaffirmation of an attachment to a forgotten and 'reactionary' symbol, an attachment so out of harmony with the national sentiment of a country from which he had been absent since the age of ten, was a bitter blow to the Royalists' hopes. They saw at once that the French people would never consent to abandon the tricolour, which now evoked so many glorious memories, and that until the Comte de Chambord consented to modify his attitude there would be no prospect of his becoming king. Thus there was an extraordinary situation: 'Henri V' invoking the name of Henri IV to justify his fidelity to the white flag, whereas Henri IV, who thought Paris worth a mass, was the very man to think Paris worth the tricolour, the more so since this was a flag under which Royalists of both groups had just served with such distinction during the Franco-Prussian war; 'Henri V' thus as good as turning down a throne which was virtually his for the asking and for which he had waited forty years; 'Henri V's' supporters, loth to believe that he really meant what he said and therefore themselves

[1] cit. BRABANT, F. H.: The beginning of the Third Republic in France, p. 327.

commending the tricolour and doing their utmost to keep the way open for his restoration; while Thiers, the man chosen by them to be head of the Provisional Government more and more clearly exhibited his preference for a Republic.

For the moment there was, then, no alternative but the continuation of the provisional régime: but as a result of a bargain at the end of August its nature was rather more clearly defined. The majority of the Assembly were anxious to secure beyond a doubt that when any constitution came to be framed they should be the framers—the door might then be left open for monarchy. Accordingly they formally arrogated to themselves the constituent power which was strenuously denied them by the Republican Radicals, Gambetta at their head, and in return they conferred upon Thiers the title of President of the Republic. In fact this was to prove a fresh stage in the consolidation of the Republic first provisionally established on September 4th, 1870. But the position remained a strange one, for, as a correspondent of the London House of Rothschild wrote shortly after the passage of the new law, anything might happen: 'We are living under a Provisional Government run by an old gentleman of seventy-four!'[1] In fact the old gentleman of seventy-four, who had been the protégé of Talleyrand and the rival of Guizot, was still remarkably vigorous.

Omniscient, a shrewd debater, and tireless talker until overcome by sleep, M. Thiers with his vast experience thoroughly enjoyed the position of being *faute de mieux premier*.[2] As temperamental as a prima donna, he always dominated his Cabinets and generally succeeded in controlling the Assembly. 'No personal power' was ever so personal as that of M. Thiers, said one of his critics on the Right. While negotiations concerning the fulfilment of the peace treaty had still to be completed he was indeed indispensable. But long before the territory was finally liberated there came an open breach with the Right which foreshadowed his downfall. The President's conduct was indeed increasingly unsatisfactory from the Royalist point of view. The return of Gambetta to the Assembly after the elections of July 1871 had led to a rapid growth of Radical Republicanism. A great series of speeches delivered at banquets in various parts of the country—the continuation of a state of siege debarred public meetings—the foundation of a paper called the *République Française*, and the results of further by-elections, including one in Paris where Thiers' own friend and Foreign Minister

[1] *Letters from Paris*, 1870-75, ed. by R. HENREY, p. 171.

[2] *Vanity Fair* published an excellent cartoon of him over this legend on January 6th, 1872.

was beaten by an obscure Radical named Barodet, showed that the
'ex-Dictator' was by no means a spent force. Now a Conservative
Republic ruled by Thiers might be supportable to the Royalists as a
necessary stopgap, but the kind of 'red' Republic which they believed to
be represented by Gambetta was anathema to them, and when Gambetta
called for the dissolution of the Assembly and the definite establishment
of a Republic they demanded that Thiers should govern as a resolute
Conservative and combat Radicalism without mercy. Thiers' refusal
to give any undertaking to do so led to a definite breach which was
widened virtually beyond repair when on November 13th, 1872, in
his presidential message to the Assembly at the beginning of a new
session he declared himself unequivocally in favour of a Republic. 'The
Republic exists,' he said, 'it is the legal government of this country; to
wish for anything else would be tantamount to revolution, the most
formidable of all revolutions.'[1] Such a flagrant violation of the Pact of
Bordeaux meant war between Thiers and the majority, war mitigated
only by the anxiety of all not to prejudice the final negotiations with
Germany for the evacuation of French territory. M. Thiers had always
impressed upon Louis Philippe that the King reigns but does not govern;
the Right now began to administer to M. Thiers a dose of his own medicine. On March 13th, 1873, a law was passed preventing the President
from communicating directly with the Assembly except on special
occasions. Thus he became less of a Prime Minister and more of a
President and was no longer able to sway the Assembly as he pleased
by his skill as a debater. Two months later the climax came in a debate
on a motion demanding that the Government should pursue a resolutely
Conservative policy. Unable to wean M. Thiers back to the paths of
strict Conservatism if not of Monarchy, the Right brought about his
downfall. He resigned at once and that same evening, the 24th May,
the Duc de Magenta, Marshal MacMahon, was elected President in his
stead. Three hundred and ninety votes were cast in MacMahon's favour,
but virtually the whole of the Left abstained.

There could be no greater contrast than that between M. Thiers and
his successor, who was eleven years his junior. Marshal MacMahon
was a devout Catholic and Conservative who had served many régimes,
commanded with distinction in Italy, contrived to maintain a certain
prestige in spite of his capitulation at Sedan, and been appointed Commander-in-Chief of the Government troops in the campaign against
the Commune. Honest and loyal, he was as limited in conversation as

[1] cit. HAUSER, H., MAURAIN, J. and BENAERTS, P.: *Du libéralisme à l'impérialisme*
(1860-78), p. 180. cp. *Mémoires du Duc de Broglie*, II, p. 126.

M. Thiers was expansive. He accepted the Presidency because he had been persuaded by his wife and the Right that it was his duty to do so, but whereas M. Thiers adored politics the Marshal knew little of them and was bored by them. He was the despair of Ministers and politicians who, out of Cabinet hours, had the greatest difficulty in getting him to talk of anything but the weather, food and hunting.[1] For most of the Right, however, in default of Restoration, the Marshal appeared far more likely to be a satisfactory provisional President than M. Thiers. With his election we enter upon the period of the truly conservative Republic, the Republic of the Dukes, as it has been called by M. Daniel Halévy, since, in addition to the President, the Duc de Magenta, three other Dukes were now to play a prominent part in the government of the country and in a second attempt at bringing about a Restoration, namely the Duc de Broglie, who, though nominally only Vice-President of the Council, was to lead MacMahon's first ministry, the Duc Decazes, Foreign Minister from 1873 to 1877, and the Duc d'Audiffret-Pasquier, President first of the National Assembly and then of the Senate.

Now that Thiers was out of the way the Right appeared to have a clear field for the application of their own policies. Although the Radicals had won some more by-elections, the death in 1873 of Napoleon III, who after his release from captivity in Germany had joined his wife in England, a sick and broken man, made it possible for the time being for the thirty Bonapartist deputies to co-operate with the Right. The new Broglie Ministry thus included even a Bonapartist as well as Legitimists and Orleanists. Its head was a man of great culture as well as of ancient lineage, yet with little experience of parliamentary politics and hampered by a diffidence which was too often and too easily mistaken for disdain. For him the term Republican was synonymous with revolutionary. To him it appeared that 'Religion, the army, the magistrature, the ascendancy of the educated upper classes, in fact everything which was in any degree representative of moral authority, everything which commanded respect'[2] was odious to the Republican party. For him, therefore, the immediate programme was that of the vigorous offensive against Radical Republicanism upon which Thiers had refused to embark. Termed the 're-establishment of moral order' it was a fight for the continued authority of the upper classes and the Church. It entailed a thorough-going purge of the administration and the magistrature in which many posts had, since September 1870, continued to be held by Republicans. It entailed the resumption by the Government

[1] *vide* CAMBON, P.: *Correspondance*, 1870–1924, I, pp. 63–4.
[2] *Mémoires du Duc de Broglie*, II, p. 44.

of all appointments of mayors and a determined effort to check Republican Press propaganda. Furthermore, it meant open support for the Church which was so often the subject of bitter Radical attacks. Civil funerals were permitted only in the waking hours. The numerous expiatory cults which had grown up after the war and the great pilgrimages to Lourdes, Paray-le-Monial and elsewhere received official encouragement. The catastrophe of 1870 was attributed by many of the Right to the general laxity of thought and morals which had been characteristic of the Second Empire, and now, by way of reaction, they were, in the words of one of them, M. de Marcère, overcome 'by a passionate desire for virtue'.[1] It was in something of this spirit that on July 4th, 1873, the Assembly voted for the construction, as 'a measure of public utility', of the Basilica of the Sacred Heart, the great church on the hill of Montmartre which dominates the city of Paris to this day. Thus the dissolute revolutionary capital, which had let the Commune separate Church and State and use its churches as clubs and debating halls, was in a sense made to do public penance for its infidelity and sacrilege. At the same time, under the sway of moral order, Ultramontane hopes of a crusade for the restoration of the Temporal power revived. In many of its aspects this strange resurgence of aristocratic and clerical ascendancy recalls the days of Louis XVIII and Charles X.

Meanwhile the question of the Restoration of the monarchy came to the fore once again. In August 1873 a journey made by the Comte de Paris to Frohsdorf, the Comte de Chambord's Austrian home, where the Orléans prince greeted 'Henri V' as 'the representative of the monarchical principle in France', seemed at last to ensure the complete fusion of the two main monarchist parties. A period of muddled negotiation between the Pretender and Royalist emissaries ensued, which led the majority of Royalists in France to believe that the difficulty of the white flag had been overcome and that restoration was imminent. Elaborate preparations were made by enthusiastic supporters to welcome the King when he came into his own again. Dresses and carriages and flags and bunting were got ready for the triumphant day. Stocks rose on the Bourse, responsive to the belief that Restoration by ending the provisional state of things would bring greater stability and prosperity. But all these expectations were doomed to bitter disappointment. On October 27th Chambord reiterated his earlier declaration. In no case would he abandon the white flag. If he did so he believed that he would be no more than legitimate king of the Revolution, liable to be swept aside by any gust of popular disapproval. 'Without my principle,' he

[1] cit. *Letters from Paris*, 1870-75, ed. by R. HENREY, p. 181.

is stated to have said in private, 'I am but a fat man with a limp.'[1] Thus Royalist hopes were finally dashed. When all was ready the Comte de Chambord, clinging with all the smiling serenity of a Pius IX to an outmoded principle, made his accession to the throne of his ancestors finally impossible. No wonder Thiers had already gleefully dubbed him the Washington of the Third Republic.[2]

In the circumstances the Orleanists would have gladly substituted the Comte de Paris immediately for the Comte de Chambord, but they had no possible chance of imposing such a solution, since despite his intransigence the Legitimists still regarded Chambord as their chief. There was no alternative, then, but to try and ensure that MacMahon, 'that Bayard of these modern times', as Chambord once described him,[3] should keep the King's place warm as long as possible in the hope that the *Deus ex Machina* of Death might intervene and remove Chambord and that meanwhile the Republic should continue to be governed in a spirit of moral order. Accordingly in November a bill was passed prolonging MacMahon's term of office for seven years. This further extension of the provisional appeared to be a striking witness to the truth of the French adage '*Il n'y a que le provisoire qui dure*', but in fact the Assembly could not for ever be debarred from its self-appointed task of constitution-making, and a Commission of thirty was also appointed to report on the organization of 'public powers'. Although the majority of the members of this Commission were Royalists, they could not spin out their labours indefinitely, and in January 1875, when their proposals came before the Chamber, the decisive debates upon the proper Constitution of the French state at last began.

From the debates of 1875 there emerged two laws concerning the organization of the public powers and one relating to the organization of a second Chamber or Senate. These, together with two later so-called 'Organic Laws', which dealt with the procedure for electing Senators and deputies, form what is generally known as the 'Constitution of 1875';[4] and the 'Constitution of 1875', with but few modifications, was to be that under which Frenchmen were to live and have their being for no less than sixty-four years. It was the Constitution not of the monarchy but of the Republic.

The Monarchist intention was far from such a result. The Right

[1] DE ROUX, MARQUIS: *Origines et fondation de la Troisième République*, p. 169. I am indebted for this reference to Canon F. H. Brabant.

[2] BOURGIN, G.: *La Troisième République*, p. 43.

[3] BOURGIN, G.: *La Troisième République*, p. 56.

[4] For the text of these laws see Appendix VII.

wished merely to support the 'Seven Year' Marshal by providing him with conservatively designed institutions to assist his task of government. They intended, in fact, to prolong the provisional and give it further definition, but not to prejudice the future beyond the seven years' term; therefore their proposal for the organization of public power contained no mention of the word 'Republic'. But the Right had continued to lose ground during the last year. The Broglie Ministry, like so many later Ministries of the Third Republic, had succumbed to a momentary coalition of extreme Left and extreme Right. Further, the alliance with the Bonapartists had been short-lived, since the coming of age of the Prince Imperial and fresh election results had revived his party's aspirations. Indeed in the electoral field the Bonapartists were now the only Monarchist party to make any headway, with the consequence that many Orleanists, rather than encourage a revival of the Empire, tended again to gravitate towards the Republic. And so it was that as a result of such a general situation and of much complicated manœuvring, an amendment known as the Wallon amendment introducing the word 'Republic' into the new legislation was carried by 353 votes to 352. 'The President of the Republic,' said the amended article, 'is elected by an absolute majority of votes by the Senate and the Chamber of Deputies met together as a National Assembly. He is appointed for seven years. He is re-eligible.' Thus by a single vote the Republic crept in furtively and as though by a side door, for its mention in this way, however apparently incidental, meant in fact that the constituent National Assembly formally recognized it as the proper and continuing mode of government. The President was already in office. As soon as elections to a Chamber and Senate had been held the new constitution would begin to function.

On December 31st, 1875, the National Assembly met for the last time. The provisional régime which had endured for the best part of five years was finally at an end. The Assembly has too often been lightly dismissed by Republican historians as a concourse of 'rustics', reactionary representatives of a dying order, whose only desire was to put back the clock and prolong a state of uncertainty in their own narrow interests. In fact, few French parliamentary Assemblies have ever included so many men of eminence in all walks of life, generals, ecclesiastics, historians, economists, philosophers, as well as the expected lawyers, journalists and professional politicians. Ability and distinction were by no means the monopoly of any one party. Debating was of a remarkably high order, and in conjunction with the various governments of Thiers and MacMahon, the Assembly had directed the fortunes of the country in a period of singular difficulty. The measure of its achievement is best understood when the position of France in December 1875 is compared with her situation in February 1871 when the new Assembly first met at Bordeaux. Then the picture was one of defeat, disorganization and hopelessness; now it was one of striking recovery, reorganization and revival of optimism. Finally, as the result of much strenuous labour, the Assembly had hammered out a set of constitutional laws which were to serve France more than three times as long as any since the Great Revolution. Perhaps it was just because they were in the nature of an agreed compromise rather than of a doctrinaire Diktat that they proved so durable.

Marshal MacMahon's soldierly sense of duty made him strikingly tenacious of office. When he became President his motto was said to be, '*J'y suis, j'y reste*'—but after the voting of the Constitutional laws and the elections to the new Chambers the mot was wittily turned: '*J'y reste, mais je n'y suis plus.*'[1] He had managed well enough with the Duc de Broglie and other Conservative Ministers, but the working of the new institutions brought him face to face with men of a very different type. Confronted with a growing tide of Republicanism that was by no means conservative, he was soon irritated and perplexed. In fact, the Republicans had won further striking victories since the Wallon amendment of January 30th, 1875. The Senate of 300 members of at least forty years of age, was to consist of seventy-five life members nominated by the Assembly and of 225 who were to be elected for nine years. The elective part of the body was to be renewable by thirds every nine years. Both the provisions for life senators and those for the composition of the electoral colleges were designed to weight the Chamber in a conservative sense. It was therefore a bitter blow to the Right in the Assembly when a coalition of Republicans and Bonapartists secured the nomination of no less than fifty-seven Republican life senators. The elections of January 1876 redressed the balance so as to secure a Conservative majority in the Upper House as a whole, but it was far less safe than the Right had hoped. Nor was this all; the elections to the Chamber of Deputies, held in February and in March, resulted in a sweeping victory for the Republicans who won no less than 360 seats, whereas the Monarchists obtained only 153, seventy-five of which went to the Bonapartists. This was largely the success that follows success—now that the Republic had been legally established many electors would have seen no sense in not supporting it. At the same time it was no doubt due also to the prestige of Thiers and to the

[1] CAMBON, P.: *Correspondance*, 1870–1924, I, p. 69.

growing popularity and authority of Gambetta, who towered head and
shoulders above most of his colleagues, both as an orator and as an adroit
politician.   The Monarchists had no popular leader to put up against
such men, and their clericalism had earned them unpopularity; their
inability to establish a monarchy discredited them and their attempts at
exercising official pressure frequently reacted against them.

The passage of the laws of 1875 had virtually settled the question of
the régime.   A restoration of monarchy by constitutional means was
now out of the question and MacMahon was hardly the man to lend
himself to a *coup d'état*, although, at one moment, as we shall see, he does
seem to have allowed himself to contemplate one upon a different issue.
There was still, however, another question of vital importance to be
resolved and that was one of the balance of power in the new Constitution.   The confrontation of a Conservative President and Senate by a
much more Radical Chamber threatened a conflict which was soon
to develop.

After a brief experiment with a Ministry headed by a representative
of the Left Centre, the Marshal reluctantly brought himself in December
1876 to request a moderate Republican, Jules Simon, to form a Cabinet.
The policy of the new Ministry, however, whose term of office coincided
with a fresh clerical offensive against Radicalism, was too liberal for the
Marshal's tastes and when it acquiesced in a motion denouncing 'Ultramontane manifestations' he resolved to be rid of it.   On the 16th May,
1877, he sent a letter to his Prime Minister which was tantamount to a
dismissal and, although he had not been defeated in the Chamber,
Simon took it as such and resigned.   The Marshal's letter included a
phrase which declared that if he had no responsibility towards Parliament he had a responsibility towards France for which he must have
regard.   This had an ominous Bonapartist ring about it and when the
Marshal then proceeded to commission the Duc de Broglie to form a
Cabinet, adjourned the protesting Chamber for a month and finally
secured the Senate's assent to its dissolution, it was evident that a first-
class constitutional conflict had arisen.

Once again the old issue of 1830 was raised.   The Marshal was
strictly within his rights.   M. Thiers had been given the right to appoint
and dismiss Ministers as he chose; he had done so freely without incurring
hostility and the Marshal had succeeded to the same powers which had
not been taken away from him by any subsequent legislation.   Similarly, one of the laws of 1875 empowered the President to dissolve the
Chamber before the expiration of its term, provided the Senate con-
curred.   But was he justified in choosing his Ministers as he wished in

defiance of the majority of the Chamber and in using his power of dissolution simply in order to try and obtain a Chamber which would work
with those Ministers? From the Republican point of view the Marshal's
claims naturally made a mockery of parliamentary government.

Thus in the summer of 1877 there took place one of the most strenuous and exciting electoral campaigns in modern French history. The
Duc de Broglie's Ministry, almost a replica of his Cabinet of 1873, used
to the full all the traditional means of pressure so highly developed under
the Second Empire and natural to any party in power. Once again
there were sweeping changes in administrative personnel, and official
candidates were general. Even the President himself took a hand in
the struggle, making speeches in various parts of the country. But all
these efforts met with little success. Although Gambetta's confident
boast in June that the 363 Republican deputies of the last Chamber
would return 400 strong in the new was not fulfilled and the Republicans
lost 36 seats, the loss was far too small to give the Right the majority.
They polled only 300,000 votes less than their opponents,[1] but won
only 207 seats. Thus a fresh clash was bound to occur when the Broglie
Government met the new Chamber. 'When the sovereign voice of
France has been heard,' cried Gambetta in one of his election speeches,
'submission or resignation must follow.' But were these the only
alternatives? Or would the Marshal, like Charles X, try yet another
dissolution or a military *coup d'état*? It is certain that he had about
him some who urged these high-handed solutions, but he resisted the
tempters and when the Broglie Government met its inevitable defeat
as soon as it encountered the new Chamber, he sought to temporize
by forming a new Cabinet in which most of the Ministers were not
members of either house and of which the head was an obscure general.
This was no less unacceptable to the Chamber, who made short shrift
of it by refusing to vote the budget unless the Ministry was chosen from
the majority. Now indeed submission or resignation were the only
alternatives. The Marshal submitted, and on December 13th, 1877, the
formation of a Ministry under Dufaure, which included Gambetta's
former colleague at Tours and Bordeaux, Freycinet, was a triumph for
parliamentary democracy.

This crisis of 1877 and the Marshal's submission were of vital importance for the future of the 'Constitution of 1875'. Henceforth no
President could hope to have any success in pitting his personal responsibility against that of the Chamber. The crisis deepened the distrust

---

[1] The Republican vote was approximately 4,000,000, the Conservative
3,700,000. cp. HALÉVY, D.: *Décadence de la liberté*, p. 32.

of 'personal power' which was already so marked among Republicans since the *coup d'état* of 1851, and thus left an unhappy legacy, whereby it became all the more difficult for the chief executive office to be held by a man of commanding personality. It meant that the Presidential power to dissolve the Chamber fell into desuetude; that Ministries would henceforward be formed from the majority in the Chamber (almost invariably from a coalition of groups which together formed a majority); and that the President of the Council would henceforth select all his Ministers, not, as hitherto, leaving the President of the Republic free to appoint to certain offices, such as the departments of Foreign Affairs, War and the Navy: in short it meant a decisive change in the balance of forces in the Constitution. The Executive had been humiliated and the Legislature was henceforth to be the preponderant power in the State, especially the Chamber with its guaranteed life of four years. How much this was to affect the character of the Republic we shall see when we come next to consider the Republic of the Republicans.

BRABANT, F. H.: *The Beginning of the Third Republic in France.* London, 1940.
BROGLIE, DUC DE: *Mémoires*, Vol. II, 1870–5. Paris, 1941.
DESCHANEL, PAUL: *Gambetta.* Paris, 1919.
DREYFUS, ROBERT: *La République de Monsieur Thiers* (1871–3). Paris, 1930.
GAMBETTA, L.: *Lettres*, 1868–82, ed. D. Halévy and E. Pillias. Paris, 1938.
HALÉVY, D.: *La fin des notables.* Paris, 1930.
HALÉVY, D.: *La République des Ducs.* Paris, 1937.
HANOTAUX, G.: *Histoire de la fondation de la Troisième République.* Paris, 1925.
HENREY, ROBERT: ed., *Letters from Paris, 1870–5, Written by C. de B., a Political Informant to the Head of the London House of Rothschild.* London, 1942.
POMARET, CHARLES: *Monsieur Thiers et son siècle.* Paris, 1948.
SAINT-VALRY, G. DE: *Souvenirs et réflexions politiques.* Paris, 1886.

X

THE REPUBLIC OF THE REPUBLICANS

THE triumph of parliamentary government in 1877 was also a triumph for the Republicans—for the Republic represented by Thiers and Gambetta. In 1871 Thiers had appeared to be poles apart from Gambetta, the man whom he had dubbed a 'raging madman', but since that time, through his breach with the Right, he had moved towards the Left while Gambetta had moved away from it. 'If the Republic is a form of government,' wrote the Duc de Broglie in his memoirs, 'the French Republican Party is not a party capable of governing,' and he made it clear that for him the term Republican was still synonymous with Revolutionary.[1] 1792, 1830, 1848, 1870, 1871 all seemed to bear this out; but since 1871 Thiers and Gambetta each in his way had done their best to divest it of its revolutionary connotation. Thiers' first contribution had been to make the form of government respectable; his second was to begin to make the Party respectable, and in this he found an unexpected but powerful ally in Gambetta. In 1869 Gambetta had subscribed to the famous Belleville electoral programme, which included demands for the election of all public officials, the suppression of standing armies and the abolition of 'privileges and monopolies'; but by 1875 he had shed much of his Radicalism and taken upon himself a new task which, as an acute observer, Saint-Valry, remarked in May of that year, was fundamentally much the same as that of Ollivier a few years earlier. It was to organize and discipline the democracy; to give it 'cadres'; to raise from it 'a new governmental personnel, a new ruling class'.[2] The heroic age of the Republican movement, the age of the men of 1848, of the Armand Barbès and the Louis Blancs was now over. The 'seventies were to be years of preparation of another kind, of preparation for the ascension to power of what Gambetta called 'a new social stratum'. Essentially this meant the rise of the class from which Gambetta himself had sprung, the class of the *petit bourgeois*, of the small shopkeepers, the clerks and the artisans, the class which

[1] *Mémoires du Duc de Broglie*, II, p. 43. cp. also pp. 89–90.

[2] SAINT-VALRY, G. DE: *Souvenirs et réflexions politiques*, I, p. 119 ff.

had shown its economic importance by the way in which it swelled the ranks of investors and by its active part in the work of reconstruction after the war. Gambetta was determined that these people who were such a vital element in the life of the nation, and potentially in the Republican movement, should be fit to share in the responsibilities of democratic government and that Republicans generally should show themselves ready for power. In seeking this end he ceased to be a Radical and became what he called an Opportunist—a name which was to stick to his followers down to the 'nineties. In other words he was now the advocate of a policy of realism: doctrinaire tenets were shelved in favour of immediately practical tasks and the electorate was reassured that if Gambetta was a stalwart opponent of monarchy and clericalism he was far from being revolutionary and red. Thus in the crisis of 1877 there was co-operation between the veteran Thiers and Gambetta, and it was believed that, if all went well, Thiers would before long once again preside over a Republican government in which Gambetta would then take a chief place. The mantle of Thiers would give Gambetta respectability beyond question, and would ensure the final establishment of a Republic which would be fully Republican in spirit as well as in name, and would guarantee rather than menace social order. Unfortunately this great partnership was never consummated, for Thiers died suddenly during the election campaign of 1877. It was left for Gambetta to complete the work with the aid of lesser men and under a President in whom he was to find an enemy instead of a friend.

But before Republican policies could be freely introduced it was necessary for the Republicans to capture the two strongholds of power which still remained in the hands of their antagonists. In little over a year after the Presidential 'submission' of 1877 their victory was complete. As a result of the first triennial elections to the Senate, in January 1879, they gained a comfortable majority of fifty or so in the Upper House. At once they proceeded to exploit their success and to reverse the work of Conservative governments by filling the administration and judiciary with loyal Republicans. This was but a natural swing of the pendulum, but when the Cabinet went further and proposed to remove a number of elderly generals, his old comrades, MacMahon could stand no more. A lonely figure now, more and more uncomfortable in an uncongenial, if not actively hostile political world, he had retained his post so long only from a sense of duty. But this tampering with the army was the last straw and after refusing to sign the decree of removal on January 30th, 1879, the Marshal, first president of the Republic under the 'Constitution of 1875', resigned his office nearly two years before his term was due to expire. Chosen originally by the National Assembly to keep the succession open for a sovereign, he had the humiliation of handing over his post to an elderly Republican lawyer of humble ancestry. That same evening the Chamber and Senate, meeting together as a National Assembly or Congress, elected M. Jules Grévy to be his successor.

Thus, with the disappearance from the political stage of the Duc de Magenta the Republic of the Dukes came finally to an end. And its end meant more than the end of a particular form of Republicanism—of Republicanism without Republicans. It was a social as well as a political revolution; for although Conservatism was still, as we shall see, to be a considerable force in the country owing to its continued association with the clergy, the army, big banking interests, and for a brief time still, with some members of the civil service, the old aristocracy were never again during the Third Republic to wield power and govern the country as they had in the 'seventies. They might still serve with distinction in the army and the diplomatic or colonial services, but in all the multiplicity of Cabinets between 1879 and 1940 it is very rare to find even the particle 'de' in front of a Minister's name. The new social strata had no such adornments.

Now that the Republicans held all the levers of power they were concerned to consolidate their victory and free to carry out a truly Republican policy. They, too, had early assumed the cloak of virtue and, like the Monarchists, attributed the débâcle of 1870 to the levity and licence of the Second Empire. Accordingly they liked to picture their régime as one in which austere excellence and elevated morals would go hand in hand with Republican simplicity. But foreign observers soon became sceptical of the virtues and showed little enthusiasm for the simplicity in so far as M. Grévy's drab and economical establishment at the Élysée was its model. At the same time, though far from revolutionary, the Republic was placed under the sign of the old revolutionary slogan 'Liberty, Equality and Fraternity' and all Republicans would have held that one at least of its missions was now to give real content to those words by the establishment of a true political democracy.[1] It is, however, a particularly striking fact, especially when we remember 1848, that in 1879, thirty years later, no Republican group of any significance in parliament goes seriously beyond this political aim. The Radicals of 1869 in a singularly laboured phrase of the Belleville programme referred to the social question in only the vaguest terms.

[1] BARNI, J.: *Manuel républicain* (1872): '*L'admirable devise de nos pères: Liberté, Égalité, Fraternité, en résume les principes fondamentaux.*'

Ten years later their successors, the Radicals of 1879, the Opportunists
and the Moderates are hardly more explicit or, if they are, the social
part of their programmes definitely takes second place. The reasons
are not far to seek. The social revolutionary aspect of the Second
Republic was the one which had done most to turn the electorate against
Republicanism, just as its social revolutionary possibilities had done
most to rouse them against the Commune, with the result that until
1879 most of the socialistically inclined Republicans were in exile.
The others—Radicals, Opportunists and so on—sprung almost wholly
from the bourgeoisie themselves, had for the most part received their
political education by participating in a political struggle against the
Second Empire. Thus they and their successors in power in the 'eighties
and most of the 'nineties either, like Thiers, distrusted social change;
or were simply not interested; or feared it since it was dangerous. In
fact, as we have seen, the Republicans' success in the critical struggle
against the Monarchists in the 'seventies was not a little due to the
conversion of important Orleanists. Such a conversion would have
been impossible had social and economic change loomed large in the
Republican programme, for the Orleanists were closely associated with
the big bourgeoisie. Of this no doubt the Opportunists were well
aware. There is also another factor which may perhaps help to explain
why political and not social problems were the main preoccupation:
France was still predominantly a land of peasants—a land in which
some sixty-five per cent of the population were still country dwellers
with little direct interest in the social problems of workers in the
towns.

Hence the first measures of the Republicans in power are concerned
with the political consolidation of victory, the political education of the
democracy and the extension of political liberties. In the first place
the advent of the Republic of the Republicans is confirmed by a number of acts which have a symbolical significance. The return of the
Chambers to Paris in 1879 and the partial amnesty for Communards,
followed by a full one two years later, were evidence of the spirit of
Fraternity which actuated the new régime, marked the reconciliation of
government and capital, and showed that the Republicans proposed to
welcome at least all Republicans into the fold. In 1880 the observance
of July 14th, the anniversary of the Fall of the Bastille, as a day of
national festival for the first time since the Great Revolution (it had been
observed as a religious festival in 1790), and its celebration amongst
other things by a great military review, emphasized both that the Republic was the heir of the Great Revolution and that it was a patriotic

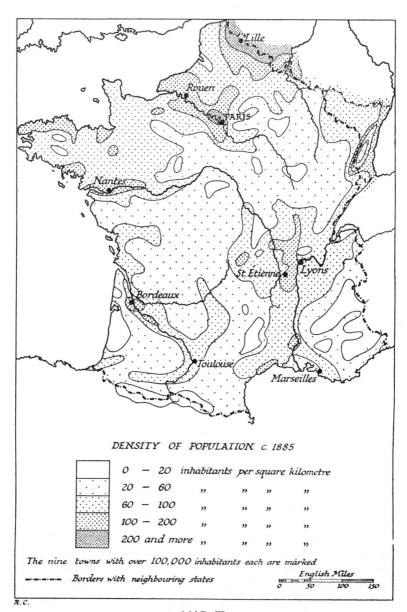

DENSITY OF POPULATION c. 1885

	0 — 20 inhabitants per square kilometre
	20 — 60 „ „ „ „
	60 — 100 „ „ „ „
	100 — 200 „ „ „ „
	200 and more „ „ „ „

The nine towns with over 100,000 inhabitants each are marked

—·—·—·— Borders with neighbouring states

English Miles
0   50   100   150

R.C.

MAP III

régime, proud of the revival of a national army. Similarly the inauguration of a big programme of public works by Freycinet showed
that the Republic had a care for the well-being of its citizens and the
dignity of the State, and last, but not least, may have served to convert
many lukewarm electors by giving them work.[1] An egalitarian,
democratic breeze blew through the Senate and certain administrative
services when by a constitutional revision in 1884 the creation of more
life senators was abandoned, provision being made for the remaining
quarter of the Upper House to be elected for nine years just like their
brethren, and when recruitment by competitive examination was introduced into the Diplomatic Service and later into other branches such
as the Conseil d'État, the Cour des Comptes, and the Inspection des
Finances. No less important were the laws restoring or extending
certain freedoms; the laws of 1884 leaving all French communes, except
Paris, free to elect their mayors (although they were still subject in
various ways to a considerable measure of prefectorial control) and
admitting a partial freedom of association by the grant to workers in
the same profession of the right to form unions for the defence of their
economic interests. But of all the reforms of these early years those
to which many Republicans attached supreme importance, which were
most contentious, roused the deepest passions and had the most far-
reaching consequences, were undoubtedly the education laws sponsored
by Jules Ferry.

After Thiers and Gambetta Jules Ferry was undoubtedly the third
most commanding figure among the founders of the Republic. Born
near St. Dié in the Vosges, trained like Gambetta at the bar, he had won
his political spurs in the same opposition struggle at the end of the
Second Empire and shown a faculty for mordant wit in a series of
articles with the felicitous title of 'Les Comptes fantastiques d'Haussmann'. But in 1870, while the younger man was virtual ruler of the
provinces, Ferry had had the narrower and more ungrateful task of
being responsible for Parisian administration. This included the distribution and eventually the rationing of food supplies, and inevitably brought
him unpopularity with a populace ill-accustomed to such privations.
Hence the nickname 'Ferry-Famine', soon to be followed by that of
'Ferry-Massacre' on account of his part in putting down the attempted
insurrection of January 22nd, in Paris. But, in spite of this unpopularity
with a section of the Parisians, Ferry's stature and influence continued
to grow in the 'seventies. He, too, took an active share in convincing
the electorate of the Republicans' fitness to govern and in time he

[1] cp. HALÉVY, D.: Décadence de la liberté, pp. 45–6.

became the acknowledged leader of one of their two main parliamentary groups, the Gauche Républicaine, the other being Gambetta's Union Républicaine. Finally he entered the Waddington Cabinet of February 1879, the first of Grévy's presidency, as Minister of Public Instruction and continued to hold this post both in the succeeding Ministry and in the Cabinet after that, which he himself headed. Thus, in spite of Cabinet changes, he was in charge of the country's education for nearly three years. This was time enough in which to put through a sweeping programme of reform.

'The most urgent of all reforms,' Gambetta had declared when he accepted the Belleville programme of 1869, 'must be the liberation of universal suffrage from every sort of tutelage, obstacle, pressure and corruption.' Universal suffrage had in 1849, 1851, 1852 voted and would again in 1870 and 1871 vote Royalist or Bonapartist. The problem was to ensure that it should vote Republican and the remedy persistently prescribed by Republicans was compulsory primary education, and moreover primary education which should be not only compulsory but also free[1] and above all in the hands of laymen. In fact we are now approaching another momentous stage in the great battle of Church and Revolution which had been waged on many fronts almost continuously throughout the century. During the Restoration and the July Monarchy, as we have seen, one of its main aspects had been the struggle for control of secondary and higher education: now the scene broadens to take in the field of primary education. In Republican eyes illiteracy—estimated by Ferry in 1879 at fifteen per cent of the population—and clerical influence in education were the main obstacles in the way of the conversion of France into a free political democracy. The flirtation of Church and Republic in 1848 had been but a brief romantic embrace. Everything that had happened since had tended to force the two farther apart.

On the one hand the Church viewed with increasing alarm the development of new forces which seemed to be still further hastening the disintegration of France as a Christian society. Enthralled by the vista of indefinite material progress opened up by the Industrial Revolution and all its attendant discoveries, the young intelligentsia believed that science and free inquiry were the keys to all things. In their brave new world God and religion had little place and the fact that so many of them were Republican and therefore politically opposed to the Conservative Catholics increased their intellectual hostility. So it is

---

[1] The abolition of fees had already been encouraged by Victor Duruy during the Second Empire and effected in 8,000 Communes.

that the majority of the brilliant young men trained at the Ecole Normale after 1848 and the majority of the Republican leaders—that is, those who were not Protestants—and the small Protestant minority was to play a part in the Third Republic out of all proportion to its numbers— were agnostics, and many of them devotees of the pseudo-scientific creed of Positivism which was founded by Auguste Comte and had an extraordinary influence in the second half of the century. This new intellectual attitude undoubtedly widened the breach between the Conservatives and the Republicans for many of whom, too, cult of the Great Revolution had become almost a religion, and, in so far as it affected their political thinking, intensified the political offensive of the Left against the Church. Long before 1870, many writers such as Edgar Quinet, Vacherot, Prévost-Paradol and others had demanded the separation of Church and State; it was one of the requirements of the Belleville programme, and, as we have seen, was actually put into effect by the Commune in Paris. Moreover, the anti-clerical materialistic propaganda was highly organized. The Ligue de l'Enseignment, founded by Jean Macé in 1866, the sectarian teaching of the freemasons, who were wholeheartedly Republican and whose numbers increased from some 50,000 to some 200,000 between 1871–7, the publication of a host of cheap brochures and booklets written for popular consumption, contributed to the diffusion through ever-widening circles of French people of an intellectual and moral outlook wholly at variance with the traditional teaching of the Church. No wonder then that in the rise of the modern Republican State the Church and the Conservatives saw the gravest threat to all that they held most dear.

On the other hand, the growth of Ultramontanism among French Catholics, their loyalty to a Pope who was so openly at war with Liberalism, who had promulgated the Syllabus of Modern Errors and the Decree of Infallibility, their violent campaigns for the defence or for the restoration of the Temporal power before and after 1870, their unconcealed support of the Royalists, and their outbursts against Radicalism led the Republicans to see in them a reactionary force which was constantly guided by political ambitions and irreconcilably hostile to most of the ideas for which they themselves stood. Moreover, since 1848, it was a force which in many ways appeared to have gained ground. The Loi Falloux of 1851 had, as we have seen,[1] confirmed their freedom to have their own schools. The number of religious orders, some legally authorized and some not, had greatly increased during the

[1] P. 84, *ante.*

Second Empire so that in 1878, in addition to the ordinary clergy, there were no less than 128,000 nuns and 32,000 monks (compared with 34,000 and 3,000 respectively in 1851) while some two out of five million French schoolchildren were being taught in Catholic *écoles libres* mainly run by the regular clergy. The value of the property held by the authorized communities was no less than 421,000,000 francs, or £16,840,000,[1] while the unauthorized bodies, of whom the Jesuits were the most notable, accounted for another 160,000,000 francs. The education of women, and the organization of charitable relief, were still, as they had been for centuries, almost wholly in the hands of the Church. The strength of clerical passion and anti-clerical feeling had already been strikingly demonstrated in the 'sixties under the Second Empire, when more passion was aroused over clerical than over almost any other issues in that momentous decade. After their experience of the rule of Moral Order between 1873 and 1877 there was hardly a Republican who could not have been firmly convinced that the power of the Church had increased, was increasing and ought to be diminished. Accordingly, when in 1876 Gambetta, echoing a cry already uttered in the 'sixties, thundered 'Clericalism—there is the enemy', he knew that he would rally Republicans of every shade. It was therefore both natural and logical that the first big offensive of the Republicans to consolidate their power should be anti-clerical in direction. But it was also a happy coincidence that such a policy was likely to win the approval of such powers as Germany, Italy and Austria, which were at this time concerned with their own struggles of Church and State, and that once the French Republican was engaged upon his favourite sport of *manger du curé* he would have less inclination to think about *revanche* or social problems. Finally, in addition to the desire to suppress illiteracy and to restrict clerical influence there was a further argument in favour of compulsory education—victorious Prussia had had it before the war of 1870, and it was widely said that her victory was the victory of the Prussian schoolmasters as well as of the Prussian generals.

So the most significant of the education bills brought forward by Jules Ferry was the bill, eventually passed in 1882, which made primary education free, compulsory and secular—that is to say, which banned religious and clerical supervision from all state primary schools. But another of his measures directed at strengthening state control over higher education won still greater notoriety since it contained article No. 7, which forbade members of unauthorized congregations to direct

---

[1] the contemporary sterling equivalent.

or teach in any educational establishment. After a tremendous debate this article was rejected by the Senate, but Government and Chamber were not prepared to admit defeat and immediately decided in favour of a rigid enforcement of the Concordat. Thus once again, as in 1828 and 1845, there is a State offensive against the unauthorized congregations, of whom the Jesuits were the chief, once again an attempt to apply a law which had so often remained unobserved. In March 1880, decrees were issued ordering the dissolution and disbandment of the Jesuits within three months and of all other unauthorized congregations who failed within a prescribed time limit to obtain permission to reside and operate in France. Conservatives and Catholics were passionately indignant, a number of communities refused to obey the decrees, some 400 magistrates and officials resigned rather than enforce them, and, when troops had in some instances to be called in to secure the expulsion of male communities (the female were unmolested), it seemed almost as though a new war of religion was at hand. But the Government remained unmoved—the nineteenth century was not the sixteenth—it had the full support of the Chamber and the numbers actually dissolved were small enough. Moreover, the resignation of Conservatively disposed magistrates and officials simply gave the Government an opportunity to replace them by others whose Republicanism was not in doubt. Indeed, in his second premiership, in 1883, Jules Ferry went further; he suspended for three months the legislation providing that magistrates should be irremovable, thus giving himself the opportunity to remove another 614 whose clerical sympathies had been too pronounced for Republican taste.

These measures were only part of a general offensive against clericalism. Two other educational laws of some importance deprived Catholic Universities of the right to confer degrees and made State provision for the first time for secondary education for women. (Yet much later, in a book published in 1930, M. André Siegfried could still write that there was no type of Frenchman more representative than the anticlerical deputy whose wife was a devout Catholic and had her daughters educated in a convent.[1] The tradition of conventual education for women was deeply rooted and not to be broken in a day.) Furthermore, the clergy were eliminated from representation on the reformed council for the direction of higher education and from the administration of charitable organizations. Military chaplains were abolished, Sisters of Mercy were gradually ousted from hospitals, divorce was re-

[1] *Tableau des partis en France*, p. 65.

established and the estimates of the Ministry of Public Worship were cut down. This offensive, backed by all the powers of the State, inevitably met with considerable success. The influence of the clergy upon many sides of French life diminished and there is no doubt that between 1880 and 1900 the decline in religious practice, already noticeable under the Second Empire, continued and was if anything accelerated. This was natural enough for, as M. Daniel Halévy has pointed out, the secular school, by eliminating from school teaching such fundamental words as 'God, soul, hope and prayer', suppressed the very instruments of religious thought.[1] In their place came as pale substitutes the jargon of civics and State morality. Furthermore, in the village schoolmasters the Republic now had a valuable new instrument for increasing its hold. Addressing a gathering of these men Ferry made quite clear what was expected of them: 'As citizens you have been enfranchized by the French Revolution; as teachers you are going to be emancipated by the Republic of 1880: how could you not love and through your teaching bring others to love the Revolution and the Republic? This policy is a national policy.'[2] When many schoolmasters, often the only educated people in the village apart from the priest, acted as secretaries to the local Mairie their value as local political agents was further enhanced. Moreover, although, officially, State schools were to be neutral so far as religious questions were concerned, the very circumstances of their creation as agencies for a secular State meant that the teaching in them often enough had a distinctly anti-clerical bias. In Great Britain parson and schoolmaster were often allies—in Republican France they were almost certain to be rivals and foes. And here indeed lies the tragedy of the France of the Revolution, a tragedy whose darkness was deepened by the laws of 1880–81. The abolition of religious instruction in state schools makes absolute the educational cleavage between the two Frances —clerical and secular, black and red—and, in spite of the multitude of acute social and economic questions which have come to overlay it, this dichotomy is still of fundamental importance. At the time, in the 'eighties, the introduction of what Broglie called 'the Godless school', and all the accompanying anti-clerical measures, inevitably led most of the clergy and devout laity to regard the Republic as a rule of Satan,

---

[1] *Société d'histoire de la Troisième République, Bulletin No. 16*, p. 135.

[2] cit. RECLUS, M.: *Jules Ferry*, p. 220. Thus, as M. Daniel Halévy has remarked (*Histoire d'une histoire*, p. 64), 'The University, daughter of the Revolution, teaches the Revolution.'

its 'Fraternity' and the emphasis on 'Unity' within the 'Patrie' in its new text-books as mere hollow mockeries. Once again, as for all previous régimes, the great problem was that of achieving a genuine national unity. Can the Third Republic ever succeed in having more than the negative quality of being the régime which divides Frenchmen least? Can it ever be a régime accepted freely by all parties, however vigorously they contend with one another within the Republican framework?

Much must obviously depend on the tact and political wisdom of the contending forces. On the Republican side the one man, who, had he lived long enough, might eventually have had the authority and power to rally the Conservatives was he who had launched the offensive against clericalism. Great hopes were entertained that Gambetta would at an early stage of the new régime form a strong Government which would do much both to consolidate the Republic at home and to make it a force to be conjured with abroad. But Grévy, who envied Gambetta's popularity and believed him to be dangerous because more than any other man he was identified by public opinion with the idea of *revanche*, refused to call upon Gambetta to form a Ministry and 'the great man' of the régime saw his supporters in office while he himself remained President of the Chamber. Inevitably he exercised influence upon policy through the men whom he had himself educated for government; but as Ministry succeeded Ministry and Gambetta still was not summoned, the intriguers, the jealous, and the henchmen of Grévy put it about that Gambetta preferred to evade responsibility and exercise a hidden dictatorship. When at last in November 1881 Grévy decided to ask him to form a Cabinet it was in the knowledge that Gambetta's influence had been largely diminished by his own manœuvring. 'The Great Ministry', which public opinion had expected to be composed of all the foremost Republican politicians, could not be formed and instead Gambetta had to content himself with a Cabinet of personal friends and men who were comparatively little known. It lasted only two months and within less than a year of its fall Gambetta, still no more than forty-four, was dead of acute peritonitis. During these last years he had become steadily more moderate: meeting and fascinating the Prince of Wales and aristocrats like the Marquis de Galliffet and the Comte du Lau, welcoming and appreciating the great importance of the accession of Leo XIII to succeed Pope Pius IX, declaring that anti-clericalism was not an article for export, perhaps entertaining hopes that even the Alsatian question could be settled by diplomacy. All competent observers were agreed that with him there passed away the one commanding figure of the Republic who was sufficiently generous and broad-minded to have created something like a real unity in France.[1] After his death Jules Ferry was the man who stood out as the ablest of the Republicans and it was to him that the men of Gambetta's 'Union Républicaine' rallied, so that for two years he was able to maintain a strong Government based upon a solid Opportunist majority. Then he in turn fell in circumstances which throw singularly little lustre upon the Chamber and virtually ended his political career.

The occasion of Ferry's fall was an incident in the process of colonial expansion which was the last great achievement of these early years of the Republican Republic, and which Ferry himself did more than any other politician to support and encourage. As we have seen, the first years after the débacle of 1870 were necessarily years of *recueillement*, overseas as well as at home. The general opinion was that France must now conserve all her resources ready for any emergency in Europe, that she must think of *revanche* as her foremost duty, remember that Germany was the great enemy and keep her eyes fixed on 'the blue line of the Vosges', and it was in harmony with such a view that the Broglie Government in 1874 reduced France's Far Eastern commitments by the evacuation of Tonkin. Yet there was still a handful of men who, moved by the spirit of adventure, the love of exploration, the hope of financial gain, or the desire to extend French influence in the world, sought to carry on that expansionist movement which had received such a powerful impetus under the Second Empire; and at home there were men with vision enough to back them in spite of popular distrust or apathy. Moreover, as France's material recovery progressed and she became a factor once again to be reckoned with in international affairs, other powers took a hand in encouraging or discouraging these aspirations. In 1878, the year of the first great exhibition to be held in Paris under the Republic, when France formally re-entered the councils of the European powers by attending the Congress of Berlin, both Lord Salisbury, ready to compensate France for Great Britain's own annexation of Cyprus, and Bismarck, anxious to divert her attention from the Vosges and to estrange her from Italy, encouraged her to move into Tunis. With this the building of a new colonial Empire was resumed.

Ever since the conquest of Algiers France had cast an eye upon Tunis, still nominally a dependency of the decaying Turkish Empire, but the subjugation of Algeria had been so long and costly that she had hesitated to take on more North African territory. Moreover, a formidable insurrection in Algeria in 1871 merely increased the general reaction

[1] cp. e.g. BODLEY, J. E. C.: *The Church in France*, p. 52.

against overseas adventures. In the striking last chapter of his 'France Nouvelle' Prévost-Paradol had urged that France had no hope of maintaining her relative position in the world unless there were a speedy and sufficient increase in the number of Frenchmen. Her great opportunity, he said, was to colonize Algeria which was rich, close at hand and easily defensible, and then he went further: 'May the day soon come when our fellow citizens, too straitly confined in our African France, will overflow into Morocco and Tunisia and found the Mediterranean Empire which will be not only a satisfaction to our pride, but certainly in the future state of the world, the last resource of our greatness.'[1] Prophetic wish! for although the increase in the number of Frenchmen was to be obtained not by colonization—the French were, as ever, slow to expatriate themselves[2]—but by assimilation and a Roman extension of citizenship, in 1940 the African and Mediterranean Empire, built by the Third Republic almost in despite of public opinion, was indeed to appear the last resource of French greatness! Yet in the years from 1878 to 1881 it was not considerations of the kind foreshadowed by Prévost-Paradol, so much as the wish to ensure that Tunisia should be French rather than Italian, which induced France to go ahead and begin a new forward policy which was approved by Gambetta as well as by Ferry. Italy, too, was showing expansionist ambitions, and her considerable interests in Tunisia suggested that she, too, might wish to annex it. So it was, that, after a short military campaign involving some 40,000 troops, France in May 1881 induced the Bey of Tunis to sign the Treaty of Bardo which converted his territories into a French protectorate, and by the end of the year, after punitive expeditions against tribes of the interior, virtually the whole country was under French control.[3] But, whereas anti-clericalism was a policy which united Republicans, colonial expansion divided them, and the Radicals, holding aloft the standard of narrow *revanchard* patriotism, combined with the Right in attacking the Tunisian venture, attributing the worst possible motives to Ferry and his supporters and so weakening his position that he was obliged to resign in November 1881. Only the

[1] *La France nouvelle*, p. 416.

[2] And when they did so, they often preferred to go to a country where they would not be liable to military service. It is noteworthy that nearly a million Frenchmen emigrated to the New World during the nineteenth and twentieth centuries, mostly to the U.S.A. and the Argentine. cp. CHATELAIN, A.: *Les migrations françaises*, Annales January-March, 1947.

[3] See Map IV.

intervention of Gambetta had saved the maintenance of the protectorate itself from being called into question.

The fall of the Ferry Cabinet under such circumstances and the passionately bitter campaigns of Left and Right had momentous consequences at the eastern end of the Mediterranean. The vast extravagance of another nominal vassal of the Turkish Sultan, the Khedive of Egypt, had brought him under the control of his French and English creditors and given France and Great Britain such an influence in the Nile delta and valley as to cause a nationalist rising in protest. Gambetta's policy during his short-lived ministry was to co-operate with Great Britain in a vigorous defence of European interests, but his successor, Freycinet, remembering Tunis, was far more timorous. He refused to join England in a naval bombardment of Alexandria, and, when eventually after much hesitation he plucked up courage to ask for credits for an expeditionary force to join with the British in an occupation of the Suez Canal area, the demand was rejected by the Chamber. Thus, once again, a Cabinet headed by one of the most prominent, if not the most forceful, of the Republican politicians was defeated on a question of overseas policy. Great Britain remained in Egypt alone and reaped the profits of a vigorous policy, whereas France had thrown away her opportunity to share in them. Unfortunately the knowledge that her loss was due to her own indecision and timidity served only to increase France's jealousy of her more successful rival and the sour grapes of Egypt were to play an important part in embittering Anglo-French relations during the next twenty years. Yet it is indeed doubtful whether those relations would have been much more cordial even if France had stayed in Egypt and exercised condominium there with Great Britain. The tradition of colonial rivalry was still very strong overseas and a condominium, instead of bringing the two countries closer together, might no less easily have been a cause of constant friction and intrigue.

Nevertheless, French expansion was not to be checked by the Chamber's censures either on the Tunisian or the Egyptian question. By now, after mature reflection, Ferry had become a convinced colonialist. He saw in colonial policy the inevitable result of the policy of industrialization to which France like the other great countries of Western Europe was irretrievably committed, and the secure majority which he enjoyed for a considerable time during his second premiership meant that the years 1883–5 witnessed a fresh forward movement. France's foothold in Madagascar, where Great Britain was again her chief rival, was strengthened; the explorations of Brazza in the Congo basin were so effectively followed up that the International Congress of Berlin in 1884-5 consented to give formal recognition to the creation of a French Congo—a colony larger than France herself, cheaply won at a cost of some 300,000 francs;[1] and last, but not least, in the Far East Tonkin was reconquered and a protectorate established over Annam. This advance in the Far East, however, led to an undeclared war with China, Annam's suzerain, and it was not until the summer of 1885 that the Chinese finally recognized France's new predominance. Before the achievement of this striking success, Ferry, the man at home who was mainly responsible, had been cast to the winds by a frenzied Chamber in one of the most extraordinary outbursts of passion and panic ever witnessed in a French Parliament. The report of a minor reverse at Langson in Tonkin followed by an urgent demand for reinforcements from the general on the spot, at once roused all the enemies of the Republic, all the enemies of the Ferry Ministry (which was not unnaturally tending to lose ground after two years of office) and all the antagonists of colonial expansion, both within and without the Chamber, in the press and in public meetings, to whip up a passionate campaign suggesting that Ferry's insensate imperialism after a prodigal expenditure of men and money was now leading France to a humiliating defeat. When the Government at once ordered reinforcements and asked the Chamber for a fresh credit of 200 million francs, the storm burst. All Ferry's opponents and all those who remembered Mexico and then thought of Germany rose up against the Prime Minister in fury and revolt. He was denounced as a tool of Germany. In a speech of extreme bitterness the formidable Radical leader Clemenceau even went so far as to accuse the Cabinet of high treason. All sense of proportion, all sense that the verdict should not be given until the facts were fully known, were swept aside and Jules Ferry, who already had certain but secret information that China was about to sue for peace, could only bow before the tempest and resign. Outside in the streets crowds shouted for the death of 'Ferry-Tonkin' and Ferry never fully recovered from the wave of unpopularity which virtually swept him out of public life. While, ironically enough, the same Chamber which had rejected his demand for credits granted them a few weeks later to his successor, the new Chamber of December 1885 rejected a motion for the evacuation of Tonkin by only one vote. Thus, as precariously as the Republic itself, the Republic's new Far Eastern Empire came to stay.

So, with the overthrow of Jules Ferry there ends the age, as we may call it, of the Founders of the Republic; but not the age of

[1] BAUMONT, M.: *L'essor industriel et l'impérialisme colonial*, p. 96.

Opportunist government. That, as we shall see, was to continue for several years more in spite of much discomfiture, disturbance and discredit.

BAUMONT, MAURICE: *L'essor industriel et l'impérialisme colonial* (1878-1904). Paris, 1937.

BRUUN, G.: *Clemenceau*. Harvard, 1943.

DESCHANEL, PAUL: *Gambetta*. Paris, 1919.

GAMBETTA, L.: *Lettres*, 1868-82. ed. D. Halévy and E. Pillias. Paris, 1938.

JACKSON, J. HAMPDEN: *Clemenceau and the Third Republic*. London, 1946.

RECLUS, MAURICE: *Jules Ferry*. Paris, 1947.

SAINT-VALRY, G. DE: *Souvenirs et réflexions politiques*. Paris, 1886.

VIZETELLY, E. A.: *Republican France, 1870-1912*. London, 1912.

XI

THE YEARS OF CRISIS AND SCANDAL

THE achievements of the Third Republic during the first ten years of the 'Constitution of 1875' were thus considerable: a great programme of public works, re-entry into the concert of Europe, and the acquisition of new overseas dominions all helped to restore prestige; while legislation at home, if it did little to make for unity among Frenchmen, at least strengthened the Republican hold on place and power and prepared the education of a new generation whose fidelity to the régime would be beyond question.

But there was a reverse side to this medal. Reviving material prosperity was tempered by a severe agricultural depression, which also affected many other parts of Europe and for which the huge influx of cheap wheat and meat from the newly developed prairies of the American Middle West was largely responsible. In France, where tenant-farmers were particularly hard hit, this depression had been aggravated by a deadly outbreak of phylloxera which wrought havoc in most of the vineyards and caused French wine production to fall from eighty-three million hectolitres in 1875 to twenty-four million in 1889; and the distress in country districts was made still worse by the crash in 1882 of the Union Générale Bank to which thousands of small farmers and rural investors had committed their savings. This depression had two main effects: it accelerated the movement of population from countryside to town, from agriculture to big industry; and it reduced the demand for many kinds of consumer goods, thus bringing on a parallel depression in industry. In consequence, by 1885 there was considerable economic distress and social discontent among various classes of the community; and the number of hostile critics of the régime had considerably increased.

The Republic, indeed, had its critics and foes on the Left as well as on the Right. The Radicals held that the Opportunists had stopped half-way; they still wanted separation of Church and State, a revision of the Constitution whereby the Senate would be abolished as a reactionary institution, and a much more thorough purge of administrative personnel. Further Left still there were many groups which had either come into being or gained new vigour as a result of the return of the Communard exiles in 1879 and 1881; and the workers had begun to organize anew in Congresses and unions. In 1879, under the influences of Jules Guesde, a workers' congress at Marseilles had declared in favour of the formation of a Socialist Party to conduct a class struggle in accordance with the collectivist doctrines of Karl Marx. Accordingly, in the following year, the Parti Ouvrier Français was founded, and for the first time Marxism was to become an important disruptive influence within the French State and Society. But it had no monopoly and while the economic distress afforded a fertile field for propaganda, there were rivals or dissident groups, the Blanquists, the Anarchists, the Possibilists after 1881, and the Alemanists after 1890, who competed with the Guesdists for influence among the working classes. The main characteristics of French Socialism during this time are its divisions, the mutual excommunications of its various sects, and the general distrust of parliamentary methods and advocacy of revolutionary violence. Faced by bitter and often highly destructive Radical criticism in Parliament and by a growing number of quasi-revolutionary groups outside, it was no wonder that the Opportunists sometimes believed that the danger to the régime came as much from the Left as from the Right.

The reverse side of the medal also showed itself in the working of parliamentary sovereignty which had been far from shedding lustre on Republican democracy. In fact the crisis of 1877 had been a calamity, for it had in effect deprived the 'Constitution of 1875' of its most valuable safeguard against the irresponsibility of the legislature. Once the menace of dissolution was removed the deputies were veritable kings of the Republic, free to do what they liked for four years. 'The Chamber' it has been well said, 'did not want any person or institution to be potent save itself; to the degree that a large assembly can govern a country, the Chamber would govern it. What the Chamber could not do would not be done—and in the Radical Republican tradition there was a strong element of anarchical suspicion of all government. Above all, that tradition was suspicious of the government of one man.'[1] The result was that the Palais Bourbon became a preserve in which shifting groups played elaborate games of intrigue in order to gain office and in which Ministries were overturned with light-hearted impunity. The system of 'interpellation', which enabled any deputy to call upon a Minister to explain his policy on any issue and necessitated an immediate general debate before the business of the day could be proceeded

[1] BROGAN, D. W.: *The Development of Modern France*, p. 166.

with, also contributed to instability, the more so that if the vote in the debate went against the Government it was expected to resign, no matter how trivial the issue. Thus legislation of national interest and continuity of national policy were alike at the mercy of political manœuvring; envy in Bodley's words 'condemned excellence to obscurity and exposed capability to ostracism',[1] and the Third Republic became a byword for ministerial instability.

Moreover, with the instability of Cabinets went the mediocrity of the deputies. The contrast between the calibre of the men of the National Assembly of 1871-5 and the Parliaments of the 'eighties and 'nineties was glaring. The Republic might produce great administrators and ambassadors—its legislators were of a far lower order. Paul Cambon, Gambetta, Lord Lyons, all deplored it, and while some like Cambon or Renan believed that 'the advance of mediocrity was the law of democracies',[2] others like Gambetta thought that a change in the electoral law would provide a remedy. Under the system known as *scrutin d'arrondissement* whereby each arrondissement elected a deputy (or deputies, if its numbers exceeded 100,000) the nomination of Republican candidates for parliament tended to fall into the hands of small committees of petty bourgeois officials, shopkeepers, schoolmasters or rentiers, often self-appointed, whose one concern was to secure the return of a deputy who would look after local interests. Thus a parochial outlook or *esprit de clocher* too often prevailed over a national view in constituency and in Chamber alike. Gambetta believed that the substitution of the method known as *scrutin de liste* would lead to the election of men of greater intellect and broader vision and, when he was Prime Minister, he brought in a bill for the revision of the electoral procedure. The bill was rejected and the 'Grand Ministère' fell, but three years later what a jealous Chamber had refused to Gambetta it granted to Brisson. Accordingly the elections of 1885 were conducted on a departmental basis, each department being entitled to one deputy for every 70,000

[1] BODLEY, J. E. C.: *France*, p. 287. How many conscientious Ministers of the Third Republic might have echoed the words of the Duc de Richelieu: 'One is obliged to exert all one's strength and all one's faculties to maintain one's position, and there is neither the time nor the means to accomplish anything useful. . . . You would be very much mistaken if you supposed that during the five months since we have been Ministers we have spent any time on administering, there has been no time for it physically. Each one is so occupied by his petty Ministerial interests, by the Chambers and by the speeches he has to make that he has no time to concern himself with the State.' cit. FOUQUES DUPARC, J.: *Le Troisième Richelieu*, p. 96.

[2] CAMBON, P.: *Correspondance*, 1870-1924, I, p. 131.

inhabitants and the electors voting at the principal town or departmental capital for as many deputies as the whole department was allowed. It was not clear, however, that the quality of the deputies in the new Chamber of 1885-9 was notably superior to that of their predecessors and, in the reaction after the Boulangist crisis of those years, the Chamber hastily returned to *scrutin d'arrondissement*, which in spite of many subsequent demands that *scrutin de liste* be given a new trial was to remain the method of election to the Chamber until 1919.

Consequently the electoral habits of constituencies became confirmed, and in the 'nineties men as different as Zola and the Vicomte de Vogüé were still to complain of the mediocrity of their parliamentary representatives; the power of local caucuses grew and under what a well-known writer was to call 'La République des Comités'[1] the *esprit de clocher* seemed more than ever to prevail.

These defects of the parliamentary régime had, as we have seen, already begun to appear during the first decade—as early as 1883 Bismarck had spoken contemptuously of France's democratic evolution *ad absurdum*[2] and, taken in conjunction with the economic distress and social discontent of the 'eighties, they go far to explain the fact that in spite of many notable successes the Third Republic was soon to suffer a series of crises and scandals which shook it to its foundations. The internal history of the last fifteen years of the century is overshadowed by the Boulangist crisis, the Panama Scandal and the Dreyfus Affair.

The main results of the elections of 1885 were not the return of better deputies, but the revival of the Right, who, although they secured only 202 seats, polled but 600,000 votes less than the Republicans, and the election of some 180 Radicals. The strength of the Conservative vote was probably due as much to Catholic discontent with the Government as to any increase of Monarchist feeling; for although the death of the Comte of Chambord in 1883 had eliminated the obstacle of the white flag, and the tragic end of the young Prince Imperial in Zululand in 1879 had removed the Pretender who had the best prospect of making a popular appeal to Frenchmen, the Monarchists could not have been said to have made much advance in popular esteem. Their new head, the Comte de Paris, though conscientious, cultivated and liberal, was little known to the French people as a whole and had no personal magnetism. None the less, the Government were sufficiently scared by the election results and the renewal of Royalist hopes and activities to seize upon an

[1] M. Daniel Halévy.

[2] cit. BAUMONT, M.: *L'essor industriel et l'impérialisme colonial* (1878-1904), p. 153.

incident in 1886 as a pretext for the expulsion of the Comte de Paris and all other heads of former ruling houses from France together with their heirs, and to decree that no member of their families should join the army or navy, occupy any public employment or be eligible for parliament. The strength of the Radical vote, which reflected social and economic discontent and the unpopularity of overseas expansion, meant that the Opportunists by themselves had no clear majority in the new Chamber. They were, therefore, obliged to depend upon the support of Right or Left. As it was still inconceivable that a Republican party should make a working alliance with the Conservatives, the Radicals were in effect masters of the situation, and men asked, as they had asked once before of Gambetta, whether the Radical leader, the redoubtable Clemenceau, would now form a Cabinet or whether he would prefer to remain behind the scenes, pull hidden strings and exercise *le pouvoir occulte*. Once again the answer was the same. The aged Grévy, who now unhappily, as we shall see, for his own reputation, was re-elected President of the Republic in December 1885, feared Clemenceau no less than he had feared Gambetta and nothing would induce him to choose him as Prime Minister. Thus Clemenceau, most unfortunately perhaps for the Republic, was condemned to wield power without responsibility, making and remaking Cabinets without being in them himself and putting his own nominees into office.

The first notable consequence of this Radical mastery was the inclusion in the coalition Cabinet formed by Freycinet in January 1886 of General Boulanger, an officer with a brilliant record of personal gallantry, son of a Breton father and a Welsh mother, still under fifty, tolerably good looking and possessed of great personal charm. Although he had not scrupled to solicit the Orleanist Duc d'Aumâle for help in his career, Boulanger now professed strong Radical views and Clemenceau imposed him on Freycinet as Minister of War because he believed that Boulanger was the man the Radicals required to carry out a more thorough Republican reform of the army. So to some extent he was: he made many changes in the Ministry of War, improved the armament and brightened the living conditions of the ordinary soldier; he also prepared a new scheme for implementing the Radical wish to reduce the term of military service to three years, and for making it really compulsory for all by doing away with exemptions and giving the anti-clericals the delight of seeing the priest with a pack on his back (*le curé sac au dos*). These were measures that might have been applied by any vigorous Republican, but Boulanger was no ordinary Minister of War and he acted in no ordinary way. Every move was accompanied by extraordinary publicity, every move was calculated to win popular favour. The result was that after he had been only six months in office he had achieved an extraordinary reputation: people talked, said Lord Lyons, as though he were about to become a Cromwell or a Monk;[1] and when the General appeared at the military review at Longchamps on July 14th a martial, blond-bearded figure on a black horse, the Parisians went mad with delight. All the cheers were for Boulanger, scarcely any for Grévy, the President of the Republic. The song 'En revenant de la revue', composed that evening by the chansonnier Paulus, became the anthem of a new cult of hero worship. Naturally the Opportunists were alarmed and urged Freycinet to be rid of a Minister whose popularity looked dangerous and whose self-advertisement ill became a servant of the Republic. But Freycinet feared the Radicals, and Boulanger, scenting opposition, for a time drew in his horns, and used his personal fascination for a more discreet consolidation of his position in social and political circles. He was so successful in doing this, while keeping the goodwill of the Radicals, that in December he retained his position in a new coalition Cabinet— 'a Freycinet ministry without Freycinet'. Meanwhile it was being put about that Boulanger was the man of Destiny who would recover France's lost provinces, and exiled Alsatians and Lorrainers and patriotic societies like Déroulède's 'Ligue des Patriotes', founded in 1882, suggested that the hour of *revanche* was at hand. Bismarck's reply was characteristic—the system of government in the Reichsland was deliberately made more harsh; a bill was sent to the Reichstag for the increase of the German army, the Triple Alliance with Austria, Hungary and Italy was renewed in February 1887 and a German Press campaign was launched against French 'warmongers'. Once again, as in 1875, there was a veritable war scare, and both in February and in April, when the Germans arrested a French police official named Schnaebele, the situation was tense. It is probable that Bismarck wished only to wage a war of nerves which would so frighten the French as to induce them to be rid of Boulanger whom he regarded as the chief danger to peace. Indeed had not wiser counsels than Boulanger's prevailed in the French Cabinet it is possible that war might have broken out. Fortunately for France Grévy and some of the Ministers kept their heads better than Napoleon III and Gramont in 1870 and France was spared a new defeat. The French public, however, knew nothing of what had gone on in the Cabinet. What they believed, when Bismarck was conciliatory over the Schnaebele affair, was that in Boulanger France at last had a man who could

[1] NEWTON, LORD: *Lord Lyons*, p. 519.

make the German Ogre draw back. The new confidence of 1887 was in striking contrast to the timorousness of 1875. The affair at once made Boulanger a national hero and new songs acclaimed him as 'General Revanche'. By now, however, the Opportunists were thoroughly alarmed and soon determined to get rid of Boulanger by bringing about the fall of the Ministry. Grévy was only too delighted to be quit of a man whom he regarded as a dangerous demagogue, but it was not so easy to find a new Prime Minister willing to take the responsibility of offending the Radicals and forming a Government without Boulanger. At length after a prolonged crisis during which there was continuous popular clamour for Boulanger's retention, the Marseillais Rouvier, who was to be one of the ablest Finance Ministers of the Third Republic, succeeded in forming a Ministry, but only at the expense of breaking with the Radicals and depending on the tolerance of the Right. For the first time since 1875 Republicans were the allies of Monarchists against other Republicans.

The public were disappointed and furious at Boulanger's exclusion from the new Ministry and the cult of the popular hero grew apace, not withstanding his fall from power. Afraid of what might happen on July 14th, 1887, the Government hastily posted him to Clermont Ferrand, but the Parisians did their best to prevent him from leaving the capital. Astonishing scenes took place at the Gare de Lyon on the evening on which he was due to depart. Immense crowds gathered and 3,000 people stood or lay on the lines in front of Boulanger's train so that it should not go. It was only by a stratagem which enabled him to mount an engine on another line that the embarrassed General was able to get away at all and take up his new command. This extra-ordinary manifestation showed that Boulanger had become the focus of a formidable revolt of public opinion against parliamentarianism. As such, others besides the Opportunists now saw in him a danger to the régime. While the journalist Rochefort, still a powerful iconoclastic force, remained true to Boulanger, Clemenceau and the more responsible Radicals withdrew their support and condemned the demonstrations at the Gare de Lyon. The July 14th celebrations went off without any undue disturbance and it might have been hoped that relegated to a provincial command—the Government would have done better still to have sent him overseas—the General would soon be forgotten. But new events soon occurred to cast further discredit on the régime and to provide Boulanger with an opportunity for return to the limelight. In the autumn of 1887 it was discovered that a deputy named Daniel Wilson, who had married Grévy's daughter and been allowed by his father-in-law to reside at the Élysée, had abused his position as the President's son-in-law to traffic in honours, to solicit subscriptions to the newspapers he owned and to conduct a vast correspondence free of charge by employing the President's frank. The Chamber appointed a Commission of Inquiry and Wilson was eventually condemned to two years' imprisonment, but acquitted on appeal. Meanwhile the scandal naturally enough led to the demand that Grévy should resign, and since he showed no inclination to do so the majority in the Chamber engineered the defeat of the Rouvier Cabinet and decided that it should be impossible for the President to find a new Prime Minister. For some days there was an unparalleled situation: crowds demonstrated in front of the Élysée and sang mocking songs such as 'Ah! quel malheur d'avoir un gendre!'; eligible deputies went on strike and refused the President's entreaties that they should form Cabinets, but still the old man of eighty-one remained obdurate. Not until November 27th did he promise his resignation for December 1st. Who was to be his successor? Suddenly the Radicals and the Right realized that Jules Ferry was likely to be the strongest candidate, and Boulanger re-emerged to take part in agitated conferences about the possibility of forming a Ministry which would after all serve under Grévy. Anything would be better than the hated Ferry.

When these manœuvres came to nothing and Grévy's farewell message was at last read to the Chamber on December 2nd, there were violent street demonstrations, organized both by Déroulède's 'Ligue des Patriotes' and by the revolutionary Blanquists of the extreme Left. There is little doubt that these signs of Ferry's unpopularity and the hostility of the extremely Radical Paris municipal council conjured up visions of serious disorders and frightened the National Assembly when it met at Versailles the next day to elect a new President. In addition Ferry's enemies were able to work upon the now traditional jealousy of a strong man. Senators and deputies therefore adopted Clemenceau's suggestion that the choice of a new President should fall on an outsider, and though his recommendation of Sadi Carnot 'He is not very bright, but he bears a Republican name' (popularly repeated as 'let's vote for the stupidest') was scarcely enthusiastic, it vividly illustrated the attitude of the legislature towards the executive and won the day. Ferry's return to a prominent position was prevented. Instead, Sadi Carnot, son of a deputy of 1848 and grandson of Lazare Carnot, the 'organizer of victory' in the Great Revolution, became the third President of the Third Republic. A member of a Republican dynasty, a bourgeois of some standing and unimpeachable integrity, he was in fact to preside over the Republic with considerable dignity and to achieve a much wider popularity than his predecessor.

Boulanger meanwhile had formed connexions both with the Monarchist Right and with the Bonapartists. He had given the Monarchists to understand that as soon as he was back at the Ministry of War he would make a *coup d'état* and effect a Restoration; while he accepted a Bonapartist suggestion that he should stand for election to the Chamber in as many by-elections as possible and so obtain such a strong personal position that he must either be admitted to the Government or sweep it away. Thus there began the extraordinary 'plebiscitary' campaign of 1888, largely financed by a Royalist Duchess, which seemed to introduce into French electioneering the vulgar hustling of American methods and in which Boulanger, soon placed on the army's retired list for indiscipline, headed a new 'National Republican Party', and carried six out of seven by-elections in various parts of the country on a programme demanding a dissolution of the existing Parliament, a revision of the Constitution and the election of a Constituent Assembly. Detached observers all bore witness that the country was swept by a kind of delirium—'It is 1851 all over again and worse,'[1] wrote the staunch Republican, Paul Cambon. The climax came in January 1889 when the Boulangists decided to test the feeling of the capital itself and the General stood at another by-election in a traditionally Republican constituency. Once again he was elected by an enormous majority amid scenes of indescribable enthusiasm. On the evening of January 27th, when the results were known, enormous crowds gathered outside the General's headquarters singing—'C'est Boulanger qu'il nous faut, Oh! Oh! Oh!', and shouting insistently: '*A l' Élysée! A l' Élysée!*' Had he but given the word that night it would seem that with the complaisance of the Paris Police he could have carried all before him and played Cromwell or Monk as he wished. But the 'gallant General', (*le brave Général*) as he was called by the song-writers, was deaf to all entreaties and refused to do anything unconstitutional. His followers had been leaning on a broken reed, a man who had no real political ideas or political courage, who adored popularity, intrigue, and playing to the gallery, but genuinely feared to be branded as a second 'man of December 2nd', and who was a slave to an ailing mistress, believed by all his entourage to have been the *femme fatale* who finally held him back on that historic night.

'He who hesitates is lost'; and so it was with Boulanger. January 27th, 1889, had given the régime a severe shock and all Republicans

[1] CAMBON, P.: *Correspondance*, 1870–1924, I, p. 318.

who remained loyal to it temporarily sank their differences and rallied in its defence. In February a new Cabinet of so-called 'Republican concentration' was formed; *scrutin de liste* was once more abandoned in favour of *scrutin d'arrondissement* in order to minimize the danger of future electoral steeplechasing; a bill was passed forbidding multiple candidatures; an energetic Minister of the Interior, Ernest Constans, prosecuted the 'Ligue des Patriotes'; and preparations were for the first time made to implement article 12 of the Constitutional Law of 16th July, 1875, whereby the Senate could act as a High Court for the trial of attacks against the safety of the State. In the meantime Boulanger himself gave the death blow to his movement and to the hopes of his supporters. It was rumoured that he was to be arrested. Instead of staying in Paris he and his mistress took train for Brussels. Had he stayed in France and boldly faced arrest and trial he might still have remained a popular hero, triumphant if acquitted, glorified by a crown of martyrdom if condemned. Indeed the evidence that he had actually plotted against the State was so flimsy that he should have been able to tear the prosecution case to ribbons. But he refused to return to France in spite of the most pressing appeals of his followers. 'Instead of being the saviour of France he preferred to save his own skin.'[1] The enthusiasm of January melted away in the disappointment and discredit of April. Although Boulanger himself was once again elected in a Paris constituency, in the general elections in September his party only won some forty seats. The Boulangism of Boulanger was effectively killed by the General's own lack of political courage and the end of the story was dreary and lamentable. Boulanger was duly condemned by the High Court—a condemnation which was hardly justice, but the Republic required a conviction; the movement fizzled out amid the mutual recriminations of the General's last adherents, and in September 1891 he committed suicide on his mistress's Belgian grave.

The astonishing enthusiasm which marked the Boulangist movement of 1888 had amazed and perplexed detached contemporary observers; for the General was no more than a regular soldier with a fine record of personal bravery who had shown some energy and humanity during a seventeen months' tenure of the Ministry of War, and those who met him were surprised by his limited intelligence though they might admit his personal charm. But the enthusiasm was not so much for what Boulanger had done as for what thousands of Frenchmen hoped he would do; and so long as his programme remained vague every hope was still possible. Thus he became the focus and symbol

[1] BAUMONT, M.: *L'essor industriel et l'impérialisme colonial* (1878-1904), p. 155.

for all the aspirations of all the discontented; for those who hoped that a flame of purification would purge the State of corruption and give it new strength and dignity; for those who still longed for *revanche*; for those who wanted a revision of the Constitution; for Monarchists and Bonapartists who believed he was working for their private ends; and even for many extremists of the Left who looked for a transformation of the social order. And so it was that Boulangism was a movement which had cut across existing party groupings and divided them all according to temperament, the liberal sheep who opposed him from the authoritarian goats who flocked to his support. As such it was the last great upsurge of a Bonapartist spirit in France—a Bonapartism, but without a Bonaparte. And so, too, though Boulangism was a fiasco, it had stirred the country to such depths that it left enduring marks upon French politics. It gave birth to a new nationalism which was to be a continuing force and which was now to be the monopoly of the Right. Hitherto during the greater part of our period the noisy patriots, the militarists eager for crusades to carry arms through Europe, have generally been the Bonapartists or Jacobin Republicans, parties of the Left under Bourbon and Orleanist government or under Republics of Moral Order: but from the crucible of Boulangism the Right, Monarchists or Right-wing Republicans like Déroulède, emerge as the standard bearers of *revanchard* patriotism, and in consequence, by reaction, the pacifist anti-militarist tendencies of the Left, already perceptible among the Republicans of the Second Empire are much reinforced. So, too Boulangism marks the beginning of a revolution in Paris. In the new era of rapid communications Paris is no longer the supreme political force overthrowing Governments and imposing new ones upon the laggard obedient provinces; although still true to itself in tending to be in opposition, its opposition begins to swing to the Right. Paris was the last city to elect a Boulangist deputy, and after the Dreyfus Affair the city which had given birth to the Commune became a stronghold of Nationalism and Conservatism. In other ways, too, Boulangism was of great importance. By menacing the very existence of the Republic it strengthened the conservative instincts of the Republicans, and so the Radicals, who had before been clamorous for constitutional revision and for the abolition of the Senate as a reactionary brake upon progressive legislation, soon abandoned revision; for all Republicans defence of the Republic came to mean defence of the Constitution of 1875, which the political scientist might therefore soon be inclined to classify as a distinctly 'rigid' form of government. But while Boulangism was thus a force which made for the conservation of existing institutions it gave a leftward impetus to political parties. The Royalists had compromised themselves seriously by participating in a movement which had raised false hopes and caused them to jettison or modify some of their traditional principles. Left farther than ever from the prospect of a speedy restoration of monarchy some of them, as a result of their disappointment and under new influences, were, as we shall see, soon disposed to rally to the Republic. At the same time, dissatisfied with the Opportunists, many of the *petits bourgeois* were to transfer their votes to the Radicals, while the allegiance of the workers passed more and more to the growing group of Parliamentary Socialists.

Immediately, the reassertion of Republican authority and the débâcle of Boulangism led to a striking revival in the popularity and prestige of the Republic. The centenary of the Great Revolution of 1789 was celebrated with éclat in a variety of ways, notable among them being a banquet to all the mayors of France.[1] At the same time a great exhibition which attracted 25,000,000 visitors, vividly displayed the wealth of France and endowed the capital with a new and wonderful landmark in the Eiffel Tower. The new President of the Republic took part in many of the ceremonies of commemoration throughout the country and made an excellent impression by his dignified bearing. The passage at last of the bill reducing the term of military service to three years and suppressing most of the exceptions hitherto permitted was a highly popular measure which may well have contributed to the Republican success in the elections of September. A new stability seemed to have been achieved when the Tirard Ministry of 1889 lasted for a whole year and the Freycinet Ministry which succeeded it for very nearly two. Nor was this all; with the experiment of what French historians know as the 'Ralliement' the Republic, more confident in its new strength, showed a more conciliatory disposition, and numbers of Conservatives and Catholics were led to abandon their hostility to the régime; and these signs of renewed vigour helped French diplomacy to lead France from isolation to the conclusion of an alliance with one of the greatest of European states. The Ralliement and the Franco-Russian Alliance were, as we shall see, two of the most remarkable attempts to consolidate the success of 1889.

The shock of Boulangism had brought home to many Republicans, and in particular to the Opportunists, the fact that the Republic was set on too narrow a basis for security. Although the Monarchists had

---

[1] A remarkable meal, at which 15,000 people sat down to table, 80,000 plates were used and 45,000 bottles of wine uncorked.

lost a number of seats in the 1889 elections, the poll showed that a third of the French people were still hostile to the régime. For some time, indeed, various Opportunist leaders had shown a desire for appeasement in the struggle of Church and State; and even Ferry, the architect of the education laws, had more than once urged the need to open the doors of the Republic to all men of goodwill. Now, after the strain of the Boulanger crisis, both sides were tired of war and the conciliatory attitude of the moderate Republicans was met with equal goodwill on the part of the octogenarian Pope who, since his election in 1878, had shown himself one of the wisest Pontiffs and ablest diplomats of the century. Leo XIII had always resolutely refused to condemn the Republic as a form of government. It was with his approval that in 1890 one of the greatest of the French bishops of the time, Cardinal Lavigerie, the Primate of Africa, spoke in a formal toast to surprised naval officers of the need for unqualified adherence to that form of government which was willed by the nation; and in subsequent pronouncements in 1891 and 1892 the Pope himself explicitly ordered the Catholics of France to recognize the Republic: the constituted authority should be accepted as representing the authority derived from God. This behest was so unpalatable to most of the hierarchy and many of the faithful that they were slow to obey, some arguing like Mgr. Freppel, the Bishop of Angers, that the Republic was no mere form of government but a whole system of irreligion, others questioning the Papal right to pronounce on a matter of secular allegiance. Thus, although in 1892 some men of note such as the great Catholic orator, the Comte de Mun and the leader of the Right in Parliament, the Baron de Mackau, rallied to the Republic, there were still many who remained intransigent in their hostility and unswerving in their loyalty to the Pretender. Moreover, the task of those who were eager for the success of appeasement was not made easier by the incurable suspicion of the Radicals, who saw in the Pope's injunctions no more than a wily attempt to manœuvre the Trojan horse of clericalism into the Republican fortress. For men like Clemenceau and Léon Bourgeois the Great Revolution of 1789 represented a *bloc* of doctrines and achievements which must be accepted in its entirety by the convert. In Clemenceau's words it was still an active force because the same men (the men of the Revolution) constantly found themselves face to face with the same enemies.[1] In so far as the Opportunists in the Chamber of 1889–93 had no clear majority and were dependent on Radical support it was, therefore, difficult for them to go very far in the way of conciliation. After 1893, however, the Opportunists,

[1] cf. HALÉVY, D.: *Histoire d'une histoire* . . ., p. 55.

or Progressists as they now came to be called, had a clear majority and the Ralliement could make new headway when what Spuller, a moderate Minister of Public Worship, termed 'a new spirit' was in the air. This spirit was shown not by the repeal of anti-clerical legislation—no Government dared go so far as that—but by a new tolerance, if not laxity, in its application. But for the Dreyfus Affair, which was once again to throw France into turmoil, it is possible that the moderate Progressists, reinforced by a growing number of Ralliés, might have continued to govern France for many years and that a certain Catholic influence might once again have made itself felt in the councils of government. As things turned out, however, these years of Ralliement were to be no more than an interlude between periods of bitter strife. The experiment of 'appeasement' was incomplete and won only limited success. Yet, even so, it was not unimportant: it weakened the Monarchists still further and, although the Ralliés were too few and divided among themselves to enable the formation of a strong Catholic Centre party, their adhesion to the Republic strengthened the Conservative element among the Republican moderates and accentuated the cleavage between the Progressists and the Radicals. It was the first real attempt of the Republic to work for the achievement of a united France.

If the attempt to reconcile Frenchmen with Frenchmen was a failure, the attempt to ally France with Russia was a notable success. Although, as we have seen, France had re-entered the European comity of nations in 1878, she was still isolated in 1889. Europe was still dominated by the Germany of Bismarck, and Bismarck had bound all the other Great Powers save Great Britain to his own system. Austria, Hungary and Italy were harnessed by the Triple Alliance while a Reinsurance Treaty, which ensured Russian neutrality in case of a French attack upon Germany, kept Russia in check. Great Britain remained aloof, but their colonial rivalries gave Bismarck little fear that she and France would ever become close friends. None the less, many Frenchmen, from Thiers and Gambetta to Decazes and Boulanger, had believed that eventually France must find a natural ally in Russia and few opportunities were missed to court the Tsarist state. Yet, if the rulers of Russia were far from friendly to Austria and chafed under the German hegemony, they had little respect for France, which Giers, the Russian Foreign Minister, had described as a 'mass of rottenness'.[1] Moreover, the old suspicions of French Republican and 'atheist' governments died hard and, as late as 1890, the Tsar told the German Chancellor that he would never ally

[1] cit. BAUMONT, M.: L'essor industriel et l'impérialisme colonial (1878-1904), p. 142.

with a Republic.[1] In that very same year, however, events occurred which were soon to lead him to do this very thing. That spring the new German Emperor, William II, 'dropped the pilot'. Bismarck was Chancellor of Germany and arbiter of Europe no longer, and the German ship of state seemed likely in less experienced hands to steer a disquietingly erratic course. The change in policy was strikingly marked by Germany's omission three months later to renew the Reinsurance Treaty with Russia. Meanwhile, France's new stability, the Pope's readiness to recognize her form of government, the revival of her military power together with her willingness to restrain Russian Nihilist activities in France and to provide facilities for the manufacture of new weapons and loans to finance the growing industrial development of the Tsarist Empire—all these were facts which made a favourable impression upon the Russian Government. When in 1891 the Kaiser renewed the Triple Alliance and began a demonstrative courtship of England, Russia, afraid of being left in isolation, rapidly drew closer to France. In July a French naval squadron visited Kronstadt and a sensation was caused when the Tsar himself visited the French Admiral's flagship and listened bareheaded to the Marseillaise. In the following month an agreement for mutual consultation was concluded; a document very vague in its terms, but none the less sufficiently important for Freycinet and other French statesmen to declare publicly that a new situation had arisen and that France who had been 'isolated and almost forgotten' was now, 'thanks to the reorganization of her army and the wisdom of her diplomacy',[2] once more an important factor in the European balance of power. French opinion was by now enthusiastically Russophil and public and Government alike were eager for a definite alliance. In fact the French authorities had immediately after the conclusion of the entente proposed to the Russians that it should be followed up and made more effective by a military convention. But the Tsar and Giers were in no hurry to bind themselves too closely—the Panama scandal and other incidents in France reinforced their hesitancy—and it was not until January 4th, 1894, that an exchange of secret notes accepting the military agreement made the Franco-Russian alliance a reality. The form of the effective instrument of the alliance, the military convention, had a great advantage from the Russian point of view: there was no need for it to be debated by the French Parliament before it could come into effect. In the meantime, in October 1893, a Russian naval squadron had paid a return visit to Toulon, and the Admiral in com-

[1] LANGER, W. L.: The Franco-Russian Alliance, 1890-4, p. 105 n.
[2] FREYCINET, C. DE: Souvenirs, II, 1878-93, p. 475.

mand and the men who accompanied him on a tour of various French cities received a delirious welcome. A few years later the alliance received its formal consecration in an exchange of visits between the heads of state. The Tsar and Tsarina came to Paris in 1896 and President Félix Faure was received in St. Petersburg in 1897.

The visit of the Russian naval squadron to France in 1893 was reported by *The Times* to have given rise to 'the most remarkable outbreak of international feeling ever witnessed'.[1] The enthusiasm for the alliance on the French side was much more noticeable than that of the Russians and yet, although during the next twenty years the Russians were the main gainers economically, since some £400,000,000 of French capital was subscribed to Russian loans by French investors, and also diplomatically, since the security given them by the Alliance enabled them to act with much greater freedom in Asia—the intensity of French feeling is easily intelligible. Quite apart from the hopes of the Nationalists and patriots, of Madame Adam and her *Nouvelle Revue*, of Déroulède and his 'Ligue des Patriotes' and of all the exiled Alsatians and Lorrainers, that the day of *revanche* would now be brought immeasurably nearer, it was clear to all that the Russian connexion had greatly enhanced the prestige both of France and of the Republic even though France might appear to be no more than the junior partner, the 'brilliant second' of the alliance. But possibly still more important was the general feeling of relief that France was no longer alone in a hostile world. Now at long last the French people felt a sense of security such as they had not experienced for more than a quarter of a century.[2]

Unfortunately, however, the prestige of France's reorganized army and of her diplomatic service was not equalled by that of her Parliament: The Boulangists had not succeeded in eliminating corruption in high places, but the disclosures resulting from the failure of the Panama Canal Company in 1889 were to give the handful of Boulangist deputies in the Chamber of 1889–93 a superb opportunity of exposing a scandal and thereby covering the régime with fresh obloquy.

The construction of a Panama Canal by a company directed by Ferdinand de Lesseps of Suez Canal fame, with the help of Eiffel and other eminent French engineers of the day, should have been a great national enterprise, a triumph of French engineering skill, a source of wealth, and a means of strengthening French influence in Central and South America. Unfortunately the difficulties and expense of the undertaking, which was begun in 1881, proved to be far greater than

[1]cit. LANGER, W. L.: *The Franco-Russian Alliance*, 1890–4, p. 356.

[2] SIEGFRIED, A.: *Tableau des partis en France*, p. 106.

Lesseps' estimate. The Company was constantly obliged to raise further loans and on each occasion the charges made by banks and publicity agents were more onerous: of the 1,040 million francs raised only 640 million were eventually spent on construction work. In spite of the importance of the enterprise for French prestige the authorities refused to give it any official support, and it was not until December 1888 that the Chamber authorized an issue of lottery bonds. When they, too, were lamentably undersubscribed, the Company, unsupported by the State, had no alternative but to go into liquidation. The shareholders appealed to Parliament to safeguard their interests and eventually Lesseps, together with his son and certain other officials of the Company, were condemned for obtaining money by false promises and for malversation of the funds. Very few dispassionate inquirers could now agree that these charges had been substantiated, and in fact they were shortly afterwards quashed on technical grounds. But it was not the trial of 'the great Frenchman', as Lesseps was generally known, and of some of the most noted engineers of the day which stirred the political world to its depths, but another case which arose incidentally out of the Panama investigations. In September 1892 a rabidly anti-semitic paper, the *Libre Parole*, accused the Company of having distributed *pots de vin* to parliamentarians through a Jewish financier named Baron Jacques de Reinach. When the Chamber reassembled after the autumn recess there were immediate interpellations, and on November 18th it was agreed that debate on the Panama question should be held on November 21st. On the 19th Reinach was found dead and Cornelius Herz, another financier of Jewish origin, who had been blackmailing him, promptly fled to England. On the 21st the Government, after a tense sitting in which a Boulangist Deputy had alleged instance after instance of corruption, giving the facts but refusing to disclose the names of the colleagues implicated, were obliged to agree to the appointment of a Commission of Inquiry. In the subsequent revelations it became clear that large sums of money had been distributed through Reinach, Herz and other agents for the Company to various members of Parliament in return for promises to vote for the authorization of its lottery bonds. Proceedings were instituted against five deputies—including three Ministers or former Ministers—and five Senators—including two former Ministers, a former Prefect of Police and a former Governor-General of Algeria—but in most of these cases they were dropped and in the end only one man, a former Minister of Public Works, who confessed to having accepted 375,000 francs, was condemned. But though Commissions of Inquiry and law courts were lenient, charges had been made and mud had been thrown which stuck. The career of Floquet, the President of the Chamber and a former Prime Minister, was virtually ended by the Affair, that of Rouvier checked for ten years, while a number of lesser men bore the stigma of having been *chéquards*, the receivers of tainted money. Most notable of all was the eclipse of the destroyer of Cabinets, the man whose tongue, sword and pistol (he was a skilled duellist) were feared by all, the Radical leader Clemenceau, who had been much too closely associated with the dubious Herz and was now on the basis of trumpery and forged documents denounced by his numerous enemies as a tool of the British Foreign Office. In the general elections of 1893 Clemenceau's meetings were punctuated by cries of 'A—Oh yes!' and he was not returned to the Chamber in which he had sat continuously since 1876.

Although previous régimes had had their notable scandals the Restoration its Ouvrard, the July Monarchy its Teste and Cubières, none made such a lasting impression or did so much to poison the air as Panama. The country as a whole was apathetic enough, and the discredited Opportunists were returned in even stronger force in the 1893 elections; but in the political world the Affair created an atmosphere which, in the words of Lord Bryce, 'lasted for years, like the smoke that continues to hang over the spot where a high-explosive shell has struck the ground. A scandal so tremendous seemed to confirm the vague suspicions that had existed before; and it tended to render probable charges subsequently made. . . .'[1] Immediately, it had a number of political consequences: it deprived parties of some of their old leaders and brought new and younger men to the fore; on the Progressist side, for example, along with Dupuy, the Presidents and Foreign Ministers of the twentieth century, Deschanel and Poincaré, Delcassé and Barthou now made their first appearance—Poincaré and Barthou so young that they were known as the 'two boys'—and in the Radical camp a Léon Bourgeois succeeded Clemenceau; it gave a new impulse to anti-semitism which had been growing ever since Édouard Drumont, the editor of *La Libre Parole*, published his vitriolic *La France Juive* in 1886; it also encouraged the growth of a new Nationalism, which in some ways foreshadowed the ideas of German National Socialism, by its defence of the essentially French mode of life, its cult of French soil and its French dead, and its rejection of alien influences, whether Jewish or Gentile; it probably hindered the Ralliement even as it delayed the consummation of the Franco-Russian alliance; and it certainly reinforced the pessimism about the future of France and her institutions which marks the observations

[1] cit. JACKSON, J. HAMPDEN: *Clemenceau and the Third Republic*, p. 79.

of so many contemporary writers. France in the 'nineties was, as General de Gaulle has written, like the Infanta weeping in the Palace Gardens, overcome with melancholy, while enjoying the good things of life.[1]

Panama also, perhaps, gave a further impetus to the growth of Parliamentary Socialism and encouraged various social theorists to put their ideas into practice. During the next few months and years the rise of the Socialists and their alliance with the Radicals in Parliament, the bombs of Anarchists, the growth of Trade Unions and of federations of unions of workers in the same localities known as Bourses du Travail, and the strikes of workers in various industries together with much talk of a general strike, all combined to force the social question upon the attention of the public and upon Parliament. In the 1893 elections Radicals and Socialists joined forces and the results led to an increase in the Socialist representation from twelve to forty-nine, among them a great orator, Jaurès, an able lawyer, journalist and organizer, Millerand, and the apostle of Marxism, Jules Guesde. The continued co-operation of the Radicals with these Socialists further emphasized the cleavage between the two main Republican parties, Progressists and Radicals. At the same time the Anarchist outrages which began in 1892 and cul-minated in the assassination of President Carnot in June 1894, the violent Socialist attacks against his successor, Casimir-Périer, the wealthy grand-son of Louis Philippe's Minister, and the formulation by Millerand in 1896 of a minimum Socialist programme for the peaceful conquest of power, all tended to force the Progressists and moderates back upon a programme of Republican defence which also implied the defence of the existing social order. Thus the political situation in the middle 'nineties was frequently disturbed and confused. Conservative hopes that Casimir-Périer would prove to be the strong man who would restore the authority of the Executive were disappointed by his resignation in January 1895 after only six months of office. Eventually, however, after a minority Cabinet of Radicals, the first predominantly Radical Cabinet of the Third Republic, had failed to secure the Senate's approval for a bill for pro-gressive income tax, and had been forced to resign by its subsequent refusal to vote certain military credits the conservative Republican forces rallied round a new Cabinet headed by Jules Méline, the champion of the agricultural interests. In so doing they followed a natural if un-conscious reaction—taking as their leader for a policy described as being 'neither revolution nor reaction' the man who had done most to benefit the naturally conservative rural majority of the French people. Under

[1] DE GAULLE, C.: *France and her army*, p. 82.

him, as Bainville put it, 'agriculture governed France. And all that could
be done by means of corn and hay he did'.[1] Eighteen ninety-six and
eighteen ninety-seven were thus years of relative prosperity and stability
which might well have continued much longer, but for the growing
tempest of the Dreyfus Affair. The social problem in these years had
come more to the fore and the opposition of conservative bourgeoisie
and rural interests to the left-wing workers had been sharper, but this
opposition had if anything delayed the passage of social legislation and
the Dreyfus Affair, like Boulangism and Panama, once again relegated
social questions to the background.

In 1894 the intelligence services of the French War Office discovered
that there had been a leakage of military information to the German
Embassy. After some investigations a young Jewish staff officer named
Alfred Dreyfus was arrested. The news of the arrest leaked out and
there was at once an outcry in the anti-semitic press which demanded
his head and attacked the Minister of War, General Mercier, because of
reports that the General was not yet satisfied of Dreyfus's guilt and
might be prepared to release him. In December Dreyfus was tried by
secret court martial and condemned to deportation for life. In the
following month, January 1895, he was publicly degraded and then
dispatched to Devil's Island off the coast of French Guiana, where he
was kept in solitary confinement. In view of the attitude of the Press,
of the statements of General Mercier who had told the *Figaro* that he had
crying proofs of Dreyfus's treason, and of the verdict, almost all Frenchmen were convinced of the Jewish officer's guilt and accepted the sentence
without question. There, so far as the general public was concerned,
the matter remained until the end of 1897. But the weakness of General
Mercier in wishing to dispose of the matter and avoid trouble with the
Press by securing a speedy conviction had laid a train which was to lead
to an explosion far more tremendous than the original one which he or
his colleagues had feared to face. Dreyfus's family were convinced of
his innocence and at once went to work to find evidence which would
clear him. At the same time, quite independently, an intelligence
officer, Colonel Picquart, had come across conclusive evidence that a
document in writing identical to that of the famous *bordereau*, or
memorandum, which was one of the main papers on which Dreyfus's
conviction had been based, had been written by a needy artillery officer
of foreign extraction and dubious morals named Esterhazy. Picquart
at once examined the Dreyfus case files and, surprised at the slenderness
of the evidence against Dreyfus, came to the conclusion that Dreyfus

[1] BAINVILLE, J.: *La Troisième République* 1870–1935, p. 198.

had been wrongly condemned, that Esterhazy was the real culprit, and that there ought to be a revision of the Dreyfus case. But his superior officers were afraid of the discredit which might follow upon an admission that military justice had erred. They prevaricated, then told Picquart that further formal proof of Dreyfus's guilt had been obtained and, when he was still not satisfied, sent him away on a mission and subsequently posted him to North Africa. The new document, later known as 'le faux Henry', was in fact a forgery, newly inserted in the Dreyfus dossier by Picquart's successor as head of the Intelligence Bureau, Colonel Henry.

Picquart, however, was able to communicate his suspicions to his lawyer, who in turn told the story to the Vice-President of the Senate, Scheurer-Kestner. Scheurer-Kestner, convinced of its substance, at once made representations to General Billot, Mercier's successor at the Ministry of War and to Méline, the Prime Minister. But General Billot had already stated in answer to an interpellation in the Chamber a year earlier that Dreyfus had been justly and legally condemned and he now stuck to his guns, while Méline, like most politicians anxious above all to avoid another scandal, stood by the Minister of War. By now, however, there was in being a small 'Dreyfusard' party determined to work for a revision of the trial—Dreyfus's brother and his friends joined forces with Scheurer-Kestner, and brought a formal charge against Esterhazy, public opinion began to be interested and while the majority of the Press was opposed to Dreyfus, the novelist, Zola, took up his cause and Clemenceau re-entered politics with a remarkable series of articles. in a paper called L'Aurore, demanding that, whatever the circumstances, the truth should be told. In the Chamber, however, Méline declared that there was no such thing as a Dreyfus Affair—the case of Esterhazy was the only one to be considered—and Billot reaffirmed his belief in Dreyfus's guilt and appealed to the Chamber to stop the campaign which was being pursued 'against the national honour and the honour of the army'. In January Esterhazy in turn was tried by secret court martial, acquitted and hailed as a hero by enthusiastic crowds. This, the Government and the War Office hoped, would be the end of the matter. But they were greatly mistaken. Two days' later Zola published his famous open letter to the President of the Republic in which he accused a number of Generals and high officers of deliberately procuring the condemnation of Dreyfus on the basis of a second document not communicated to the defence and declared that the court martial of 1898 had acted on superior instructions in acquitting Esterhazy.

'J'accuse', as Zola's letter was called, was described by Anatole France as 'a revolutionary act of incomparable power'. It was a challenge which no Government could ignore. It roused passions to fever heat and forced all who were concerned for the character of the Republic to take sides. The guilt or innocence of Dreyfus became an article of belief about which even families were bitterly divided, for the issue had now been raised far beyond the personality of the individual Dreyfus and his sufferings. For most Frenchmen Dreyfus became no more than a symbol, either of the eternal Jewish traitor, or of the denial of Justice. On the one hand the Nationalists, the patriots, the anti-semites, the Catholics and all those who put social order before everything, believed that the whole affair was a deliberate plot to throw France into disorder and discredit the army, a plot hatched, said the anti-semites by an international Jewish syndicate. On the other the Dreyfusards held that injustice had been tolerated for alleged reasons of State and that if Reason of State were allowed to dominate in French affairs the citizen had no security against any form of arbitrariness; the Republic was no better than the Ancien Régime.

For the time being, however, the great bulk of public opinion, Republican as well as Conservative, was still against Dreyfus. Zola was twice tried and condemned for slander—the second time in default —and the verdict was hailed with delight by crowds which shouted for 'Death to Zola' and 'Death to the Jews'. In the summer of 1898, however, new and sensational developments occurred; a new Radical Minister of War, Cavaignac, abandoned the attitude of his predecessors and attempted to establish Dreyfus's guilt by public disclosure of some of the evidence in the Chamber. This, as Clemenceau wrote, at once made revision of the Dreyfus trial inevitable. 'That was inescapable from the day when the Government undertook to supply proof instead of being content with mere affirmations.'[1] And so in fact it turned out. The Dreyfusards were no longer up against a stone wall: they now at last had the chance of dissecting the evidence; and Picquart wrote to the Prime Minister, Méline's successor Brisson, offering to prove that one of the documents mentioned by Cavaignac did not refer to Dreyfus, that another had been falsified and that a third, the 'faux Henry', was a forgery. Shortly afterwards a War Office intelligence officer confirmed the forgery of the third. Colonel Henry was questioned by Cavaignac, confessed and, on being confined to the fortress prison of Mont Valérien, committed suicide. The anti-Dreyfusards were thunderstruck by this news so damaging to their case, and Esterhazy, the real villain of the piece, scenting a change in the wind, slipped away to England, where

[1] L'iniquité, p. 460 (July 8th).

he lived quietly under the name of Comte de Voilemont until his death in 1923.

Although the '*faux Henry*' was not one of the documents on which Dreyfus's conviction had been based, so much play had been made with it that discovery that it was a forgery convinced Brisson and many deputies that a retrial was necessary. Not so the Minister of War; Cavaignac resigned rather than hear of a revision of the case and the two Generals who succeeded him speedily followed suit. Meanwhile a formal request from Madame Dreyfus for revision had been handed to the Cour de Cassation and eventually a civilian Minister of War in the new Dupuy Government of Republican concentration, formed in November 1898, agreed to hand over the secret dossier to the Court. Revision was thus inevitable, but much might depend on who conducted the trial. Legally the case should have been dealt with by the section of the Court of Cassation, known as the Criminal Chamber, but this contained a number of Protestants and free-thinkers and so in February 1899 the anti-Dreyfusards managed to secure the passage of a special law transferring it to the whole court. A few days' later still further excitement was caused by the sudden death of the President of the Republic, Félix Faure, in the course of an intimate meeting with a lady who was not his wife. As the President was Conservatively minded and had very little sympathy with the Dreyfusards the anti-Dreyfusards at once declared that the Dreyfusards were responsible for his death. Although there was no evidence of this, the influential Royalist writer, Charles Maurras, went on repeating it up to 1930. The death of the President, however, influenced feeling still more and the ensuing presidential election in which Émile Loubet defeated Jules Méline was tantamount to a Dreyfusard victory in that it was a defeat of the more Conservative candidate, of Méline, who as Prime Minister had done his best to prevent the Dreyfus Affair from being reopened. A few days' later Faure's funeral gave the Nationalist Déroulède, an ardent anti-Dreyfusard, the chance to attempt a *coup d'état*. But the coup of Reuilly, in which the novelist Maurice Barrès was one of his accomplices, was a lamentable failure, ill-prepared and without even a Boulanger to capture the imagination of troops and crowds. Its only significance was to show that there were still groups of men faithful to the Boulangist tradition and that the general effervescence and state of feeling was such that they judged the time ripe for a coup; while Déroulède's acquittal in May was one more instance of the frequent partiality of French justice during these impassioned months.

In June the long-drawn-out affair began to move to its climax. The

Court of Cassation, in spite of the anti-Dreyfusard February law and of the violence of the anti-Dreyfusard party, showed its independence, quashed the trial of 1894 and ordered a rehearing. The anti-Dreyfusards were furious and a Baron Christiani insulted the new President of the Republic by striking him on the head with a cane at the Auteuil races, an absurd and pitiable incident, but one which had immediate consequences in Parliament. The Dupuy Ministry, accused of not having given the President sufficient protection, was defeated and resigned. After a prolonged Ministerial crisis one of the ablest barristers of the day, Waldeck-Rousseau, who had made his début in Gambetta's 'Grand Ministère', formed a Cabinet which was to mark a turning-point in French politics and to stay in office for the record length of nearly three years.

The immediate determination of the new Government was to restore public order which had been sadly disturbed by anti-Jewish riots and demonstrations of Dreyfusards and anti-Dreyfusards, and to dispose of the Dreyfus Affair as soon as possible. The Nationalist agitation, Déroulède's coup and rumour of further plots against the régime gave it the opportunity to pose, like the Tirard-Constans Cabinet of 1889, as a Cabinet of Republican defence. Accordingly, before the second Dreyfus trial opened, some sixty-seven people were arrested for plotting against the régime and three of them, including Déroulède, were in January 1900, condemned by the High Court and banished or imprisoned for ten years. On August 7th, 1899, the retrial of Dreyfus, which aroused extraordinary interest throughout the world, began at Rennes and in September the new court martial gave their verdict. While two out of seven of the judges had voted for Dreyfus's acquittal, the majority found him guilty of 'intelligence with the enemy with attentuating circumstances' and sentenced him to ten years' detention. Except among the anti-Dreyfusards there was a wave of furious indignation at such a verdict when so many had expected acquittal. Shortly afterwards, however, the President of the Republic pardoned Dreyfus and at the end of the year the Government secured an amnesty for all concerned, their main object being that the whole Affair should be forgotten as speedily as possible. But the eager Dreyfusards were far from satisfied with such a result and in consequence of further strenuous efforts on their part there was a second revision of the case by the Court of Cassation in 1906. This time the Rennes verdict was also quashed, but the Court did not order a retrial. Instead the Chamber passed a special resolution for Dreyfus's rehabilitation; he was decorated with the Legion of Honour and he and Picquart were both promoted in rank.

This Affair, of the many Affairs in French history the one which is known simply as 'The Affair' without qualification, dragged on for twelve years from the original trial to the final rehabilitation, and during at least three appeared almost entirely to dominate the French political scene. Yet, though the educated classes not only in France but throughout a large part of the world were passionately roused by it, the great mass of the French people were unmoved and little interested in a question which soon became so complicated as to be far beyond their understanding. They tended to dismiss it as a soldiers' and politicians' quarrel which was no concern of theirs, and it is noteworthy that in the general elections of 1898 it was a very minor issue. None the less it was profoundly important for the development of French politics and its effect upon the orientation of the Third Republic.

The fragmentary and conflicting character of the evidence disclosed to the public was equally perplexing for the educated classes; hence the great majority of those who took sides did so in the last resort according to their ordinary political prejudices. Thus the Nationalist Barrès could write that his mind was made up even before he knew the judicial facts: 'I adhered to the opinion of the men whom society had pointed out as competent,'[1] and for him, as for so many others, at any rate at first, the competent judges were the army officers. But it was when serious doubts came to be cast upon the competence of the army that political passions came into play. While the foremost men of letters, artists, and 'intellectuals' went into battle on one side or the other—the 'Ligue pour la défense des Droits de L'Homme et du Citoyen' being countered by the 'Ligue de la Patrie Française'—each distilling the issue into a war of abstract principles (*Fiat justitia ruat coelum* against the idea that it were better that an innocent man should die 'and that the whole nation perish not')—all the forces of the Right tended to rally together against a new offensive of a Republican spirit which they disliked; while eventually the Radicals and Left, once again shocked by the strength of Conservatism (and the violence of the clerical, Nationalist, and anti-semitic elements in it) determined to break it once and for all.

This clash of principles led to an exposure of military justice, but significantly enough, in spite of this and all the subsidiary lawsuits, it did not provide any general demand for a revision of French judicial procedure. To the end of the Republic the liberty of the citizen was to remain unprotected by any habeas corpus and at the mercy of a police system endowed with arbitrary powers reminiscent of the Ancien Régime.

[1] BARRÈS, M.: *Scènes et doctrines du nationalisme*, I, p. 218.

At the same time the Affair soon provoked, as Clemenceau foresaw, an admirable opportunity for party intrigue, and this increased its complexity. 'It was utilized,' wrote Bodley, 'by the Reactionaries against the Republic, by the Clericals against the non-Catholics, by the anti-Clericals against the Church, by the military party against the Parliamentarians and by the revolutionary Socialists against the Army. It was even conspicuously used by rival Republicans against one another.'[1] Like the Boulangist movement it cut across parties.

The triumph of the Dreyfusards meant that the Republic was to swing back to the militant anti-Clericalism of the first decade. It signalized the decline and, as we shall see, the division of the Opportunists and an advance of the Radicals to a position of ascendancy. Once again the enemy was on the Right and there must be no foe to the Left. Above all, the Conservative forces were routed and there was an end of the moderate conciliatory Republic of the 'nineties under which the Ralliement had been such a notable experiment. All the latent bitterness and old hatreds revive and the Dreyfus Affair is the prelude to the most formidable of the secular Republic's offensives against its old enemies with whom we have so often already seen it at grips.

[1] cit. LESLIE, SHANE: *Memoir of John Edward Courtenay Bodley*, p. 269.

BARRÈS, MAURICE: *L'appel au soldat*. Paris, 1926.

BARRÈS, MAURICE: *Leurs figures*. Paris, 1943.

BAUMONT, MAURICE: *L'essor industriel et l'impérialisme colonial* (1878–1904). Paris, 1937.

CLEMENCEAU, GEORGES: *L'iniquité*. Paris, 1899.

DANSETTE, ADRIEN: *Le Boulangisme*, 1886–90. Paris, 1938.

DANSETTE, ADRIEN: *Les Affaires de Panama*. 3rd ed. Paris, 1934.

JAURÈS, JEAN: *Les Preuves*. Paris, sd.

KAYSER, JACQUES: *L'Affaire Dreyfus*. 7th ed. Paris, 1946.

VIZETELLY, E. A.: *Republican France*, 1870–1912. London, 1912.

ZOLA, EMILE: *La Vérité en marche*. Paris, 1901.

XII

THE REPUBLIC OF THE RADICALS

THE Waldeck-Rousseau Ministry of 1899–1902 was one of the most remarkable of the Third Republic as well on account of its composition, its duration, its achievements and the direction it gave to French politics as because of the personality of its head. In addition to a number of distinguished young Radicals, such as Delcassé at the Foreign Office and the thirty-six-year-old Joseph Caillaux at the Ministry of Finance, it included General the Marquis de Galliffet as Minister of War and Millerand, the first Socialist to enter any European Cabinet, as Minister of Commerce. These last two appointments raised an outcry, yet both showed the boldness and wisdom of the new Prime Minister. In Galliffet, an old beau of the Second Empire, a gallant soldier and an aristocrat of independent views, who had been a friend both of Gambetta and the Prince of Wales, Waldeck-Rousseau had chosen a man whom he could expect to have the necessary prestige and courage to carry out reforms in an army still largely officered by aristocrats; in selecting Millerand he had recognized the importance of the parliamentary Socialists, invited them to become a respectable government party and shown his intention of tackling problems of social reform. Millerand's acceptance of office had, however, been made without the formal approval of his party and his *cas* was hotly disputed by his Socialist colleagues several of whom wished to exclude him for the crime of entering a 'bourgeois' Cabinet. In the end he was allowed to retain his party membership, but the dispute helped to retard the union of French Socialists in a single political party which Jaurès had long been working for. This was not to be achieved until 1905, when the Guesdists and Moderates, or Reformists, at length fused in what was to be known as the Section Française de l'Internationale Ouvrière (S.F.I.O.). In other words, the French Socialist party in 1905 became a single branch of the Second International which was at this time largely dominated by German Marxists, and in doing so the moderates had to yield to the intransigence of the doctrinaires, to forgo co-operation with other parties, to submit to a discipline alien to them,[1] to refuse to take part in 'bourgeois' governments and to vote against all credits for military expenditure or colonial domination.   The international character of French Socialism becomes much more marked, and with it its emphasis on the solidarity between Socialists and workers in all countries and its pacifism and opposition to what it denounces as Imperialism and Militarism.   In the years after 1905 when France is adding the last territory to her colonial Empire and when the danger of war in Europe more than once seems imminent this trend of French Socialism is, as we shall see, of great importance.

The inclusion of Galliffet in the Cabinet angered the Left, the inclusion of Millerand irritated the Right as well as some of his own brethren; and when the new Government first met the Chamber its majority was so small that it looked as though its life would be a matter of weeks, if not days.   In fact, however, it lasted nearly three years.   This triumph of duration was largely due to the forceful personality and the tactical skill of the Prime Minister.   An ardent disciple of Gambetta, who had first given him office, Waldeck-Rousseau was as silent, cold and reserved as his master had been eloquent, warm-hearted and expansive—'imprisoned in his silence as a pike is imprisoned in aspic' was Barrès' description.[2]   A Progressist, in the tradition of Gambetta, he none the less, through the circumstances in which he formed his Cabinet and by his subsequent policy, split his party and so put an end to the long period of Opportunist-Progressist ascendancy which had been virtually uninterrupted since 1879.   Although he carried with him a considerable number of Progressist followers, his Cabinet was essentially dependent on the support of the Radicals, of the new Group of Radical-Socialists, often so difficult to distinguish from the Radicals except in name, and of the Socialists.   Thus he prepared the way for the preponderance of the so-called Republican bloc of Left-wing groups in which the Radicals were long to be the dominant element and whose theory of political strategy was to be summed up in the phrase 'No enemies to the Left'. Under his government the country enjoyed a period of relative quiet after the turmoil of the Dreyfus Affair, the régime was consolidated anew and the international position of the country was strengthened.

The return to stability in 1899–1900 was in many ways reminiscent

[1] The Socialists became the first party in France to have any regular standing party organization for electroral and other purposes.   The results of unity and good organization were soon reflected at the polls.   They obtained 59 seats in the Chamber in 1906, 76 in 1910, and 104 in 1914.

[2] *Leurs figures*, p. 185.

of the return to stability after the Boulangist crisis. Once again the
firmness of a government of Republican defence disposed of real or
imaginary plotters, put an end to disorder in the streets and restored
public confidence. Once again a great banquet of the mayors of France
demonstrated the loyalty of the people's representatives in local government; and once again a great exhibition in Paris, that of 1900, turned
the attention of Frenchmen away from politics to the contemplation of
the benefits of material prosperity.

In other respects, however, the consolidation of the Republic at
home recalled 1879 rather than 1889. The Dreyfus Affair had shattered
the Ralliement and all hopes of entente with the Right. As in the days
of Moral Order and the crisis of 1877, the clergy and the army appeared
to many Republicans to have shown themselves in their true light as
impenitent adversaries of the ideal of a liberal democratic régime.
They had exercised political pressure and they must be called to order.
If Waldeck-Rousseau had shown any inclination to forget that it was
Gambetta who had denounced clericalism as the enemy, his Radical
supporters, as fanatically sectarian as ever, were at hand to remind him
of the saying. Anti-clericalism was in fact the cement which bound
the different elements of the Republican bloc together and so long,
therefore, as the religious question was to the forefront, so long was the
bloc likely to hold together. Accordingly the measures taken to curb
the Church and to purge the army were, as in 1879 and afterwards,
among the most significant of the acts of the new Government. Numerous changes were made in the high command of the army, and, most
important of all, the power of promotion was transferred from the
military commission, which had hitherto been responsible, to the Minister of War. This meant that under a politically minded Minister army
rank might depend upon an officer's political views rather than on his
professional competence. In fact this new power was to be flagrantly
abused by General André, the man appointed by Waldeck-Rousseau
to succeed Galliffet upon his resignation in 1900; André, an ardent
Positivist, did not scruple to use freemasons to act as spies and draw up
reports upon the political opinions of army officers. These reports,
collected on a card index at the Grand Orient Lodge headquarters, were
then consulted by the Minister when making promotions. The revelation of this practice by a Nationalist deputy in 1904 naturally caused a
sensation and André was obliged to resign; but the knowledge that the
Ministries of the Bloc Républicain had tolerated such espionage caused
much bitterness both among the public and within the army itself.
The Dreyfus Affair had already discredited and divided the army and

encouraged the spread of pacifism and anti-militarism among the public —the practices of an André perpetuated and intensified the divisions. In dealing with the Church the Government was, like so many earlier French Governments, mainly concerned with the religious orders, which were now officially stated to number 3,216 different congregations with a total membership of nearly 200,000 in France. Waldeck-Rousseau himself had denounced them as a political danger—a rival power within the State—and in pointing to their milliard francs' worth of property he seemed deliberately to evoke memories of the *émigrés* 'milliard' of Restoration days and to encourage the hopes of anti-clerical despoilers. In 1900 the powerful order of the Assumptionists, who had shown their enterprise by organizing pilgrimages to Lourdes and elsewhere[1] and whose paper *La Croix* had been one of the most influential clerical organs, was convicted of having subsidized Nationalist candidates in election campaigns and was dissolved. More important, however, was the effect upon the orders of the law of 1901 relating to the Contract of Association. Ever since 1871 the problem of securing satisfactory legislation to permit of freedom of association had been discussed but left unsolved. No fewer than thirty bills had been brought forward and either defeated or allowed to drop. The only exception was the law sponsored by Waldeck-Rousseau in 1884 which had accorded legal freedom to professional syndicates. Now, as Prime Minister, the architect of that law, an able legist concerned with the problems of order in the State, was eager to complete his work. The bill, which he first put forward in 1899 and which, after much debate and many amendments, mainly of an anti-clerical nature, was finally passed in July 1901, was both a general statement of public law and an offensive measure against the religious orders. While it laid down freedom of association as a general principle, it restricted such freedom to native societies: associations controlled or partly composed of foreigners were excluded, and in consequence the law ruled that each congregation must apply for legal authorization or be dissolved. The Government's wish that such applications should be submitted to the Conseil d'État was overruled with the result that they were subjected not to the supposedly dispassionate scrutiny of a legal body, but to the examination of the Chamber of Deputies with its political prejudices. Furthermore, an anti-clerical deputy had succeeded in tacking on to the final bill a clause which had no strict relevance to the liberty of association as such, but was rather a refurbishing of the famous Article 7 of Jules Ferry, rejected by the Senate in 1881. Henceforward no member of any unauthorized

[1] LECANUET, E.: *L'Eglise de France sous la Troisième République*, p. 361.

congregation was to be permitted to teach. The bill, as it eventually passed, could justifiably be described by the anti-clerical historian, Debidour, as 'the most decisive act of anti-clerical policy since 1870'.[1]

This law on Associations had already gone further than Waldeck-Rousseau's intention and it was soon to be seen that he had launched an anti-clerical offensive which he was no longer able to control and was presently to deplore.

The revival of the clerical question had roused intense interest and feeling throughout the country and brought no less than ninety per cent of the electorate to the polls in the general elections of 1902. The result was an overwhelming victory for the Bloc Républicain, who obtained nearly 370 seats compared with the 220 which went to the Conservatives and Moderates, although in actual votes these Right-wing groups polled only 200,000 less. Waldeck-Rousseau might perhaps have been able to continue in office for a further long term had not fatigue and ill-health compelled him to retire. Possibly, too, he hesitated to face such a solidly anti-clerical rank and file, for the Radicals were now the strongest element in the bloc, and the result of the elections was universally understood to have been a vote in favour of the continuation of an anti-clerical policy which he may well have thought had now gone far enough. Unfortunately, he was himself to give it still further impetus by his recommendation of a successor. Like another able barrister, the last Prime Minister but one of the Third Republic, Paul Reynaud, Waldeck-Rousseau partly ensured the frustration of his own work by his faulty judgement of men. The appointment of André as War Minister was one serious blunder, the recommendation of Emile Combes as the next President of the Council was another.

The *petit père* Combes, as he was known to his familiars, an elderly and comparatively little known Radical Senator, had begun life as a seminarist and a professor of theology and now had all the renegade's fanatical hatred of his former faith. The victory of the Bloc made it certain that the Chamber would be likely to press for a strict application of the Association Law; Combes's accession to power meant that it would be applied with rancorous severity and that there would soon be a general offensive against the Church on all fronts in order to fulfil the Prime Minister's desire for what he called the complete triumph of 'the spirit of the Revolution'. By the end of 1902 all schools (some 12,000 in number) conducted by unauthorized congregations had been closed. In the following March the Government sent to the Senate the applica-

[1] cit. PHILLIPS, C. S.: *The Church in France*, 1848-1907, p. 263. For its text see BODLEY, J. E. C.: *The Church in France*, Appendix III.

tions for authorization of the five male orders whose existence it was still prepared to tolerate, the Trappists, the White Fathers, the African Missions, and two others, while it referred to the Chamber the remaining requests, which were all duly rejected in spite of vigorous protests from the Holy See, the clergy and numerous outside bodies. In consequence fifty-four male congregations were dissolved, comprising some 20,000 friars and monks distributed through 1,500 houses in various parts of the country. In the following June eighty-one applications from female congregations were likewise rejected *en bloc*, and a year later a law was passed forbidding all congregations to give teaching of any kind. Those which had been legally recognized as teaching orders were to be compelled to give up their teaching work within ten years. The last speeches of the dying Waldeck-Rousseau were eloquent protests against the perversion of his own legislation, but they were made in vain. Combes was not to be deterred from his task of fighting clericalism until it was completely disarmed.

The policy of Combes naturally irritated the Vatican and brought the question of separation of Church and State once more to the fore. Yet, although the demand for separation had remained an integral part of the Radical programme ever since 1869, it is possible that the Concordat of 1801 might still have been maintained for some while longer but for the personality and policy of the new Pope, Pius X. Even a Combes could see, as many an Opportunist had seen before him, that the Concordat gave the State certain powers of control over the Church which it might do well not to relinquish.

The great Leo XIII, who had once been hailed by Gambetta as a 'consecrated Opportunist', who had done his best to bring about peace between the French Catholics and the Third Republic, and who had given such a notable impulse to new movements of a Catholic Socialist character by the Encyclicals in which he declared that it was the duty of the Church to have a care for the social problem and a concern for the material as well as spiritual welfare of the working classes, had died in August 1903 at the age of ninety-three. His successor, the sixty-nine year old Pius X, though a man of saintly life, was far less tactful and far more limited in vision. Following the tradition of Pius IX rather than of Leo XIII, he was concerned not so much to adjust the policy and functions of the Church to the changing conditions of a new century as to defend the stronghold of faith from the subtle assaults of an individualist modern world and to stand out inflexibly for the maintenance of Papal rights and prerogatives. Thus it was that the man who promptly condemned the modernist thought of the Abbé Loisy and was presently

to pass sentence upon the 'Sillon', one of the most fruitful of the endeavours of French Catholic laymen to develop a vigorous movement of
Catholic Socialism and the precursor of the important political party
of the Fourth Republic, the Mouvement Républicain Populaire, soon
came into conflict with the French Government on other issues. Already
before Leo XIII's death Combes had begun a quarrel over the interpreta-
tion of the Concordat, a sort of twentieth-century investiture dispute,
in which he had claimed to nominate Bishops to French sees without
any previous consultation with the Papal representatives in France.
This claim was resisted by the Pope, and the quarrel became more bitter
when Pius X threatened to withhold canonical institution from any
bishops who were appointed by the French Government without his
prior approval. Still more important was the incident of March 1904
when the Pope in his character as 'Prisoner of the Vatican' sent a secret
note to the Governments with whom he was in diplomatic relation protesting against a visit by President Loubet to the King of Italy in Rome.
Loubet was the first head of any Catholic State to enter the Quirinal
since 1870 and the Pope denounced his visit as an act 'offensive' to the
Holy See whose capital city the Italian State had seized in defiance of
'all rights'.[1] The disclosure of this note by Jaurès' paper, the Socialist
Humanité, caused acute tension between France and the Vatican. As a
result of this and of a further incident in which two French bishops,
known to have Republican sympathies, were summoned to Rome to
account for alleged improprieties of conduct, events moved rapidly to
a climax: diplomatic relations with Rome were severed, Radical and
anti-clerical passions were further roused and in November 1904 Combes
introduced a bill for the separation of Church and State. Although he
fell two months later, discredited for having applied to the control of
civil administration 'Bonapartist' methods of espionage not unlike those
practised by André in military matters, he was still able to exert strong
anti-clerical influence in the Senate, and the much more moderate ministry under Rouvier, who succeeded him, dared not abandon the proposal
for separation which had just been unanimously endorsed by a Radical
Party Congress, although the French public as a whole was remarkably
indifferent to the issue.

The new Government, however, showed its comparative lack of
enthusiasm by leaving the main work of piloting the bill through
Parliament to a new deputy, a comparatively young journalist and lawyer
named Aristide Briand, who acted as *rapporteur*. Briand had begun his
career at St. Nazaire as a militarist Socialist, but he was, in reality, too

[1] cit. ZÉVAÈS, A.: *Histoire de la Troisième République*, 1870-1926, p. 448.

nonchalant to be an ardent doctrinaire and it was not long before he was
to throw off his Socialist allegiance. Now, aided by the combination
of an exceptionally musical voice and unusual expressiveness of face and
gestures, he showed extraordinary suppleness and tactical skill, fascinated
the Chamber by his eloquence and established a parliamentary reputation.
The momentous law of December 9th, 1905, which eventually emerged
was thus largely his work. It declared that the Republic ensured freedom of worship and guaranteed its free exercise subject to regulations
necessary for the preservation of public order. At the same time,
however, the Republic ceased to recognize or subsidize any form of
worship, Roman Catholic, Protestant or Jewish, there was an end of
the *budget des cultes*—and church revenues and endowments were to
be handed over to new *associations cultuelles* which were to be framed
within a specified time limit by the laity of parishes in order that religious
services might be maintained. An inventory of all Church property
was meanwhile to be made in order to facilitate the reallocation of assets.

In fact the separation of Church and State, deplored by Bodley as
the 'first serious breach made in the administrative fabric constructed
by Napoleon',[1] meant the substitution of one set of legal relationships
for another, and when they saw that separation was inescapable the main
concern of French churchmen was that the financial loss involved in the
change should be as slight as possible. Unfortunately for them, however, their material position was considerably prejudiced as a result of
the attitude of the Pope and of the absence, since the severance of diplomatic relations, of any official channel of negotiation between the French
Government and the Vatican. It was in fact regrettable that relations
between the French Republic and the Holy See were such that an arrangement which had worked for over a century was terminated by the uni-
lateral act of one of the parties to the Concordat instead of by an agreement. The result was that, without waiting to consult the French
episcopate, the Pope vehemently denounced the principle of separation
and refused to recognize the *associations cultuelles*. Although the
taking of the inventory of Church property had led to disturbances in
some parts of France, where the faithful regarded it as a sacrilegious pro-
ceeding, any hopes that the Pope may have had that there would be a
revulsion of feeling in favour of the maintenance of the Concordat were
doomed to disappointment by the results of the general election of 1906.
This reaffirmed the supremacy of the Bloc and soon led to the formation
of a new Ministry in which Briand became Minister of Public Instruction
and Worship and in which Clemenceau took office for the first time as

[1] BODLEY, J. E. C.: *The Church in France*, pp. 3, 114.

Minister of the Interior. The continued refusal of the Pope to sanction the formation of the proposed *associations cultuelles* meant that there was now no legal body to which the Church's property could be assigned or its buildings transferred. In consequence, since the Church refused to comply with the terms of the law, the State sequestered its property, handing over its funds to public relief organizations and its buildings to the local municipalities. Only the Churches remained for the use of the clergy and even these were not legally in Church ownership.

Thus the Pope's uncompromising attitude had the extraordinary result that 'The Catholic Church was without legal status of any kind; it could hold no property; it was "literally an outlaw"'[1] existing merely upon the sufferance of the theoretically 'neutral' state. Materially it was extremely hard hit. The clergy were now dependent entirely upon the support of the faithful and many of them in poor districts were condemned to a life of great poverty. The natural consequence was that recruits fell off, the number of the clergy declined and many parishes could no longer be served. On the other hand the general quality of the priesthood, reduced though it was in numbers, was greatly improved, since in general only those who had a real vocation and were prepared to face a life of hardship and privation were now prepared to enter the ministry. In the long run, although the elimination of organized Christian influences from French life was quickened, the momentous separation of 1905 was probably beneficial to both sides. Republican Governments and Chambers no longer spent a disproportionate amount of their time in sterile quarrels with the Church, while the Church, though materially poorer and numerically weaker, now enjoyed a real freedom from State interference and in its altered condition was soon to show a new intellectual vigour and to attract into its fold some of the finest minds in France. Finally, although anti-clericalism was still to remain a force to be conjured with in France and persists until this day, the removal of the main grievances of the anti-clericals did contribute to a general appeasement once the bitterness attendant upon separation had had time to die. In so far as this happened, the work of Waldeck-Rousseau, Combes, Briand and Clemenceau during the years 1899 to 1907 was a real contribution to Republican consolidation, not merely in the sense that it helped to bring about a succession of electoral victories of the Republican Bloc and to demonstrate the powerlessness of the old enemies who had played such a conspicuous part in opposition to the régime during the first thirty years of its existence, but because it removed the root cause of many of the main difficulties with which the Republic

[1] PHILLIPS, C. S.: *The Church in France, 1848-1907*, p. 287.

had had to contend. The new settlement was neither just nor generous, but in the end it worked better than the old.

Meanwhile, during these same years, important steps were taken to strengthen the position of France in Europe and for these she was largely indebted to another disciple of Gambetta, Théophile Delcassé, who became Foreign Minister in 1898 and retained the post through the best part of four successive Ministries, a notable example of the way in which ministerial instability and apparent fluctuations of policy might sometimes be corrected by continuity of action in a particular department. Delcassé, indeed, a little dark, spectacled, buttoned-up, secretive person of unimpressive professorial appearance and enormous industry, showed remarkable pertinacity in pursuing his aims. He did his utmost to reinforce the Franco-Russian alliance, ensuring the continued validity of the military agreement between the two powers, and in 1901 and 1902 there was a fresh exchange of visits between the Tsar and the President of the Republic. Still more important was the success he achieved in effecting a rapprochement with Italy and in bringing to an end a long period of friction with Great Britain.

Relations with Italy, strained ever since France had established her protectorate in Tunisia, had deteriorated still more since Italy's adherence to the Triple Alliance in 1882 and the denunciation in 1887 by the violently anti-French Crispi of the Franco-Italian Treaty of commerce, which led to eleven years of trade warfare more damaging to Italy than to France. In 1896, however, the Italian defeat of Adowa in Abyssinia led to the fall of Crispi and put an end for the time being to Italy's bellicose attitude. The way lay open for a revision of Italian policy, and a speedy improvement in Franco-Italian relations ensued. In that same year an agreement regulating the status of Italians in Tunisia was tantamount to a recognition by Italy of France's position in the Beylicate. Two years later, in November 1898, Delcassé was able to conclude a new commercial treaty and sent as Ambassador to Rome another of Gambetta's disciples, Camille Barrère, who remained there for more than a quarter of a century and most ably assisted him to put the relations of the two countries on a new footing of confidence and friendship. The most important immediate results were the conclusion in 1900 of a secret agreement whereby France promised Italy a free hand in Tripolitania in return for recognition of her own claims in Morocco, and the confidential assurance given by the Italian Government in 1902, when it once again renewed the Triple Alliance, that it did not consider itself bound thereby to take part in any aggression against France under any circumstances whatsoever. This entente, which practically invalidated the effect of the Triple Alliance in so far as Italy was a potential ally for Germany against France was more openly demonstrated by the visit of part of the Italian fleet to Toulon in 1901 and by the exchanges of visits between the King of Italy and President Loubet, which, as we have seen, had such momentous consequences for the relations of Church and State in France. The German Chancellor, Prince Bülow, who had some inkling of what was going on but could not prevent it, attempted to treat the rapprochement as an innocent flirtation: 'In a happy marriage,' he told the Reichstag, 'the husband should not be upset if his wife enjoys an innocent waltz with another man.' But, as a French historian has remarked, 'the flirtation was to develop into a liaison'.[1]

Still more important was the rapprochement with Great Britain. Ever since the end of the Restoration when France had resumed her advance as a colonial power, in spite of periods of more or less close entente in Europe, the traditional spirit of jealous rivalry had tended to dominate her relations with Britain overseas. In the great period of colonial expansion during the last quarter of the nineteenth century the extension of the new French overseas Empire had not been halted by the furore about Tonkin which led to the dramatic fall of Jules Ferry in 1885; and by 1894 the rulers of the Third Republic had become sufficiently conscious of their imperial responsibilities to set up a separate Ministry of Colonies. The creation of the Indo-Chinese Union in 1887 was followed in the 'nineties by the conquest of Dahomey (1890), the establishment of the Ivory Coast as a separate colony (1893), the occupation of Timbuctoo (1894), and the annexation of Madagascar (1896). Throughout the world, from the fisheries of Newfoundland to the rivers of Siam and the islands of the Malayan Archipelago, French and British sailors, explorers and traders, met and competed; and although agreements such as that for the establishment of a condominium in the New Hebrides in 1887, the Constantinople Convention of 1888 neutralizing the Suez Canal, and the Convention of 1890 delimiting French and British spheres of interest in the Niger Valley brought temporary local appeasements, on the whole relations between the two countries tended to grow steadily worse. The loss of Egypt continued to rankle with the French, and rivalry in Madagascar and trouble in Siam added fresh causes of friction. Already in 1893 the British Ambassador in Paris, Lord Dufferin, had described the feeling of all classes towards Great Britain as one of 'animosity and bitter dislike'.[2] During the next five

[1] cit. BAUMONT, M.: L'essor industriel et l'impérialisme colonial (1878-1904), p. 323.

[2] cit. LANGER, W. L.: The Diplomacy of Imperialism, 1890-1902, I, p. 49.

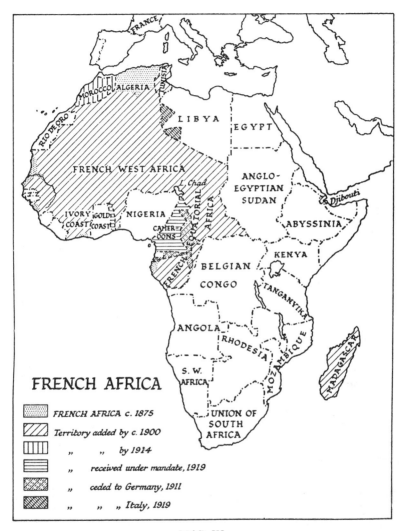

FRENCH AFRICA

	FRENCH AFRICA c. 1875
	Territory added by c. 1900
	„ „ by 1914
	„ received under mandate, 1919
	„ ceded to Germany, 1911
	„ „ „ Italy, 1919

MAP IV

years events in Africa were to bring the two countries to the verge of
hostilities. The penetration of French explorers, traders and missionaries
to the heart of Africa from bases on the Senegal in the west or the Congo
in the south had opened up visions of a vast French African Empire
which might extend not only north and south from the Congo to
Algeria, but also east and west from the Senegal to the Nile and beyond.
But in attempting to penetrate into Sudan and the Upper Nile Valley,
the French were entering upon territory which was regarded as its own
preserve and sphere of influence by the power which held Egypt. Great
Britain stood in the way; and when 1898 a small French expeditionary
force under Captain Marchand was encountered by Kitchener of Khar-
toum at Fashoda in the Sudan the British Government demanded its
withdrawal. Fortunately, Delcassé, like Grévy in 1887, kept his head
despite popular anger and never lost sight of the fact that so long as the
Germans continued to hold Strasbourg and Metz they were France's
only permanent enemy. France could not engage in war against the
greatest naval power in the world, and any attempt to do so for spheres
of influence in a remote part of Africa could lead only to the loss of
her newly won Empire. The Minister persuaded his colleagues in the
Dupuy Cabinet, and Marchand was ordered to retire. A few months
later a new Anglo-French Convention left the Tchad area to France and
confirmed Britain's control of the Upper Nile. Thus Fashoda decided
that East Africa should remain predominantly British while West Africa
would continue to be predominantly French. France, now obliged to
abandon her efforts at eastward expansion, was to find plenty of scope
for her energies during the next forty years in opening up the vast un-
explored interior between the Niger and the Mediterranean countries
and in rounding off her African domain by the establishment of a protectorate in Morocco.

War was thus averted, but at the price of a severe blow to French
prestige, and during the next few years French opinion was more than
ever virulently hostile to Great Britain and showed its animosity by its
open sympathies with the Boers during the Boer War of 1899–1902.
Soon after Fashoda, the President of the Republic himself, Félix Faure,
went so far as to tell a Russian diplomat that Great Britain, not Germany,
was France's real enemy;[1] and some of the anti-British propaganda of
the Boer War period was so forceful that the Germans thought it worth
while to reprint it when they occupied France in 1940.[2] On their side

[1] cit. BAUMONT, M.: L'essor industriel et l'impérialisme colonial (1878–1904),
p. 301.
[2] e.g. L'Assiette au beurre, No. 119, of 1903.

the British did not hide their contempt and pity for a country which after so many scandals was now in the throes of the Dreyfus Affair.

But the drain of the Boer War upon British resources, the loss of prestige which it involved and the revelation of British unpopularity abroad necessitated a revision of British policy. Isolation was now becoming more dangerous than splendid, and, after negotiations for some sort of Anglo-German alliance had broken down as had efforts to reach friendly agreement with Russia, she had turned in 1902 to Russia's new enemy in the Far East and concluded an alliance with Japan. This inclined her all the more to try and compose her differences with Russia's ally France, so that she should not be faced with the hostility of the French as well as of the Triple Alliance powers. Meanwhile France on her side had for some time been preoccupied by the growing anarchy in Morocco and by the disposition of other powers to interfere in what she had long designed as her own preserve. Italy, as we have seen, already recognized her claims, but there remained Spain, Great Britain, and, last but not least, the Germany of William II, now belatedly seeking a 'place in the sun'. If Great Britain also could be induced to recognize the preponderance of French interests in Morocco, the way might lie open to a wider understanding which would be advantageous to both powers, since in Europe itself, politically and commercially, there was no real reason why they should not be friends. Thus the Moroccan question on the one hand and the German menace on the other disposed both Governments to seek a settlement of outstanding questions. In arriving at an Entente both were well served by new men, France by its new ambassador in London, Paul Cambon, appointed to the Court of St. James in 1898, and Great Britain by her new sovereign, Edward VII, whose genial tact and readiness to visit Paris in 1903 did much to overcome the French people's hostility to England and to prepare the way for political understanding.

In April 1904 a comprehensive agreement was signed. In return for a formal recognition of her position in Egypt Great Britain gave France a free hand in Morocco, and in an accompanying convention and declaration disputes in Newfoundland and Africa and in Siam, Madagascar and the New Hebrides were finally settled. The old colonial rivalry was brought to an end with the closing stages of the great period of expansion and as a result there came into being the Entente Cordiale. The relations of the two countries were revolutionized. They gradually developed the habit of co-operation: henceforward they would be more inclined to combine for the defence of their Empires, and their friendship meant a new alignment of the Great Powers. It was soon to

be seen that Great Britain had definitely cast her weight into the European balance on the side of the Dual Alliance. The logical corollary
was a similar agreement between Great Britain and Russia, signed in
1907, towards which French diplomacy naturally contributed. With
its conclusion the Triple Alliance of Germany, Austria-Hungary and
Italy was faced by a Triple Entente of France, Great Britain and Russia.
The division of the European Great Powers into two rival and heavily
armed camps was complete.

Agreements with Italy, Spain and Great Britain: all these could
appear, and were hailed as 'so many "jalons" planted on the path to
peace'.[1] Following soon after the Hague Peace Conference of 1899,
which had been unexpectedly summoned by the Tsar to call a halt to
the continuing increase in armaments, and had led to the Hague Convention for the peaceful settlement of international disputes, they might
appear to suggest that world peace was more secure than at any time since
Bismarck's fall and that it might be preserved for another generation.
But there was one power which had not had any part in these Moroccan
negotiations, and which was affronted at her exclusion and at the cold-
ness with which Delcassé received the advances she made to France;
and that power, Germany, was also the power who had been the chief
obstacle to a limitation of armaments by the Hague Conference of 1899
and whose naval and commercial rivalry with Great Britain was yearly
growing sharper. Irritated by a diplomatic revolution, which seemed
to diminish her relative importance, but heartened by Russia's defeat
at the hands of Japan in 1905 and by its revelation of Russia's military
weakness, she sought to break first the Franco-Russian alliance and then
the Anglo-French entente. Her efforts to do so and their failure were,
as we shall see, to lead to growing tension. The armaments race continued and the ineptitude of German diplomacy, compared with the
success of French, led Europe nearer to war because of the suspicions and
fears of isolation and encirclement which resulted in the minds of
Germany's rulers. For the time being, however, the conclusion and
maintenance of the Entente Cordiale appeared to be an important new
guarantee of continued European peace.

Thus in appearance the Third Republic was strengthened at home
and abroad as a result of the policy of Waldeck-Rousseau and his successors. But, although in spite of the questionable practices of Combes
the Radicals returned stronger than ever after the elections of 1906, the
signs of strength were, as so often before, offset by signs of weakness

[1] cit. BAUMONT, M.: *L'essor industriel et l'impérialisme colonial* (1878-1904),
p. 360.

which led shrewd observers to question the solidity of the régime and to doubt the value of France as an ally.

The Bloc and the Radicals had entrenched themselves in place and power, but they had not, any more than their predecessors, succeeded in uniting all Frenchmen in allegiance to the Republic. The parliamentary régime was still a subject of attack from enemies on both flanks. On the Right, although the Monarchists of the old school had been virtually eliminated as a parliamentary force by the elections of 1902 and 1906, a new movement had come to infuse fresh vigour into Royalism and equip it with a highly developed intellectual doctrine. The group of the Action Française, an extreme nationalist paper founded in 1899, who announced their conversion to the cause of monarchy in 1904, never became a factor of any importance inside a parliament which they effected to despise; but by their teachings and writings, their intellectual vigour, their narrow concept of 'integral Nationalism', and their violent attacks on the Republic, their leaders, Charles Maurras, Léon Daudet, and others, were to exercise a considerable influence for the best part of forty years. On the Left, and more immediately menacing, were the Syndicates with their traditional sympathy with Anarchist theories, later reinforced by the teachings of Georges Sorel, author of a famous work called *Réflexions sur la Violence*. In 1895 the formation of a Confédération Générale du Travail (C.G.T.) or Trades Unions' Congress, followed in 1896 by that of a general 'Fédération des Bourses du Travail', under the guidance of an able young consumptive named Fernand Pelloutier, marked the development of Syndicalist organization upon a national scale; and when in 1902 the Fédération des Bourses du Travail amalgamated with the reorganized C.G.T. a small body (in 1904 it had only 150,000 members) came into being which has ever since exercised an influence upon French economic and political life. From the first there was a conflict within the C.G.T., just as there was in the political Socialist groups, between the moderates and the radicals, between those who favoured moderate tactics and were prepared to co-operate with the Parliamentary Socialists and those who preferred to rely solely upon direct action by economic means. At the Amiens Congress of the C.G.T. in 1906 the revolutionary Syndicalists won a notable victory, and, in the so-called Amiens Charter, carried a resolution in which the Congress formally disowned connexion with any political doctrine and advocated the general strike as the instrument by which it hoped to achieve its ultimate aim, the expropriation of the capitalist. class and the reconstruction of society on a syndicalist basis. This resolution was the signal for the intensification of industrial unrest

which had already been growing in 1906. The next two years were
marked by strikes and disturbances in many parts of the country, strikes
of electricians, of workers in the building and food industries, and of
navvies in 1907 and 1908 in big towns such as Paris, Marseilles, Le
Havre and Dunkirk, disturbances in 1907 among the vine-growers of
the south who had lately formed a union and were suffering from a
fresh depression, and last, but not least disquieting to the Government,
a strike of post-office workers in 1909, followed by a call from the C.G.T.
for a great general strike. These syndicalist strikes and disturbances,
which in many cases were accompanied by anti-militarist propaganda,
presented a challenge to the authority of the State which Clemenceau,
Prime Minister from October 1906 to July 1909, had no hesitation in
accepting. In many cases troops were employed to deal with strikers;
the new and illegally formed Primary Teachers' Union was refused
permission to affiliate with the C.G.T.; a number of Trade Union
leaders were arrested and civil servants who struck were dismissed.
Thus Clemenceau, who had so often in his early years been a destructive
force, typifying the Radical distrust of strong government, now, in
his 'sixties, experienced what it was to be defied by disruptive elements.
He kept order and the general strike was a fiasco; but he split the Bloc,
for his policy of repression became more and more distasteful to the
Parliamentary Socialists. However much they disapproved of certain
aspects of the Syndicalists' theory and action, they refused to disown
them by supporting the Prime Minister. Clemenceau throughout his
ministry was the object of attacks by Jaurès and others, which were
scarcely less bitter than those he himself had once launched against Jules
Ferry. The clash of policies was accentuated by the clash of personalities,
for the optimistic, warm-hearted, eloquent Jaurès, a sort of doctrinaire
professorial Gambetta, was the very antithesis of the dry, sceptical,
authoritative, old Jacobin fighter Clemenceau. And so in the end
Clemenceau found himself in the paradoxical situation of leaning more
and more on the support of his old enemies, the Progressists, and of being
attacked more and more violently by his old allies, the Socialists. When
his government fell, defeated, like so many French Cabinets, on a comparatively minor issue, he was succeeded by Briand, whose suppleness
and talk of appeasement suggested that he might be the man to repair
the breaches in the Bloc. Such hopes were unfulfilled. In 1910 there
was a fresh wave of strikes, notably on the railways, and Briand, who, a
decade earlier had been one of the ardent Socialist advocates of the
general strike, had by now, like Millerand, moved away from the
Socialists, and, like Clemenceau, was to find how different social problems

looked from the seat of government. He dealt no less firmly—withstood the strikers and refused to allow civil servants who had been punished to resume their posts. As a result he, too, failed to win Socialist support and lost that of many Radical-Socialists. His fall in February 1911 definitely marked the end of the Bloc for the time being and opened a new period of instability. During the three years before the outbreak of the Great War of 1914 there were no less than seven Cabinets, and the facts that some of them were headed by former Progressists such as Poincaré and Barthou and that Poincaré was in 1913 elected President of the Republic showed to what an extent the Bloc had for the moment disintegrated.

Thus the social problem had once again come to the fore during the years following the Dreyfus Affair; under Millerand's guidance at the Ministry of Commerce some important measures had been taken to deal with labour problems: a Direction du Travail or Labour Department had been set up under the presidency of Arthur Fontaine, one of the most remarkable of the civil servants of the régime; a Conseil Supérieur du Travail had been established on which Trade Unions were given representation and much encouragement was given to Union organization. Furthermore, in 1900, the Waldeck-Rousseau Cabinet had secured the passage of a law for the gradual reduction to ten hours of the working day of all employees in mixed establishments. But since then, although many proposals for social legislation had appeared in Ministerial programmes, scarcely any important measures of social reform had reached the statute book, apart from a law providing for old-age pensions introduced by Clemenceau and passed in April 1910, under the Briand Ministry. The dispute of Church and State had been a growing preoccupation between 1901 and 1905 and where the social question again forced itself on public attention in 1906 and afterwards it had been mostly in the ugly form of strikes, and remedies had been sought in repression rather than in legislation.

The triumph of the Dreyfusard party at the opening of the century had been accompanied by a 'great wave of democratic feeling' which had seemed to promise much in the way of achievement. But by 1911, as a Left-wing French historian has admitted, 'only bitterness was left'.[1] Parliament had seemed to spend itself in sterile disputes and intrigues.

In fact, the defects of the French parliamentary system, which we have already noted as productive of violent discontent in the 'eighties and 'nineties, had by now become still more deeply rooted. The legislature was still unchecked, or where controlled it was so not by the executive but by the pressure of sectional interests in the electorate.

[1] BOURGIN, G.: La Troisième République, p. 180.

The habit of interpellation had increased; so too had the number of parliamentary standing commissions which tended more and more to arrogate to themselves a power to interfere in administration. In consequence deputies were coming to win a patronage of administrative posts, which meant that they were constantly solicited by their electors and constantly under the temptation to bestow places for political motives. Moreover, as the class of professional politicians grew, so more and more deputies were guided in their conduct by the financial need to keep their seats. Hence the increasing inclination of the nation's representatives on the eve of a general election to vote for the lavish expenditure of public funds on objects likely to win the votes of constituents, irrespective of the state of the national finances, which had in fact steadily tended to deteriorate since the turn of the century; and hence their increasing dependence upon those local electoral committees whose interests tended, as we have seen, to be so petty. In addition to the local committees and the standing parliamentary commissions we must also note the emergence of another form of committee evolved by the Bloc, the Délégation des Gauches. This was composed of representatives of the four main groups of the Bloc and acted in such constant consultation with the Government that it undoubtedly to a large extent dictated Government policy and so exercised a new form of *pouvoir occulte*. Furthermore, the temptation which was to be so notable in the early years of the Fourth Republic, for sectional groups of the community to seek to capture the machinery of State or to exercise pressure upon policy for their own ends was already discernible. By disavowing a Minister, the executive committee of the Radical and Radical-Socialist groups might destroy a Cabinet, and many syndicates were so highly disciplined as virtually to dictate the votes of their members. Thus the highly centralized state structure, perfected by Napoleon and so carefully and deliberately preserved by succeeding régimes, seemed to be crumbling away under the dissolving action of a myriad groups and committees.[1] The State had granted freedom of association, but there was soon to come a time when certain associations seemed to be strongholds of a new feudalism able to defy the State. Under this Republic of Committees, which in its demagogic aspect deserved the title once given it by a clever writer of 'La République des Camarades',[2] national interests appeared more than ever to be obscured by those of groups and indi-

[1] The Radical policy of Combes, known as 'Combisme', was described approvingly by the Radical philosopher Alain as nothing else but the continuous control of the elected by the elect. HALÉVY, D.: *Décadence de la Liberté*, p. 63 n.

[2] Robert de Jouvenel.

viduals. Denounced or derided by the Syndicalists and the Action Française, disappointing the most clear-sighted and patriotic of the Republicans, the machine of government once again seemed sadly in need of an overhaul. No Bonaparte was at hand to recast it from the beginning; no statesman was strong enough to impose a constitutional reform which would strengthen the executive and limit parliamentary irresponsibility; and so once again the politicians who sought to redress matters turned to juggling with the electoral procedure. In 1910 Briand, in a striking speech, had declared the need for a strong 'purifying breeze' to pass across 'all the little foul and stagnant ponds which are being formed and spreading more or less over the country'. The remedy, eagerly sponsored alike by the Right and by the Socialists, was the introduction of proportional representation, but in spite of a favourable vote in the Chamber in 1912 and of continuous propaganda, it was strenuously opposed by the Radicals whose organization was largely built up on the basis of *scrutin d'arrondissement*; and it was rejected by the Senate, which had now for many years shown itself the sort of Conservative body it was originally intended to be—except that the order of things it conserved was fundamentally Republican—resolutely opposing all change whether in the form of an income tax, of votes for women, or a new electoral procedure. So the elections of 1914 were once again held under the old system, and, incidentally, they led to a re-formation of the Bloc. The Socialists were ready to abandon their ardour for electoral reform in order to back the Radicals upon an issue about which they felt more strongly. Events abroad and the increasing risk of war had brought the question of the army once more to the fore.

The anti-militarism, which had grown notably in the late 'eighties and 'nineties, partly in reaction against Boulangism, partly as the result of the unpopularity of conscription with young men of letters who wrote novels[1] throwing a somewhat lurid light upon conditions in the army, and last but not least because of the Dreyfus Affair and the development of Socialism with its internationalist pacifist teachings, came to a climax with the bill passed in 1905 by which the length of military service was reduced from three to two years and in the reduction of military expenditure and neglect of the navy. The law of 1905, which incidentally suppressed exemptions, thus making compulsory service for the first time practically as well as theoretically equal for all, had been introduced in 1901 at the time of the Franco-Italian repprochement and became effective just after the conclusion of the Anglo-French Entente.

[1] e.g. *Curieuse*, by J. PELADAN (1886); *Le cavalier Miserey*, by ABEL HERMANT (1887), and *Sous-offs*, by LUCIEN DESCAVES (1890).

Following not long after the Hague Peace Conference and upon this improvement in France's diplomatic position it might equally with the Entente be held to be a factor for peace. But in the momentous year 1905, the year also of the separation of Church and State and of the formation of a united French Socialist party, the international situation deteriorated.

Now that France had the goodwill of Great Britain and Italy for her designs on Morocco, she was anxious to consolidate her position as quickly as possible. But Germany, sore at not having been consulted by Delcassé in spite of her treaty rights in Morocco, was unwilling to abandon her own Moroccan ambitions without a struggle, and eager to break the Anglo-French Entente if she could. In March 1905 the Kaiser had visited Tangier and delivered a resounding speech in which he declared that Germany regarded the future of Morrocco as an international question. When Delcassé refused to agree to the subsequent German proposal for an international conference, the German Government demanded and obtained his resignation from the Rouvier Cabinet who were alarmed, knowing France's military unpreparedness, and put little trust in Delcassé's assurances of English support. This enforced resignation was a blow to French pride and prestige, but in the ensuing conference, which met at Algeciras in 1906, Germany gained little, since the majority of the Powers represented agreed that the organization of police services in Moroccan ports should devolve upon France and Spain. Thus France's dominant interest was recognized, although nominal supervision by a Dutch or Swiss Inspector-General, and the fact of the conference itself, preserved a semblance of international control, and her new duties gave her the opportunity to strengthen her foothold in Morocco. Moreover, instead of being weakened, the Entente Cordiale was reinforced by the crisis, since, although the British Government resolutely resisted the French suggestions that entente should be converted into alliance, they did agree to allow military staff conversations: even though they were in no way to bind the two Governments, this action of the British Government was significant.

In 1909 a change in German policy suggested that the Moroccan question need no longer give trouble, but this hope was illusory. For Germany the Bosnian crisis of that year relegated Moroccan affairs to a secondary place and the German Government agreed to the conclusion of a Franco-German convention whereby they recognized French political preponderance in Morocco in return for the grant of facilities for German nationals to co-operate with French in obtaining economic concessions. But this *détente* did not last long. When in 1911 a rebellion against the Sultan led the French to seize the opportunity of strengthening their grip on the country by sending an expeditionary force, avowedly to rescue the Europeans blockaded in Fez, Germany once again stepped in, declared that France's action was contrary to the Algeciras Act of 1906, sent a gunboat, the *Panther*, to Agadir, nominally to protect German interests in Southern Morocco, and said that it would be withdrawn only when France offered suitable compensation: in return for formal recognition of freedom of action by France in Morocco she must receive the whole of the French Congo. In spite of the pro-German sympathies of the Prime Minister, Caillaux, the French Government were unanimous in refusing such an exorbitant demand. For some days there was something of a war scare reminiscent of 1875 and 1887. But a clear indication by Great Britain that she thought Germany's claims excessive and would go to France's help if she were attacked, caused the German Government to think twice about imposing their demand by force. Eventually, after long and difficult negotiations, a new Franco-German Convention was signed in November 1911. Germany at last gave France a free hand in Morocco and agreed that she might set up a protectorate there. In return there was a territorial readjustment on the borders of the German Cameroons, whereby a considerable area of the French Congo passed under German rule.[1]

The Agadir crisis was important for a number of reasons. It led in March 1912 to the formal establishment of a French Protectorate in Morocco similar to those already set up in Tunis and Annam. General Lyautey was appointed the first Resident and by 1914 the country was almost wholly under effective French control. A new area of 440,000 square kilometres and some 5,000,000 people was thus added to the French dominions and the vast French African Empire was now finally rounded off eighty-four years after the conquest of Algiers. But this success had been bought at a price which was dear and in conditions which were disquieting and humiliating. Caillaux had hoped, as had Rouvier in 1905, that the opportunity of discussions with Germany might lead to a general settlement of disputed questions and open a new era in Franco-German relations, but nothing came of such hopes and he himself had to resign as a result of the disclosure that he had conducted the German negotiations largely behind the back of his own Foreign Minister, De Selves. In fact the effect of Germany's 'big stick' diplomacy was to lead a large number of Frenchmen to see that German policy was a threat alike to French security and to European peace, to induce the French Government to attempt still further to strengthen its ties

[1] See Map IV.

with Great Britain[1] and Russia, and to encourage a campaign by the
Nationalists and the Right for the reimposition of three years' military
service.   The laws of 1912 and 1913, by which the Austro-Hungarian
and German Empires made further increases in the size of their armies,
alarmed the French military authorities and, eventually, in 1913, they
sponsored a bill for the re-establishment of three years' service which
became law in August of that year.   But this three years' law met with
most strenuous opposition from the Socialists and from some of the
Radicals.   Men like Jaurès held firmly to the old Radical Republican
view that a truly Republican army should consist merely of 'the nation
in arms' and that there should be no professional force; and believing
that alliances and competition in armaments were the main causes of war
they pathetically hoped that the solidarity of Socialists and workers
in the two countries would lead to a Franco-German rapprochement.
For them, therefore, it was important that France should take no step
which might be construed as 'provocative', while Marxists and revolutionary Syndicalists like Gustave Hervé believed that there had to be a
choice between war and revolution and that any measure calculated to
reinforce the army must be opposed because they held it to be *ipso facto*
strengthening the militarist domination of the capitalist State.

This new law was far from popular, for it increased the financial
burden of the country—and in the autumn of 1913 the Radicals, hitherto
divided on the military question, allowed electoral considerations to
prevail in shaping their policy.   They calculated correctly that opposition
to the three years' law would pay them best and made it one of the chief
points of their programme.   Their decision enabled the Bloc to be
re-formed and to win a striking victory in the general elections of May
1914.   The Socialists gained some 30 seats and the Radicals of various
shades came back 260 strong.   When the new Chamber met it seemed
certain that the law was doomed.   Indeed the first Cabinet to confront
the new Chamber fell that same day because it announced its intention
of maintaining the law.   Here, however, we come to one of those rare
moments when the personality of the President of the Republic was
of extreme importance.   Poincaré, the firm, tenacious Lorrainer who
had been elected President in January, 1913, had long been preoccupied by the dangers of the international situation and was
fully convinced that the three years' law was necessary for national

---

[1] For instance by the naval agreement of 1912, whereby the French concentrated
their main naval forces in the Mediterranean while Great Britain transferred
part of her Mediterranean squadron to the North Sea.   Such an arrangement
gave France a strong moral claim to British support should war break out.

security. In spite of the attitude of the Chamber and of Jaurès' admon-
ition reminding him of Gambetta's warning to a former President who
ventured to oppose the Lower House, that he must submit or resign,
Poincaré was determined not to give way without a struggle. He
chose as his next Prime Minister, Viviani, a Socialist who was ready to
play for time. Then on June 28th another event occurred which saved
the law. The death at Sarajevo of the heir to the throne of the Austro-
Hungarian Empire by the hand of a Serbian assassin provoked a new
crisis for which there was to be no solution save that of war.

   Although the Bloc, the French peace party, won such a success in
the elections it must not be thought that the question of the three years'
law and the general problem of national defence had left the country
indifferent. Far from it; indeed the passions aroused were strikingly
illustrated by a dramatic incident which contributed to the fall of the
Doumergue Ministry in December 1913 : the wife of the Finance Minister,
Caillaux, exasperated at the campaign conducted against her husband
by a Right-wing paper, the *Figaro*, forced her way into the Director's
office and shot him dead. Like the Choiseul-Praslin crime on the eve
of the Revolution of 1848 and the murder of Victor Noir in 1870,
Madame Caillaux's action, as a French historian has pointed out, 'marked
the paroxysm of a drama of internal politics which was the prelude
to the drama being prepared on the other side' of the frontier.[1] Nor
was it the last or the most important crime of its kind. On July 31st,
on the very eve of the cataclysm, a half-witted fanatic, led astray by the
violence of the attacks by the Nationalist Press against the 'pro-German
Socialist traitor' shot Jaurès in a restaurant. The great orator's trust in
the solidarity of Socialists in all lands was vain and by a strange irony
the new pacifist Chamber, of which he had been one of the most notable
members, spent virtually all its life wrestling with the problems of war
and the defence of an invaded country.

   [1] RECLUS, M.: *La Troisième République de 1870 à 1918*, p. 274.

ALAIN: *Éléments d'une doctrine radicale.* 6th ed. Paris, 1933.
BARRÈS, MAURICE: *La grande pitié des églises de France.* 14th ed. Paris, 1914.
BAUMONT, MAURICE: *L'essor industriel et l'impérialisme colonial* (1878-1904). Paris, 1937.
BODLEY, J. E. C.: *The Church in France.* London, 1906.
BRUUN, GEOFFREY: *Clemenceau.* Harvard, 1943.
CAILLAUX, JOSEPH: *Mes Mémoires.* Vols. I–II. Paris, 1942.
CAMBON, PAUL: *Correspondance, 1870–1924.* Vol. II (1898–1911). Paris, 1940.
PORTER, C. W. R.: *The Career of Théophile Delcassé.* Philadelphia, 1936.
RENOUVIN, P., PRÉCLIN, E. and HARDY, G.: *L'Époque Contemporaine II; La Paix
   Armeé et la Grande Guerre* (1871–1919). 2nd. ed., Paris, 1947.

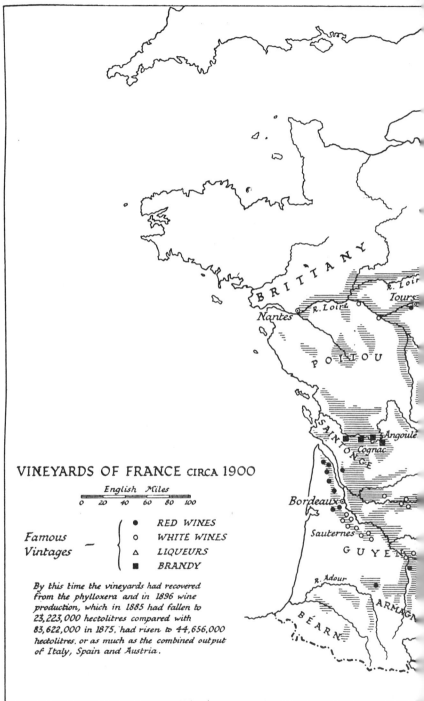

VINEYARDS OF FRANCE CIRCA 1900

English Miles

0   20   40   60   80   100

●	RED WINES
○	WHITE WINES
△	LIQUEURS
■	BRANDY

Famous Vintages —

By this time the vineyards had recovered from the phylloxera and in 1896 wine production, which in 1885 had fallen to 23,223,000 hectolitres compared with 83,622,000 in 1875, had risen to 44,656,000 hectolitres, or as much as the combined output of Italy, Spain and Austria.

BRITTANY

R. Loir.
Tours
Nantes   R. Loire
R. Loire

POITOU

SAINTONGE   Angoulê
Cognac

Bordeaux

Sauternes

GUYEN

R. Adour
ARMAG

BÉARN

R.C.

MAP V

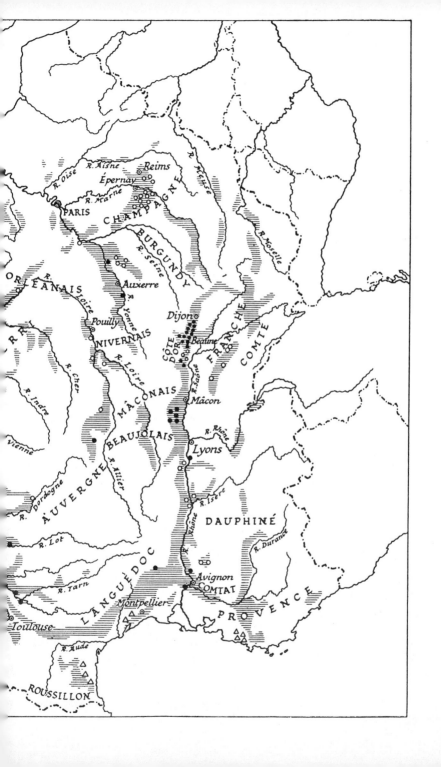

R. Oise
R. Aisne
Reims
Épernay
R. Marne
CHAMPAGNE
PARIS
BURGUNDY
R. Seine
ORLÉANAIS
Auxerre
R.
R. Loire
Pouilly
R. Yonne
NIVERNAIS
Dijon
CÔTE D'OR
Beaune
FRANCHE COMTÉ
R. Moselle
R. Aube
R. Moselle
R. Loire
R. Cher
R. Indre
R. Saône
MÂCONAIS
Mâcon
BEAUJOLAIS
Vienne
AUVERGNE
R. Dordogne
R. Allier
Lyons
R. Rhône
R. Lot
R. Isère
DAUPHINÉ
R. Rhône
R. Durance
LANGUEDOC
R. Tarn
Avignon
COMTAT
Montpellier
PROVENCE
Toulouse
R. Aude
ROUSSILLON

XIII

FRANCE IN 1914

IN 1815, on the morrow of the Napoleonic Wars, we paused to take a brief glance at French society. Now, in 1914, when France is once again about to enter a great European conflict, it is fitting that we should halt for a moment and consider the changes wrought in that society after nearly half a century of Republican Government.

In 1914, on the eve of the first World War, France was a land of some 39,600,000 people. Thus her population had increased by 10,000,000 in a hundred years, but she was no longer the most populous country in Europe apart from Russia. She had been outstripped by Great Britain who now had some 43,000,000 people, and, still more conspicuously by her great enemy Germany, the number of whose inhabitants had soared to 70,000,000. Moreover, the birth-rate had fallen from 26 per 1,000 in the decade 1861–70 to 18·7 per 1,000 in 1912.[1] This fall was, however, partly offset by a simultaneous decline in the death-rate, with the result that the figures of the total population since the turn of the century had been more or less stationary. Unfriendly critics pronounced France to be decadent and declared that the decline in her birth-rate was due to the corruption of her morals. In fact various causes had contributed to this decline. The growing standard of comfort among the bourgeoisie led to a restriction of the size of middle-class families—the bourgeois being often content with an only child. The Code Napoléon with its provision for the equal division of property among a man's heirs had a similar limiting effect upon the size of peasant families, since excessive sub-division meant that holdings became too small to provide a livelihood. Other subsidiary causes which may have had a restrictive effect were the growth of alcoholism among sections of the working class[2] and the relatively high price of bread under the protectionist system which defended French agricultural interests after 1892. In a world free from war and rumours of war

---

[1] SEIGNOBOS, C.: *Histoire sincère de la nation française*, p. 455.

[2] The average consumption of alcohol was tripled between 1870 and 1914.

such a decline and such numerical inferiority compared with Germany need not have greatly mattered. But, coupled with a comparable industrial inferiority, in the world of 1914 they were a cause of grave anxiety.

France, as we have seen, could already by 1870 be reckoned a big industrial power. So she was still in 1914; but for her, unlike her industrialized neighbours such as Great Britain, Belgium and Germany, agriculture was still the biggest 'industry'. Twenty-two million one hundred thousand of her people still lived in the country and even as late as 1939 more than fifty-five per cent of the population was to be found in villages or small towns of less than 4,000 inhabitants.[1] In 1911 only twenty-six per cent lived in towns of over 20,000. There were good reasons for this approximation of France, unlike the other big industrial nations of the West, to a balanced economy. Her Governments had long looked upon the peasantry as the backbone of the country and had aimed at maintaining virtual self-sufficiency in foodstuffs; and at the same time her poverty in natural resources, especially coal, meant that she was handicapped in comparison with many of her neighbours. Although the new coal pits of the Nord and Pas-de-Calais had been opened up at the end of Louis Philippe's reign, these deposits were hard to work and France's output in 1913 was only 41,000,000 tons compared with the 279,000,000 tons produced in Germany and the 292,000,000 in Great Britain.[2] She was particularly poor in home supplies of good coking coal, and, furthermore, large parts of the country were remote from any of the coal-producing areas. Thus industrialization had proceeded less rapidly than in neighbouring countries. Big industries of course there were, as we have seen long since, and they continued to develop much as did big industries elsewhere. For instance, the formation of 'comptoirs' foreshadowed the development of the large Cartel or Trust. But the continued, if not growing, importance of luxury trades for export markets and the tendency of manufacturers in many other industries to concentrate mainly upon the requirements of the home market[3] meant that France was still predominantly a land of small industries. Although work at home had become increasingly rare, as late as 1931 no less than

[1] MAILLAUD, P.: *France*, p. 17.

[2] CLAPHAM, J. H.: *Economic Development of France and Germany, 1815–1914*, p. 234.

[3] In the twenty years before the 1914–18 war French exports increased by 66 per cent; but those of Germany and Belgium increased by 124 per cent and 129 per cent respectively.

60 per cent of France's industrial workers were to be found in firms which employed less than twenty persons.[1] This meant that the tradition of fine craftsmanship was still very live, that French individualism still persisted in industry, and that a vast number of employers still had direct personal relationships with their men. The possession of a balanced economy meant that the country was much less liable than many others to suffer from the fluctuations of world markets and the evils of unemployment. But it also meant that, if war were to come, France with her multitude of small factories and her relatively small number of industries equipped for rapid mass production on a big scale would be much less fitted than Great Britain or Germany to turn out the vast quantities of armaments and munitions without which it could not be waged. 'As early as 1913,' it has been said, 'the ratio of industrial potential as between Germany, England and France was computed at —Germany 3, England 2, France 1.'[2]

This, of course, did not mean that enormous strides had not been made in the continuation of that industrial development, which we saw was so notable under the Second Empire, and that the lives of most Frenchmen were not greatly affected by these further material transformations. The development of iron and steel made possible the manufacture of a host of new tools and revolutionized the building industry. By 1913 France's output of steel fell not far short of that of Great Britain and the exploitation of the Briey basin after 1892 had made her the greatest exporter of iron ore in the world. Her consumption of raw cotton had trebled and the handloom weavers had almost disappeared as a result of increasing mechanization. Mechanization had also transformed the silk industry and the woollen industry, now largely concentrated in Roubaix and Tourcoing, and the manufacture of artificial silk had begun in 1890. France had developed chemical industries which were themselves to transform a host of others, and electricity, one of the wonders of the 1889 Exhibition, was soon to supersede gas as a widespread means of lighting and to provide the basis for another industry of great importance. But, compared with Great Britain and Germany, lack of coal and suitable raw materials put her at a disadvantage in the production of heavy chemicals, while she was slow to make the most of her advantages in the use of the hydro-electric power which might be easily harnessed from her abundant mountain rivers. Although Paris had its first underground and the Paris-Lyons-Marseilles railway company began to electrify its lines in 1899, by 1914 France lagged behind

[1] MAILLAUD, P.: *France*, p. 75.
[2] MAILLAUD, P.: *France*, p. 76.

Germany and Switzerland in her development of power and the great
period of electrification was not to begin until after 1918. At the same
time industrialization and the distribution of industrial products were
further facilitated by the growing improvement of communications.
By 1890 the mileage of railway track had doubled since 1870, largely
by the construction of local lines at heavy loss to the State, the canal
system had been standardized and extended and rivers improved to
fit them for traffic. About the same time the motor-car had made its
appearance: by 1914 there were some 99,000 vehicles in the country
and the Paris taxis could be ready to make their contribution to the victory of the Marne.[1] Already the long-distance cable and the telephone
had conquered space, though here again France was behind Great Britain
and Germany. Already aviation, the cinema and the wireless were
exciting the interest of pioneers. Blériot had flown the Channel, the
Lumière brothers had made the cinema a practical possibility and Branly
had contributed to the development of wireless. But while these new
inventions foreshadowed still more extraordinary things to come they
had not yet developed sufficiently to affect the everyday life of the
ordinary Frenchman.

Nevertheless, in spite of the importance of industry and the industrial
worker, it is rural France which still presents, outside Paris, the most
characteristic pictures of French society. Big industry was largely confined to five departments of the North, to the periphery of the Massif
Central, and to a few large cities such as Paris, Lyons and Marseilles.
Elsewhere agriculture in all its variety was the occupation of the majority
of working Frenchmen. The structure of agricultural society had
altered little during the century. The large estates reconstituted in the
early part of the nineteenth century were still a feature of the landscape
in certain districts, although many of them had changed hands and
passed out of the possession of impoverished nobles into that of prosperous business men. The number of independent peasant proprietors
and tenant farmers had tended to increase while that of the métayers and
landless labourers had declined: but this had been no revolution, merely
a gradual process. So, too, the configuration of holdings was little
changed. France had had no enclosure movement like Great Britain
and many of the peasant holdings were still widely scattered. They were
also on the average, compared with British farms, exceedingly small.
Out of a total of nearly four million holdings no fewer than two and a
half million were less than twenty-five acres in extent. Such small
units effectively prevented the growth of anything like a rural proletariat,

[1] A number of taxis were used to transport reinforcements.

except in specialized occupations or areas like the big vineyards of the
south, the big farms near Paris or among the foresters: but at the same
time their existence and the prevalence of scattered holdings meant that
farming was bound to be more conservative in character than in many
other countries, since lack of capital hampered the introduction of
machinery and new technique. Nevertheless, great progress had been
made especially after the end of the long depression of the 'seventies
and 'eighties and the protection accorded by the Méline tariff of 1892.
Much of this was due to State encouragement. In 1879 the Government
had sponsored vine defence syndicates to combat the phylloxera. After
Waldeck-Rousseau's law of 1884 had permitted the formation of professional unions, agricultural syndicates, co-operatives and insurance
societies had received Government encouragement. And so by 1914
ploughing with oxen, cutting corn and hay with scythes and sickles, and
threshing with flails or antiquated horse machines, were much less
common. Moreover, although the numbers of the rural population
had begun to decline absolutely after 1875 and although the area under
wheat declined steadily after 1862, the yield increased, largely owing
to improvements in technique and the abandonment of fallow. Thus,
in spite of the fact that the yield per acre was less than in Great Britain,
Belgium or Germany, France was still the greatest wheat-producing
country in Europe outside Russia. At the same time the French vineyards had recovered so effectively from the phylloxera that by 1906
they suffered from over-production.

The Industrial Revolution and the slow but steady fall in the agricultural population, had other important consequences. Good roads,
an increasing number of railways and the telegraph, all facilitated specialization and so certain districts became famous for market and flower
gardening and for dairy produce. At the same time the decline in the
population meant that more land was put to pasture and there was a
notable increase in the numbers of horses, cows and pigs. Nevertheless, the drift of the labourers to the towns and the not infrequent reluctance of younger sons of peasants to return to the land after doing their
military service affected parts of the country in another way. Any
Englishman travelling in France must have been struck by the spaciousness of a land in which the population was two and a half times less
dense than in his own country. Still more must he have been surprised
at the not uncommon spectacle of villages half or wholly deserted.
During the 1914-18 war the American Ambassador was to record his
astonishment at finding nearly all the houses of Vieux Perouges in the
Auvergne in ruin 'from the combined action of time and abandon-

ment'.[1] After the war which took such toll of peasant life these melancholy scenes were to be still more frequent. Yet the highly important fact that Belgians, Spaniards, Italians and even Poles came across the borders to work on the land did something to arrest the depopulation and showed that conditions of labour in France might nevertheless be more attractive than in their own countries. By 1914 there were well over 1,000,000 of these foreign workers.

France, indeed, was as a whole still a singularly rich and prosperous country in which a great number of people lived cheaply and well. The peasant was better clothed, fed, and housed, and more independent than ever before of the *curé* and the *château*. 'You no longer,' wrote Clapham, 'praised a man by saying he was "as good as good bread," because it no longer seemed a high compliment. You no longer talked of the "black bread of adversity", because black bread was not made in France. The most unfortunate Frenchman ate the white wheaten bread that was served to princes in the middle ages, and ate it freely. Besides his abundance of good bread, the average Frenchman, during the second half of the nineteenth century, increased his consumption of wine and potatoes by fifty per cent; his consumption of meat, beer and cider by a hundred per cent; his consumption of spirits by two hundred per cent; his consumption of sugar and coffee by three hundred per cent.'[2] The urban wage-earner had his share in this increase as well as the peasant and the bourgeois. The standard of living had notably increased for every class, except perhaps the old aristocracy, and the general optimism and belief in indefinite material advance had been widespread, especially in the 'eighties and 'nineties: it is still evident to the traveller who observes the number of cafés rejoicing in such names as 'De l'Avenir' or 'Du Progrès'. This prosperity had what would seem grave defects to most European Governments forty years later. As we have seen, it probably contributed to the decline in the birth-rate. It also led to a great increase in the number of small *rentiers*. The family business was never so characteristic in France as in England, and now more than ever it was the ambition of many a small business man and prosperous *petit bourgeois* to work as hard as possible in order to cease work as soon as possible. His one aim was to retire early, acquire a small piece of land and in Candide's well-known phrase 'cultivate his garden'. Many men of under fifty might thus be found throughout France who spent their time

[1] *The War Memoirs of* WILLIAM GRANVILLE SHARP, p. 147.

[2] CLAPHAM, J. H.: *The Economic Development of France and Germany*, 1815–1914, pp. 402–3.

pottering in gardens, fishing and playing bowls or busying themselves with local politics.[1]

More than ever, of course, in the France of 1914 it was the bourgeoisie who dominated the scene, ruled the world of politics, industry, letters and the arts, enjoyed the good things of life, and set the tone in dress, manners and customs for the rest of their country. Their ascendancy and the growth of communications was leading in France, as in every country, to a growing uniformity so that local customs and costumes and local traditions and dialects began to disappear. The nobility after the end of the 'République des Ducs' had more and more lost their separate political and social importance, although some of them still maintained a closed circle in the Faubourg St. Germain in Paris[2] and carried on something of a country-house life in the châteaux which still remained to them. More and more, however, they tended to become merged with the bourgeoisie; many of them married into the families of industrialists and business men, and some even took to business themselves. It was the industrialists and business men who most frequently had bought their châteaux and their collections of furniture or works of art. The great banking and industrial families were still more influential than before. After the British it was the French financiers who were the bankers of the world. The amenities and pleasures provided for the wealthy increased. Yachting and racing joined hunting among their main sports, while fishing, shooting and dancing remained popular with all classes and cycling races aroused intense enthusiasm. The manners of the richer bourgeoisie were aped by the *petite bourgeoisie*, but the distinguishing mark between them, according to an eminent French historian, was the absence of a *salon* or drawing-room in the *petit bourgeois'* home.[3] Increasing uniformity of customs was accompanied by a much greater freedom of address and by a greater gentleness of manners, a more humanitarian outlook which coincided with a revolution in the art of medicine which did much to relieve human suffering under medical treatment. Yet amid all these changes the essential element in the social structure, the family, stood firm, and the Frenchwoman in general was so satisfied with her position in the family, which often enabled her to manage her husband's business or at least share in

[1] HUDDLESTON, SISLEY: *France and the French*, p. 31. His comment on this tendency after 1918 also holds good of the years before 1914.

[2] Reminiscent of the circle of the Listomères so well described by BALZAC in *Le Lys dans la vallée*.

[3] SEIGNOBOS, C.: *Histoire sincère de la nation française*, p. 467.

the direction of his work, that she showed little interest in agitating for the vote.[1]

Thus, materially and socially, the century has seen great changes and the greatest of all have been those which occurred under the Third Republic. During the forty-four years since its proclamation the Republic had indeed witnessed much besides scandals and political crises and party struggles; and, lest in the preceding chapters we should have seemed to be too much preoccupied by the political vicissitudes of those years, we must add a word more about some other aspects of French destiny during that same time. The developments of education and of a cheap and sometimes scurrilous and venal Press meant that literacy was now widespread among the lower classes. Culture, however, remained the monopoly of the bourgeoisie. Never before had there been such a spate of journals and reviews and books of all kinds. Never before had writers, artists and composers been so abundant or treated with more respect. The French of all classes were singularly free from social snobbery or colour prejudice: and if there was a definite snobbery it was an intellectual one, arising from the bourgeois cult of the man of letters. Yet there was good reason for such an attitude. Paris was as ever a centre for the practise of the arts and a market for their productions, and France of the Third Republic had continued to show that intellectual distinction in an extraordinary variety of subjects for which she had now so long been distinguished. With the death of Victor Hugo in 1885 there had disappeared the last and greatest of the Romantics. But, as we have seen, the Romantic movement had long since given way to Realism and Realism in turn had passed into the still more realistic and 'scientific' Naturalism, which had a widespread influence throughout Europe, and of which Zola was the leader among French novelists. Meanwhile Guy de Maupassant and Alphonse Daudet had become great masters of the short story, and the discovery of the Russian novel in the years following Hugo's death contributed to an interest in the new 'science' of psychology. Thus the novels of men like Barrès and Bourget marked in their turn a reaction from the Naturalist School, a reaction which was enormously strengthened in another sphere by the work of Henri Bergson, whose philosophical teaching stressed the importance of the irrational factors in the development of man. In poetry, too, the Symbolists and men like Verlaine and Mallarmé had moved away from Realism and had emphasized anew the value of art for art's sake, while another novelist, Pierre Loti, appeared to escape from

[1] HUDDLESTON, SISLEY: *France and the French*, p. 58. cp. LESLIE, S.: *Memoir of J. E. C. Bodley*, p. 371, for Bodley's views on the French women.

it by setting the scenes of most of his tales amid the exotic luxuriance of distant lands.   Nationalists like Barrès, Bourget, Péguy and Maurras had been confronted by internationalists like Anatole France and Romain Rolland.   Sardou had been one of the most prolific and popular writers for the theatre, in which Sarah Bernhardt was now the queen among actresses, and Rostand had produced his *Cyrano de Bergerac*.   Nor were the artists behind the men of letters.   The Impressionists had continued to exercise an extraordinary influence under the lead of men such as Manet, Monet, Renoir and Degas.   The great figures of Cézanne, Van Gogh and Gauguin had followed.   Seurat had been the exponent of Pointillisme, and Picasso, Braque and Matisse had begun to perplex, shock or delight a wide public with their new Cubist paintings.   In sculpture France had produced the greatest master of modern times in Rodin, and in music she had given birth or a home to more composers of distinction—Massenet, Saint-Saens, Bizet, César Franck, G. Fauré, Vincent D'Indy and Debussy—than perhaps at any time in her history.   Furthermore, distinction in the world of creative imagination had been nearly matched in that of learning and the sciences.   Taine, Renan and Fustel de Coulanges had continued their work as historians and been succeeded by men such as Sorel, Hanotaux and Lavisse.   J. H. Fabre had won renown for his study of insects; Vidal de la Blache for his work as a geographer; Durkheim and Tarde for their studies of social psychology; and Marcel Bertrand as a geologist.   Henri Poincaré had shown himself one of the foremost mathematicians of the age. Pasteur had continued his great work in microbiology and the Institut Pasteur had been founded in 1888 by international subscription in recognition of his services to mankind.   Marcellin Berthelot had been the father of synthetic chemistry, and last but not least the Curies had opened up a vast new field of scientific and medical inquiry by their discovery of radium in 1898.

Thus it can be seen that ministerial instability and political crises had done nothing to stultify the continued flowering of French inventive genius.   Beneath the superficial instability there was the solidity given by prosperity and a conservative social structure; and that solidity was further strengthened by the continuance of the centralized administration and by the influence of many distinguished civil servants.   It was in these years that, in addition to the institution of the secular primary school and the reforms of secondary education which, as we saw, formed such an important part of the anti-clerical offensive of the 'eighties, higher education was transformed by the creation of Universities in the proper sense of the word, by the foundation of many more or less specialized schools such as the École des Sciences Politiques, and by a great improvement in the facilities for scientific study. It was in these years that the great battle between the champions of a classical and a 'modern' education began anew, until in 1902 the modernists won a notable victory when the Minister for Education decided that Latin and Greek need no longer be required for the Baccalauréat or matriculation examination. Yet on the whole France lagged behind her more industrialized neighbours in technical education. The war of 1914–18 was necessary in order to give it a development on a wide scale.

It was the civil servants and teachers who did the work in making the new educational facilities effective. It was the civil servants and soldiers who at the same time administered and consolidated the vast new Empire which had been built up by Jules Ferry and his successors, the second largest in the world. Here, too, there was a great battle waged over policy. Were the peoples of the Empire to be assimilated and to become Frenchmen just as the conquered peoples of Rome eventually became Roman citizens or were they to develop on the lines of the peoples of the British Empire towards some kind of self-government within a French Commonwealth? On the whole the assimilationist policy tended to prevail and so alongside the experiments in the government of native peoples conducted by the British Colonial Office very different experiments were being carried out by the civil servants and administrators of France.[1] But the words 'French Empire' or Lyautey's later summary of the assimilationist ideal—'France is a nation of 100,000,000 inhabitants'—must not blind us to the fact that this Empire was created piecemeal and contained the utmost diversity of race, religion, language, economic resources and cultural development. Nor indeed was it all subject to a single Ministry of Colonies. Protectorates like Morocco and Tunisia were the responsibility of the Ministry of Foreign Affairs while Algeria, since it was regarded as an extension of Metropolitan France, came under the Ministry of the Interior. Thus, however much uniformity might be aimed at on paper, in practice a considerable variety of treatment was inescapable.

This vast and varied Empire was a reservoir of manpower and economic resources of great potential importance: but here too the War of 1914–18 was necessary before either French Governments or French public opinion became fully alive to their value in supplementing the deficiencies of the mother country. Originally colonies, in so far as they were not acquired for purely political or strategic reasons, had

[1] The treatment of the native peoples, for instance in the Congo and Indo-China, has been sharply criticized by some Frenchmen for its inhumanity.

been primarily regarded as useful markets for France's own products;
and when the capacity for absorption of French manufactures or foodstuffs fell below expectation public opinion had lost interest. As we
have seen, it was only in relation to the German problem that the movement for colonial expansion and the development of the Empire really
became matters of prime concern either for the average politician or
for the general public. Thus, since the Empire held but a small place
in the consciousness of the ordinary Frenchman in 1914 we will not
attempt to examine its problems in any further detail. The soldiers
and the civil servants on the spot often did admirable work but they were
hampered by the lack of interest at home: moreover this lack of interest
often went hand in hand with the reluctance to grant funds for development.

Here we come to a last point to be made in this brief survey. The
France of 1914 was a land of wealth and prosperity, but the French State
by comparison with the people was poor. Of old the main contact
of the people with the State had been through the person of the tax-
gatherer and the State had been disliked and distrusted accordingly.
Natural thrift, individualism and distrust of the State had all combined
to create a strong public resistance to direct taxation and a strong desire
to restrict State expenditure. In fact that expenditure had increased
from between 1875 and 1913 by an average sum of no less than sixty-
eight million francs per annum and in nearly a century it had risen from
864 millions to what the men of 1819 would have regarded as the astron-
omical figure of 5,191 millions.[1] This was largely due to the great
development of social services and pension and other payments under
the Third Republic. But it is arguable that had the politicians been
willing to brave public opinion and to push through an income tax in
the 'eighties or 'nineties instead of waiting until July 1914 on the very
eve of war, France would not only have had a better system of budgeting
—already the practice of voting supplementary credits and extraordinary
expenditure apart from the Budget proper was tending to falsify the true
picture of the financial situation—but would also have been able to
afford to spend more money on technical, scientific and colonial development. In view of the ordeal by which she was about to be faced such
money would have been well spent, such additional contributions by a
wealthy people to the national exchequer well repaid.

And so we see France on the eve of the Great War, a rich and prosperous people full of intellectual vigour; but a people sharply divided politically, distrustful of the State and disquietingly inferior to her Eastern

[1] MARION: *Histoire financière de la France depuis 1715*, VI, v. ff.

neighbour in population and industrial resources and potential.   If we discount the operation of outside factors the odds must be overwhelmingly against her.

AUGÉ-LARIBÉ, M.: *L'evolution de la France agricole*, Paris, 1912.

CLAPHAM, J. H.: *The Economic Development of France and Germany*, 1815-1914. Cambridge, 1921.

HUDDLESTON, SISLEY: *France and the French*.   London, 1925.

MORAZÉ, CHARLES: *La France bourgeoise, XVIIIe-XXe siècles*.   Paris, 1946.

SEIGNOBOS, CHARLES: *Histoire sincère de la nation française*.   15th ed.   Paris, 1933.

XIV

THE GREAT WAR OF 1914-18

ON the 28th June, 1914, the Archduke Francis Ferdinand was assassinated. Once again, as so often in recent years, there was a strained situation in the Balkans, but not so strained as to deter Poincaré, the new President of the French Republic, with his Prime Minister, Viviani, from carrying out an engagement to visit Russia. An opportunity to reaffirm and strengthen the Russian alliance was not lightly to be discarded and on the 18th July they set sail for the Baltic. On the 23rd Austria-Hungary delivered an ultimatum to Serbia and within a few days, in spite of Serbia's acceptance of all the Austrian demands, save one, the situation looked so threatening that the French Government, whose offers of mediation had proved vain, telegraphed urgently to the President and Viviani to return. On the 28th Austria-Hungary declared war on Serbia and on the following day Russia, anxious to check further Austrian aggrandisement in the Balkans and loth to stand by while fellow Slavs were crushed, ordered a partial mobilization which was converted into total mobilization on the 30th. The Russian action, unfortunately, did not lead Austria to call off hostilities. Instead it extended the area of tension. On the 31st Germany intervened with two ultimata, one demanding that Russia should immediately demobilize, the other asking for a statement from the French Government of the attitude they would adopt in case of war between Germany and Russia.

France had no intention of abandoning her Russian ally, but she was still eager to strain every nerve to avoid war. In order to show her will for peace she had withdrawn all troops to a distance of ten kilometres behind the Franco-German frontier, but the last chance of preventing German intervention and a general European war appeared to lie in persuading Great Britain to make a clear declaration that she would come to France's aid if she were attacked. The pressing appeals of the French Government were backed by a personal letter from President Poincaré to King George V, but in vain. British opinion was still greatly divided and by no means ready for intervention in a continental war arising out of an incident in the Balkans: the British Government felt unable to give the assurances for which France was so anxious, and the German declaration of war on Russia on 1st August meant that a general European war was inevitable. That same day the French Government ordered a general mobilization and for the first time in history proclaimed a general state of siege throughout the country. Events now moved with extraordinary rapidity: on the 2nd German troops entered Luxembourg and demanded free passage through Belgium; and on the 3rd August, on the pretext that French aeroplanes had bombed Nuremberg, the German Government declared war on France. On the 4th, treating their solemn guarantee of her neutrality as a 'scrap of paper' they marched into Belgium. In face of this flagrant breach of international good faith, and of the menace to the Channel ports which it implied, the British Government could hesitate no longer. From that day all three powers of the Triple Entente were at war with Germany and Austria-Hungary, and on the 3rd September the Entente was converted into an Alliance by an agreement that no one of them would conclude a separate peace.

Thus for the third time within a century France was faced by a German invasion. But in contrast with 1815 and 1870 she was no longer alone and the knowledge that she had two powerful allies was a factor of immense moral and psychological importance in enabling the French people to meet the first tremendous shocks of the German onslaught with confidence and determination.

If Germany calculated that Republican France, so lately torn by dissension over the military law, so notorious for ministerial instability and seemingly so riddled by pacifism, would be an easy victim still more divided by war, she was bitterly disillusioned. The national emergency, the new aggression by the power which had seized Alsace and Lorraine in 1871 and had four times since then, in 1875, 1887, 1905 and 1911 threatened France with war again, brought all Frenchmen together. Ideological differences were sunk and the response to Poincaré's appeal for an *union sacrée* in face of the foe was immediate and moving in its sincerity. The most ardent anti-militarists like Gustave Hervé paid tribute to the patriotism of a Nationalist like Déroulède, the Syndicalists and Socialists rallied to the defence of the country, and presently a militant anti-Clerical like Combes would accept a Cabinet post only if a prominent Right-Wing Catholic, Denys Cochin, were also included.[1] The Government, who had been ready to arrest a number of leading Syndicalists, pacifists, and suspected spies, named in a black list known as 'Carnet B', wisely left all Frenchmen on the list

[1] *The War Memoirs of* WILLIAM GRANVILLE SHARP, p. 43.

at liberty and also instructed prefects to suspend the laws against congregations. In the first seven months of the year there had been 654
strikes involving some 160,000 workers, but in the remaining five there
were no more than eighteen. Workers and peasants, bourgeois and
nobility, Catholics and freemasons, indeed every section of French
society, with very few exceptions, did its best during these first months
to place the cause of national unity before all else. In addition to the
confidence derived from the fact of having allies there were other important factors to account for this unity. There were few who did
not regard the territory of France as something sacred and its violation
by an invader as sacrilege; and so the defence of French soil was an almost
religious duty. Furthermore, French patriots could hope that the hour
of *la justice immanente*, in which Gambetta had proclaimed his faith,
was now at hand and that the injustice of 1871 would at last be repaired.
France had never herself sought *revanche* by aggression, but now that
war had been forced upon her she hoped to obtain it. Finally, just
because it had been so patently forced upon her she could claim, as
Poincaré did in his message of August 4th, that her cause was the cause
of Right. This belief that she was fighting for justice and for the maintenance of a democratic way of life which was threatened by a militarist
Imperialism, undoubtedly helped to rally the Left. It was well that
this was so, for in the trials ahead France was to need every addition of
strength which unity could give.

In area, population and resources the Allies had an immense superiority. Their European populations alone exceeded those of the Central
Powers by more than 100,000,000; additional manpower and raw
materials of all kinds might be drawn from their overseas dominions,
which together covered a considerable part of the globe; and they had
the mastery of the seas in spite of the strength of the German fleet.
But men and materials were of no avail unless they were trained and
adapted for military purposes. The Germans and Austrians, who had
long been preparing for war, were at the outset only slightly inferior in
the numbers they could put into the field and this inferiority was more
than compensated by their greater weight of armament and more
efficient military organization. As in 1870, Germany counted upon
this, on superior mobility, and on the advantage given her by having
the initiative. She confidently expected to be able to destroy the
French armies within six weeks. Once France was out of the war she
would be able to dispose of Russia and Great Britain at her leisure.
Thus everything depended upon the power of France to withstand the
initial shock.

The immediate French mobilization of some 3,700,000 men, 2,887,000 of whom were reservists,[1] took place without a hitch during the first fortnight of August. By the middle of the month the army numbered some forty-six regular infantry and ten cavalry divisions. In addition there were twenty-five divisions in reserve. On its left flank it co-operated with the Belgian army of six divisions and the British Expeditionary Force of five divisions. Against these eighty-two infantry divisions under three different commands Germany massed nearly the whole of her forces, seventy-eight divisions under a single command.[2] The French High Command were well aware that the main German assault was likely to be in the west and that a German invasion of Belgium was probable, but they made a grave error in believing that for political reasons the Germans would not advance in Belgium beyond the Meuse. Consequently the bulk of the French forces was concentrated too far south and the Germans were able to carry out a vast sweeping movement on their right flank through Belgium and to win the so-called Battle of the Frontiers. At the end of August the French and British troops were in retreat almost all along the line. By the beginning of September most of Belgium was in German hands, the Belgian army was blockaded in Antwerp, and the army of Von Klück had swept down through Northern France, crossed the Marne at several points and penetrated almost to the gates of Paris. On September 2nd, at the instance of the Commander-in-Chief and anxious not to repeat the error of 1870 and risk being blockaded in the capital, which it was agreed to defend to the last, the Government left Paris for Bordeaux.

For a few agonizing days it looked as though Germany's confident expectation of a speedy decision in the west was going to be justified. But in Joffre, the massive, imperturbable French Commander-in-chief, the German Von Moltke had found his match. At exactly the right moment when Von Klück had extended his forces too far Joffre launched a counter-offensive against the German right flank. The Battle of the Marne was a momentous victory for the Allies, and when the German troops failed to break through at Verdun, and their subsequent drive to seize the Channel Ports was frustrated at Ypres and Dixmude in November, it was clear that the enemy had been out-generalled. The

[1] FONTAINE, A.: *French Industry during the War*, p. 26. By the end of the war 7,935,000 men had been called up.

[2] These figures are taken from P. RENOUVIN: *La crise européenne et la grande guerre*, pp. 187-8, 208.

superior coolness of Joffre had saved France from disaster, but unfortunately neither the French nor the British had the men or material
to follow up their advantage. By the end of the year the opposing
armies were interlocked in a struggle on a front which extended from
the English Channel across North France to the Vosges and the Swiss
frontier and which was to undergo comparatively little change of
contour until the last phase, in spite of titanic efforts by both sides to
break it. The 'miraculous' victory of the Marne meant that the war
in the west was to be converted from a war of movement, which nearly
all the prophets on both sides, soldiers, politicians and economists alike,
had confidently expected to be over by Christmas 1914, into a war of
trenches which was to drag on for nearly four years.[1]

The deadlock on the western front and the consequent prospect of
a long struggle changed the whole perspective of the war and made it
necessary for the French and other Allied Governments to adjust themselves to an entirely novel situation. In a long war their superior manpower and resources might very well be the decisive factor: and so the
training and equipment of men, the provision of munitions and the
maintenance of food and other essential supplies became problems of the
first magnitude, while the quest for new allies, the enforcement of an
economic blockade and attempts to create diversions in other parts of
Europe became important objects of policy.

The process of adjustment was no easy one. Hitherto Governments,
eager for and relying on a quick decision, had thrown most of their
manpower into the forces and been content to fight on stocks of munitions and other war supplies, while in France full-scale mobilization had
caused a temporary paralysis of commerce and industry and led to a
sharp rise in unemployment. The problem for France was aggravated
by heavy losses in men and material. The tremendous battles of the
first four months had cost her 455,000 men killed or missing and another 400,000 wounded.[2] They had saddled her with nearly 900,000
refugees, including some 150,000 Belgians, some 600,000 of whom
were virtually destitute and had to be given relief.[3] Furthermore,
they meant that she was obliged to continue the war the poorer for the

[1] It is only fair to recall that 'Had it not been for Russia's immediate offensive
in East Prussia [in accordance with the stipulations of her military convention with
France], the German invasion of France would probably have been as complete
in 1914 as it was in 1940.' NAMIER, L. B.: *Diplomatic Prelude: 1938-1939*, p. x.

[2] FONTAINE, A.: *French Industry during the War*, p. 27.

[3] FONTAINE, A.: *French Industry during the War*, p. 37.

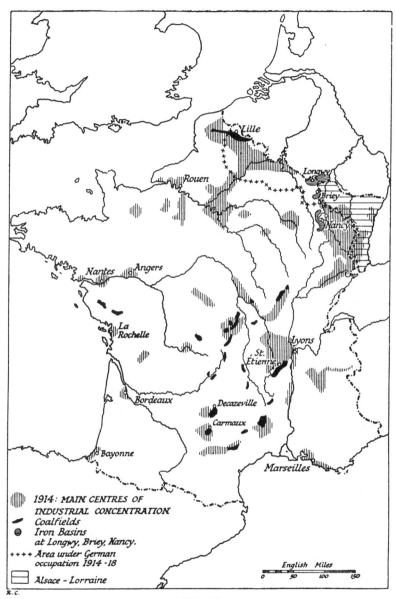

Lille

Rouen

Longwy

Briey

Nancy

Nantes

Angers

La
Rochelle

Lyons

St.
Etienne

Bordeaux

Decazeville

Carmaux

Bayonne

Marseilles

1914: MAIN CENTRES OF
INDUSTRIAL CONCENTRATION
Coalfields
Iron Basins
at Longwy, Briey, Nancy.
++++ Area under German
occupation 1914-18
Alsace - Lorraine

English Miles
0   50   100   150

R.C.

MAP VI

loss of ten departments which had been wholly or partly invaded. These covered no more than 11·5 per cent of French territory,[1] but they included some of the most fertile land and some of the most important industrial areas in the country. In 1913 they had produced no less than 20·4 per cent of the wheat crop, 25·52 per cent of France's oats and 49·48 per cent of her sugar-beet production.[2] They contained 16·3 per cent of her manufacturing capacity, 21·1 per cent of the labour employed in manufacturing industries and 41 per cent of the steam motive power utilized in those industries.[3] Their loss meant the loss of an important part of the metallurgical, coal-mining and textile industries most vital for war production.

Thus the prospect of a long war materially modified and extended the tasks of government. As Tocqueville had written more than seventy years earlier: 'War cannot fail to add enormously to the functions of civil government; almost inevitably it concentrates in the hands of the latter the direction of the whole population and the direction of everything.'[4] So it was now; and the remarkable achievement of the Third Republic was that it was able to adapt itself to the new conditions without any fundamental change of constitution. There were many, even in France, who had doubted the capacity of the Republican régime to direct the country in time of war and the doubt had only recently again been expressed in a volume by the Socialist deputy, Marcel Sembat, to which he gave the arresting title of *Faites un Roi, sinon faites la paix*. These gloomy prophets were to be confounded. The Government, for a few months on its own responsibility and then for the remainder of the war in more or less close collaboration with the legislature, was able to conduct the war without any fundamental modification of the parliamentary régime of 1875.

When the Chambers met in special session in August 1914, they had authorized the Government to maintain the state of siege for the duration of hostilities, to proclaim a moratorium, to suspend the freedom of the Press, to incur certain kinds of expenditure without reference to them, and to obtain short-term loans or special advances from the Bank of France. The emergency at the end of the month and the German threat to Paris had impelled Viviani to reform his Government in accordance with the principles of Union Sacrée so as to include some of the

---

[1] FONTAINE, A.: *French Industry during the War*, p. 20.

[2] AUGÉ-LARIBÉ, M.: *Agriculture and Food Supply in France during the War*, p. 55.

[3] FONTAINE, A.: *French Industry during the War*, p. 20.

[4] cit. RENOUVIN, P. *The Forms of War Government in France*, II.

most eminent statesmen, Briand, Delcassé, Millerand and Ribot, as well as two prominent Socialists, Marcel Sembat and the veteran Jules Guesde, and very soon afterwards a Presidential decree terminated the parliamentary session.   During the critical four months which followed the Government were forced to improvise all kinds of measures in order to meet the exigencies of war and they did so without reference to the Chambers.   Their powers over the Press developed into a wide censorship; they instituted summary courts martial at the front on Joffre's request; they set up all manner of new public services and by decree considerably modified existing legislation about army recruitment and freedom of trade.   From September 2nd to December 22nd 'all powers were concentrated in the hands of the Government: it was invested, on its own authority, with a kind of dictatorship'.[1]   And, such was the desire for strong government, such the continuing force of *union sacrée* that this dictatorship was accepted virtually without protest or question.

The need to improvise continued, as did legislation by decree. Gradually, under the pressure of military requirements, the State exercised increasing direction of the economic life of the country, requisitioning crops and purchasing coal supplies, fixing maximum prices and erecting a multiplicity of controls.   Often these overlapped and duplicated one another, causing muddle and delay; but such defects, as we in this country know full well, are inseparable from any improvised war-time bureaucracy; and in the France of 1914-18 controls were indispensable. Private enterprise, so highly individualist and so little organized for associative purposes, though it did much, had neither the capital nor the authority necessary for directing the French economic war effort unguided by State supervision and aid.   Gradually, then, as the war proceeded, the State, without any doctrinaire intention, accustomed Frenchmen to state interference and even to the idea of nationalization. It also accustomed an increasing number to look to it for aid and benefits—pensions and relief of all kinds which had to be paid either out of charity or as incentives to fresh effort.   These things were of great importance.   But in the new period of war, which followed the battles of movement, the Government no longer acted wholly on their own. According to the Constitution, the Chambers were bound to reassemble in the second week in January and there is no evidence that the Government had any intention of prolonging their dictatorship beyond that date.   On the contrary, they took the Chambers into partnership, allowed them to sit in permanent session, determining their own vacations, and granted Senators and deputies who were serving in the forces

[1] RENOUVIN, P.: *The Forms of War Government in France*, p. 99.

the right to obtain furloughs in order to take part in parliamentary business. The executive still enjoyed considerable independence; party quarrels were silenced by the 'Union Sacrée'; deputies were loth to overturn Cabinets when the country was in danger; and unwelcome criticism could be checked by alleging reasons of military secrecy: none the less, the Chambers once again played a part in public affairs and gradually showed an increasing wish to extend their control. This reassertion of Parliament's desire to check the executive and to call it to account was to have important effects upon the direction of the war.

The most urgent requirements for the continued effective prosecution of the war were, as we have seen, those of manpower and munitions. By the beginning of 1915 the supply of light artillery was nearly exhausted and there was a shortage of most kinds of munitions. The initial unemployment had been largely reduced and there was a pressing need for more skilled labour. Women did much to help fill the gap made by mobilization, and engaged in all manner of occupations usually reserved for men. They became bakers, wheelwrights, masons, gang foremen, train drivers and much else besides. But the need for skilled labour in war factories could only be met by releases of men from the army and in July arrangements were made for 500,000 men to return to industry. Eighteen months later the decline in food production also gave cause for anxiety—not only was there the loss of the north-east departments, but the mobilization of agricultural labour without reserve had meant that most of the farms of France were left to the care of old men, women and children. They made heroic efforts, but inevitably the yield of crops declined and land went out of cultivation. Hence, in spite of attempts to check the fall in production by the use of prisoners of war and of what little foreign and colonial labour could be obtained, another 300,000 men had to be set free from the army to work on the farms.

As the casualties on the western front mounted, the problem of manpower became more and more acute, and in their attempt to maintain the numerical strength of the forces the army authorities had time and time again to relax their standards of physical fitness. Behind the lines man hours were saved by greater standardization, the remodelling of plant and more scientific factory organization. The conditions of some French industries were transformed by the introduction of American methods. But all these measures were merely palliatives. France could not have borne the strain of maintaining the western front and keeping up the manufacture of munitions and agricultural production had she been alone. Already, before the end of 1915, Joffre had ex-

pressed his doubts of the country's ability to endure a long war of attrition unless the Allies took a large share in operations on land. France's
manpower problem was only soluble with the help of her Allies.
Fortunately that help was now speedily forthcoming, and, although
throughout the war the French continued to hold by far the longest
section of the western front,[1] Great Britain was soon able to send large
numbers of men across the Channel. By the autumn of 1915 the original
divisions of Old Contemptibles had swelled into the first thirty-five of
Kitchener's army; by the spring of 1916 they numbered seventy. Meanwhile the Russians had borne the brunt of the German offensive of 1915.
They had been obliged to give up the whole of Poland, Galicia and
Lithuania, and had suffered enormous losses of men and material. But
once again the Germans failed to deliver a knock-out blow. The
eastern front still remained in being to occupy a large number of divisions.
Without it, it is very doubtful whether the western front could have
withstood the whole weight of the enemy forces.

The problem of munitions was not solved before Parliament had
displayed its concern and shown the revival of its influence upon policy.
At first this influence was exerted mainly through its standing committees.
In particular the Army Committees of the two Chambers were active
in criticizing the conduct of the War Ministry, the alleged inefficiency
in dealing with the munitions shortage, and the weakness of the civil
authorities in tolerating the growth of an enormous military bureaucracy. Their attacks led in August 1915 to the resignation of Millerand,
the War Minister, whose general policy had been to leave Joffre and the
army authorities a very free hand. His resignation was soon followed
by that of the whole Cabinet. It was succeeded by a second Union
Sacrée Ministry, headed this time by Briand and including two octo-
genarians, Combes of anti-clerical fame and Freycinet, a historic link
with the national defence of 1870.

Meanwhile the area of conflict was steadily widening. In October
1914, Turkey had joined the Central Powers, thereby barring the easiest
way of communications between France and her remote Russian Ally;
and British and French attempts to reopen it by seizing the Straits had
met with a sanguinary check in the Dardanelles. In May 1915 Italy
entered the war, selling her alliance to the Allies who had offered the
highest price in the large territorial gains promised by the Secret Treaty
of London of April that year; and in September Bulgaria, eager for

[1] FONTAINE, A.: *French Industry during the War*, p. 28. 'At the Armistice the
Belgian army occupied 30 kilometres of front, the British army 90 kilometres,
the American army 100 kilometres, the French army 330 kilometres.'

revenge on her old enemy Serbia, cast in her lot with Germany, thereby
bringing about the final collapse of the Serbs. Thus, on balance, the
advantage in the other European theatres of war by the end of 1915 lay
very definitely with the Central Powers. In the West, too, victory
for the Allies seemed as remote as ever. Attempts to create useful
diversions to relieve the Russians were of little avail, and, as the stalemate
continued, so parliamentary suspicions of the wide powers and jealous
independence exercised by Joffre and his subordinates tended to grow.
In September the Government demanded that Joffre should release
four divisions to serve as part of an Anglo-French Expeditionary Force
to be sent under General Sarrail to Salonika in the hope of relieving the
harassed Serbs; but Joffre at once protested against the new arrangements
and the difficulty was solved by a decree of December 2nd extending his
authority to cover the new army of the Near East. From the first big
clash of civil and military authority Joffre had triumphed and emerged
a Generalissimo. So, too, early in 1916 Briand stood by him when
Galliéni, the Minister of War, who had criticized the weakness of certain
defensive positions near Verdun, was proved to have been right and
submitted to his colleagues a memorandum on the 'reorganization of
the High Command'. It was Galliéni and not Joffre who resigned.

It was well for France that this was so, for the calm manner in which
Joffre adhered to his plans in the face of great provocation saved her
from a new disaster. In February 1916 Falkenhayn, Moltke's successor
as German Commander-in-Chief, launched his great offensive against
the seemingly vulnerable Verdun salient, to the retention of which he
rightly believed the French would attach great importance. He reckoned that the attempt to defend it against an enormous concentration of
German men and armament would lead to such heavy losses—a proportion of 5 to 2—that France would be bled white and no longer able to
continue the struggle. But he, too, like Moltke, miscalculated: the
French casualties were indeed heavy, 275,000, but in that remorseless
six months' battle the German losses were almost as many.[1] Moreover,
Joffre coolly persisted with his own plan for an offensive on the Somme,
and the fact that he was able to deliver it in July, even though only on a
much reduced scale, finally frustrated Falkenhayn's plan. The Germans had to divert troops to the north; on the Somme the Allied artillery
was, for the first time, superior; and in the ensuing battle the enemy lost
no less than 267,000 men and 6,000 officers.[2] Verdun was saved and its

[1] RENOUVIN, P.: *La crise européenne et la grande guerre*, p. 331.

[2] RENOUVIN, P.: *La crise européenne et la grande guerre*, p. 338.

stubborn defence for ever afterwards remained a glorious symbol of French gallantry and powers of resistance. But the Somme was costly, too, for France, and once again the Allies had failed to break through. Ever since Galliéni's resignation, criticism of the High Command had increased and Parliament now at last vigorously asserted the right of the legislature to exercise some measure of control over the executive and to curtail the liberty of the military power. By June 1916 it had established its claim to sit in Secret Committee in order to debate matters which could not safely be discussed in public, and in this Secret Committee the Government once again had to face interpellations as in pre-war days. At the same time the Army Committees obtained authorization both to inspect conditions in munition factories and arsenals in the interior and to investigate 'the preparation of means of defence and offence, whether industrial or military' in the zone of operations itself.[1] Much could be said in criticism of this parliamentary interference in military matters, but on the whole there is little doubt that its general effect was salutary. It provided a useful corrective to military complacency and helped to check the arbitrariness and inefficiency or wastefulness of military administration. It was, however, a severe blow to the Commander-in-Chief and by the end of the year, after the failure of the Somme offensive, it was clear that Joffre's position was seriously shaken. The Government decided to relieve him of his command, but mindful of the great services he had rendered they made him Marshal of France. With his removal civil authority asserted itself still more vigorously. There was no longer a unified command over all French armies, but each front had its separate Commander-in-Chief, while the general direction of the war was left to the Minister of War, who now 'unhesitatingly travelled about the front, visited the army commanders, and called for the plans of attack'.[2] In April 1917 the Minister was aided in his task by the appointment for the first time of a Chief of Staff, first of all Pétain and subsequently Foch.

Thus, largely as the result of parliamentary pressure, there had been vital changes in the High Command. Unfortunately at the same time the prolongation of the war began to impair the unity of Frenchmen. While the principle of the Union Sacrée was as yet uncontested in Parliament there were disquieting signs of a rift outside. As early as the autumn of 1914 a handful of Syndicalist leaders, including the secretary of the powerful Union des Métaux, had protested against

---

[1] RENOUVIN, P.: *The Forms of War Government in France*, p. 133.

[2] RENOUVIN, P.: *The Forms of War Government in France*, p. 88.

the collaboration of the Socialist Party in the Government of National Defence. During the following two years Socialists and Syndicalists in neutral states had begun to organize propaganda denouncing the 'Imperialist' war and calling for a speedy peace without indemnities and without annexations. This propaganda gradually had some effect in the belligerent countries, all of which were by the end of 1916 beginning to experience internal difficulties. In December it was significant that nearly half the delegates at the French Socialist Party's annual congress voted in favour of resuming relations with Socialists in other (including enemy) countries, and that nearly half also opposed the continued participation of the Socialists in the Government. It was clear that the days of *union sacrée* were numbered, and in the following September the Socialists declined to take part in a new Painlevé Cabinet.

Meanwhile the military position in the West had been seriously affected by events in the East. By the autumn of 1916 most of Roumania which had joined the Allies in August had been overrun, and Russia, isolated and disorganized, was so crippled by social and political discontent, that her Allies were led to fear the outbreak of revolution and the conclusion of a separate peace. In such circumstances the tonic of success in the West was all the more desirable, but unfortunately all the more difficult to achieve.

General Nivelle, however, Joffre's successor as Commander-in-Chief on the western front, was a man of sanguine temperament. Eager to put an end to the 'war of attrition', he was wedded to the idea of a big offensive, which, in accordance with a principle adopted at one of the inter-allied military conferences now held at increasingly frequent intervals, was to be simultaneous with offensives on all fronts. But the outbreak of the threatened revolution in Russia and the overthrow of the Tsardom in March 1917 paralysed activity both on the Italian and on the eastern Russo-Roumanian front, since the Italians feared to draw upon themselves the whole weight of the Austro-Hungarian army. Moreover, a strategic withdrawal by the Germans in the sector of the German front on which Nivelle proposed to attack, further modified the chances of success. None the less, in spite of the criticisms both of several of his own subordinates and of Haig, the British Commander-in-Chief, Nivelle, persisted in carrying out his plan. The offensive launched in April, from which he had so optimistically expected a triumphant success, was a complete failure. On May 15th Nivelle, his authority gone, was relieved of his command and succeeded by Pétain, who had distinguished himself at Verdun, while Foch became Chief of Staff.

These events, the paralysis of Russia and the bitter disappointment at this fresh check in the West, coinciding as they did with abortive peace soundings and with more intensive Socialist and defeatist propaganda, had disquieting consequences in France. In May and June there were disturbances among workers in Paris and the St. Etienne district and a large number of strikes, and on May 20th several regiments refused to return to the line, while two at Soissons mutinied and threatened to march on Paris. These troubles among workers and soldiers were certainly not unconnected, but there is no evidence to show that they were part of an organized conspiracy. The enthusiasm of the first months had long since given way to a dogged resignation. The cumulative horror of the seemingly endless blood-letting was beginning to tell and to make men weary; and when the workers in the factory or the *poilus* home from the front saw how many behind the lines were living in comfort and making handsome profits while boasting of their patriotism, they became disillusioned and bitter. Herein lay the fundamental cause of the wavering of morale, the cause which made such men momentarily an easy prey to the subversive influence of a Russian brigade which was fighting with them on the western front and to the defeatist propaganda circulated by the Fédération des Métaux and the extremist Comité de Défense Syndicaliste. In both cases the authorities acted leniently: the Government refused to employ force against the workers and adopted a conciliatory attitude towards the Unions; and in a few weeks the troubles died down: in the army only twenty-three of the 150 mutineers condemned to death by court martial were executed; and Pétain soon restored discipline by wise improvements in the conditions of service—food was bettered, leave and rest periods were given more regularly and generously, and closer contact was established between officers and men. None the less, the failure of the Nivelle offensive and the unrest following upon it meant that for several months the French army was reduced to a comparatively passive role and that the British forces during that period had to bear the main brunt of operations. Moreover, the disturbances, the defeatist propaganda and the leniency of the Minister of the Interior caused disquiet in political circles. Here too, there were signs that the determination of some was beginning to waver. Men like Caillaux were ready to think of a compromise peace; and the revelations of the summer and autumn with their suggestions of treason and conspiracy led to a growing demand for stronger leadership. In July Clemenceau made a violent attack upon the Minister of the Interior, Malvy, denouncing both his weakness in dealing with the defeatist Syndicalists and his personal association with the Anarchist editor of a suspect paper, *Le Bonnet Rouge*. As a result of this and of a Press campaign which ensued, Malvy resigned on August 31st, and his resignation was soon followed by that of the whole Ribot Cabinet which had been in office since Briand retired in March.

The next Ministry, headed by Painlevé, was weaker than any of its war-time predecessors because, as we have seen, the Socialists now definitely broke the Union Sacrée and refused their support. It was also weakened by the revelation of further instances of treachery, notably the acceptance by a dubious individual named Bolo Pasha of ten million francs from the Deutsche Bank for the purpose of buying the majority of shares in *Le Journal*. Attacked by the Socialists on the Left and by all those further to the Right who were anxious for much more forceful treatment of the defeatists, it fell in November, the only Cabinet during the war to be overthrown on an adverse vote in the Chamber. By this time the outlook at home and abroad was gloomy indeed. At home the atmosphere was poisoned by suspicion and mistrust; abroad, although the failure of the unrestricted submarine campaign launched by Germany in January had saved Great Britain from dire peril and the entry of the U.S.A. on the side of the Allies in May had opened up an immense hope, prospects had darkened with the Italian defeat at Caporetto in October and the Bolshevik Revolution in November. The Italian defeat revealed that the morale of the Italian troops had also gravely deteriorated, and necessitated the diversion of a number of French and British divisions to the new line of resistance on the Piave. The Bolshevik Revolution made the withdrawal of Russia from the war a practical certainty. When this happened Germany's war on two fronts would be at an end and she would be free to transfer almost the whole weight of her forces to the West. The first handful of American troops had landed in France in June 1917, but they had been a mere handful, and no one could say whether others would follow in sufficient force to provide the necessary reserves to meet the German offensive which must inevitably be delivered in 1918. In this grim and depressing situation a tonic was essential. Fortunately one was to hand. On the 14th November the President, Poincaré, called upon Clemenceau to take over the government of France. 'So long as victory is possible,' Poincaré had written in August 1914, 'he (Clemenceau) is capable of upsetting everything! A day will perhaps come when I shall add: Now that everything seems to be lost, he alone is capable of saving everything.'[1] The day

---

[1] cit. JACKSON, J. HAMPDEN: *Clemenceau and the Third Republic*, p. 168.

had come. In the words of Winston Churchill: 'The last desperate stroke had to be played. France had resolved to unbar the cage and let her tiger loose upon all foes, beyond the trenches or in her midst.'[1]

Clemenceau, the stormy petrel of French politics for over forty years, was now an old man of seventy-six, but he had a toughness and dynamic energy far beyond that of many who were half his age. A Jacobin Radical in the classical tradition of 1793, he had, in his paper *L'Homme Libre* which, when censorship interfered, at once reappeared as *L'Homme Enchainé*, and as President of the Army Committee of the Senate, been an incessant gadfly since the outbreak of war, goading all, sparing none with his relentless exposures of inefficiency and ruthless demands for greater energy. Now he had but one aim—victory; and home and foreign policy alike were summed up in his famous phrase: '*Je fais la guerre!*'

The effect of Clemenceau's accession to power was immediate; a sigh of relief passed through the country and public confidence was rapidly restored. France now had the strong government which she so urgently required and the war was to end as it began under a virtual dictatorship: only Clemenceau did not silence the Chambers or abandon the appearance of co-operation with them. Some months earlier they had refused a demand by Briand for authority to take all necessary measures by decree; but now, on February 10th, 1918, they granted to Clemenceau the power to legislate by decree in all spheres of economic activity, and he induced them to abandon the Secret Committee practice which hampered the work and authority of the Government. Nor was there any revival of the *union sacrée*; the Socialists still held aloof, but they were a minority over whom at such a moment Clemenceau could ride roughshod. Such was the emergency and such the public trust in Clemenceau that he was able to impose his will upon Parliament almost without question; and as his Cabinet, like Gambetta's 'Grand Ministère', was composed of much lesser men than himself, the dictatorship was virtually that of a single man. Clemenceau in himself was a Committee of Public Safety.

Waging war at home meant short shrift for those whose will to wage it had faltered. Painlevé had fallen because of his weakness in combating defeatism. Clemenceau at once made examples. Malvy and Caillaux were arraigned before the High Court; Bolo Pasha, Mata Hari and other spies and traitors were executed; and rough justice was dealt to many

[1] cit. JACKSON, J. HAMPDEN: *Clemenceau and the Third Republic*, p. 171.

lesser suspects. Many who were innocent may well have suffered, but there could be no Dreyfus Affair in time of extreme peril. Public opinion demanded strong government and this was what Clemenceau was determined to give. Reason of state and the requirements of public safety, which he had denounced so vigorously in the days of Dreyfus, were now overriding in their urgency.

Waging war against the enemy meant above all doing the utmost to hasten American aid and to secure unity of command on the decisive western front. With the approach of spring the situation became ever more critical. The Russians had concluded an armistice in December 1917; on March 3rd 1918 they signed the peace of Brest-Litovsk and withdrew from the war. On the 16th March Roumania capitulated and five days later the Germans launched their threatened offensive. They struck with tremendous force between Arras and Le Fère at the point of junction between the British and French armies, surprised the British, routed Gough's troops, and drove a wedge between the Allied forces. The situation looked so serious that Clemenceau prepared for the necessity of moving the Government once more from Paris. But the crisis settled the question of military co-ordination. At an historic conference at Doullens on March 26th, attended by Poincaré, Clemenceau, the British War Minister, Lord Milner, and the British and French Commanders-in-Chief and Chiefs of Staff, Foch was entrusted with the task of co-ordinating the operations of the Allied armies on the western front; on April 3rd he was given the strategic direction of these operations, and on the 17th he formally became 'General in Chief of the Allied armies'. Thus unity of command was at last established and confidence restored. In Foch, a Pyrenean like Joffre, calm, quick and imaginative, the Allies had the man they needed. But, although a swift move by French troops filled the gap on the Somme, gruelling days were still ahead. The attack near Arras was only the beginning of the German offensive and Ludendorff was prepared to throw in his whole strength to force a decision before American soldiers could reach Europe in sufficient numbers to turn the scale. An attack on the Lys in April, held by the British at Kemmel Hill, was followed in May by the catastrophe of the Chemin-des-Dames. The French in turn were surprised and the Germans broke through to the Marne once more and penetrated as far as Château Thierry, only fifty miles from Paris. The capital was again in danger and the enemy began to bombard it at long range. Behind the lines morale began to waver anew. At once there were clamours for scapegoats and demands that Foch and Pétain should be relieved of their commands. At such a moment Clemenceau was indomitable; he refused to listen to the Deputies' demands for a public debate or a Secret Committee. The Generals had his complete confidence, and he told the Chamber that it must be patient: 'There is only one thing that matters: that is the final success, the last victory.' To get it, he was prepared, like Gambetta in 1871 and like a great Englishman later, to wage war unconquerably: 'The Germans may take Paris,' he told General Mordacq, 'but that will not prevent me from going on with the war. We will fight on the Loire, we will fight on the Garonne, we will fight even on the Pyrenees. And if at last we are driven off the Pyrenees, we will continue the war at sea.'[1]

His confidence and patience were amply justified. The Germans were held at the gates of Paris, and their last big attack in Champagne in July was a failure followed by a speedy French counter-attack which brought them to the brink of disaster and obliged them to abandon almost all the territory they had conquered since the 27th May. Already, in June, American troops had distinguished themselves in the battle area between Rheims and Soissons, and in July the first independent units had been in action at Château Thierry. By the 1st August no less than 1,145,000 men had been landed in France and nineteen divisions were ready to be sent to the front. Reinforcements were following at the rate of 250,000 a month. The tide had turned: the time had come, wrote Foch, 'to abandon the defensive attitude hitherto imposed by numerical inferiority and to go over to the offensive'[2]—the time to which he had looked forward from the moment when he had assumed the Supreme Command. By the beginning of September the German forces were in full retreat and the German Government and High Command had realized that all chance of winning the war had gone. In the middle of the month Austria-Hungary was suggesting peace negotiations; by the end, the Allied Army of the Near East, now under the command of General Franchet d'Espérey, had helped to bring Bulgaria to her knees, and the German Government themselves, abandoned by their allies, had decided, too, to ask for an armistice and peace. On November 11th the armistice was signed and France's long ordeal was over. Through the help of her Allies, the tenacity of leaders such as Joffre and Poincaré, Clemenceau and Foch, and the gallantry and courage of the great mass of her people, soldiers and civilians, men and women alike, she had survived and emerged victorious. For four years she had sustained the greatest part of the western front; her troops had

[1] cit. JACKSON, J. HAMPDEN: *Clemenceau and the Third Republic*, p. 179.

[2] cit. RENOUVIN, P.: *La crise européenne et la grande guerre*, p. 545.

fought at the Dardanelles, in Serbia, in Italy and at Murmansk; they
had conquered Togoland and helped to take the Cameroons. Her
ships had guarded the Mediterranean. Her Empire had remained loyal,
and with a handful of men Lyautey had completed the pacification of
her latest dependency and even raised Moroccan troops to fight in
Europe. Her institutions had survived virtually unchanged, and shown
that they were supple as well as strong. But the cost of her efforts was
tremendous. She was victorious, but exhausted. One million three
hundred thousand of her best men were dead and 740,000 maimed;
289,000 houses had been destroyed and 3,000,000 acres of good land
rendered unfit for cultivation.[1] She was short of labour and raw
materials; plant and rolling stock urgently needed renewing. The
growth of public expenditure had been enormous and had had to be
met by loans and the issue of paper money with a consequent rise of
prices and danger of inflation. Her public debt had increased from
$33\frac{1}{2}$ milliard francs in 1913 to over 219 milliard in 1919.[2] She owed 33
milliard francs to foreign countries and a once favourable trade balance
now showed a deficit of 21 milliards.[3] Her economy had been seriously
disrupted, her society in many ways revolutionized by the incidence
of State control. All the European belligerents were in a similar
plight, but in the West it was France which had been the battlefield and
France with her declining population was least able to support the loss
of manpower. After the armistice it remained to make peace and to
garner the fruits of victory; but on a sober reckoning it was to appear
highly doubtful whether they could ever compensate her for the losses
of war. 'My work is finished,' said Foch to Clemenceau, on 11th November when he handed him the completed document of the armistice.
'Your work is beginning.'[4] Clemenceau could be relied on to do his
best, but even he could not secure a peace which fully satisfied French
requirements.

[1] RENOUVIN, P.: *La crise européenne et la grande guerre*, p. 605.

[2] RENOUVIN, P.: *La crise européenne et la grande guerre*, p. 604.

[3] The percentage ratio of imports to exports had increased from 123 in 1912
to 472 in 1918. FONTAINE, A.: *French Industry during the War*, p. 18.

[4] cit. JACKSON, J. HAMPDEN: *Clemenceau and the Third Republic*, p. 186.

AUGÉ-LARIBÉ, M. and PINOT, P.: *Agriculture and Food Supply in France during the
    War*. Yale, 1927.
BIDOU, H., GAUVAIN, A. and SEIGNOBOS, C.: *La Grande guerre* (Vol. IX of LAVISSE, E.:
    Histoire de France contemporaine. Paris, 1921).

BRUUN, GEOFFREY: *Clemenceau*. Harvard, 1943.

CRUTTWELL, C. R. M. F.: *A History of the Great War, 1914–18.* 2nd ed. Oxford, 1936.

FONTAINE, ARTHUR: *French Industry during the War.* Yale, 1926.

JACKSON, J. HAMPDEN: *Clemenceau and the Third Republic.* London, 1946.

JÈZE, G. and TRUCHY, H.: *The War Finance of France.* Yale, 1927.

POINCARÉ, R.: *Au service de la France; neuf années de souvenirs.* 10 vols. Paris, 1926–33.

RENOUVIN, P.: *The Forms of War Government in France.* Yale, 1927.

RENOUVIN, P.: *La crise européenne et la grande guerre* (1904–18). Paris, 1934.

XV

FROM VICTORY TO THE ECONOMIC SLUMP OF 1929

FRANCE had been three times invaded by German troops and four times threatened with war by German Governments during the space of a century. Whereas 1870-71 had cost her less than 50,000 men,[1] 1914-18 had meant death for 1,300,000, and the strain of the four years' war just ended had, as we have seen, been almost unbearable. Her troops had re-entered Alsace and Lorraine and no ally would deny her right to their recovery. But the achievement of *revanche* and fulfilment of *la justice immanente* still left unsolved the wider problem of Franco-German relations. Germany was defeated and for a moment torn by revolution, but her population was still far greater than that of France—where the casualties of war had led to an increase in the fall of the birth-rate—her territory was virtually untouched by the devastations of war and she retained an enormous industrial potential. What guarantee could there be that in twenty or thirty years' time, when she had recovered her strength, this great, efficient, industrious nation, with her memory of vast ambitions frustrated, would not in her turn seek *revanche* and make a fresh bid for the world domination so nearly within her grasp in 1914 and in 1918? Unless there were to be an immediate and enduring rapprochement between the two countries, a thing impossible for Frenchmen who were in a state of impassioned hatred engendered by the strain and horrors of war, the only solution could be one of force. France must have material guarantees strong enough to ensure her security and Germany must be crippled and kept down. This problem of security against a recurrence of German aggression is the central and thorniest problem of the peace negotiations between France and her Allies, and because those negotiations fail to provide a solution, it overshadows the whole of subsequent French history.

The armistice of November 11th, 1918, had been greeted by most of the peoples of Europe with an immense relief and with an immense hope; relief that the carnage was over, hope that a new device of international organization would make the repetition of such slaughter for

[1] INGE, W. R.: *Lay Thoughts of a Dean*, p. 95.

ever impossible. Had not President Wilson in his famous message to Congress on January 8th proposed as the last of his Fourteen Points the formation of a new holy alliance of peoples, a League of Nations, whose object would be to afford 'mutual guarantees of political independence and territorial integrity to great and small states alike'? [1]

For most Frenchmen, at any rate at first, the League was, however, only alluring if it could be made to ensure security by the use of force; and when it was clear that Wilson and Lloyd George would have nothing to do with Léon Bourgeois' plan to endow the League with its own army and the power to enforce military sanctions, Clemenceau, the leader of the French delegation, lost all interest in its organization. For him it was clear that the Franco-German problem must be settled by other means and that the end of security could be achieved only by hard bargaining at the conference table. So it was that he demanded that Germany should pay the whole cost of the war, that the Saar district with its coal mines should be ceded permanently to France, and that the whole of the left bank of the Rhine should be detached from Germany, occupied permanently by the Allies, and constituted as a separate state or states. This solution of the Rhineland problem was considered by Foch to be essential for French security and his view was shared by Poincaré, a large number of politicians, and the great mass of French opinion. But British and American ideas on these questions were very different—annexations and separations of territory went clean-counter to the principle of self-determination which was so dear to President Wilson's heart and which had been newly consecrated in the Fourteen Points; while to Lloyd George an independent Rhineland spelt a new Alsace-Lorraine, and permanent occupation a commitment which no British Government could undertake. Thus it came about that Clemenceau, 'terrifying figure' though Lloyd George sometimes found him to be, was forced to compromise on every one of his main demands. By the Treaty of Versailles, signed on June 28th, 1919, in the Hall of Mirrors, where forty-eight years earlier Bismarck had proclaimed the German Empire, France formally recovered sovereignty over Alsace-Lorraine, and as a result of Germany's renunciation of her colonies added almost the whole of Togoland and the Cameroons to her African Empire [2]; but instead of Germany's paying for the whole cost of the war, the Allies were to receive reparations for all damage done to civilians and their property; instead of obtaining full sovereignty over the Saar

[1] For text of the Fourteen Points and of the League of Nations Covenant see BUTTERFIELD, H.: *Select Documents of European History*, 1715–1920, p. 194 ff.

[2] See Map IV.

district, France had to be content with the ownership of its coal mines and with its government by a League of Nations Commission for fifteen years, at the end of which a plebiscite was to decide whether the inhabitants preferred incorporation in France or in Germany; and instead of securing the separation of the Rhineland and its permanent military occupation, she could obtain only the demilitarization of the right bank to a depth of fifty kilometres and the military occupation of the léft bank and the bridgeheads for fifteen years. Two important clauses were, however, secured by Clemenceau, stipulating that, if Germany failed to fulfil her treaty obligations or if the 'guarantees against unprovoked aggression' were not considered sufficient, the territory on the left bank might be reoccupied or its evacuation deferred.

'The guarantees against unprovoked aggression'—these were a cardinal factor in the negotiations. Wilson and Lloyd George, impressed by the strength of the French desire for security, had come forward with the offer of a joint Anglo-American undertaking to go to France's aid if on any future occasion she was again the victim of an unprovoked German attack. But it had been conditional on Clemenceau's withdrawal of his demands for a separate Rhineland and permanent military occupation. Clemenceau was obliged to choose. Before the war French statesmen had in vain sought for such an undertaking from Great Britain. Its offer now by the representative of the U.S.A. as well as of Great Britain exceeded his fondest hopes. With the automatic assistance of the two most powerful states in the world France's security might well seem assured. She accepted the offer and gave up the main French demands concerning the Rhineland; with the result that, although British and American opinion long regarded Clemenceau as the unrelenting advocate of a harsh and tyrannical peace, he was attacked by many of his countrymen for his weakness and leniency. It was only after protracted and passionate debates that the Treaty was eventually ratified by the French Parliament in October 1919. Unfortunately for France the American Congress was still more critical of it and in March 1920 the Treaty of Versailles and the League of Nations were repudiated by the American Senate. With them went the American guarantee to France and in consequence the British offer, which had been conditional upon American participation in the general scheme for international security, ceased to hold good. France had fallen between two stools. She had failed to secure the strategic frontier which her military experts regarded as indispensable and the pledges given her in return for its abandonment had not been honoured. Painfully and laboriously she had to seek for some other solution of the German problem. In the transformed and disunited Europe with which she was now confronted and in the divided state of her own public opinion this was to be no easy quest.

With the end of the war and the collapse of the Central Powers in 1918, the old European order had vanished and the balance of power, not only in Europe but also in the world, was greatly altered. A large part of the European Continent lay prostrate, disorganized by revolution and impoverished by war. On the other hand the countries of the New World had grown rich as their exports to the European belligerents had risen by leaps and bounds. Among them there towered the U.S.A., now a creditor nation and a world power of the first magnitude, but showing by her repudiation of the Versailles Treaty and the League of Nations that she was not yet ready to accept the permanent responsibilities which her new rank implied. In Central and Eastern Europe where formerly there had been the three great Empires of Germany, Austria-Hungary and Russia, there were now, in addition to a Republican Germany and a Bolshevik Russia, no less than ten relatively small states, all more or less intensely nationalistic and jealous of each others' pretensions. Their existence was a triumph for the Wilsonian principle of self-determination, but it made the problems of European unity more complex and it left a series of weak powers on Germany's eastern border instead of two strong ones. Moreover, the task of creating a new and harmonious order on the ruins of the old was rendered infinitely more difficult by the October Revolution of 1917 and the definite triumph of Bolshevism in Russia by 1920. The spread of Communism with its call for revolution in all capitalist states had at once been recognized as a threat to the established way of life in every country west of the Pripet Marshes. This threat, as we shall see, was parried and Communism triumphed only in a single country. But its entrenchment there, in the very country which had so lately been France's ally, on whom she had long relied to maintain the balance of European power, was regarded as a standing menace to the internal order of European states and therefore a profound cause of internal disunion. So it was that, although the temporary settlement of Germany, the disappearance of Austria-Hungary and the outlawry of the Russian pariah gave France for the moment an unquestioned preponderance on the Continental mainland, the distant outlook was far less reassuring. The day might come when France would have to choose between German military and Russian social aggression. More than ever before, her politics were to become subordinated to direction by forces beyond her own frontiers.

Meanwhile her situation was none the easier for the difficulties of transition from war to peace at home. On October 24th, 1919, hostilities terminated officially and measures enacted by law or decree for the duration of the war ceased to have effect.   Military and economic demobilization proceeded apace and the business of reincorporating the lost provinces and repairing the damage in the occupied departments was begun.   Demobilization from the forces was completed within a year of the armistice; requisitioned railways were restored to their owners, but in such bad condition that they soon had to be completely reorganized; import control restrictions were removed; and almost all the war-time ministries and services, except those concerned with further employment and the recruitment of foreign labour, closed down.   The recovery of Alsace and Lorraine did not wholly make up for the decline of population by 2,000,000 between 1911 and 1921 and France became increasingly dependent on foreign help for certain types of labour, especially in the mines.[1]   On the other hand she gained the valuable iron ore and metallurgical works of Lorraine and the textile factories and newly-developed potash mines of Alsace.   It was, as we shall see, much less difficult to integrate these assets in French economy than to solve the psychological problems of incorporating populations whose mode of life had for nearly half a century been conditioned by a different set of laws.   Materially, indeed, the process of transition was in many ways easier than might have been expected.   The unemployment feared as a result of speedy demobilization was mitigated by the need for labour for reconstructing the devastated regions and by the introduction of a shorter working day.   Yet there was also much social unrest and in 1919 there were more than 2,000 strikes involving well over 1,000,000 workers. Inevitably discipline in factory and workshops tended to relax after the war-time effort and discontent was aggravated by the facts that the eight-hour day introduced in accordance with the Treaty of Versailles was too often ignored by employers, that there was a steady increase in the cost of living, which caused much hardship to those dependent on small fixed incomes, that wages failed to catch up with the increasing rise in prices, so that in 1920, if not in 1919, real wages had fallen below the 1911 level,[2] and last but not least that there was a good deal of Com-

[1] By 1931 there were no less than 1,600,000 foreign wage earners in France, including 287,000 Poles, 194,000 Spaniards, 156,000 Belgians, and 475,000 Italians. I am indebted for these figures to the Research Department of Chatham House.

[2] The real wages of workers in industry and agriculture were, with few exceptions, higher in 1921 than in 1911, but the delay in adjusting remuneration to the increasing price rise brought them below the 1911 level in 1920.   The net salaries of Government employees, except those in the lowest categories, was considerably lower than in 1911.   FONTAINE, A.: *French Industry during the War*, p. 69.

munist propaganda which had a disturbing effect. The most striking
result of Communism was to split the ranks of the Socialists. At the
Socialist Party Congress at Tours in 1920 there was a clash between
the moderates, who believed in parliamentary methods, upholding the
Versailles settlement and remaining loyal to the Second International,
and the extremist majority who sought to establish the dictatorship
of the proletariat by violent means, denounced the peace as a capitalist
contrivance for the maintenance of bourgeois supremacy, and professed allegiance to a new Third International whose headquarters
were in Moscow. Immediately, Socialism was weakened, for the split
affected both the party and the C.G.T. The new Communist party,
founded in 1920, recruited its adherents from the dissident Socialists, and
the C.G.T.U. (Confédération Générale dú Travail Unitaire), affiliated
to the Moscow Profintern, was set up as a rival to the C.G.T. A new
and disciplined party was thus introduced to the Left of the Socialists
and, most important of all, it appeared to take its orders from an organization controlled by a foreign power. If we discount the political activities of Ultramontanes and religious orders this was an entirely new and
sinister development in French party politics.

In parliament, too, there was a reaction against war-time discipline,
the discipline which Clemenceau had carried on beyond the armistice.
But the life of the Chamber of 1914 was drawing to a close, after having
already been prolonged beyond its normal term, and a general election
was fixed for 1919. For a moment it seemed as though a new and in-
vigorating spirit was going to sweep through French politics. The old
method of election by *scrutin d'arrondissement,* so dear and so safe
for the Radicals, was set aside in favour of a new and complicated system
of proportional representation, which told heavily in favour of the most
disciplined group and resulted in a sweeping majority for a new bloc
called the Bloc National. This election of the so-called 'Chambre bleu
horizon' was the counterpart of the Khaki election of 1918 in Great
Britain. The majority of the new deputies were ex-servicemen of
varying political origins who had come together, abjuring their old
parties, in order to carry forward into the realm of politics the fraternity
in arms acquired at the front. The new bloc was a sort of derivative of
union sacrée which cut right across the old pre-war Bloc des Gauches
because it split the Radicals. For this reason, and because it included
several Royalists and many Catholics but excluded the Socialists, its
character was distinctly Conservative. For the first time in the history
of the Third Republic since the establishment of the Constitution of
1875 a Conservative majority had been returned to a French Chamber.

In fact the nearest analogy to this first Chamber after the war of 1914–18 was the first Assembly after the war of 1870. In both cases the stress of war and anxiety about the international future had simplified the issues and so momentarily obscured the normal trend of party politics. In both cases a great many men had been elected who were newcomers to politics. Just as the return of the Royalist majority in 1871 (and also in 1815) had been a vote for peace and order, so the return of the Chamber Bleu Horizon was also a vote for peace and order—for a firm insistence on the execution of the terms of the Treaty and for order in the face of the Communist menace. But as they were absorbed into normal peace-time occupations it was soon to be seen that the 'Anciens Combattants' would lose their solidarity under the solvent influences of civilian life and the propaganda of the traditional parties, and would resume their old political habits. Meanwhile, the return of the Bloc National had appeared momentarily to unite the soundest elements in the nation in defence of its fundamental interests. The fact that the Bloc included a number of practising Catholics suggested, moreover, that the splendid record of the clergy during the war had finally disposed of the old anti-clericalism.

Almost the first important task of the new Chamber was the election of a President to succeed Poincaré, whose term was due to expire in January 1920. Two candidates were nominated, Clemenceau and Deschanel, a former Progressist whose main qualifications were his exceptional elegance and the tact with which he had frequently presided over the Chamber. The National Assembly, Nationalist though it was, rejected Clemenceau and took Deschanel. So ended the long public career of the most notable of the statesmen of the Third Republic. In accordance with custom on the election of a new President, Clemenceau, now seventy-nine years of age, at once resigned his premiership and retired into private life. He had in the end fallen a victim to the same treatment which he had on a memorable occasion meted out to Jules Ferry—once again a Republican Assembly had treated one of her greatest men with its ancient prescription of fear and ingratitude. Only by occasional public utterances and conversation with his friends did the wonderful old man continue to show how much clearer-sighted he was than most of his contemporaries and what leadership the nation had lost during the years of doubt and hesitancy to come. France could have had no abler pilot through the shoals of European politics; and, if it is argued that at home his presidency might have provoked a constitutional crisis, the answer is that one was to come in any case. Within a few months there was yet another Presidential election. Clemenceau

had advised the National Assembly in 1887 to vote for the stupidest—
ironically enough when the Assembly of 1920 chose Deschanel in preference to him they voted for a man who shortly afterwards had a
breakdown and had to be removed to a mental home.   On the next
occasion they were not afraid to vote for a strong man; they elected the
man who had succeeded Clemenceau as Prime Minister, the former
Socialist, Millerand, and he, like MacMahon, was to clash with the
succeeding Chamber.

With the signature of the Treaty of Versailles, the election of the
Chambre Bleu Horizon, the retirement of Clemenceau and the repudiation of the Treaty by the American Senate, we enter upon a new phase
of French history which is marked by sharp fluctuations of domestic
and foreign policy, fluctuations which correspond to growing cleavages
of opinion at home.

The Chambre Bleu Horizon and Senate had rejected Clemenceau,
not because of his nationalism, but because of his authoritarianism and
his Jacobin anti-clericalism which still persisted.   They still wanted a
nationalist and a man of authority to keep order and defend French
interests; in Millerand they found the person they needed both as Prime
Minister and subsequently as President.   He pursued a firm policy of
insisting on the exact fulfilment of the Treaty and he acted vigorously
in the face of threats to social order.   Thus in April 1920 he replied to
the German Government's unauthorized dispatch of 20,000 men to
keep order in the Ruhr by the immediate occupation of Frankfurt and
Darmstadt; and when in January 1922 in the midst of an economic
crisis, Briand, in conference with Lloyd George at Cannes, showed
disquieting signs of an inclination to make concessions to Germany on
the reparations question, he promptly recalled him, and Briand resigned
without having been defeated in the Chamber.   It was he who then took
the unprecedented step of calling upon a former President of the Republic,
Poincaré, to form a Ministry, and his choice was largely determined by
the fact that Poincaré could be relied on to take a strong line in dealing
with Germany.   So indeed he did; Poincaré, the sternly patriotic
Lorrainer, who had presided over the destinies of the country during
the Great War was also a cold clear-headed legist, and would go to
the limit in exacting fulfilment of the Treaty of Versailles.   Thus it was
that in 1923, when Germany defaulted in the payment of reparations, he
sent French troops to occupy the Ruhr, in spite of British disapproval,
already manifested in 1920 on the occasion of the march into Frankfurt
and Darmstadt.   It was Millerand also who helped to check the spread
of Bolshevism by sending a French military mission to Poland in 1920

under General Weygand.   The Poles were then at war with the Russians
and the help given to them by Weygand contributed much to their
victory in the Battle of Warsaw which effectively checked the Russian
advance.   Thus Millerand fully represented the policy of the Bloc
National and indeed it was to his undoing that he identified himself with
them too closely.   Gradually, as the life of the 1919 Chamber wore on,
the Radicals sat more loosely to the Bloc; and eventually they left it
altogether and renewed their friendship with the Socialists.   So when
the time came for the next general elections in 1924 they had reverted
to their old attitude of 'No enemies to the left' (with the exception now
of the Communists), and with the Radical-Socialists and Socialists they
formed a combination called the Cartel des Gauches which was but the
old pre-war Bloc Républicain under another name.   In the meantime,
as peace-time habits became more general, the Radical committees and
electoral machinery had regained much of their influence.   Moreover,
Poincaré's policy of the strong arm did not succeed: the Ruhr occupation met with passive resistance on the part of the Germans, it made an
additional call upon French manpower and finance and it did not achieve
its object of making Germany pay.   It was therefore not hard for its
opponents to declaim against 'Poincaré la guerre' and to represent the
occupation as a foolhardy, costly adventure: and at a time when France
was beginning to comprehend her own weariness, to know that beyond
all else she desired peace without adventures and to suffer from an
acute financial crisis, their attacks had considerable influence.   They
were also able to make much capital out of the budgetary deficit, the
continued rise in prices, the depreciation of the franc and the Poincaré
Government's imposition of additional taxation in order to remedy the
situation.   Consequently, in the 1924 elections the Cartel obtained a
handsome majority in the Chamber, although its poll was not much
more than in 1919.   At once it sought to exploit its victory.   The
Socialists had long been hostile to Millerand as a deserter from their
ranks; he was mistrusted on account of his authoritarian tendencies
and his open advocacy of a revision of the Constitution which would
increase the powers of the President of the Republic; and the whole
Cartel maintained that he had, during the elections, shown his sympathies
too openly with the Bloc National.   They were therefore determined
to have his head.   One of their papers, the *Quotidien*, came out with a
demand for 'all the places and at once'; and this meant that they claimed
even the Presidency of the Republic.   So there arose a first-class constitutional crisis which recalled both 1887 and 1877; 1887, because when
Millerand sought to form a Ministry from among the majority in the

new Chamber he was unable to do so since the potential Prime Ministers went on strike and refused to serve under him; 1877, because he then abandoned the attempt, formed a minority Cabinet, and like MacMahon, attempted to induce the Senate to concur in a dissolution of the Chamber. The Senate refused and Millerand had no alternative but to resign. But the Senate had still some care for the balance of power in the State. If the Cartel then proceeded to procure the election of one of their own nominees from the Chamber, the President of the Republic would become a mere creature of the legislature. The Senate therefore put up its own President, Doumergue, against the President of the Chamber, Painlevé, and secured his election by a large majority. A Radical Government was at once formed by Edouard Herriot, the Mayor of Lyons, with Socialist support. The general outline of French political groupings resumed its 'normal' pre-war aspect, and the resemblance was strengthened by the fact that the Radicals once again stirred up the issue of Church and State.

This advent of the Cartel to power led to notable changes in policy at home and abroad. The new Government made haste to terminate the unpopular Ruhr occupation and to accept the revised scale of reparation payments proposed by the so-called Dawes Plan. The German policy of the Bloc National might well be held to have failed. So far from making Germany pay it had only embittered her, involving France in financial loss and estranging her from Great Britain, which thought that France was abusing her position as the dominant state on the Continent and tended in consequence to back the weaker Germany in the interests of the balance of power. The Herriot Government sought to achieve the main end of security by conciliation instead of by force. It agreed to the admission of Germany to the League of Nations, it renewed diplomatic relations with Russia and sought to revive the Entente with Great Britain. Its predecessors had aimed at security, first by obtaining a new form of guarantee from Great Britain once the old one had been nullified by the American repudiation, and secondly, by the conclusion of alliances with some of the new states in Eastern Europe whose very existence was so largely dependent upon the maintenance of the Versailles settlement. It was in pursuance of this policy that in 1921 they had entered into a formal alliance with Poland, which was accompanied by a military convention and the grant of a loan to enable Poland to purchase French supplies; that in 1924 this was followed by a Treaty with Czechoslovakia; and that closer political and economic relations had been developed with the two other members of the so-called Little Entente, Rumania and Yugoslavia. They had not, however,

been successful in obtaining a new guarantee from Great Britain,
which took the view that France's security was adequately assured by
the League of Nations Covenant with its guarantee and sanctions clauses,
and which insisted on linking any specific proposal with the settlement
of a number of outstanding European problems. Thus frustrated, they
had turned to the League itself, there seeking to extract security concessions from Great Britain by blocking the progress of the disarmament
talks, by which the British Government set great store, and to strengthen
the League Covenant which they regarded as full of loopholes. But
although they had been able to block disarmament, they had made little
headway with security. Draft Treaties of Mutual Assistance and
Geneva Protocols alike were wrecked by the reluctance of successive
British Governments to take on any new commitment. By 1925,
however, since the advent of the Cartel, much closer relations had been
established with Great Britain and something of the spirit of the old
Entente had returned—thenceforward until the end of the Republic it
was notable that relations between the two countries were much easier
when a Government of the Left was in power in France. This was
perfectly understandable: the Left were more conciliatory in their
approach to the German problem, more genuinely inspired with belief
in the Wilsonian ideals, which after all had so much in common with
the great Liberal tradition of the French Revolution, and in consequence wholehearted supporters of the League of Nations; on the
other hand the Right were those whose thought was more strongly
coloured by the violent 'integral Nationalism' preached by the 'Action
Française'—as far back as Fashoda and the Boer War it had been this
Right who had been the most vociferous in their hostility to the British
Empire. It was the Right, too, who had adopted an intransigent attitude towards Germany which the British found exceedingly difficult
to understand or appreciate, and who distrusted the League of Nations
as a mere 'talking shop'. So now it was a Government of the Left
which came nearer than any Government of the Bloc National to achieving through friendship with Great Britain the guarantees it so persistently
sought.

The Locarno Agreements of October 1925 appeared to be a great
triumph for Briand, now Foreign Minister in the second Cartel Government, and for Austen Chamberlain, the British Foreign Secretary. They
comprised a series of agreements whereby Great Britain, France, Italy,
Belgium and Germany mutually guaranteed Germany's western frontiers. In this way France at last secured a British undertaking of support
against any unprovoked attack and Germany formally recognized the

permanence of the frontier arrangements made at Versailles. This seemed to mean that she had effectively been brought back into the European States system and to open up the prospect of a new and more cordial phase in Franco-German relations. Gradually, it appeared, the unity of Europe was being reforged by amicable agreement on the basis of existing Treaties, and Locarno gave rise to a wave of optimism and confidence. Moreover, its maintenance was so important that Briand, the man of Locarno, throughout the vicissitudes of home politics was to remain at the Quai d'Orsay for nearly seven years—the longest tenure of the Foreign Office in the history of the Third Republic.

Thus the foreign policy of the Cartel Governments achieved some notable success, but at home they were much less happy in their handling of affairs, and their domestic policy was to bring them to confusion long before the term of the Chamber of 1924 expired. They were soon confronted by trouble in Alsace and Lorraine, revolt in Syria, and a serious financial crisis.

The trouble in Alsace and Lorraine was largely of their own making. The war, with its need for *union sacrée*, and the conciliatory attitude of both Church and Governments during the decade 1914–24, had allayed much of the old bitterness arising out of the Separation of Church and State. Many of the dissolved religious orders had been allowed to return. Priests and Catholic laymen had given magnificent service in the field of battle. The Pope had in 1923 permitted the formation of diocesan associations to take the place of the *associations cultuelles* originally envisaged in the Separation law,[1] and diplomatic relations with the Vatican had been re-established. But Herriot and the Radicals still retained much of their old sectarianism, and, thinking perhaps that there was still nothing like a display of anti-clericalism for binding the groups of a Left-wing Cartel more closely together, they lost no time in opening an offensive against the Church, threatening to apply the Laws against the Congregations in all their strictness and to recall the French Embassy from the Vatican. These threats were mainly harmful in that they diverted attention from more important issues; but there were more serious consequences when Herriot proposed to extend all the anti-clerical legislation passed between 1871 and 1914 to the recovered provinces, and when his successor did away with the High Commissioner's Office, substituting a Directorate-General with its headquarters in Paris. In Alsace and Lorraine the Concordat of 1801 still remained in force, slightly modified by arrangements made during the German occupation. The population contained a large number of devout

[1] See *ante*, p. 203.

practising Catholics who in German days had had close association with the powerful German Catholic Centre Party. Already the business of reincorporating the two provinces had occasioned friction and misunderstanding between French officials and the local populations and this now came to a head, especially in Alsace. The protests were so widespread that Herriot was unable to impose his policy, but the very fact that he had intended to introduce it left a legacy of unrest and disaffection which was to afford an opportunity for the growth of home rule or autonomist movements, and subsequently for the development of a German 'Fifth Column'.

In Syria, too, anti-clericalism worked harm as the tactless conduct of the new High Commissioner, General Sarrail, perhaps appointed because of his anti-clerical sympathies, led in 1925 to a violent rising throughout the south of the country which it took several months and cost many lives to suppress. But the main source of the trouble which brought the Cartel to grief was not anti-clericalism but finance. Finance, which before the war had interested few but the experts, was now a matter of growing public concern. The continued rise in prices, the over-valuation of the franc, lavish expenditure and the flight of capital abroad called for firm remedies, but the doctors of the Cartel were divided—the Radicals attempting to eke out their existence by a series of expedients such as short-term loans from banks; the Socialists calling for drastic measures such as a capital levy and a compulsory consolidation of Treasury bonds, which alarmed the financial interests of the country and only increased instability. From April 1925 to July 1926 there was a series of crises owing to the inability of the Chamber to come out firmly in favour of a decided policy because of the risk of splitting the Cartel. Ministry followed Ministry and plan upon plan was put forward in vain. At length in July 1926 when the franc had fallen from 70 francs to the pound in May 1924, when the Cartel came into office, to 250 and the French Treasury was almost empty, the Radicals came to a decision. Fundamentally, in spite of the mystique of Leftism which served them so well at election times, they were Conservative in their instincts and had many ties with the financial world. They rejected the Socialist prescriptions and rallied round Poincaré and orthodox finance. Once again the former President of the Republic was called in to govern with a strong hand; and because of his prestige, because his Republicanism was irreproachable, and because he was able to form a government of Union Nationale, public confidence was very quickly restored. Indeed the Chamber itself went so far as to grant to him what it had refused to Briand and Caillaux six months earlier, namely the power to take all necessary measures for ending the financial crisis by decree-laws. Such power had never been granted in peacetime before—only once in 1918, as we have seen,[1] in the darkest hours of the war, had similar authority been granted to Clemenceau. This abdication by the legislature, conscience-smitten at the results of its own incompetence, was a significant event. Poincaré used his dictatorial powers sparingly, but their very existence afforded a precedent which might be revolutionary in its consequences.

For nearly three years, thanks to Poincaré's restoration of confidence and to his policy of strict economy and cheap money, the country enjoyed a period of relative calm and prosperity. The process of reconstruction had been completed, and French export trade had notably expanded both as a result of this and of the devaluation of the franc. At home Poincaré stabilized the franc at a fifth of its pre-war value, set up a sinking fund, concluded a number of commercial agreements stabilizing tariffs, and began the construction of a great defensive line near the eastern frontier known as the Maginot Line. Abroad, the completion of Germany's disarmament in accordance with the Versailles Treaty, the preparations for a conference on general disarmament, the Kellogg Pact outlawing war, the formation of the International Steel Cartel by producers of Germany, France, Belgium, Luxemburg and the Saar, the conclusion of treaties of alliance with Roumania (June 1927) and Yugoslavia (March 1927), all seemed to strengthen France's position and to renew or perpetuate the greater confidence in European stability which had been engendered by Locarno; and in 1929 Briand was even to go so far as to expound to the League Assembly a somewhat Utopian scheme of European Union. At home, too, the return to the traditional electoral machinery of *scrutin d'arrondissement* (a proposal backed by both the main parties, Radicals and Socialists, in the late Cartel) for the elections of 1928 emphasized the orthodoxy of the new dispensation, which a French historian has compared to 'the Conservative Republic dreamt of by Thiers, realized for a moment in the time of Méline and broken by the Dreyfus Affair'.[2] But, underlying the so-called Union Nationale, there were deep clefts, and an economic blizzard was soon to blow, causing financial distress and political unrest in every country in the world.

The Union Nationale was far from being an *union sacrée*; in spite of its name it was primarily an alliance of groups of the centre, the first

[1] *ante*, p. 249.

[2] MADAULE, J.: *Histoire de France*, II, p. 348.

to govern since Thiers' day.[1] Moreover, the crisis of 1925-6 and the
break-up of the Cartel had caused much bitterness on the Left. Never
before had the Left groups been faced by a financial crisis of such magnitude and they attributed their failure and Poincaré's success in settling it
to the hidden power of financial interests. They were easily led to
believe that reforms had been blocked by the so-called 'Mur d'argent'
erected by the bankers and industrialists, and that these men would
continue to oppose any and every measure which would tend to a
redistribution of wealth. And since the financial crisis had paralysed
government, and orthodox finance meant retrenchment, it was easy to
argue that the 'Mur d'argent' was opposed to all kinds of social reform.
Thus the events of 1924-8 widened the age-long gulf between different
groups of Frenchmen on the social question, and in 1928 shattered the
Union Nationale, for although the elections of that year had been an un-
doubted triumph for Poincaré, in November at the Radical Party
Congress the militant members on the Left wing of the party took
advantage of an imprudently 'clerical' measure of the Prime Minister
to declare against its continued participation in the Government. By
associating themselves with the Union Nationale the Radicals had, as
we have seen, joined a movement which was essentially one of social
and economic conservation. Once the immediate aims were achieved
the old tendency of the party to regard itself as a revolutionary party
of movement which must have no enemies or as few enemies as possible
to the Left reasserted itself. The support of the Socialists for *scrutin
d'arrondissement* brought the Socialists and Radicals together again
and the departure of the Radicals from the Poincaré Government in
November foreshadowed the re-formation of the Cartel. There was
the same swing back to coalition of these two parties as in the years before
the war. The Radicals as the centre party are constantly torn between
opposing forces and the course of French parliamentary history is governed by the fluctuations of their alliances. Unfortunately for France,
the opposing forces on the two flanks, under the impact of economic
crises and of new developments abroad will tend to become more and
more violently antagonistic. France is torn between them with such
tension that in the end she is wellnigh in a state of veiled civil war. For
if the Left was embittered, the Right had never disarmed. Always
anti-democratic and anti-parliamentary in its tendencies, much attracted,
indeed, by the rise of Italian Fascism, it had violently attacked the Cartel
Governments on all aspects of their policy. In particular, it had denounced the Locarno Agreements for the position of equality they gave

[1] SEIGNOBOS, C.: *Etudes de politique et d'histoire*, p. 311.

to Germany and for their omission to guarantee Poland's western frontier, and it pursued Briand with unrelenting hostility until his death. Although it had been thrown into disarray in 1926 by the Papal condemnation of the Action Française, whose political doctrines were wholly amoral, the return of economic instability and of threats to security from abroad soon gave it a fresh opportunity to exert its influence. In November 1929 the slump in the U.S.A. led to an economic and financial crisis of the first magnitude. In June 30th, 1930, the last French troops left the Rhineland and two months later 107 National-Socialist Deputies were elected to the German Reichstag. Storm clouds were gathering which threatened both Briand's Locarno settlement and Poincaré's restoration of French prosperity. And in July 1929 Poincaré had to retire from the Premiership on account of ill-health while Briand, tired and ageing, would not long remain to face the tempest. In the lean years ahead the guidance of French destinies was to fall into the hands of younger and lesser men.

Meanwhile the war and the monetary crises which followed had increased the tempo of social change, impoverishing the man who depended on dividends or a pension and rendering the producer, notably the peasant, more independent. 'Never,' wrote the French historian, Seignobos, 'not even during the French Revolution, had the State dealt such a blow to private property; stabilisation reduced the value of investments by four-fifths while death duties ate into inheritances.'[1] In consequence the tendency to social levelling continued; while the growing uniformity of dress and manners was accelerated by American production methods and the influence of such new inventions as the wireless and the cinema. In sport France now for the first time began to make a mark with champions such as Suzanne Lenglen and Borotra in lawn tennis and Carpentier in boxing. To science she still made distinguished contributions, particularly in the realm of physics with the work of Jean Perrin, Paul Langevin, and those eminent brothers, the Duc de Broglie and Prince Louis de Broglie. Intellectually, however, the war in many ways acted as a disruptive agent, and this was especially noticeable in French literature. Already the philosophy of Bergson with its exaltation of intuition had exercised a profound effect upon novelists like Proust, most of whose work was first published after 1919. Already Gide, who was the most influential literary figure of the 'twenties, had derived much of his inspiration from the amoralism of the German Nietzsche. Such philosophies, together with the growing interest in psychology, had encouraged escapist cults of sensation and extreme artistic and literary

[1] *Histoire sincère de la nation française*, pp. 488–9.

movements like that of the Surrealists with their enthronement of the
unconscious. The war, with its bloodshed and destruction of much of
the old European order had further contributed to undermine traditional
human values and to drain much of the post-war literature of ethical or
national content. There was still an abundance of artistic talent; the
sense of form remained strong and was conspicuously displayed in French
films or in the work of writers such as Mauriac and Giraudoux, but in
the realm of ideas there was what a French author has called a 'fever of
intellectual denationalization'[1] Such a phenomenon was by no means
peculiar to France at this time, but in a society where the national
traditions had been so deep-rooted, and part of which was so highly
intellectual, the disarray caused by the jettisoning of old values and by
the restless search for new ones outside the French traditions may well
have had a deeper and ultimately more damaging effect than elsewhere.
When we come in the next chapter to look upon a picture of growing
darkness it will be wise to bear in mind the importance of this moral
and intellectual disorder as a possible element in the tragedy of 1940.

[1] MAILLAUD, P.: *France*, p. 96.

GATHORNE-HARDY, G. M.: *A Short History of International Affairs*, 1920-39. 3rd ed.
    Oxford University Press, 1942.
HUDDLESTON, SISLEY: *France and the French*. London, 1925.
JORDAN, W. M.: *Great Britain, France and the German Problem*, 1918-39. Oxford
    University Press, 1943.
JOSEPH-BARTHÉLEMY: *Le Gouvernement de la France*. New ed. Paris, 1939.
MIDDLETON, W. L.: *The French Political System*. London, 1932.
PICKLES, DOROTHY M.: *The French Political Scene*. London, 1938.
SEIGNOBOS, C.: *La signification historique des élections françaises de 1928*, in *Études de
    politique et d'histoire*. Paris, 1934.
RITCHIE, R. L. G.: *France, A Companion to French Studies*, London, 1937.
SIEGFRIED, A.: *Tableau des partis en France*. Paris, 1930. [Translated into English
    under the title of *France, A Study in Nationality*. Yale, 1930.]
VAUCHER, P.: *Post-War France*. Oxford University Press, 1934.
WALTER, GÉRARD: *Histoire du Parti Communiste Français*. Paris, 1948.
WOLFERS, A.: *Britain and France Between Two Wars*. New York, 1940.

XVI

THE FINAL CATASTROPHE

THE economic crisis was more damaging to the more highly industrialized nations than to France. She was much less dependent than the United Kingdom or Germany upon foreign trade and it was not until 1931 that she seriously began to feel the pinch. By then successive currency depreciations abroad had eliminated the competitive advantage which had been enjoyed by French exports, and these were further hampered by the trade barriers which foreign countries began to erect in defence of their national economies. At first, therefore, the most alarming consequences of the crisis for France lay in its political effects in Europe and above all in Germany. There the depression assumed disastrous proportions, and by 1932 the number of unemployed had risen to 4,000,000. Germany was no longer able to meet her obligations and in 1932 reparations were virtually abrogated by the Lausanne Conference, which reduced the amount due from thirty-eight milliard francs to three milliards, payable in thirty-seven years after a three years' moratorium. The crisis played directly into the hands of the growing National Socialist party which had laid responsibility for it at the door of the Treaty of Versailles and of the weak Weimar Republic and preached a militant Nationalism. By 1932 the National Socialist leader had polled no less than thirteen million votes in the German presidential election. His party appeared to be not only the party of German rearmament but also that of German *revanche.*

But it was just at this time that the question of disarmament came to the fore. In 1932 the long-prepared Conference forgathered, and France found herself confronted by a formidable dilemma. On the one hand Germany had been declared to have completed her obligations under the Treaty of Versailles and once this declaration had been made the other signatories were formally bound by the same Treaty to disarm themselves, while if they failed to do so, but still wished to trea Germany as an equal, there could be no reason for not allowing her to rearm up to their limit. On the other hand Germany's industrial potential and her manpower were far greater than France's, and if the National Socialist party came into power what guarantee could there be that it

would observe any limit or submit to international control? Once
again France sought to link the question of disarmament to that of
security and once again put forward a plan for the creation of an international force and for strengthening the political authority of the League
of Nations, but it was coldly received by Great Britain, who still looked
askance at all proposals to turn the League into a sort of super-state.
Before the Conference entered on its next phase critical elections had
taken place in both Germany and France.

In France there were two elections, the general elections to the
Chamber and an unexpected election to the Presidency of the Republic,
since Paul Doumer, who had been elected in preference to Briand in
May 1931—yet one more example of a vote for the lesser man—was
assassinated by a Russian *émigré* named Gorguloff between the first
and second ballot.   The first ballot had shown a majority in favour of
the reformed Cartel or Union des Gauches, but it was the old Chamber
which joined with the Senate in electing the President and their choice
fell, as on many occasions before, upon the President of the Senate, a
moderate named Albert Lebrun.   The second ballot reinforced the first;
the Cartel returned triumphant to the Chamber and Herriot became
Prime Minister for the second time, once again forming a Radical
Ministry which was supported by the Socialists, but did not include any
of their representatives.   It was 1924 over again; only the Cartel did
not now claim 'all the places' and were content to leave Lebrun in the
Élysée.   It remained to be seen whether in this new European situation
this new Government of the Left would embark upon such a reversal of
politics as had marked the administrations of 1924-6.

In Germany parliamentary elections were held in July and here they
took an opposite course.   The flow of the tide towards the extremes of
National Socialism on the one hand and Communism on the other hand
had continued: but the National Socialists were in the ascendancy;
they won 230 seats and became the largest party in the Reichstag.   Six
months later President Hindenburg appointed Adolf Hitler Chancellor
of the German Reich.   The problem of disarmament was going to be
still more difficult and by now the economic crisis was beginning to hit
French economy.

Once again, indeed, it was the misfortune of the Cartel to be confronted by acute financial difficulties and once again they were unable
to resolve them because of the disagreement of Radicals and Socialists
concerning the remedies to be adopted.   Once again this inability meant
the lack of a stable majority and a succession of ministerial crises.   In
December 1932 Herriot fell because of his wish to honour France's

war debts to the U.S.A., whereas a majority held that war debts were linked to reparations and that, as it was due to American insistence that Germany had been granted a moratorium on the payment of reparations, France had no obligation to pay the U.S.A. so long as she received nothing from Germany. Between December 1932 and February 1934 no fewer than four Cabinets, those of Paul-Boncour, Daladier, Albert Sarraut and Chautemps, had followed one another in rapid succession without being able to impose a strong policy leading to financial recovery. Half-way through the life of the second Cartel Chamber it was once again high time for the Left parties to admit their impotence and call a Poincaré not only to rescue the finances but also to regenerate the régime and to mobilize all the energies of the nation before it was too late. But there was no Poincaré at hand, and it was necessary for an insurrection to add political to economic crisis and expose more clearly the depths to which the Republic had sunk, before a new saviour could be brought to power.

Once again all the old symptoms of disease which had shown themselves in the days of Gambetta and Ferry, and in the time of the Panama scandal and the Dreyfus Affair, had manifested themselves—mediocrity of the deputies, *esprit de clocher*, parliamentary corruption, ministerial instability, paralysis of legislation. Reform of all kinds, social, constitutional, financial, was blocked by the conservatism of deputies and senators who had vested interest in the maintenance of a régime which gave the Chambers virtual dictatorship, and who flattered themselves that because they were elected by the nation they were necessarily also the elect of the nation. At the same time the situation of France in the world was rapidly deteriorating. Her birth-rate continued to decline and her security was increasingly imperilled. The failure of the League of Nations to deal with the Manchurian crisis in 1931-2, and the failure of Tardieu and Herriot to reinforce the League by investing it with military powers, had shown that it was but a broken reed. The abortive Four Power pact to which Ramsay MacDonald had induced France to adhere in 1933 had alarmed her Eastern allies and had led Poland to conclude a pact of non-aggression and friendship with Germany in 1934, while the economic crisis had further weakened France's ties with the Little Entente powers since she was no longer able to give them financial aid. Finally, Germany's abrupt decision to leave the Disarmament Conference and the League of Nations in October 1933 emphasized the menace of militant National Socialism and its contempt for the European order established at Versailles. Once again, as in the days of Boulangism, public opinion, especially in Paris, became more and more impatient with the manœuvrings of parliamentarians and with a régime which showed such lack of policy and absence of leadership; and the growing hostility manifested itself in the reviving strength of the Action Française and in the formation of new Leagues, of which the most notable was the association of ex-servicemen known as the Croix de Feu led by Colonel de La Rocque. When the Stavisky scandal of 1933 followed those of Hanau in 1928 and Oustric in 1930, both of which involved more or less prominent politicians, and when it was widely believed that the 'suicide' of the financial adventurer Stavisky had been 'arranged' by the police with the connivance of the Prime Minister, Chautemps, in order to prevent him from making revelations of parliamentary corruption on a scale reminiscent of Panama,[1] indignation came to a head. There were street demonstrations in Paris on January 12th, 22nd, and 27th, 1934, and they continued even after Chautemps's resignation. According to one of the most recent historians of France, M. Madaule, it appears probable that there was a definite plot to overthrow the régime concerted mainly by elements on the extreme Right and Left and that the Minister of the Interior in the Cabinet of Daladier, who succeeded Chautemps, was himself privy to it.[2] But, if there were such a plot, it fell through owing to disagreement among the conspirators and to administrative changes made by Daladier. Instead, the malcontents of the Right, the Croix de Feu, and, significantly enough, the municipal Councillors of Paris, called for a monster meeting on the Place de la Concorde to demonstrate once again against the Stavisky scandal. But though the proclaimed intention of the demonstrators was to march up the Champs Élysées to the tomb of the Unknown Soldier, the crowd soon surged towards the Palais Bourbon and threatened to break through the police cordon. Thereupon the police opened fire and eleven people were killed and 300 wounded. Had not Daladier taken precautions and had the Chamber not been guarded, there might well have been a repetition of the scenes of February 1848 and September 1870. As it was the *journée* of February 6th, 1934, was the first occasion since 1848 on which blood had been shed in the streets of Paris in a manifestation which menaced the existence of the régime.

The casualties naturally exasperated the demonstrators and heightened the tension. Rioting continued and there were threats of more serious trouble and counter demonstrations by the Left, which were to culminate in a general strike on the 12th. Meanwhile, notwithstanding the fact

[1] In fact it was a smaller affair and the main victims of Stavisky's frauds were insurance companies cp. WERTH, A., *France in Ferment,* p. 62.

[2] MADAULE, J.: *Histoire de France,* II, p. 366.

that at the very moment when the crowds were massed in the Place de la
Concorde he had been given a vote of confidence, Daladier, who spoke
little and bore a slight resemblance to Napoleon, thereby conveying the
illusion that he was a strong man, resigned. Thus the executive abdicated
and still further betrayed its weakness. For the first time in the history
of the Third Republic a government which enjoyed parliamentary
support had yielded to pressure from outside Parliament. The President
of the Republic had to look outside the ranks of the parliamentarians who
had so ignominiously fumbled with the governmental machine during the
past four years. Once again, a former President of the Republic was
summoned to save the situation. Millerand's successor, the elderly and
genial Doumergue, like Cincinnatus from his plough, was called from
his rural retreat near Toulouse and hastened to Paris to become Prime
Minister and form a new Government of National Union, which included members of all parties except the Socialists and Communists.
Louis Barthou, one of the Progressist 'boys' of the 'nineties, became
Minister of Foreign Affairs, Tardieu and Herriot Ministers of State, and
Marshal Pétain, one of the heroes of the 1914–18 war, accepted the
Ministry of War. The effect on the public was immediate. Disturbances ceased, confidence was restored and the Chamber, thoroughly
scared by the danger through which it had passed, once again invested
the Government with power to legislate by decree. Henceforward
it shows itself more and more disposed to abdicate part of its functions
in this way, thereby singularly perverting the character of parliamentary
democracy.

But although Doumergue's Government did much to restore the
financial situation and, as we shall see, improve France's diplomatic
position, it failed to dissolve the armed leagues, reduce the cost of living
or effect any constitutional reform. More than ever a revision of the constitution, a reform of the structure of the regime, such as Millerand and
many others had advocated, seemed indispensable if the old diseases were
not once again to cripple the body politic as soon as parliament resumed
full sovereignty. Revision had been the insistent cry of the Boulangists
and the Ligue des Patriotes nearly half a century earlier; revision was
undoubtedly one of the main desires of many of the demonstrators of
February 6th, 1934, but the Republic was incapable of reform of this
kind and even the very modest proposals put forward by Doumergue
for strengthening the executive were blocked, mainly by the opposition
of the Radicals, who had such strong vested interests in the *status quo*.
On November 7th the Doumergue Cabinet fell. In spite of the shock
of February 6th the parliamentary régime was to stumble along as

before, unreformed, but tempered now by increasing recourse to the device of legislation by decree, a device which really concealed a greater menace to parliamentary sovereignty than any which was likely to arise from a moderate measure of constitutional reform.

The other limiting feature about the Doumergue Cabinet of 'Union Nationale' was that it was by no means a Cabinet of *union sacrée*. Socialists and Communists were both excluded and began to draw together in opposition to the Government and to its financial deflationary policy, which, however effective, was soon highly unpopular. Hitherto, ever since the split in the Socialist ranks in 1920, the main characteristic of the relations between the two chief working-class parties had been their bitter antagonism. Their new alliance, confirmed by an agreement of 1935 and their participation in the so-called Rassemblement Populaire of the same year, was a momentous event which was to lead to an amalgamation of the dissident C.G.T.U. with the C.G.T., to be decisive for the result of the general elections of 1936, and to thrust the social problem once more into the forefront of French politics, already troubled by so many other issues. The deflationary policy soon disquieted the Radicals, who were quick to perceive its unpopularity and hastened to dissociate themselves from the Union Nationale and to return to the application of their old principle of 'No enemies to the Left'. Hence, with the formation in 1936 of the Front Populaire, there came into being a new Bloc of the Left-wing parties, a new Cartel des Gauches, but vitally different from the Cartels of 1924 and 1932, in that it now for the first time included the Communists. Moreover, the strength of the Communists' appeal to the electorate in May 1936 had been much reinforced by momentous developments abroad. Before we consider the programme of the Front Populaire and the reasons for its electoral triumph we must glance at the evolution of French policy and the growth of international tension since the 6th February, 1934.

Louis Barthou, Foreign Minister in the Doumergue Cabinet, an energetic and cultivated man of the older Republican school, lost no time in attempting to strengthen France's weakening security by reinforcing her eastern alliance system and by seeking to negotiate a sort of Eastern Locarno which would give the Versailles frontiers in Eastern Europe, including Germany's eastern frontier, the same sort of guarantees as those devised for Germany's western frontier in 1925. He visited Warsaw, Prague, Bucharest and Belgrade, and, in order to compensate for Poland's new leanings towards Germany and to extend the area of eastern security, brought Russia into the negotiations and obtained her admission into the League of Nations a year after Germany had left it.

As part of the general plan France was ready to guarantee Russia's western frontier in exchange for a Russian guarantee of the Franco-German frontier. But Germany's reply to Barthou's invitation to take part in the negotiations was a virtual refusal, and Poland's was so hedged about with conditions and counter-suggestions that the general scheme came to nothing. None the less, it had had the most important results. Russia's emergence from her long isolation and her consent to join the League showed that Stalin, too, was seriously disturbed by Hitler's advent to power in Germany. It held out a prospect of immense importance for French security and foreshadowed a renewal of the classic Franco-Russian Alliance of 1894–1918, for, although the general Eastern Locarno came to nothing, two of the powers concerned in the negotiations with France, Russia and Czechoslovakia, had been favourable to Barthou's proposals and were ready to do their part. The momentous result was the signature, in May 1935, of the Franco-Russian Pact of mutual assistance, and of a similar Russo-Czech Pact dependent for its operation upon French intervention should aggression occur.

But by then, owing to the inadequacy of French police precautions, Barthou was no longer alive to make the most of this new orientation. In October 1934, in the very course of strengthening French bonds with Yugoslavia and welcoming her sovereign to French soil, he was assassinated at Marseilles and the King fell with him. At a critical moment in European history Yugoslavia lost a strong king and had to substitute a weak Regency; and in the same hour France lost a vigorous French Foreign Minister, one who had never played such a commanding role as Briand, Poincaré or Millerand, but who was the last notable figure of the generation which made its political début before 1900. His successor was a very different person. Doumergue now entrusted the direction of foreign policy to a dark Auvergnat named Pierre Laval, a man of obscure origin who, like Briand, had begun his career as a Socialist agitator on the extreme Left but had gradually moved farther to the Right until he was now a moderate with Right-wing sympathies. It was he who signed the Franco-Russian Pact, visited Moscow immediately afterwards and obtained from Stalin a momentous declaration in praise of France's rearmament plan—for two months earlier, on March 16th, Hitler's reintroduction of compulsory military service in Germany had effectively put an end to any further serious projects of disarmament under the auspices of the League of Nations. Thus far Laval continued Barthou's policy, but he was also concerned to conjure the growing German menace by other means and showed no haste to ratify the Franco-Russian Pact. Above all he was anxious to improve relations with Italy.

Ever since Versailles Italy had shown her discontent with a peace settlement which had failed, she considered, to do justice to her legitimate
territorial aspirations.   She was thus what, in the parlance of the 'thirties,
was called a 'have-not' power, anxious for a revision of the peace treaties.
Moreover, since 1922 she had overthrown democratic government and
established Fascism.   In spite of the fact that in July 1934, when the
Nazis had attempted a Putsch in Vienna, Mussolini had massed troops
on the Brenner Pass, there was still a grave risk that sooner or later
ideological sympathies and a common desire for treaty revision would
force Germany and Italy into one another's arms.   Meanwhile Franco-
Italian relations had been distinctly strained in the 'twenties and there
was still room for their improvement.   Thus it was that already, in
January 1935, Laval had visited Rome and sought, like Delcassé and
Barrère forty years earlier, a settlement of outstanding questions and a
new entente.   The Rome agreements of that month brought the two
powers closer together than at any time since 1919, and for a while there
was much talk of a Latin Bloc, which, in French Catholic and Conservative circles at least, was regarded as a potential bulwark against Bolshevism as much as against Nazism.   The two powers undertook to co-
operate for the maintenance of Austrian independence—the Nazi Putsch,
if successful, would have meant the immediate annexation or Anschluss
of Austria to the German Reich—and of friendly relations with the
Danubian states for whose favour they had been hitherto competitors.
They agreed upon a new status for Italians in Tunisia and upon a small
rectification of the frontier between Libya and French Africa in Italy's
favour.   But this agreement was reached only at a price, and Laval's
willingness to pay it was to land him in a grave dilemma.   He agreed
that Italy should have a free hand in Abyssinia.   In other words, she
should be free to carve out for herself the colonial empire in East Africa
which she had failed to found under Crispi in the 'nineties.   The move
was in the best tradition of pre-war Bismarckian diplomacy.   Even as
Bismarck had sought to avert the danger of French *revanche* by encouraging France to go to Tunis and Egypt, so Laval sought to divert
'have-not' Italy from her grievances in Europe and to reduce the risks
of a German-Italian alliance by encouraging her to go to Abyssinia.
But 1935 was very different from 1878 or from 1904, the year of the
Anglo-French Entente which had given France herself a free hand in
Morocco.   Abyssinia, like Italy and France, was now a member of the
League of Nations in which France had played a dominant role and whose
Covenant she had sworn to observe.   If collective security throughout
the League of Nations was to mean anything at all, it meant that, if

Italy attacked Abyssinia and Abyssinia appealed to the League, France must go to Abyssinia's aid and enforce sanctions against the aggressor. If she refused to do so and clung to her new friendship with Italy, she would be turning her back on the whole of her post-war policy which had been directed to the achievement of collective security through the League as well as to the conclusion of alliances with Germany's neighbours; she would wreck the newly concluded Franco-Russian Pact, estrange Great Britain, perhaps irremediably, and find herself either in complete isolation or forced back upon a rapprochement with Nazi Germany, no comfortable bedfellow. There is little doubt that Laval hoped that he might not be faced with a direct choice: after all, in September 1931, the League had failed to impose sanctions against Japan when she seized Manchuria, and the preservation of the newly-formed Stresa front of Great Britain, France, and Italy in Europe might seem to be of much more importance in restraining Germany and keeping the peace of the world than an Italian 'colonial' escapade in Abyssinia. Unfortunately for him, however, the Italian attack on Abyssinia, when it came in September 1935, caused such strong public resentment in Great Britain that the British Government, whom France had so long vainly sought to convert to a strengthening of the League Covenant, now for the first time since the League came into being, took a 'strong' view of that Covenant. But Great Britain could not act effectively without France, and so there was still a chance for a *modus vivendi* which would save the face of Great Britain and the League without mortally offending Italy. But, unfortunately for Anglo-French relations, details of the Hoare-Laval negotiations to this end leaked into the French press, and their premature disclosure roused such a storm of protest in Great Britain that Sir Samuel Hoare, the British Foreign Secretary, was compelled to resign. Laval, by now Premier as well as Foreign Minister, was reluctantly forced to make the choice he sought to evade, and France joined Great Britain, albeit very halfheartedly, in applying economic sanctions to the power with whom she had so lately acted in concert.

The consequences of the Abyssinian affair were indeed serious for France and for Europe. The half-hearted application of sanctions did nothing to prevent the Italian conquest of Abyssinia but merely further discredited the League of Nations and proved the ineffectiveness of collective security. On the other hand, the fact that France applied sanctions at all alienated her from Italy and precipitated the Italian rapprochement with Germany which the Rome Agreements had been designed by the French to prevent. Worse still, the Hoare-Laval crisis, following close upon an Anglo-German naval agreement concluded without French approval, made many Frenchmen, particularly of the Right, see in Great Britain the enemy who had undermined France's position in Europe by forcing her to choose between Italy and the League.   There was a wave of Anglophobia among the Nationalists of the Right, which was so violent as almost to recall the passions of the Boer War, while on the other side of the Channel Englishmen were aggrieved that the unco-operative attitude of France had allowed Italy to snap her fingers at the cherished League. In the winter of 1935-6 Anglo-French relations were more strained than at any time since Poincaré's occupation of the Ruhr, if not since the foundation of the Entente Cordiale in 1904.   The consequences of this tension were soon to be seen in that part of Europe which most nearly affected France's vital security.   On March 7th, 1936, using as a pretext the French Chamber's vote in January in favour of the ratification of the Franco-Russian Pact, Germany, without any previous notice, proceeded to the military reoccupation of the Rhineland.   This action was an un-doubted breach of the Locarno Agreements of 1925, but it could be questioned whether it was a flagrant breach requiring immediate British aid to France and Belgium.   It was a test case of Hitler's ability to break international agreements with impunity, and the time and the ground were well chosen.   Not only were Anglo-French relations strained, but British public opinion, which had never understood the French anxiety about the Rhineland, and which was unfamiliar with the texts of the Locarno agreements, as of most treaties, tended to regard Germany's action as no more than an assertion of reasonable rights over part of her own territory and was by no means disposed to take a firm line.   In these circumstances, and faced by the hesitations of their own Foreign Minister and General Staff, the French Government—an ephemeral Cabinet headed by the Radical, Albert Sarraut—also hesitated, and finally contented themselves with a protest.   Thereby they missed their greatest opportunity of checking the victorious tide of National Socialism before it overflowed the German borders.   All the evidence subsequently disclosed goes to suggest that Hitler's army was still too weak to resist a French advance in force, and that, had a Poincaré been in power, France might have administered a rebuff such as would seriously have weakened the Nazi movement.   Instead the prestige of the Nazi régime was enhanced and the Germans were able to entrench themselves in the Rhineland, build the great defensive Siegfried Line and prepare fresh attacks upon existing treaties.   Otherwise, the main consequence of their breach of Locarno was to bring the two main western signatories to-gether again.   Although Great Britain was not ready to act in March

1936 the British Government promptly reaffirmed their recognition of the validity of the Locarno Agreements, and, in return for a reciprocal assurance from France, offered to initiate staff talks in order to consider ways of concerting military action should unprovoked aggression compel either power to fulfil its obligations. France readily responded and in December 1936, the French Foreign Minister told the Chamber that all French forces would at once go to the aid of Great Britain were she the victim of an unprovoked attack. Henceforward, in view of the growing power of Germany and the estrangement of Italy, France had no alternative but to follow the lead of Great Britain in her attempts to preserve European peace. It was the easier for her to do so since she now once again had a Government of the Left.

There were many reasons, old and new, which explained this new success of the Left at the polls. Once again the mystical charm of carrying on the movement of the Great Revolution by casting a vote on the Left had exercised its traditional attraction. Once again, as in 1889 or 1902, the men of the Left had successfully posed as the defenders of Republican liberties, not this time against Royalism or clericalism but against the menace of growing Fascist tendencies among elements of the Right with their semi-military Leagues such as the Croix de Feu and the more sinister Hooded Men, or Cagoulards, and their avowed sympathies for Fascist Italy at the time of the Abyssinian crisis. Anti-Fascism took the place of anti-clericalism as the cementing force in the new Bloc. But more important still were the widespread economic discontent and the hopes of remedying it held out by the economic and social programme of the Popular Front. Since 1931 France's economic situation had been steadily deteriorating under the impact of the world slump. Whereas in most other countries the bottom of the depression had been reached by 1933, in France the bulk and value of foreign trade, whose recovery was hampered by price disparities, continued to fall in spite of some measure of success eventually achieved in lowering production costs by a deflationary policy. The luxury trades were hard hit, the tourist traffic fell off sharply because France's adherence to the gold standard made her one of the dearest countries in Europe, the tonnage of her mercantile marine and the value of her income from freights declined, and by the beginning of 1936 there were 500,000 unemployed in receipt of relief and many others out of work. All this had coincided with a sharp fall in agricultural prices in 1932 and a prolonged period of unrest amongst the agricultural community. The threat of devaluation had encouraged speculation and involved a loss of gold from the Bank of France, and the subsequent insistence on

a deflationary policy with its accompanying economies, cuts in staff
and reduction of salaries, had been extremely unpopular with many of
the workers and also with many *petits bourgeois* and others dependent
on fixed incomes. Accordingly, many of the votes cast for the Front
Populaire had been votes for the abandonment of deflation and for
increases in wages. Finally, the victory of the Front marked an up-
surging of all the forces which had so long and so vainly called for
social reform. The brief movement of idealism and aspiration towards
social collaboration, by which the relations of employers and employed
and Government and unions had been characterized on the morrow of
the armistice, had quickly been dissipated, and they had swung back to
their pre-war condition of tension and distrust. Individual employers,
in a spirit of benevolent paternalism, might treat their workers admirably,
providing them with garden cities, dispensaries, family allowances, and
insurance schemes, but the majority looked on the eight-hour day with
disapproval and were reluctant to adjust the wages of their men to meet
the rises in living costs. Attempts to force an improvement in conditions by widespread strikes in 1919 and 1920 had failed and the following fifteen years had been on the whole a period of 'social stability and
working-class apathy'.[1] The Cartel Governments of 1924 and 1932,
submerged by other problems, had not added any important measure
of social reform to the statute book; and a bill in favour of compulsory
holidays with pay for workers in industry and commerce, which was
voted by the Chamber in 1931 and might have had an important psychological effect had it immediately become law, had been turned down by
the Senate. Since 1919 almost the only important pieces of social legislation were comprised in two laws of 1928 and 1930 providing for a system
of compulsory insurance and in a further law of 1932 instituting a general
system of family allowances. Thus the Front Populaire, with its slogan of
'Bread, Peace and Liberty' and its programme for the nationalization of
key industries and improvement of working-class conditions, seemed
to offer to a vast number of Frenchmen, to many of the bourgeoisie and
peasants as well as the workers, the one solution of their material difficulties, the one hope of relief from hardship, discontent and years of struggle.
For this reason alone its victory was of considerable significance.[2]

[1] LAROQUE, PIERRE: *Les rapports entre patrons et ouvriers*, p. 303. GOGUEL,
F.: *La politique des partis sous la III* République*, I, p. 354.

[2] It is to be noted that the Right still remained a considerable force. 'The
decrease in their voting strength was only 124,409 votes from 1928 to 1932, and
178,419 from 1932 to 1936,' when they still polled about 43 per cent of the total
votes. cp. MICAUD, CHARLES A.: *The French Right and Nazi Germany*, p. 12 n.

The new coalition was in many ways similar to the Cartels of 1924 and 1932, but there was an important difference in the balance of forces within it. For the first time it was the Socialists and not the Radicals who were the largest single party; while further still to the Left, Communist representation had increased from ten to seventy-two. This striking Communist success was not due merely to social discontent. The Franco-Russian Pact and Stalin's declaration approving the French decision to rearm had been of real importance, both because they gave the Communist party in France a new respectability and because they led it to one of those abrupt reversals of policy which were such conspicuous features of the history of Communist groups all over the world. The French Communists, hitherto anti-democratic, contemptuous of the Republic and violent opponents of rearmament, now came forward as champions of democracy and Republican liberty, claimed to be legitimate heirs of the French Revolution, sang the 'Marseillaise' and were among the foremost to urge the acceleration of national defence; while in their hatred of the extremists of the Right they even declared themselves ready to co-operate with Catholics in order to combat the menace of Fascism. This volte-face certainly did much to account for their success at the polls. Furthermore, their success emphasized the growing tendency for France, like Germany earlier in the 'thirties, to be torn between two extremes which were international in their connexions; while the preponderance of the Socialists clearly indicated that the long ascendancy of the Radicals was drawing to an end. As the largest single party, after the elections of 1924 and 1932, had been the Radicals, it was they who had formed the Government: but now the rise of massive groups to their Left forced them more obviously into the position of being the Conservatives that they really were; and the Socialist predominance meant that the first Front Populaire Government was to be headed not by the Radical Herriot, but by the Socialist Léon Blum. Nevertheless the Radicals were still a very important element in the coalition; the new Government was not exclusively Socialist, but a Socialist-Radical combination. The Communists gave it their support but declined to take part in the Cabinet. The application of Socialist legislation would therefore only be possible in so far as it was tolerable to the Radical Ministers.

In a speech to the Socialist Congress immediately after the elections Léon Blum described the Front Populaire as 'not merely a combination of parties, but a powerful mass movement'.[1] And such indeed it

[1] cit. PICKLES, DOROTHY M.: *The French Political Scene*, p. 134; for text of the Front Populaire programme see THOMSON, D., *Democracy in France*, pp. 252 ff.

appeared to be when, without waiting for the formation of the new
Government or for instructions from their Unions, the workers in the
aeronautical industries, the nationalization of which had been demanded
in the electoral programme of the Front Populaire, downed tools; and
when their example was followed in a host of other industries, especially
in the region of Paris.   There was a great wave of spontaneous stay-in
strikes by workers who were flushed with electoral victory and thought
that they were masters at last.   'The people' as in 1848 and 1871, believing themselves in control got out of control; and although the strikes
were singularly free of violence either towards individuals or towards
machinery, the forces of order, the bourgeoisie, as in 1848 and 1871,
took instant alarm.   And this time their alarm was all the greater and
more comprehensible because they now saw France threatened with
social disorder and anarchy at the very moment when the international
situation was growing more menacing.   Just as the workers saw the
hand of the foreigner behind the Fascist formations of the Right, so the
bourgeoisie saw the hand of the foreigner behind the strikes which inter-
rupted the rearmament programme. Discounting the Communists'
new-founded patriotism, they suspected the influence of Russia and the
deliberate fomenting of social revolution. Thus the advent of the
Front Populaire, instead of inaugurating a new period in which long-
needed social reforms would bridge the gulf between classes in France
and by reinforcing political with social democracy, create a new unity
among the French people, only increased their divisions, confirmed the
fears and suspicions of Right and Left and accelerated the drift towards
extremes.   Significantly enough it was in the very month in which the
first Blum Government took office, in June 1936, that a new anti-Com-
munist group, the Parti Populaire Français was founded by an ex-
Communist deputy named Jacques Doriot.   Within a year it claimed to
have 200,000 members.   Significantly enough, too, the fact that the
new Prime Minister was a Jew gave a new impetus to the growing
anti-semitism of the Right.   Anti-semitism, so rampant at the time of
the Dreyfus Affair, had greatly decreased by the time of the Great War,
and in the 'twenties it had been confined mainly to the comparatively
small circles influenced by such papers as the *Action Française* and the more
scurrilous *Gringoire*.   But since 1933 it had grown considerably as a result
of the influx of several thousand German and Austrian Jewish refugees.
Now that Blum was Prime Minister there were many on the Right
who talked, in language strangely like that of the German National
Socialists, of the menace to French society from Jewish Bolshevism.

For many of its most naïve and enthusiastic supporters the advent of the Front Populaire had seemed to herald the millennium. But little more than a year after it took office the Blum Government fell and gave place to a Ministry in which a much more cautious Radical policy prevailed. In fact, the Front Populaire went the way of the Cartels before it. It, too, came to grief on finance. Its social policy was costly; the outbreak of further strikes meant the continuance of the fall in exports; taxation did not produce a return sufficient to balance the budget; and, in spite of the Government's emphasis on peace, the grave international situation compelled it to shoulder the financial burden of a growing armament programme. This did not in any way mean that it had achieved nothing. It had not attempted to reform the Constitution of 1875—that was not one of its aims—nor had it radically altered the social and economic structure of the country, for, as Blum explained, its aim had been 'to administer the bourgeois State', 'to put into effect the Popular Front programme, not to transform the social system'.[1] Nevertheless it had gone a certain way towards this end by giving the Bank of France a more democratic constitution in which the State had more effective control, and providing for the progressive nationalization of the armament industries. Furthermore, through the so-called Matignon agreements, concluded by the C.G.T. and representatives of industrial employers under Government auspices on the morrow of the formation of the Blum Cabinet, and by subsequent legislation in 1936 it had greatly improved working-class conditions. Wages were raised by an average of twelve per cent; every worker was to have a fortnight's holiday with pay each year and an Under-Secretary was appointed especially to provide amenities for his leisure hours; conditions of work were to be regulated for each industry and each economic region by collective contracts between representatives of employers and employed; workers' delegates were to be elected in all factories employing more than ten people; the normal working week was reduced to forty hours; labour disputes were to be submitted to conciliation and compulsory arbitration without prejudice to the right to strike, a procedure which was subsequently to be given juridical form in 1938. All these measures represented great gains from the workers' point of view; but their application inevitably took time, and the adjustment of industry to the new conditions involved much bitterness and friction which showed itself in the continuation of strikes throughout 1936 and 1937. Much more immediately effective in producing appeasement was the Government's success in adjusting the level of agricultural prices; and in particular the stabilization of wheat prices through a newly created National

[1] cit. PICKLES, DOROTHY M.: *The French Political Scene*, p. 130.

Wheat Board. But the general economic results of the Government's legislation were disappointing: unemployment was only slightly reduced; production did not increase, and would probably have shown a decline but for the rearmament programme and the temporary stimulus provided by the devaluation of the franc in September 1936. By March 1937, after the initial measures had been carried through and under the menace of growing financial difficulties, the parties in the Popular Front could no longer agree upon further reforms and M. Blum was obliged to call a halt. Once again, as in 1926 and 1932, there was a conflict between those Socialists who wished to continue a thorough-going policy of structural change and to repair the financial chaos by drastic measures and the Radicals who favoured more limited and orthodox remedies. The substitution in June 1937 of a Government headed by M. Chautemps for that of M. Blum meant that the Radicals had won: and although Radical-Socialist co-operation continued uneasily for some months to come there was little further reform of great significance. Once again Governments were preoccupied by growing financial difficulties and, still more important, by the progressive deterioration of the international situation; and when in 1938 the second Blum Cabinet was replaced by a new Union Nationale Ministry it was clear that the Front Populaire had finally broken down. More than ever France required national unity under a strong leader. But she now had no Poincaré or Clemenceau, nor even a Doumergue: but only a mediocrè Radical named Daladier.

In many ways France had been behind other countries in social legislation and the conditions in which she allowed her people to live and work. Reforms were long overdue and the Front Populaire had done much to remove the grounds for reproaching France with social backwardness. The bitter irony of the situation was, however, that, as we have seen, the Front Populaire came to power in circumstances which intensified instead of lessening the hostilities among Frenchmen and that its reforms, which inevitably tended to reduce production, came at the very moment when increased output was vital. In consequence, the last Governments of the Third Republic were more than ever paralysed and unable to respond with decision to the series of crises provoked by German initiative; and each crisis served only to emphasize the division and confusion of French opinion.

This the first Blum Government had discovered very soon after its accession to power. In July 1936 an insurrection of the Spanish Right against the Republican Government in Spain, which in its composition closely resembled the French Front Populaire, roused passionate partisan feeling in France. Spanish affairs, as we have seen,[1] had often in the past led to French intervention, and now the militants and Left wing of the Front Populaire put strong pressure on Blum to go to the aid of the Frente Popular. Not only did they urge this in the interests of Republican and Socialist solidarity but also of French security, for it was soon clear that the rebels in Spain were being aided by Germany and Italy, who in November proclaimed their alliance in the so-called Rome-Berlin Axis. But the Right and the Catholics in France were equally strongly in favour of General Franco, the rebel leader, while the British Government were far from enthusiastic about supporting the Spanish Government. With a divided nation behind him, a lukewarm Britain on his flank, and a hostile Germany and Italy in his rear, Blum had to content himself with non-intervention and a joint Anglo-French patrol of the Mediterranean, where submarines of unknown nationality became a menace to neutral and Spanish Republican shipping. When the protracted civil war ended it was the Axis protégé who emerged victorious. In 1939, as in 1870, Germany had skilfully arranged that her intended victim should seem to be menaced on the Pyrenees as well as on the Rhine. Meanwhile, however, the Communists and Left wing of the Front Populaire long continued to hope for a reversal of the non-intervention policy; and their agitation on behalf of the Spanish Republicans, and the fact that many of them served as volunteers with the Republican forces, made it all the easier for the Right in France to denounce the Front Populaire as the party that wished to land the country in war. Here, indeed, we must note a strange reversal of roles. From the days of Boulanger, it will be remembered, it had been the Right who had supplanted the Left as the militant patriots and Nationalists; it was they who had been most eager for *revanche*, most jealous in upholding French prestige abroad, most strongly in favour of a hard peace and most critical of any relaxation of the stipulations of the Treaty of Versailles. But with the Abyssinian crisis of 1935, eager to avoid war with Italy at all costs, they reverted to the attitude which had characterized them during the first seventy years of our period and once again became the party of peace. This attitude was perfectly intelligible: the last thing the French people as a whole desired was to be involved in another great war such as that of 1914-18; collective security had broken down; the eastern system of alliances had been weakened; Russia was remote, suspect to the Right on ideological grounds and militarily a doubtful quantity; Great Britain, which had not even enforced conscription, could not be expected to give France much help

[1] See *ante*, pp. 30–31, 57, 65.

of immediate value on land; and France was sadly conscious of her numerical inferiority and the backwardness of her rearmament programme compared with that of Germany. If, in addition, she was deeply divided on social and other questions and war and defeat were likely, as in so many countries in 1918, to bring social revolution in their train, what wonder that the Right should regard the preservation of peace as the highest French interest? Unfortunately their obsession with the Communist menace was to lead them beyond this view to the view that peace and an accommodation with Germany were desirable at any price.[1] Their sense of values became distorted and they failed to see that a peace bought at the cost of submitting to intimidation and dishonouring pledges could lead only to servitude and be no true peace at all.

This inability of divided France to take a lead and react vigorously to the attacks on the European order established at Versailles now made by the revisionist powers was still more evident in 1938. The international situation progressively deteriorated. In November 1937, the Axis was extended from Rome and Berlin to Tokio, and, by veiling their territorial ambitions with the cloud of the Anti-Komintern Pact, Germany, Italy and Japan cast fresh dust in the eyes of Conservatives, many of whom were led to believe that these three states were indeed the bulwark of European civilization against a real Communist menace. A few months later, after Mr. Eden's resignation from the Chamberlain Cabinet had shown that the forces which favoured appeasement of the Axis Powers were still in the ascendant in Great Britain, the Germans marched into Austria and imposed Anschluss by annexation. The forcible overthrow of the Versailles territorial settlement had begun and France and Great Britain could do no more than protest. It was not long before the next victim was singled out for attack. In the summer Germany began her war of nerves against Czechoslovakia, unleashing the Sudeten Germans of Bohemia to claim incorporation with the Reich. Here was yet one more critical test for France. If Czechoslovakia yielded it would mean the disintegration of the Czechoslovak state, menaced at the same time by Polish and Hungarian claims on the northern and southern borders: and with Czechoslovakia the whole alliance system built by France with such care, but already gravely weak-

---

[1] Ever since 1871 there had always been Frenchmen—Gambetta, Ferry, Rouvier and Caillaux are notable examples—who had asked themselves whether it was not fatal for both countries that France and Germany should for ever remain irreconcilable foes and who at one time or another believed that reconciliation was possible. But hitherto such men had been mostly of the Left.

ened in spite of the Blum Government's attempts to strengthen it, would be in danger of falling to the ground. If, on the other hand, Czechoslovakia refused to yield and was attacked by Germany, France was bound by treaty to go to her aid. The war she was so anxious to avoid would be inevitable. In this crisis there were many on the Right in France who sought to argue that the French undertaking to Czechoslovakia was no longer binding since the Locarno system had broken down.[1] Paralysed by the divisions of French opinion, incapable of giving a firm lead, the weak Government of Daladier neglected Russia and left the initiative to Great Britain, who had no obligations to Czechoslovakia, to try and find a compromise solution which would appease Hitler, preserve the Czechoslovak state and save Europe from war. After an acute crisis in September 1938 the compromise was discovered at Munich where Chamberlain and Daladier, ignoring Russia's interests in Eastern Europe, met Hitler and Mussolini and sacrificed Czechoslovakia on the altar of a highly precarious peace. The Czechoslovak state was maintained, but shorn of territory in such a way that it became strategically defenceless. The Franco-Russian Pact had failed to operate and the eastern alliance system had broken down. Peace had been preserved, but France's prestige had immeasurably declined and her relative position in Europe had been weakened still further. If there were any in France, as well as in England, who were naïve enough to believe that Munich meant peace in their time they were speedily disillusioned. On March 15th, 1939, Hitler overthrew the Munich settlement and marched into Prague. No one in either country could any longer believe in the effectiveness of a policy of appeasement. It was clear to the dullest that Germany now aimed at nothing less than the domination of the Continent. Great Britain at once reacted vigorously, giving a guarantee to Poland and undertakings to assist Rumania and Greece, should their independence be threatened. Once again the French Government followed the British lead. They reaffirmed the Franco-Polish alliance, they gave similar undertakings to Rumania and Greece and signed a pact of mutual assistance with Turkey. But the British and French attempts to bring Russia into their new combined front against aggression were doomed to failure. On August 23rd, 1939, while their representatives were still in Moscow attempting to negotiate a military agreement, they and the whole world were confounded by the news that Ribbentrop, the Nazi Foreign Minister, had also been there and had signed a pact of non-aggression and friendship

[1] e.g. The article entitled 'Conscience angoissée' in *Le Temps* of April 12th, 1938, by Joseph Barthélemy.

with Stalin. The Western Powers had bought time independently of Russia at Munich: now Russia paid for the same commodity independently of them at Moscow. The way was free for the next German offensive which followed at once in a series of demands upon Poland. This time there was to be no second Munich. All attempts at conciliation broke down. Germany invaded Poland on September 1st, and on September 3rd, 1939, Great Britain and France declared war on Germany. But it was significant of the change in the positions of the two countries since 1914 that the British declaration preceded that of France by six hours.

Thus all the efforts of France since 1918 to build up such a system of security as would make a renewal of German aggression for ever impossible had come to naught. Once again, as in 1914, because of the aggression of a Germanic power in Eastern Europe she was at war with her traditional foe, and once again Great Britain was her chief ally in the west. But in the east instead of Russia she had only Poland as an ally,[1] and Poland was overrun and crushed in two months. Whereas, from 1914 to 1917 at least, Germany had been weakened by the necessity of fighting on two fronts, she was now very quickly at liberty to throw the whole weight of her forces against the west. Unless the Allies could upset her plans she would be free to choose her own moment and exert her utmost strength to force an immediate decision. The danger which threatened France after the outbreak of war in 1939 was still more terrible than that of August and September 1914. In the face of that earlier peril she had sunk her internal differences and achieved the impressive moral and political unity of *union sacrée*; then she had had the leadership of a Poincaré, a Viviani and a Joffre, and had worked the 'miracle' of the Marne. Now, however, she was still morally and politically divided and had only a Lebrun, a Daladier and a Gamelin, no miracle workers, but men of stature much too small for so great an emergency. The story of 1939-40 was to be tragically different from that of 1914.

Initially all seemed to go well. The army was mobilized without a hitch, and there was an appearance of political unity when the emergency war credits were voted by all parties including the Communists and when the Communist deputies went off to join their regiments. But the Russo-German Pact and the consequent Russian invasion of Eastern Poland on the one hand, and the absence of any serious hostilities in the west

---

[1] It is noteworthy that Poland never received from France a tithe of the military aid which France received from Russia in 1914, nor even a tithe of what she 'had been led to expect or at least to hope for.' B. H. SUMNER review of NAMIER, L.B.: *Diplomatic Prelude* in *International Affairs*, July 1948.

on the other, soon had a disintegrating effect. It is arguable that a real revival of French unity could have been achieved only under the stimulus of a violent German attack on the western front immediately after the declaration of war. Then, so long as the defence held, it is probable that the desire to defend the sacred soil of France would have outweighed every other consideration. But no such attack came, even after Poland had been crushed; there was not even any aerial bombardment and the French general staff had made a serious psychological error in not attempting to create a diversion while Poland was still resisting. To the Polish débâcle there succeeded the long winter months of the 'phoney' war. Such a period of expectancy would in any case have been sorely trying to the morale of a nation so impetuous as the French. In the conditions of 1939–40 it was most damaging. The Russo–German Pact and Russian invasion of Poland had led to the dissolution of the French Communist Party and to the eventual unseating and trial of a large number of Communist deputies and Senators. These were high-handed measures, but they were justified on the grounds that the Communists were the agents of a foreign power which was in league with France's enemy. None the less, Communist propaganda continued and it was now directed to attacks on the Government as 'Fascist' and on the war as an 'Imperialist' war with which the French soldier should have nothing to do. Thus during the tedious months of inaction there were, as in 1917, insidious attempts by the extreme Left to undermine the morale of the troops and the workers. At the same time, and still more disquieting because of its political influence, there grew up a peace party headed by men of the Right such as Laval who asked what point there was in beginning a war in the west, now that the war in the east was over, and suggested that peace, if necessary at the price of some concessions, a new Munich, would be preferable to defeat and the loss of many lives.[1] Thus the German subtlety in abstaining from war in the west for so many months reaped rich dividends in France. Moreover, Russia's attack on Finland at the end of November and Finland's heroic resistance still further confused the issue. For many, both in England and France, not content with being at war with Germany, were eager to go crusading against Russia, and, had Finland been more easy of access, it is probable that an Anglo-French expeditionary force would have been sent to her aid. Incidentally this diversion and the failure of the Allies to take the initiative in the west led to increasing

[1] It may be noted here that there had been a striking growth of intellectual pessimism in the 'thirties and that writers such as Sartre and Anouilh had already begun to expound their doctrines of futility.

criticism of Daladier in France and of Chamberlain in England. On
March 20th Daladier resigned, and in May, after the collapse of
the Allies' attempt to save Norway, Chamberlain made way for
Churchill.

In France the peace party had worked against Daladier and hoped
to supplant him, but the President of the Republic called upon Paul
Reynaud to form a Ministry. That choice meant that war would be
waged with greater determination, although it was disquietingly significant that in its first meeting with the Chamber the new Cabinet only
obtained an effective majority of one. It also meant that the alliance
with Great Britain would become still closer. Already on December
12th, 1939, an agreement between the French and British treasuries had
provided for a striking measure of financial co-operation. The two
Governments had also agreed in principle that both their armies should
be under a single commander, the French Generalissimo, General Gamelin. Now on the morrow of the formation of the Reynaud Cabinet
they united in a solemn declaration not to negotiate or conclude an
armistice or treaty of peace except by mutual agreement, and undertook
to maintain community of action in all spheres for as long as might be
necessary after the conclusion of peace. Hitler's hopes of shattering the
unity of the Allies without a blow were vain when Churchill and Reynaud were in power. He could not afford to wait indefinitely and on
May 10th launched the great land offensive in the west for which the
world had so long been waiting.

In many ways, in spite of the moral and political disunity by which
she was weakened, France had learnt the lessons of the last war and
was therefore more quickly prepared for the emergency of 1939–40.
The material welfare of the troops was better provided for; there was
less dislocation because the distribution of manpower was better adjusted between the needs of the army and of the war industries; and
power to legislate by decree, once again granted by a Chamber which
had agreed to prolong its own life by two years as early as March 21st,
1939, gave the Government greater freedom of action. But there was
one field in which she had learnt nothing or learnt wrong and in which
she proved incapable of learning even from the Polish campaign of 1939.
It was France's crowning disaster that her generals as well as her politicians were inferior to their task. They had prepared for another war
of trenches; they had become obsessed by the defensive mentality of
the Maginot Line and ignored the fact that it was the offensive war of
movement, the tanks and armoured cars, which had won the final victory
even in 1918. They had devoted enormous sums to the construction

of the Maginot Line, but yet had not carried it along the Belgian frontier to the sea;[1] they had been blind to the fact that it was on armoured divisions and aeroplanes that the Russians and Germans were spending their credits, and deaf to the warnings of men like Paul Reynaud and De Gaulle who had urged that the victory in modern war would go to the most highly mechanized army. Thus they had failed in their first duty of being imaginative and keeping abreast with the technical developments of modern war. When to this were added grave errors of judgement in meeting the German attack the results were fatal.

On May 10th the Germans launched their offensive through Holland and Belgium. It looked like a repetition of 1914. Then Joffre had concentrated his forces too far south and had not been prepared for the vast German enveloping movement in the north-east: now the French High Command hurried troops to parry the enveloping movement and were caught off their guard at the pivotal point where the Maginot Line came to an end. It was here, near Sedan, so full of memories of an earlier débâcle, that the Germans broke through in force with seven Panzer divisions: and, once they had broken through, their crushing superiority in armour and aeroplanes and their greater mobility were decisive. They had almost unlimited freedom of movement. The Dutch had already given in on May 15th and the Belgians were to capitulate a fortnight later, on the 28th. Meanwhile the French High Command had made a fatal mistake in not ordering the immediate withdrawal from Belgium of the French and British armies of the north as soon as it had intelligence of the German break-through at Sedan and on the Meuse. This meant that forty British and French divisions were caught by a vast encircling movement and that when their attempts to break through the German ring were unavailing they had no choice but to evacuate by sea from Dunkirk in order to escape annihilation. The 'miracle of the Marne' in 1914 had been a victory. Dunkirk, too, was a 'miracle', but it was still part of a great defeat. Already on the morrow of the Norwegian catastrophe Reynaud had broadened his Cabinet by including two new Ministers of the Right. Now he replaced the Commander-in-Chief, Gamelin, by Weygand, Foch's Chief of Staff in the last war, who had recently distinguished himself in pacifying Syria, and brought Pétain into his Cabinet as Vice-President. But it

---

[1] One of the reasons alleged was fear of offending the Belgian Government. But as M. Pierre Maillaud has pointed out: 'As Belgium never agreed to co-ordinate her own strategy with that of the French, save at the last minute, it is difficult to see how the Belgian Government could have taken exception to elementary measures of self-defence, *France*, p. 105.

was too late and these were old men, tired and disillusioned, Weygand seventy-three and Pétain eighty-four. It was a thousand fresh planes and tanks and a supply of young generals with a fresh outlook that France required, and the tanks and planes did not exist. Already by the end of May Weygand had made up his mind that the defeat was irretrievable and that there was no choice but to give in. By the end of the Dunkirk evacuation France had lost two-fifths of her effectives and eight-tenths of her material.[1] The British losses in material were almost as heavy.

The defeat of the French forces was a military defeat, the victory of the power which had an overwhelming superiority in men and materials and knew how to use them with ruthless efficiency. The demoralization caused in the French army by the 'phoney war' and by the insidious propaganda of Communist and fifth columnists weighed little against the gallantry once again displayed by the ordinary French soldier in Norway, Belgium and France. But such gallantry was powerless against such odds and the battle was lost often before it could be said to have been joined. A heavy weight of responsibility lies indeed upon the French General Staff of the late 'twenties and 'thirties.

France had suffered great military disasters before, but she had not given in. In 1870 she had witnessed Sedan and Metz but had gone on waging war to the knife, even after the capitulation of her main regular armies. Again, in 1914, she had survived the Battle of the Frontiers and in 1918 the Chemin des Dames, and wrested victory from defeat. But in 1940 she would no longer be true to herself. It was now, after the military defeat, that the demoralizing forces which we have seen at work during the 'phoney war' were to exert their influence to the country's dishonour and the ruin of the Third Republic. It was now that France needed a Gambetta or a Clemenceau and failed to find one. It was during the critical twelve days after Dunkirk that the fateful battle was fought on the home front between the men who were eager to continue the fight and those who thought only of abandonment, of obtaining power for themselves and of overthrowing the régime. On June 5th Paul Reynaud once again remodelled his Cabinet and thereby showed his poor judgement of men. For, apart from De Gaulle whom he made Under-Secretary for War, the other new Ministers were all weak men who would soon show their readiness to desert the sinking ship of state. Furthermore, like Boulanger, Reynaud was at certain moments of crisis to be fatally influenced by his mistress, who was never far away during these last days of his Premiership.

[1] KAMMERER, A.: *La vérité sur l'Armistice*, p. 61.

For the time being, however, he remained indomitable. In a tele-gram to President Roosevelt on the 10th June he declared that the Government would withdraw to one of the French provinces—he had for some time had this idea of creating a redoubt in Brittany—and that if they were driven from the national territory they would continue the struggle in North Africa or, if need be, in one of France's American possessions. On that same day the Government left Paris, which was hourly threatened by the advancing Germans, and set out like the Gov-ernment of August 1914 for Bordeaux. On that day, too, France's plight was made even worse by the decision of the 'jackal dictator', Mussolini, to stab her in the back. Italy came in on the side of her Axis partner and declared war on France and Great Britain. Two days later, in a dramatic council of war at Cangey near Tours, Weygand declared that further resistance was impossible. Pétain agreed, but the majority of the other Ministers still refused to share his view that France should ask for an armistice. In the next three days, however, the argu-ments of Weygand and Pétain gained ground. A Clemenceau would at once have replaced the defeatist generals and silenced the defeatist Ministers or excluded them from his Cabinet, but Reynaud, in spite of the advice of men like Campinchi and Louis Marin, hesitated to do so. The hesitation was fatal. By the 16th the Germans had entered Paris and the Government had reached Bordeaux; Reynaud had failed to persuade Weygand that the proper course of action was to follow the Dutch example, allowing the army to cease fire in France without any formal capitulation while the Government and what men and material could be saved continued the struggle from North Africa; he had failed to make good use of the support of the Presidents of the Chamber and Senate; he had failed to dismiss Weygand and remodel his Cabinet; and the result was that the peace party within it now gained the upper hand. The dramatic British offer of a Franco-British Union was turned down. Reynaud had allowed his authority to be gradually undermined and that evening he resigned. The appointment of the vain and aged fatalist, Marshal Pétain, as his successor, made an armistice inevitable and spelt the doom of the Third Republic. It meant the triumph of Laval and of the party who hated Great Britain, who were convinced that she, in turn, would speedily succumb, and were eager to make terms with Germany, reverse the old alliance system, erect an authori-tarian régime and earn for France a comfortable place in the new European order. It also meant the breach of the Solemn Declaration of March 28th, for France was bound to go on fighting unless she was formally relieved from her engagements by Great Britain; and the British

Government, although on the 16th they had reluctantly agreed that France should inquire about armistice terms, had made it a *sine qua non* of their agreement that the French fleet should be sent for safe keeping to British ports while any armistice negotiations were in progress. Of this cate-goric condition the Pétain Government took no account. Furthermore, they refused to preserve their own freedom by moving the Government to North Africa, in spite of the representations of the Presidents of the Senate and Chamber and of the President of the Republic himself. Pétain, urged on by Laval, clung fatalistically to the notion that it was honourable for him and the Government to share the lot of their com-patriots in metropolitan France and that France's interests could not be defended if she were abandoned. The brave men like Mandel, Minister of the Interior in the Reynaud Government, and various deputies and others, who, notwithstanding, set out for Morocco and attempted to raise the standard of resistance there, were arrested and in consequence some of them eventually met their death.

And so it was that on June 22nd, 1940, the representatives of the Pétain Government signed the most humiliating armistice in French history. France was to be cut in two; the northern and western half, including Paris and all the Atlantic coast line, being occupied by the Germans, and only the southern departments being left in nominal independence to the Pétain Government which established its head-quarters at Vichy; the fleet was to be demobilized and disarmed; and one million four hundred thousand men were to remain prisoners in German hands.[1] Two days later an armistice followed with Italy. In their brief campaign in the Alps French troops had more than held their own, and only a small area of French territory was to be occupied by Italian troops under the armistice terms. Germany had won the victory; it was only natural that she should seize the lion's share of the spoils.

The Third Republic did not long survive these humiliations. On the 1st July the Senate and Chamber met together at Vichy as a National Assembly and by 569 votes to 80 passed a new Constitutional Law giving 'full powers to the Government of the Republic to promulgate in one or more Acts, by the authority and under the signature of Marshal Pétain, the new constitution of the French State'. On the following day Pétain issued the first of his constitutional acts under that law. Thereby he abrogated the Law of 1875 defining the functions of the President of the Republic, assumed the functions of 'Head of the French State' and arrogated to himself all the effective power. The Constitu-

[1] MAILLAUD, P.: *France*, p. 77; for the text c.f. THOMSON, D., *Democracy in France*, pp. 260 ff.

tional Law had been signed by the President of the Republic, Lebrun, who had been re-elected in 1939, and, although he never formally resigned, that signature and the vote of parliament meant that the President of the Republic, and the Chamber of 1936—the Front Populaire Chamber, whose election had aroused such extravagant hopes, together had virtually abdicated and voted and signed away the Third Republic.

Thus the régime born of defeat in 1870 succumbed in the catastrophe of 1940. It had never fully succeeded in reconciling the opposing forces born of the Revolution of 1789 or in solving the social problems created by the Industrial Revolution, and because of these failures it was in its last years the less able to put up an effective resistance to the disruptive pressure of alien ideologies. It had been weakened at the outset by the constitutional crisis of 1877, which had destroyed the internal balance of power and brought about an unhealthy preponderance of the legislature: and last but not least the country over which it presided, had never completely recovered from the strain of the First World War with all that that entailed. Yet, for all its defects, it had probably given a majority of Frenchmen as much government as they wanted and the sort of government they could best tolerate for a long period of years. It had lasted more than three times as long as any other régime since 1789 and the star of France, although dimmed and tarnished, was not wholly extinct. Already on June 18th from London General de Gaulle had issued his rousing call to all Free Frenchmen to rally round him. It was one of the many tragedies of those tragic weeks that by the end of that June so very few Frenchmen were free.

GATHORNE-HARDY, G. M.: *A Short History of International Affairs*, 1920–39. 3rd ed. Oxford University Press, 1942.

JORDAN, W. M.: *Great Britain, France and the German Problem*, 1918–39. Oxford University Press, 1943.

KAMMERER, ALBERT: *La vérité sur l'armistice*. Paris, 1944.

MAILLAUD, PIERRE.: *France*. Oxford University Press, 1942.

MICAUD, CHARLES A.: *The French Right and Nazi Germany*, 1933–9. Durham, N.C., 1943.

PICKLES, DOROTHY M.: *The French Political Scene*. London, 1938.

SEIGNOBOS, C.: *Le sens des élections françaises de 1932*, in *Etudes de Politique et d'histoire*. Paris, 1934.

VAUCHER, PAUL: *Social Experiments in France*, in *Politica*. June, 1938.

WALTER, GÉRARD: *Histoire du Parti Communiste Français*. Paris, 1948.

WERTH, ALEXANDER: *France in Ferment*. London, 1934.

WERTH, ALEXANDER: *The Destiny of France*. · London, 1937.

WERTH, ALEXANDER: *The Last Days of Paris; a Journalist's Diary*. London, 1940.

WOLFERS, ARNOLD: *Britain and France Between Two Wars*. New York, 1940.

APPENDIX I

Genealogical Tree of the Houses of Bourbon and Bourbon-Orléans.

HENRI IV
b. 1553, King of France, 1589–1610.

Gaston
b. 1608, d. 1660.

Henriette-Marie
b. 1605, m. Charles I,
King of England, d. 1669.

Louis XIII
b. 1601,
King of France, 1610–43.

Philippe,
Duc d'Orléans
b. 1640, m.
d. 1701.

(1) Henriette-Anne,
(2) Charlotte, dau. of Elector Palatine,

Louis XIV
b. 1638,
King of France, 1643–1715.

Philippe,
Duc d'Orléans
b. 1674, Regent of France, 1715–23,
d. 1723.

Louis, Dauphin of France
b. 1661, d. 1711.

Louis, Duc d'Orléans
b. 1703, d. 1752.

Charles,
Duc de Berry.

Louis-Philippe,
Duc d'Orléans
b. 1725, d. 1785.

Louis, Duc
de Bourgogne
b. 1682,
d. 1712.

Philippe,
Duc d'Anjou
b. 1683, King
of Spain, 1700–46,
d. 1746.

Louis-Philippe-Joseph,
Duc d'Orléans ('Philippe Égalité')
b. 1747, guillotined, 1793.

Louis XV
b. 1710, King of France, 1715–74.

Louis Philippe I
b. 1773,
King of the French, 1830–48,
d. in exile, 1850.

Louis, Dauphin of France
b. 1729, d. 1765.

Louis XVIII
Comte de Provence
b. 1755, King of
France, 1814–24.

Charles X
Comte d'Artois, b. 1757,
King of France, 1824–30,
d. in exile, 1836.

Louis XVI
b. 1754, King of
France, 1774–93,
guillotined, 1793.

Louis XVII
('the prisoner in
the Temple'),
b. 1785, d. 1795.

Marie Thérèse   m.   Duc d'Angoulême
Charlotte   b. 1775, d. 1844.
b. 1778,
d. 1851.

Charles,
Duc de Berry
b. 1778, m. Caroline, dau.
of Francis I of Naples,
assassinated, 1820.

Henri Charles, Comte
de Chambord ('Henri V'),
b. 1820, m. Marie-Louise, dau.
of Francis IV, Duke of Modena,
d. in exile 1883.

Louise Marie Thérèse
m. 1845, Charles III,
Duke of Parma.

Antoine
Philippe,
Duc de Mont-
pensier
b. 1824,
d. 1890.

Henri
Eugène,
Duc
d'Aumale
b. 1822,
d. 1897.

Louis
Ferdinand,
Prince de
Joinville
b. 1818,
d. 1900.

Clementine
b. 1817,
m. Prince
Augustus
of Saxe-
Coburg-
Gotha.

Ferdinand
b. 1861,
Prince of
Bulgaria,
1887.

Louis,
Duc de
Nemours
b. 1814,
d. 1896.

Marie
b. 1813,
m. 1837,
Duke of
Wurtem-
burg,
d. 1839.

Louise
b. 1812,
m. 1832,
Leopold I,
King of
the
Belgians,
d. 1850.

Ferdinand-Philippe,
Duc d'Orléans
b. 1810, d. 1842.

Robert,
Duc de Chartres
b. 1840, d. 1910.

Jean,
Duc de Guise
b. 1874, d. 1940.

Henri, Comte de Paris
(the present Pretender)
b. 1908.

Louis Philippe,
Comte de Paris
b. 1838,
d. in exile, 1894.

Philippe,
Duc d'Orléans
b. 1869, d. 1926.

APPENDIX II

THE PRESIDENTS OF THE THIRD REPUBLIC

1. ADOLPHE THIERS: Appointed Chief of the Executive Power, Feb. 17th, 1871. Given title of President of the French Republic by Law of Aug. 31st, 1871. Resigned, May 24th, 1873.
2. MARSHAL MACMAHON: Elected, May 24th, 1873. Resigned, January, 1879.

Elected at Versailles in accordance with the constitutional laws of 1875.

3. JULES GRÉVY: Jan. 30th, 1879. Completed his term.
   Re-elected, Dec. 28th, 1885. Resigned, Dec. 2nd, 1887.
4. SADI CARNOT: Dec. 3rd, 1887. Assassinated, June 24th, 1894.
5. JEAN-PAUL CASIMIR-PÉRIER: June 27th, 1894. Resigned, Jan. 15th, 1895.
6. FÉLIX FAURE: Jan. 17th, 1895. Died, Feb. 16th, 1899.
7. EMILE LOUBET: Feb. 18th, 1899. Completed his term.
8. ARMAND FALLIÈRES: Jan. 17th, 1906. Completed his term.
9. RAYMOND POINCARÉ: Jan. 17th, 1913. Completed his term.
10. PAUL DESCHANEL: Jan. 17th, 1920. Resigned, Sept. 17th, 1920.
11. ALEXANDRE MILLERAND: Sept. 23rd, 1920. Resigned, June 11th, 1924.
12. GASTON DOUMERGUE: June 13th, 1924. Completed his term.
13. PAUL DOUMER: May 31st, 1931. Assassinated, May 7th, 1932.
14. ALBERT LEBRUN: May 10th, 1932. Completed his term. Re-elected, April 5th, 1939.

APPENDIX III

THE CHARTER OF 1814

AFTER a lengthy preamble the Charter follows thus:

'À ces causes,

Nous avons volontairement et par le libre exercice de notre autorité royale, accordé et accordons . . . tant pour nous que pour nos successeurs et à jamais . . . la Charte constitutionnelle qui suit.

Droit public des Français

1. Les Français sont égaux devant la loi, quels que soient d'ailleurs leurs titres et leurs rangs.

2. Ils contribuent indistinctement, dans la proportion de leur fortune, aux charges de l'État.

3. Ils sont tous également admissibles aux emplois civils et militaires.

4. Leur liberté individuelle est également garantie, personne ne pouvant être poursuivi ni arrêté que dans les cas prévus par la loi, et dans la forme qu'elle prescrit.

5. Chacun professe sa religion avec une égale liberté, et obtient pour son culte la même protection.

6. Cependant la religion catholique, apostolique et romaine, est la religion de l'État.

7. Les ministres de la religion catholique, apostolique et romaine, et ceux des autres cultes chrétiens reçoivent seuls des traitements du Trésor royal.

8. Les Français ont le droit de publier et de faire imprimer leurs opinions en se conformant aux lois qui doivent réprimer les abus de cette liberté.

9. Toutes les propriétés sont inviolables, sans aucune exception de celles qu'on appelle nationales, la loi ne mettant aucune différence entre elles.

10. L'État peut exiger le sacrifice d'une propriété pour cause d'intérêt public légalement constaté, mais avec une indemnité préalable.

11. Toutes les recherches des opinions et votes émis jusqu' à la

Restauration sont interdites. Le même oubli est commandé aux tribunaux et aux citoyens.

12. La conscription est abolie. Le mode de recrutement de l'armée de terre et de mer est determiné par une loi.

Formes du gouvernement du Roi

13. La personne du Roi est inviolable et sacrée. Ses ministres sont responsables. Au Roi seul appartient la puissance exécutive.

14. Le Roi est le chef suprême de l'État, commande les forces de terre et de mer, déclare la guerre, fait les traités de paix, d'alliance et de commerce, nomme à tous les emplois d'administration publique, et fait les règlements et ordonnances nécessaires pour l'exécution des lois et la sûreté de l'État.

15. La puissance législative s'exerce collectivement par le Roi, la Chambre des pairs, et la Chambre des députés des départements.

16. Le Roi propose la loi.

17. La proposition de loi est portée, au gré du Roi, à la Chambre des pairs ou à celle des députés, excepté la loi de l'impôt qui doit être adressée d'abord à la Chambre des députés.

18. Toute loi doit être discutée et votée librement par la majorité de chacune des deux Chambres.

19. Les Chambres ont la faculté de supplier le Roi de proposer une loi sur quelque objet que ce soit et d'indiquer ce qui leur paraît convenable que la loi contienne.

20. Cette demande pourra être faite par chacune des deux Chambres, mais après avoir été discutée en comité secret; elle ne sera envoyée à l'autre Chambre qu'après un délai de dix jours.

21. Si la proposition est adoptée par l'autre Chambre, elle sera mise sous les yeux du Roi; si elle est rejetée, elle ne pourra être représentée dans la même session.

22. Le Roi seul sanctionne et promulgue les lois.

23. La liste civile est fixée, pour toute la durée du règne, par la première législature assemblée depuis l'avènement du Roi.

De la Chambre des pairs

24. La Chambre des pairs est une portion essentielle de la puissance législative.

25. Elle est convoquée par le Roi en même temps que la Chambre des députés. . . .

27. La nomination des pairs de France appartient au Roi. Leur

nombre est illimité.   Il peut en varier les dignités, les nommer à vie ou les rendre héréditaires selon sa volonté.

28.   Les pairs ont entrée dans la Chambre à vingt-cinq ans, et voix délibérative à trente ans seulement.

29.   La Chambre des pairs est presidée par le chancelier de France et, en son absence, par un pair nommé par le Roi.

32.   Toutes les délibérations de la Chambre des pairs sont secrètes.

33.   La Chambre des pairs connaît des crimes de haute trahison et des attentats à la sûreté de l'État qui seront définis par la loi.

34.   Aucun pair ne peut être arrêté que de l'autorité de la Chambre, et jugé que par elle en matière criminelle.

De la Chambre des députés des départements

35.   La Chambre des députés sera composée des députés élus par les collèges électoraux, dont l'organisation sera déterminée par des lois.

36.   'Chaque département aura le même nombre de députés qu'il aura eu jusqu' à présent.'

37.   Les députés seront élus pour cinq ans, et de manière que la Chambre soit renouvelable par cinquième.

38.   Aucun député ne peut être admis dans la Chambre s'il n'est âgé de quarante ans et s'il ne paie une contribution directe de 1,000 francs.

40.   Les électeurs qui concourent à la nomination des députés ne peuvent avoir droit de suffrage s'ils ne payent une contribution directe de 300 francs, et s'ils ont moins de trente ans.

41.   Les présidents des collèges électoraux seront nommés par le Roi et de droit membres du collège.

42.   La moitié au moins des députés sera choisie parmi des éligibles qui ont leur domicile politique dans le département.

43.   Le président de la Chambre des députés est nommé par le Roi sur une liste de cinq membres présentée par la Chambre.

44.   Les séances de la Chambre sont publiques, mais la demande de cinq membres suffit pour qu'elle se forme en comité secret.

46.   Aucun amendement ne peut être fait à une loi s'il n'a été proposé ou consenti par le Roi, et s'il n'a été renvoyé ou discuté dans les bureaux.

47.   La Chambre des députés reçoit toutes les propositions d'impôts; ce n'est qu'après que ces propositions ont été admises qu'elles peuvent être portées à la Chambre des pairs.

48.   'Aucun impôt ne peut être établi ni perçu s'il n'a été consenti' par les deux Chambres et sanctionné par le Roi.

49. 'L'impôt foncier n'est consenti que pour un an.' Les impositions indirectes peuvent l'être pour plusieurs années.

50. Le Roi convoque, chaque année, les deux Chambres; il les proroge, et peut dissoudre celle des députés des départements; mais, dans ce cas, il doit en convoquer une nouvelle dans le délai de trois mois.

51. Aucune contrainte par corps ne peut être exercée contre un membre de la Chambre durant la session, et dans les six semaines qui l'auront précédée ou suivie.

52. Aucun membre de la Chambre ne peut pendant la durée de la session être poursuivi ni arrêté en matière criminelle, sauf le cas de flagrant délit, qu'après que la Chambre a permis sa poursuite.

53. Toute pétition à l'une ou à l'autre Chambre ne peut être faite ou présentée que par écrit. La loi interdit d'en apporter en personne à la barre.

Des ministres

54. Les ministres peuvent être membres de la Chambre des pairs ou de la Chambre des députés. Ils ont en outre leur entrée dans l'une ou l'autre Chambre, et doivent être entendus quand ils le demandent.

55. La Chambre des députés a le droit d'accuser les ministres, et de les traduire devant la Chambre des pairs, qui seule a celui de les juger.

56. Il ne peuvent être accusés que pour fait de trahison ou de concussion. Des lois particulières spécifieront cette nature de délits et en détermineront la poursuite.

De l'ordre judiciaire

57. Toute justice émane du Roi. Elle s'administre en son nom par des juges qu'il nomme et qu'il institue.

58. Les juges nommés par le Roi sont inamovibles.

59. 'Les cours et tribunaux ordinaires actuellement existants sont maintenus. Il n'y sera rien changé qu'en vertu d'une loi.'

60. L'institution actuelle des juges de commerce est conservée.

61. La justice de paix est également conservée. Les juges de paix, quoique nommés par le Roi, ne sont point inamovibles.

62. Nul ne pourra être distrait de ses juges naturels.

63. Il ne pourra en conséquence être créé de commissions et Tribunaux extraordinaires. Ne sont pas comprises sous cette dénomination les juridictions prevôtales si leur établissement est jugé nécessaire.

64. 'Les débats seront publics en matière criminelle, à moins que

cette publicité ne soit dangereuse pour l'ordre et les moeurs; et, dans ce cas, le tribunal le déclare par un jugement.

65. 'L'institution des jurés est conservée.' Les changements qu'une plus longue expérience ferait juger nécessaires ne peuvent être effectués que par une loi.

66. La peine de la confiscation des biens est abolie et ne pourra pas être rétablie.

67. Le Roi a droit de faire grâce et celui de commuer les peines.

68. Le Code civil et les lois actuellement existants qui ne sont pas contraires à la présente Charte restent en vigueur jusqu'à ce qu'il y soit légalement dérogé.

Droits particuliers garantis par l'État

69. 'Les militaires en activité de service, les officiers et soldats en retraite, les veuves, les officiers et soldats pensionnés conserveront leurs grades, honneurs et pensions.'

70. 'La dette publique est garantie.' Toute espèce d'engagement pris par l'État envers ses créanciers est inviolable.

71. 'La noblesse ancienne reprend ses titres. La nouvelle conserve les siens.' Le Roi fait des nobles à volonté, mais il ne leur accorde que des rangs et des honneurs, sans aucune exemption des charges de devoirs de la société.

72. 'La Légion d'honneur est maintenue.' Le Roi détermine les règlements intérieurs et la décoration.

74. Le Roi et ses successeurs jureront dans la solennitée de leur sacre d'observer fidèlement la présente Charte constitutionnelle.

Donné à Paris, l'an de grace 1814 et de notre règne le dix-neuvième.

Signé: LOUIS.

Et plus bas, le ministre secrétaire d'État de l'intérieur, signé: Abbé De Montesquiou. Visa: le chancelier de France, signé: Dambray.

APPENDIX IV

The Declaration of the Chamber of Deputies and the clauses of the Constitutional Charter of 1830 which modified the Charter of 1814

1. Déclaration de la Chambre des Députés du 7 Août 1830.

La Chambre des Députés, prenant en considération l'impérieuse nécessité qui résulte des événements des 26, 27, 28, 29 juillet dernier et jours suivants, et de la situation générale où la France s'est trouvée placée à la suite de la violation de la Charte constitutionnelle; considérant en outre, que, par suite de cette violation et de la résistance héroïque des citoyens de Paris, S. M. Charles X, S. A. R. Louis-Antoine, Dauphin, et tous les membres de la branche aînée de la maison royale, sortent en ce moment du territoire français—Déclare que le trône est vacant en fait et en droit, et qu'il est indispensable d'y pourvoir. Déclare secondement que, selon le voeu et dans l'intérêt du peuple français, le préambule de la Charte Constitutionnelle est supprimé, comme blessant la dignité nationale, en paraissant octroyer aux Français des droits qui leur appartiennent essentiellement et que les articles suivants de la même charte doivent être supprimés ou modifiés de la manière qui va être indiquée.

Moyennant l'acceptation de ces dispositions et propositions, la Chambre des députés déclare enfin que l'intérêt universel et pressant du peuple français appelle au trône S. A. R. Louis-Philippe d'Orléans, Duc d'Orléans, Lieutenant général du royaume, et ses descendants à perpetuité, de mâle en mâle, par ordre de primogéniture, et à l'exclusion perpétuelle des femmes et de leur descendance. En conséquence, S. A. R. Louis-Philippe d'Orléans, Duc d'Orléans, Lieutenant général du royaume, sera invité à accepter et à jurer les clauses et engagements ci-dessus énoncés, l'observation de la Charte constitutionnelle et des modifications indiquées, et, après l'avoir fait devant les Chambres assemblées, prendre le titre de Roi des Français.

2. Charte Constitutionnelle de 1830.

Louis-Philippe, etc.

Nous avons ordonné et ordonnons que la Charte constitutionnelle de 1814, telle qu'elle a été amendée par les deux Chambres le 7 août et acceptée par nous le 9, sera de nouveau publiée dans les termes suivants.

ART. 6. Les ministres de la religion catholique, apostolique et romaine, professée par la majorité des Français, et ceux des autres cultes chrétiens recoivent des traitements du trésor public.

7. Les Français ont le droit de publier et de faire imprimer leurs opinions en se conformant aux lois. La censure ne pourra jamais être rétablié.

Formes du gouvernement du roi

13. Le roi est le chef suprême de l'État; il commande les forces de terre et de mer, déclare la guerre, fait les traités de paix, d'alliance et de commerce, nomme à tous les emplois d'administration publique et fait les règlements et ordonnances nécessaires pour l'exécution des lois, sans pouvoir jamais ni suspendre les lois ellesmêmes, ni dispenser de leur exécution.

Toutefois aucune troupe étrangère ne pourra être admise au service de l'État qu'en vertu d'une loi . . .

15. La proposition des lois appartient au Roi, à la Chambre des pairs et à la Chambre des députés. Néanmoins toute loi d'impôt doit être d'abord votée par la Chambre des députés.

17. Si une proposition de loi a été rejetée par l'un des trois pouvoirs, elle ne pourra être représentée dans la même session.

De la Chambre des pairs

22. Toute assemblée de la Chambre des pairs qui serait tenue hors du temps et la session de la Chambre des députés est illicite et nulle de plein droit, sauf le seul cas où elle est réunie comme cour de justice, et alors elle ne peut exercer que des fonctions judiciaires.

27. Les séances de la Chambre des pairs sont publiques, comme celles de la Chambre des députés.

De la Chambre des députés

31. Les députés sont élus pour cinq ans.

32. Aucun député ne peut être admis dans la Chambre s'il n'est âgé de trente ans et s'il ne réunit les autres conditions déterminées par la loi.

34. . Nul n'est électeur s'il a moins de vingt-cinq ans, et s'il ne réunit les autres conditions déterminées par la loi.

35.   Les présidents des collèges électoraux sont nommés par les électeurs.

37.   Le président de la Chambre des députés est élu par elle à l'ouverture de chaque session.

Des ministres

L'ancien article 56 est supprimé.

De l'ordre judiciaire

54.   Il ne pourra en conséquence être crée de commissions et de tribunaux extraordinaires, à quelque titre et sous quelque dénomination que ce puisse être.

Droits particuliers

64.   Suppression des mots et des règlements.

65.   Le Roi et ses successeurs jureront à leur avènement, en présence des Chambres réunies, d'observer fidèlement la Charte constitutionnelle.

66.   La présente Charte et tous les droits qu'elle consacre demeurent confiés au patriotisme et au courage de gardes nationales et de tous les citoyens français.

67.   La France reprend ses couleurs. A l'avenir, il ne sera plus porté d'autre cocarde que la cocarde tricolore.

Dispositions particulières

68.   Toutes les nominations et créations nouvelles de pairs faites sous le règne du roi Charles X sont déclarées nulles et non avenues.

69.   Il sera pourvu successivement par des lois séparées et dans le plus court délai possible aux objets qui suivent.

   1.   L'application du jury aux délits de la presse et aux délits politiques.

   2.   La responsabilité des ministres et des autres agents du pouvoir.

   3.   La réélection des députés promus à des fonctions publiques salariées.

   4.   Le vote annuel du contingent de l'armée.

   5.   L'organisation de la garde nationale avec intervention des gardes nationaux dans le choix de leurs officiers.

   6.   Des dispositions qui assurent d'une manière légale l'état des officiers de tout grade de terre et de mer.

7. Des institutions départementales et municipales fondées sur un système électif.

8. L'instruction publique et la liberté de l'enseignement.

9. L'abolition du double vote et la fraction des conditions électorales d'éligibilité.

Fait au Palais-Royal, à Paris, le 14e jour du mois d'août l'an 1830.

Signé: LOUIS-PHILIPPE.

APPENDIX V

THE CONSTITUTION OF NOVEMBER 4th, 1848

Au nom du peuple français

L'Assemblée nationale a adopté, et le Président de l'Assemblée nationale promulgue la Constitution dont la teneur suit.

Préambule

En présence de Dieu et au nom du Peuple français, l'Assemblée nationale proclame:

I. La France s'est constituée en République. En adoptant cette forme définitive de gouvernement, elle s'est proposé pour but de marcher plus librement dans la voie du progrès et de la civilisation, d'assurer une répartition de plus en plus équitable des charges et des avantages de la société, d'augmenter l'aisance de chacun par la réduction graduée des dépenses publiques et des impôts, et de faire parvenir tous les citoyens, sans nouvelle commotion, par l'action successive et constante des institutions et des lois, à un degré toujours plus élevé de moralité, de lumières et de bien-être.

II. La République française est démocratique, une et indivisible.

III. Elle reconnaît des droits et des devoirs antérieurs et supérieurs aux lois positives.

IV. Elle a pour principes la Liberté, l'Égalité et la Fraternité.

Elle a pour bases la Famille, le Travail, la Propriété, l'Ordre public.

V. Elle respecte les nationalités étrangères comme elle entend faire respecter la sienne, n'entreprend aucune guerre dans des vues de conquête, et n'emploie jamais ses forces contre la liberté d'aucun peuple.

VI. Des devoirs réciproques obligent les citoyens envers la République, et la République envers les citoyens.

VII. Les citoyens doivent aimer la Patrie, servir la République, la défendre au prix de leur vie, participer aux charges de l'État en proportion de leur fortune; ils doivent s'assurer, par le travail, des moyens d'existence, et, par la prévoyance, des ressources pour l'avenir; ils doivent concourir au bien-être commun en s'entr'aidant fraternellement les uns les autres et à l'ordre général en observant les lois morales et les lois écrites qui régissent la société, la famille et l'individu.

VIII. La République doit protéger le citoyen dans sa personne, sa famille, sa religion, sa propriété, son travail, et mettre à la portée de chacun l'instruction indispensable à tous les hommes; elle doit, par une assistance fraternelle, assurer l'existence des citoyens nécessiteux, soit en leur procurant du travail dans les limites de ses ressources, soit en donnant, à défaut de la famille, des secours à ceux qui sont hors d'état de travailler. En vue de l'accomplissement de tous ces devoirs, et pour la garantie de tous ces droits, l'Assemblée nationale fidèle aux traditions des grandes Assemblées qui ont inauguré la Révolution française décrète, ainsi qu'il suit, la Constitution de la République.

Constitution

CHAPITRE I

DE LA SOUVERAINETÉ

1. La souveraineté réside dans l'universalité des citoyens français. Elle est inaliénable et imprescriptible. Aucun individu, aucune fraction du peuple ne peut s'en attribuer l'exercice.

CHAPITRE II

DROITS DES CITOYENS GARANTIS PAR LA CONSTITUTION

2. Nul ne peut être arrêté ou détenu que suivant les prescriptions de la loi.

3. La demeure de toute personne habitant le territoire français est inviolable; il n'est permis d'y pénétrer que selon les formes et dans les cas prévus par la loi.

4. Nul ne sera distrait de ses juges naturels. Il ne pourra être créé de commissions et de tribunaux extraordinaires, à quelque titre et sous quelque dénomination que ce soit.

5. La peine de mort est abolie en matière politique.

6. L'esclavage ne peut exister sur aucune terre française.

7. Chacun professe librement sa religion et reçoit de l'État pour l'exercice de son culte, une égale protection. Les ministres, soit des cultes actuellement reconnus par la loi, soit de ceux qui seraient reconnus à l'avenir, ont le droit de recevoir un traitement de l'État.

8. Les citoyens ont le droit de s'associer, de s'assembler paisiblement

et sans armes, de pétitionner, de manifester leurs pensées par la voie de la presse ou autrement. L'exercice de ces droits n'a pour limite que les droits ou la liberté d'autrui et la sécurité publique. La presse ne peut, en aucun cas, être soumise à la censure.

9. L'enseignement est libre. La Liberté d'enseignement s'exerce selon les conditions de capacité et de moralité déterminées par les lois, et sous la surveillance de l'État. Cette surveillance s'étend à tous les établissements d'éducation et d'enseignement sans aucune exception.

10. Tous les citoyens sont également admissibles à tous les emplois publics, sans autre motif de préférence que leur mérite, et suivant les conditions qui seront fixées par les lois. Sont abolis à toujours tout titre nobiliaire, toute distinction de naissance, de classe ou de caste.

11. Toutes les propriétés sont inviolables. Néanmoins l'État peut exiger le sacrifice d'une propriété pour cause d'utilité publique légalement constatée, et moyennant une juste et préalable indemnité.

12. La confiscation des biens ne pourra jamais être rétablie.

13. La Constitution garantit aux citoyens la liberté du travail et de l'industrie. La société favorise et encourage le développement du travail par l'enseignement primaire gratuit, l'éducation professionnelle, l'égalité de rapports entre le patron et l'ouvrier, les institutions de prévoyance et de crédit, les institutions agricoles, les associations volontaires, et l'établissement, par l'État, les départements et les communes, de travaux publics propres à employer les bras inoccupés; elle fournit l'assistance aux enfants abandonnés, aux infirmes et aux vieillards sans ressources, et que leurs familles ne peuvent secourir.

14. La dette publique est garantie. Toute espèce d'engagement pris par l'État avec ses créanciers est inviolable.

15. Tout impôt est établi pour l'utilité commune. Chacun y contribue en proportion de ses facultés et de sa fortune.

16. Aucun impôt ne peut être établi ni perçu qu'en vertu d'une loi.

17. L'impôt direct n'est consenti que pour un an. Les impôts indirects peuvent être consentis pour plusieurs années.

CHAPITRE III

DES POUVOIRS PUBLICS

18. Tous les pouvoirs publics, quels qu'ils soient, émanent du peuple. Ils ne peuvent être délegués héréditairement.

19. La séparation des pouvoirs est la première condition d'un gouvernement libre.

CHAPITRE IV

DU POUVOIR LÉGISLATIF

20. Le Peuple français délègue le pouvoir législatif à une assemblée unique.

21. Le nombre total des représentants du peuple sera de 750, y compris les représentants de l'Algérie et des colonies français.

22. Ce nombre s'élèvera à 900 pour les assemblées qui seront appelées à reviser le Constitution.

23. L'élection a pour base la population.

24. Le suffrage est direct et universel. Le scrutin est secret.

25. Sont électeurs, sans condition de cens, tous les Français âgés de vingt-un ans, et jouissant de leurs droits civils et politiques.

26. Sont éligibles, sans condition de domicile, tous les électeurs âgés de vingt-cinq ans.

27. La loi électorale déterminera les causes qui peuvent priver les citoyens français du droit d'élire et d'être élu. . . .

28. Toute fonction publique rétribuée est incompatible avec le mandat de représentant du peuple. Aucun membre de l'Assemblée nationale ne peut, pendant la durée de la législature, être nommé ou promu à des fonctions publiques salariées dont les titulaires sont choisis à volonté par le Pouvoir exécutif. Les exceptions aux dispositions des deux paragraphes précédents seront déterminées par la loi électorale organique.

29. Les dispositions de l'article précédent ne sont pas applicables aux assemblées élues pour la revision de la Constitution.

30. L'élection des représentants se fera par département, et au scrutin de liste. Les électeurs voteront au chef-lieu du canton; néanmoins, en raison des circonstances locales, le canton pourra être divisé en plusieurs circonscriptions, dans la forme et aux conditions qui seront déterminées par la loi électorale.

31. L'Assemblée nationale est élue pour trois ans, et se renouvelle intégralement. La nouvelle Assemblée est convoquée de plein droit pour le lendemain du jour où finit le mandat de l'Assemblée précédente.

32. Elle est permanente. Néanmoins, elle peut s'ajourner à un terme qu'elle fixe. Pendant la durée de la prorogation, une commission composée des membres du bureau et de vingt-cinq représentants nommés par l'Assemblée au scrutin secret et à la majorité absolue a aussi le droit de la convoquer en cas d'urgence. Le Président de la République a aussi le droit de convoquer l'Assemblée. L'Assemblée nationale

détermine le lieu de ses séances. Elle fixe l'importance des forces militaires établies pour sa sûreté, et elle en dispose.

33. Les représentants sont toujours rééligibles.

34. Les membres de l'Assemblée nationale sont les représentants, non du département qui les nomme, mais de la France entière.

35. Ils ne peuvent recevoir de mandat impératif.

36. Les représentants du peuple sont inviolables. Ils ne pourront être recherchés, accusés, ni jugés, en aucun temps pour les opinions qu'ils auront émises dans le sein de l'Assemblée nationale.

37. Ils ne peuvent être arrêtés en matière criminelle, sauf le cas de flagrant délit, ni poursuivis qu'après que l'Assemblée a permis la poursuite. En cas d'arrestation pour flagrant délit, il en sera immédiatement référé à l'Assemblée, qui autorisera ou refusera la continuation des poursuites. . . .

38. Chaque représentant de peuple reçoit une indemnité à laquelle il ne peut renoncer.

39. Les séances de l'Assemblée sont publiques. Néanmoins, l'Assemblée peut se former en comité secret, sur la demande du nombre de représentants fixé par le règlement. Chaque représentant a le droit d'initiative parlementaire. . . .

40. La présence de la moitié plus un des membres de l'Assemblée est nécessaire pour la validité du vote des lois.

41. Aucun projet de loi, sauf les cas d'urgence, ne sera voté définitivement qu'après trois délibérations, à des intervalles qui ne peuvent être moindres de cinq jours . . .

CHAPITRE V

DU POUVOIR EXÉCUTIF

43. Le peuple français délègue le pouvoir exécutif à un citoyen qui reçoit le titre dé Président de la République. . . .

45. Le Président de la République est élu pour quatre ans et n'est rééligible qu'après un intervalle de quatre années. Ne peuvent non plus être réélus après lui, dans le même intervalle, ni le vice-président, ni aucun des parents ou alliés du Président jusqu'au 6e degré inclusivement.

46. Le Président est nommé, au scrutin secret et à la majorité absolue des votants, par le suffrage direct de tous les électeurs des départements français et de l'Algérie.

47. Les procès-verbaux des operations électorales sont transmis immédiatement à l'Assemblée nationale qui statue sans délai sur la validité de l'élection et proclame le Président de la République. Si

aucun candidat n'a obtenu plus de la moitié des suffrages exprimés, et au moins deux millions de voix, ou si les conditions exigées par l'article 44 ne sont pas remplies, l'Assemblée nationale élit le Président de la République, à la majorité absolue et au scrutin secret, parmi les cinq candidates éligibles qui ont obtenu le plus de voix.

Avant d'entrer en fonctions, le Président de la République prête au sein de l'Assemblée nationale le serment dont la teneur suit: EN PRÉSENCE DE DIEU ET DEVANT LE PEUPLE FRANÇAIS, REPRÉSENTÉ PAR L'ASSEMBLÉE NATIONALE JE JURE DE RESTER FIDÈLE À LA RÉPUBLIQUE DÉMOCRATIQUE, UNE ET INDIVISIBLE, ET DE REMPLIR TOUS LES DEVOIRS QUE M'IMPOSE LA CONSTITUTION.

49. Il a le droit de fair présenter des projets de loi à l'Assemblée nationale par les ministres.   Il surveille et assure l'exécution des lois.

50. Il dispose de la force armée, sans pouvoir jamais la commander en personne.

51. Il ne peut céder aucune portion du territoire, ni dissoudre ni proroger l'Assemblée nationale, ni suspendre, en aucune manière, l'empire de la Constitution et des lois.

52. Il présente, chaque année, par un message, à l'Assemblée nationale, l'exposé de l'état general des affaires de la République.

53. Il négocie et ratifie les traités.   Aucun traité n'est définitif qu'après avoir été approuvé par l'Assemblée nationale.

54. Il veille à la défense de l'État, mais il ne peut entreprendre aucune guerre sans le consentement de l'Assemblée nationale.

55. Il a le droit de faire grâce, mais il ne peut exercer ce droit qu'après avoir pris l'avis du Conseil d'État.   Les amnisties ne peuvent être accordées que par une loi.   Le Président de la République, les ministres, ainsi que toutes les autres personnes condamnées par la Haute-Cour de justice, ne peuvent être graciés que par l'Assemblée nationale.

56. Le Président de la République promulgue les lois au nom du Peuple français . . .

58. . . . Le Président de la République peut, par un message motivé, demander une nouvelle délibération.   L'Assemblée délibère, sa résolution devient définitive, elle est transmise au Président de la République . . .

62. Il (le Président) est logé aux frais de la République et reçoit un traitement de 600,000 francs par an.

63. Il réside au lieu où siège l'Assemblée nationale, et ne peut sortir du territoire continental de la République sans y être autorisé par une loi.

64. Le Président de la République nomme et révoque les ministres.

Il nomme et révoque, en conseil des ministres, les agents diplomatiques, les commandants en chef des armées de terre et de mer, les préfets, le commandant supérieur des gardes nationaux de la Seine.

. . . Il nomme et révoque, sur la proposition du ministre compétent, dans les conditions réglementaires déterminées par la loi, les agents secondaires du gouvernement.

65. Il a le droit de suspendre pour un terme qui ne pourra pas excéder trois mois les agents du pouvoir exécutif élus par les citoyens, il ne peut les révoquer que de l'avis du Conseil d'État. . . .

66. Le nombre des ministres et leurs attributions sont fixés par le pouvoir législatif.

67. Les actes du Président de la République, autres que ceux par lesquels il nomme et révoque les ministres, n'ont d'effet que s'ils sont contre-signés par un ministre.

68. Le Président de la République, les ministres, les agents et dépositaires de l'autorité publique, sont responsables, chacun en ce qui le concerne, de tous les actes du Gouvernement et de l'administration. Toute mesure par laquelle le Président de la République dissout l'Assemblée nationale, la proroge ou met obstacle à l'exercice de son mandat, est un crime de haute trahison. Par ce seul fait, le Président est déchu de ses fonctions; les citoyens sont tenus de lui refuser obéissance; le pouvoir exécutif passe de plein droit a l'Assemblée nationale. Les juges de la Haute Cour de justice se réunissent immédiatement à peine de forfaiture: ils convoquent les jurés dans le lieu qu'il désignent, pour procéder au jugement du Président et de ses complices; ils nomment eux-mêmes les magistrats chargés de remplir les fonctions de ministère public. Une loi déterminera les autres cas de responsabilité, ainsi que les formes et les conditions de la poursuite.

69. Les ministres ont entrée dans le sein de l'Assemblée nationale; ils sont entendus toutes les fois qu'ils le demandent, et peuvent se faire assister par des commissaires nommés par un décret du Président de la République.

70. Il y a un Vice-Président de la République nommé par l'Assemblée nationale, sur la présentation de trois candidats faite par le Président dans le mois qui suit son élection. Le Vice-Président prête la même serment que le Président. Le Vice-Président ne pourra être choisi parmi les parents ou alliés du Président jusqu'au 6e degré inclusivement. En cas d'empèchement du Président, le Vice-Président le remplace. Si la présidence devient vacante par décès, démission du Président, ou autrement, il est procédé, dans le mois, a l'élection d'un Président.

CHAPITRE VI
DU CONSEIL D'ÉTAT

71. Il y aura un Conseil d'État, dont le Vice-Président de la République sera de droit président.

72. Les membres de ce conseil sont nommés pour six ans par l'Assemblée nationale. Ils sont renouvelés par moitié, dans les deux premiers mois de chaque législature, au scrutin secret et à la majorité absolue. Ils sont indéfiniment rééligibles.

73. Ceux des membres du Conseil d'État qui auront été pris dans le sein de l'Assemblée nationale seront immédiatement remplacés comme représentants du peuple.

74. Les membres du Conseil d'État ne peuvent être révoqués que par l'Assemblée et sur la proposition du Président de la République.

75. Le Conseil d'État est consulté sur les projets de loi du Gouvernement qui, d'après la loi, devront être soumis à son examen préalable, et sur les projets d'initiative parlementaire que l'Assemblée lui aura renvoyés. Il prépare les règlements d'administration publique; il fait seul ceux de ces règlements à l'égard desquels l'Assemblée nationale lui a donné une délégation spéciale. Il exerce à l'égard des administrations publiques tous les pouvoirs de surveillance et de contrôle qui lui sont déférés par la loi. . . .

CHAPITRE VII.
DE L'ADMINISTRATION INTÉRIEURE

76. La division du territoire en départements, arrondissements, cantons et communes, est maintenue. Les circonscriptions actuelles ne pourront être changées que par la loi.

77. Il y a: 1e dans chaque département une administration composée d'un préfet, d'un conseil général, d'un conseil de préfecture; 2e dans chaque arrondissement, un sous-préfet; 3e dans chaque canton, un conseil cantonal; 4e dans chaque commune, une administration composée d'un maire, d'adjoints et d'un conseil municipal.

79. Les conseils généraux et les conseils municipaux sont élus par le suffrage direct de tous les citoyens domiciliés dans le département et dans la commune. Chaque canton élit un membre du Conseil général. Une loi spéciale réglera le mode d'élection dans le département de la Seine, dans la ville de Paris et dans les villes de plus de 200.000 âmes.

80. Les Conseils généraux, cantonaux et municipaux peuvent être dissous par le Président de la République, de l'avis du Conseil d'État.

CHAPITRE VIII

DU POUVOIR JUDICIAIRE

81. La justice est rendue gratuitement au nom du Peuple français. Les débats sont publics, à moins que la publicité ne soit dangéreuse pour l'ordre ou les moeurs; et, dans ce cas, le tribunal le déclare par un jugement.

82. Le jury continuera d'être appliqué en matière criminelle.

83. La connaissance de tous les délits politiques et de tous les délits commis par la voie de la presse appartient exclusivement au jury. Les lois organiques détermineront la compétence en matière de délits d'injures et de diffamation contre les particuliers.

84. Le jury statue seul sur les dommages-intérêts réclamés pour faits ou délits de presse.

85. Les juges de paix et leurs suppléants, les juges de première instance et d'appel, les membres de la Cour de cassation et de la Cour des comptes, sont nommés par le Président de la République, d'après un ordre de candidature ou d'après des conditions qui seront réglées par les lois organiques.

86. Les magistrats du ministère public sont nommés par le Président de la République.

87. Les juges de première instance et d'appel, les membres de la Cour de cassation et de la Cour des comptes sont nommés à vie. Ils ne peuvent être révoqués ou suspendus que par un jugement, ni mis à la retraite que pour les causes et dans les formes déterminées par les lois.

88. Les conseils de guerre et de revision des armées de terre et de mer, les tribunaux maritimes, les tribunaux de commerce, les prud'-hommes et autres tribunaux spéciaux, conservent leur organisation et leurs attributions actuelles jusqu'à ce qu'il y ait été dérogé par une loi.

89. Les conflits d'attributions entre l'autorité administrative et l'autorité judiciaire seront réglés par un tribunal spécial de membres de la Cour de cassation et de conseillers d'État, désignés tous les trois ans en nombre égal par leur corps respectif. Ce tribunal sera présidé par le ministre de la justice.

91. Une Haute Cour de justice juge, sans appel ni recours en cassation les accusations portées par l'Assemblée nationale contre le Président de la République, ou les ministres. Elle juge également toutes personnes prévenues de crimes, attentats ou complots contre la sûreté intérieure ou extérieure de l'État, que l'Assemblée nationale aura renvoyées devant elle. . . .

92. La Haute Cour est composée de 5 juges et de 36 jurés. Chaque année, dans les quinze premiers jours du mois de novembre, la Cour de

cassation nomme, parmi ses membres, au scrutin secret et à la majorité absolue, les juges de la Haute Cour au nombre de 5 et 2 suppléants. Le 5 juges appelés à siéger font choix de leur président. Les magistrats remplissant les fonctions du ministère public sont désignés par le Président de la République, et, en cas d'accusation du Président ou des ministres, par l'Assemblée nationale. Les jurés au nombre de 36 et 4 jurés suppléants sont pris parmi les membres des Conseils généraux des départements. Les représentants du peuple n'en peuvent faire partie. . . .

96. L'accusé et le ministère public exercent le droit de récusation comme en matière ordinaire.

97. La déclaration du jury portant que l'accusé est coupable ne peut être rendue qu'à la majorité des deux tiers des voix.

98. Dans tous les cas de responsabilité des ministres, l'Assemblée nationale peut, selon les circonstances, renvoyer le ministre inculpé, soit devant la Haute Cour de justice, soit devant les tribunaux ordinaires, pour les réparations civiles.

99. L'Assemblée nationale et le Président de la République peuvent, dans tous les cas, déférer l'examen des actes de tout fonctionnaire, autre que le Président de la République, au Conseil d'État, dont le rapport est rendu public.

100. Le Président de la République n'est justiciable que de la Haute Cour de justice. Il ne peut, à l'exception du cas prévu par l'article 68, être poursuivi que sur l'accusation portée par l'Assemblée nationale, et pour crimes et délits qui seront déterminés par la loi.

CHAPITRE IX

DE LA FORCE PUBLIQUE

101. La force publique est instituée pour défendre lÉtat contre les ennemis du dehors, et pour assurer au dedans le maintien de l'ordre et l'exécution des lois. Elle se compose de la garde nationale et de l'armée de terre et de mer.

102. Tout Français, sauf les exceptions fixées par la loi, doit le service militaire et celui de la garde nationale. La faculté pour chaque citoyen de se libérer du service militaire personnel sera réglée par la loi du recrutement.

103. L'organisation de la garde nationale et la constitution de l'armée seront reglées par la loi.

104. La force publique, est essentiellement obéissante. Nul corps armé ne peut délibérer.

105. La force publique, employée pour maintenir l'ordre à l'intérieur,

n'agit que sur la réquisition des autorités constituées, suivant les règles déterminées par le Pouvoir législatif.

106. Une loi déterminera les cas dans lesquels l'état de siège pourra être déclaré, et réglera les formes et les effets de cette mesure.

107. Aucune troupe étrangère ne peut être introduite sur le territoire français sans le consentement préalable de l'Assemblée nationale.

CHAPITRE X
DISPOSITIONS PARTICULIÉRES

108. La Légion d'honneur est maintenue et ses statuts seront revisés et mis en harmonie avec la Constitution.

CHAPITRE XI
DE LA REVISION DE LA CONSTITUTION

111. Lorsque, dans la dernière année d'une législature, l'Assemblée nationale aura émis le voeu que la Constitution soit modifiée en tout ou en partie, il sera procédé à cette revision de la manière suivante: Le voeu exprimé par l'Assemblée ne sera converti en résolution définitive qu'après trois déliberations consécutives, prises chacune à un mois d'intervalle, et aux trois quarts des suffrages exprimés. Le nombre des votants devra être de 500 au moins. L'assemblée de revision ne sera convoquée que pour trois mois; elle ne devra s'occuper que de la revision pour laquelle elle aura été convoquée. . . .

CHAPITRE XII
DISPOSITIONS TRANSITOIRES

112. Les dispositions des Codes, lois et règlements existants, qui ne sont pas contraires à la présente Constitution restent en vigueur·jusqu'à cequ'il y soit légalement dérogé. . . .

113. Il sera procédé à la première élection du Président de la République, conformément à la loi spéciale rendue par L'Assemblée nationale, le 28 octobre 1848.

APPENDIX VI

THE CONSTITUTION OF 1852

1. Constitution Faite en Vertu des Pouvoirs délégués par le Peuple Français à Louis-Napoléon Bonaparte par le Vote des 20 et 21 Decembre 1851.

14–22 juin 1852.

TITRE I

ARTICLE PREMIER.—La Constitution reconnâit, confirme et garantit les grands principes proclamés en 1789 et qui sont la base du droit public des Français.

TITRE II

FORME DU GOUVERNEMENT DE LA RÉPUBLIQUE

2. Le gouvernement de la République française est confié pour dix ans au prince Louis-Napoléon Bonaparte, président actuel de la République.

3. Le Président de la République gouverne au moyen des ministres, du Conseil d'État, du Sénat et du Corps législatif.

4. La puissance législative, s'exerce collectivement par le Président de la République, le Sénat et le Corps législatif.

TITRE III

DU PRÉSIDENT DE LA RÉPUBLIQUE

5. Le Président de la République est responsable devant le peuple français, auquel il a toujours le droit de faire appel.

6. Le Président de la République est le chef de l'État. Il commande les forces de terre et de mer, déclare la guerre, fait les traités de paix, d'alliance et de commerce, nomme à tous les emplois, fait les règlements et décrets nécessaires pour l'exécution des lois.

7. La justice se rend en son nom.

8. Il a seul l'initiative des lois.

9. Il a le droit de faire grâce.

10. Il sanctionne et promulgue les lois et les sénatus-consultes.

11. Il présente, tous les ans, au Sénat et au Corps législatif, par un message, l'état des affaires de la République.

12. Il a le droit de déclarer l'état de siège dans un ou plusieurs départements, sauf à en référer au Sénat dans le plus bref délai.

Les conséquences de·l'état de siège sont réglées par la loi.

13. Les ministres ne dépendent que du chef de l'État; ils ne sont responsables que, chacun en ce qui le concerne, des actes du gouvernement; il n'y a point de solidarité entre eux; ils ne peuvent être mis en accusation que par le Sénat.

14. Les ministres, les membres du Sénat, du Corps législatif et du Conseil d'État, les officiers de terre et de mer, les magistrats et les fonctionnaires publics prêtent le serment ainsi conçu: *je jure obéissance à la Constitution et fidélité au Président.*

15. Un sénatus-consulte fixe la somme allouée annuellement au Président de la République pour toute la durée de ses fonctions.

16. Si le Président de la République meurt avant l'expiration de son mandat, le Sénat convoque la nation pour procéder à une nouvelle élection.

17. Le chef d'État a le droit, par un acte secret et déposé aux archives du Sénat, de désigner le nom du citoyen qu'il recommande, dans l'intérêt de la France, à la confiance du peuple et à ses suffrages.

18. Jusqu'à l'élection du nouveau Président de la République, le président du Sénat gouverne avec le concours des ministres en fonctions, qui se forment en conseil de gouvernement, et délibèrent à la majorité des voix.

TITRE IV

DU SÉNAT

19. Le nombre des sénateurs ne pourra excéder cent cinquante; il est fixé, pour la première année, à quatre-vingts.

20. Le Sénat se compose: 1° des cardinaux, des maréchaux, des amiraux; 2° des citoyens que le Président de la République juge convenable d'élever à la dignité de sénateur.

21. Les sénateurs sont inamovibles et à vie.

22. Les fonctions de sénateur sont gratuites; néanmoins le Président de la République pourra accorder à des sénateurs, en raison des services

rendus et de leur position de fortune, une dotation personnelle, qui ne pourra excéder trente mille francs par an.

23. Le président et les vice-présidents du Sénat sont nommés par le Président de la République et choisis parmi les sénateurs: Ils sont nommés pour un an. Le traitement du président du Sénat est fixé par un décret.

24. Le Président de la République convoque et proroge le Sénat. Il fixe la durée de ses sessions par un décret. Les séances du Sénat ne sont pas publiques.

25. Le Sénat est le gardien du pacte fondamental et des libertés publiques. Aucune loi ne peut être promulguée avant de lui avoir été soumise.

26. Le Sénat s'oppose à la promulgation: 1° des lois qui seraient contraires ou qui porteraient atteinte à la Constitution, à la religion, à la morale, à la liberté des cultes, à la liberté individuelle, à l'égalité des citoyens devant la loi, à l'inviolabilité de la propriété et au principe de l'inamovibilité de la magistrature; 2° de celles qui pourraient compromettre la défense du territoire.

27. Le Sénat règle par un sénatus-consulte: 1° la Constitution des colonies et de l'Algérie; 2° tout ce qui n'a été prévu par la Constitution et qui est nécessaire à sa marche; 3° le sens des articles de la Constitution qui donne lieu à différentes interprétations.

28. Ces sénatus-consultes seront soumis à la sanction du Président de la République et promulgués par lui.

29. Le Sénat maintient ou annule tous les actes qui sont déférés comme inconstitutionnels par le gouvernement ou dénoncés pour la même cause par les pétitions des citoyens.

30. Le Sénat peut, dans un rapport adressé au Président de la République, poser les bases des projets de lois d'un grand intérèt national.

31. Il peut également proposer des modifications à la Constitution. Si la proposition est adoptée par le pouvoir exécutif, il y est statué par un sénatus-consulte.

32. Néanmoins, sera soumise au suffrage universel toute modification aux bases fondamentales de la Constitution, telles qu'elles ont été posées dans la proclamation du 2 décembre et adoptées par le peuple français.

33. En cas de dissolution du Corps législatif et jusqu'à une nouvelle convocation, le Sénat, sur la proposition du Président de la République, pourvoit par des mesures d'urgence à tout ce qui est nécessaire à la marche du gouvernement.

TITRE V

DU CORPS LÉGISLATIF

34. L'élection a pour base la population.

35. Il y aura un député au Corps législatif à raison de 35,000 électeurs.

36. Les députés sont élus par le suffrage universel, sans scrutin de liste.

37. Il ne reçoivent aucun traitement.

38. Ils sont nommés pour six ans.

39. Le Corps législatif discute et vote les projets de loi et l'impôt.

40. Tout amendement adopté par la commission chargée d'examiner un projet de loi sera renvoyé sans discussion au Conseil d'État par le président du Corps législatif. Si l'amendement n'est pas adopté par le Conseil d'État, il ne pourra pas être soumis à la délibération du Corps législatif.

41. Les sessions ordinaires du Corps législatif durent trois mois ; ses séances sont publiques, mais la demande de cinq membres suffit pour qu'il se forme en comité secret.

42. Le compte-rendu des séances du Corps législatif par les journaux ou tout autre moyen de publication ne consistera que dans la reproduction du procès-verbal dressé, à l'issue de chaque séance, par les soins du président du Corps législatif.

43. Le Président et les vice-présidents du Corps législatif sont nommés par le Président de la République pour un an. Ils sont choisis parmi les députés. Le traitement du président du Corps législatif est fixé par un décret.

44. Les ministres ne peuvent être membres du Corps législatif.

45. Le droit de pétition s'exerce auprès du Sénat. Aucune pétition ne peut être adressée au Corps législatif.

46. Le Président de la République convoque, ajourne, proroge et dissout le Corps législatif. En cas de dissolution le Président de la République doit en convoquer un nouveau dans le délai de six mois.

TITRE VI

DU CONSEIL D'ÉTAT

47. Le nombre des conseillers d'État en service ordinaire est de quarante à cinquante.

48. Les conseillers d'État sont nommés par le Président de la République et révocables par lui.

49. Le Conseil d'État est présidé par le Président de la République et, en son absence, par la personne qu'il désigne comme vice-président du Conseil d'État.

50. Le Conseil d'État est chargé, sous la direction du Président de la République, de rédiger les projets de loi et les règlements d'administration publique et de résoudre les difficultés qui s'élèvent en matière d'administration.

51. Il soutient, au nom du gouvernement, la discussion des projets de lois devant le Sénat et le Corps législatif. Les conseillers d'État chargés de porter la parole au nom du gouvernement sont désignés par la Président de la République.

52. Le traitement de chaque conseiller d'État est de 25.000 francs.

53. Les ministres ont rang, séance et voix délibérative au Conseil d'État.

TITRE VII
DE LA HAUTE COUR DE JUSTICE

54. Une Haute Cour de justice juge, sans appel ni recours en cassation, toutes personnes qui auront été renvoyées devant elle comme prévenues de crimes, attentats ou complots contre le Président de la République et contre la sûreté intérieure ou extérieure de l'État. Elle ne peut être saisie qu'en vertu-d'un décret du Président de la République.

55. Un sénatus-consulte déterminera l'organisation de cette Haute Cour.

TITRE VIII ·
DISPOSITIONS GÉNÉRALES ET TRANSITOIRES

56. Les dispositions des codes, lois et règlements existants, qui ne sont pas contraires à la présente constitution, restent en vigueur jusqu'à ce qu'il y soit légalement dérogé.

57. Une loi déterminera l'organisation municipale. Les maires seront nommés par le pouvoir exécutif et pourront être pris hors du Conseil municipal.

58. La présente constitution sera en vigueur à dater du jour où les grands corps de l'État qu'elle organise seront constitués. Les décrets rendus par le Président de la République, à partir du 2 décembre jusqu'à cette époque, auront force de loi.

APPENDIX VII

THE 'CONSTITUTION' OF 1875

I. LOI CONSTITUTIONNELLE SUR LES RAPPORTS DES POUVOIRS PUBLICS

16–18 juillet 1875

1. Le Sénat et la Chambre des députés se réunissent chaque année, le second mardi de janvier, à moins d'une convocation antérieure faite par le Président de la République. Les deux Chambres doivent être réunies en session cinq mois au moins chaque année. La session de l'une commence et finit en même temps que celle de l'autre.

Le dimanche qui suivra la rentrée, des prières publiques seront addressées a Dieu dans les églises et dans les temples pour appeler son secours sur les travaux des Assemblées.

2. Le Président de la République prononce la clôture de la session. Il a le droit de convoquer extraordinairement les Chambres. Il devra les convoquer si la demande en est faite, dans l'intervalle des sessions, par la majorité absolue des membres composant chaque Chambre. Le Président peut ajourner les Chambres. Toutefois, l'ajournement ne peut excéder le terme d'un mois ni avoir lieux plus de deux fois dans la même session.

3. Un mois au moins avant le terme légal des pouvoirs du Président de la République, les Chambres devront être réunies en Assemblée nationale pour procéder à l'élection du nouveau Président. A défaut de convocation, cette réunion aurait lieu de plein droit le quinzième jour avant l'expiration de ces pouvoirs. En cas de décès ou de démission du Président de la République, les deux Chambres se réunissent immédiatement et de plein droit.

Dans le cas où, par application de l'article 5 de la loi du 25 février 1875, la Chambre des députés se trouverait dissoute au moment où la présidence de la République deviendrait vacante, les collèges électoraux seraient aussitôt convoqués, et le Sénat se réunirait de plein droit.

4. Toute assemblée de l'une des deux Chambres qui serait tenue

hors du temps de la session commune est illicite et nulle de plein droit, sauf le cas prévu par l'article précédent et celui où le Sénat est réuni comme cour de justice; et, dans ce dernier cas, il ne peut exercer que des fonctions judiciaires.

5. Les séances du Sénat et celles de la Chambre des députés sont publiques. Néanmoins, chaque Chambre peut se former en comité secret, sur la demande d'un certain nombre de ses membres, fixé par le règlement. Elle décide ensuite, à la majorité absolue, si la séance doit être reprise en public sur le même sujet.

6. Le Président de la République communique avec les Chambres par des messages qui sont lus à la tribune par un ministre. Les ministres ont leur entrée dans les deux Chambres et doivent être entendus quand ils le demandent. Ils peuvent se faire assister par des commissaires désignés, pour la discussion d'un projet de loi determiné, par décret du Président de la République.

7. Le Président de la République promulgue les lois dans le mois qui suit la transmission au gouvernement de la loi définitivement adoptée. Il doit promulger dans les trois jours les lois dont la promulgation, par un vote exprès dans l'une et l'autre Chambre, aura été déclarée urgente. Dans le délai fixé pour la promulgation, le Président de la République peut, par un message motivé, demander aux deux Chambres une nouvelle délibération qui ne peut être refusée.

8. Le Président de la République négocie et ratifie les traités. Il en donne connaissance aux Chambres aussitôt que l'intérêt et la sûreté de l'État le permettent. Les traités de paix, de commerce, les traités qui engagent les finances de l'État, ceux qui sont relatifs à l'état des personnes et au droit de propriété des Français à l'étranger, ne sont définitifs qu'après avoir été votés par les deux Chambres. Nulle cession, nul échange, nulle adjonction de territoire ne peut avoir lieu qu'en vertu d'une loi.

9. Le Président de la République ne peut déclarer la guerre sans l'assentiment préalable des deux Chambres.

10. Chacune des Chambres est juge de l'éligibilité de ses membres et de la régularité de leur élection; elle peut seule recevoir leur démission.

11. Le bureau de chacune des deux Chambres est élu chaque année pour la durée de la session et pour toute session extraordinaire qui aurait lieu avant la session ordinaire de l'année suivante. Lorsque les deux Chambres se réunissent en Assemblée nationale, leur bureau se compose du président, vice-président et secrétaires du Sénat.

12. Le Président de la République ne peut être mis en accusation que par la Chambre des députés et ne peut être jugé que par le Sénat. Les ministres peuvent être mis en accusation par la Chambre des députés pour crimes commis dans l'exercice de leurs fonctions. En ce cas ils sont jugés par le Sénat.

Le Sénat peut être constitué en cour de justice par un décret du Président de la République, rendu en conseil des ministres, pour juger toute personne prévenue d'attentat commis contre la sûreté de l'État.

Si l'instruction est commencée par la justice ordinaire, le décret de convocation de Sénat peut être rendu jusqu'à l'arrêt de renvoi. Une loi déterminera le mode de procéder pour l'accusation, l'instruction et le jugement.

13. Aucun membre de l'une ou l'autre Chambre ne peut être poursuivi ou recherché à l'occasion des opinions ou votes émis par lui dans l'exercice de ses fonctions.

14. Aucun membre de l'une ou l'autre Chambre ne peut, pendant la durée de la session, être poursuivi ou arrêté en matière criminelle ou correctionnelle qu'avec l'autorisation de la Chambre dont il fait partie, sauf le cas de flagrant délit. La détention ou la poursuite d'un membre de l'une ou de l'autre Chambre est suspendue pendant la session et pour toute sa durée, si la Chambre le requiert.

II. LOI RELATIVE À L'ORGANISATION DES POUVOIRS PUBLICS

25–28 février 1875

1. Le pouvoir législatif s'exerce par deux assemblées, la Chambre des députés et le Sénat. La Chambre des députés est nommée par le suffrage universel, dans des conditions déterminées par la loi électorale. La composition, le mode de nomination et les attributions du Sénat seront réglés par une loi spéciale.

2. Le Président de la République est élu à la majorité absolue des suffrages par le Sénat et par la Chambre des députés réunis en assemblée nationale. Il est nommé pour sept ans. Il est rééligible.

3. Le Président de la République a l'initiative des lois, concurremment avec les membres des deux Chambres. Il promulgue les lois lorsqu'elles ont été votées par les deux Chambres; il en surveille et en assure l'exécution. Il a le droit de faire grâce; les amnisties ne peuvent être accordées que par une loi. Il dispose de la force armée. Il nomme

à tous les emplois civils et militaires. Il préside aux solennités nationales. Les envoyés et les ambassadeurs des puissances étrangères sont accrédités auprès de lui.

Chacun des actes du Président de la République doit être contresigné par un ministre.

4. Au fur et à mesure des vacances qui se produiront à partir de la promulgation de la présente loi, le Président de la République nomme, en conseil des ministres, les conseillers d'État en service ordinaire. Les conseillers d'État ainsi nommés ne pourront être révoqués que par décret rendu en conseil des ministres. Les conseillers d'État nommés en vertu de la loi du 24 mai 1872 ne pourront, jusqu'à l'expiration de leurs pouvoirs, être révoqués que dans la forme déterminée par cette loi. Après la séparation de l'Assemblée nationale, la révocation ne pourra être prononcée que par une résolution du Sénat.

5. Le Président de la République peut, sur l'avis conforme du Sénat, dissoudre la Chambre des députés avant l'expiration légale de son mandat. En ce cas, les collèges électoraux sont convoqués pour de nouvelles élections dans le délai de trois mois.

6. Les ministres sont solidairement responsables devant les Chambres de la politique générale du gouvernement et individuellement de leurs actes personnels. Le Président de la République n'est responsable que dans le cas de haute trahison.

7. En cas de vacance par décès ou pour toute autre cause, les deux Chambres réunies procèdent immédiatement à l'élection d'un nouveau président. Dans l'intervalle, le conseil des ministres est investi du pouvoir exécutif.

8. Les Chambres auront le droit, par délibérations séparées, prises dans chacune à la majorité absolue des voix, soit spontanément, soit sur la demande du Président de la République, de déclarer qu'il y a lieu de reviser les lois constitutionnelles. Après que chacune des deux Chambres aura pris cette résolution, elles se réuniront en Assemblée nationale pour procéder à la revision. Les délibérations portant revision des lois constitutionnelles, en tout ou en partie, devront être prises à la majorité absolue des membres composant l'Assemblée nationale. Toutefois, pendant la durée des pouvoirs conférés par la loi du 20 novembre 1873 à M. le maréchal de Mac-Mahon, cette revision ne peut avoir lieu que sur la proposition du Président de la République.

9. Le siège du pouvoir exécutif et des deux Chambres est à Versailles.

x*

III.   LOI RELATIVE À L'ORGANISATION DU SÉNAT

24–28 février 1875

1.   Le Sénat se compose de 300 membres: 225 élus par les départements et les colonies et 75 élus par l'Assemblée nationale.

2.   Les départements de la Seine et du Nord éliront chacun 5 sénateurs Les départements de la Seine-Inférieure, Pas-de-Calais, Gironde, Rhône, Finistère, Côtes-du-Nord, chacun 4 sénateurs.   La Loire-Inférieure, Saône et Loire, Ille-et-Vilaine, Seine-et-Oise, Isère, Puy-de-Dôme, Somme, Bouches-du-Rhône, Aisne, Loire, Manche, Maine-et-Loire, Morbihan, Dordogne, Haute-Garonne, Charente-Inférieure, Calvados, Sarthe, Hérault, Basses-Pyrénées, Gard, Aveyron, Vendée, Orne, Oise, Vosges, Allier, chacun 3 sénateurs.   Tous les autres départements chacun 2 sénateurs.   Le territoire de Belfort, les trois départments de l'Algérie, les quatre colonies de la Martinique, de la Guadeloupe, de la Réunion et des Indes françaises éliront chacun un sénateur.

3.   Nul ne peut être sénateur s'il n'est Français, âgé de quarante ans au moins et s'il ne jouit de ses droits civils et politiques.

4.   Les sénateurs des départements et des colonies sont élus à la majorité absolue et, quand il y a lieu, au scrutin de liste, par un collège réuni au chef-lieu du département ou de la colonie et composé: 1° des députés; 2° des conseillers généraux; 3° des conseillers d'arrondissement; 4° des délégués élus, un par chaque conseil municipal, parmi les électeurs de la commune.

Dans l'Inde française, les membres du conseil colonial ou des conseils locaux sont substitués aux conseillers généraux, aux conseillers d'arrondissement et aux délégués des conseils municipaux.   Ils votent au chef-lieu de chaque établissement.

5.   Les sénateurs, nommés par l'Assemblée, sont élus au scrutin de liste à la majorité absolue des suffrages.

6.   Les sénateurs des départements et des colonies sont élus pour neuf années et renouvelables par tiers, tous les trois ans.

Au début de la première session, les départements seront divisés en trois séries contenant chacune un égal nombre de sénateurs.   Il sera procédé, par la voie du tirage au sort, à la désignation des séries qui devront être renouvelées a l'expiration de la première et de la deuxième periode triennale.

7.   Les sénateurs élus par l'Assemblée sont inamovibles.   En cas de vacance par décès, démission ou toute autre cause, il sera, dans les deux mois, pourvu au remplacement par le Sénat lui-même.

Le Sénat a, concurremment avec la Chambre des députés, l'initiative et la confection des lois. Toutefois, les lois de finances doivent être, en premier lieu, préséntées à la Chambre des députés et votées par elle.

9. Le Sénat peut être constitué en Cour de justice pour juger, soit le Président de la République, soit les ministres et pour connaître des attentats commis contre la sûreté de l'État.

10. Il sera procédé à l'élection du Sénat, un mois avant l'époque fixée par l'Assemblée nationale pour sa séparation. Le Sénat entrera en fonctions et se constituera le jour même où l'Assemblée nationale se séparera.

11. La présente loi ne pourra être promulguée qu'après le vote définitif de la loi sur les pouvoirs publics.

INDEX